Multiple Meanings of Money

Multiple Meanings of Money

How Women See Microfinance

Smita Premchander

with

V. Prameela, M. Chidambaranathan

and

L. Jeyaseelan

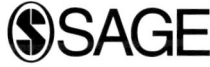

Los Angeles | London | New Delhi
Singapore | Washington DC | Melbourne

First published in 2009 by

 SAGE Publications India Pvt Ltd
B1/I-1 Mohan Cooperative Industrial Area
Mathura Road, New Delhi 110 044, India
www.sagepub.in

SAGE Publications Inc
2455 Teller Road
Thousand Oaks, California 91320, USA

SAGE Publications Ltd
1 Oliver's Yard, 55 City Road
London EC1Y 1SP, United Kingdom

SAGE Publications Asia-Pacific Pte Ltd
3 Church Street
#10-04 Samsung Hub
Singapore 049483

Published by Vivek Mehra for SAGE Publications India Pvt Ltd, typeset in 10.5/12.5 pt Minion by Star Compugraphics Private Limited, Delhi

Library of Congress Cataloging-in-Publication Data

Multiple meanings of money: how women see microfinance/Smita Premchander
 . . . [et al.].
  p. cm.
Including bibliographical references and index.
 1. Microfinance—India. 2. Women—India—Economic conditions. 3. Economic assistance, Domestic—India. I. Premchander, Smita.

HG178.33.I4M85   322.082—dc22   2009   2009026083

ISBN: 978-81-321-0169-7 (PB)

The SAGE Team: Elina Majumdar, Manali Das, Vijay Sah and Trinankur Banerjee

For the women who talked
about their lives, relationships and finances,
so that we could all learn together

Contents

List of Tables

List of Figures

List of Abbreviations

ADB	Asian Development Bank
AFC	Agriculture Finance Corporation Ltd
AIMS	Assessing the Impact of Microenterprise Services
ANM	Auxiliary Nurse and Midwife
AOP	Actor-oriented Perspectives
AP	Andhra Pradesh
APMAS	Andhra Pradesh Mahila Abhivruddhi Society
ASA	Activists for Social Action
BAIF	Bharatiya Agro Industries Foundation
BDS	Business Development Services
BPL	Below Poverty Line
BRAC	Bangladesh Rural Advancement Committee
BRCS	Bay Research and Consultancy Services
CARE	Cooperative for Assistance and Relief Everywhere
CCA	Canadian Cooperative Association
CDE	Centre for Development and Environment
CETZAM	The Christian Enterprise Trust Zambia
CGAP	Consultative Group for Assisting the Poor
CMF	Centre for Microfinance
CYSD	Centre for Youth and Social Development
DANIDA	Danish International Development Assistance
DFID	Department for International Development
DIC	District Industries Centre
DLCC	District Level Coordination Committee
DLRC	District Level Review Committee
DWCRA	Development of Women and Children in Rural Areas
EDPs	Entrepreneurship Development Programmes
FAO	Food and Agriculture Organisation of the United Nations
FWWB	Friends of Women's World Banking
GOI	Government of India
GOK	Government of Karnataka
GTZ	German Development Cooperation/German Technical Cooperation
HCR	Head Count Ratio

HDFC	Housing Development Finance Corporation
HIV/AIDS	Human Immunodeficiency Virus/Acquired Immune Deficiency Syndrome
HSBC	Hong Kong and Shanghai Banking Corporation Ltd.
ICICI	Industrial Credit and Investment Corporation of India
IFAD	International Fund for Agricultural Development
IFP	Institut Français de Pondicherry
IGA	Income Generating Activity
IIHRD	Indian Institute for Human Research and Development
IIPO	Indian Institute of Public Opinion
IIPS	International Institute for Population Sciences
ILO	International Labour Organization
IRDP	Integrated Rural Development Programme
KSWDC	Karnataka State Women's Development Corporation
LEAD	League for Education and Development
MACS	Mutually Aided Cooperative Society
MASY	Mahila Arthik Samavrudhi Yojane
MBT	Mutual Benefit Trust
MFI	Microfinance Institution
MFO	Micro-finance Organisations
MFP	Minor Forest Produce
MHHDC	Mahbub ul Haq Human Development Centre
MLA	Member of Legislative Assembly
MYRADA	Mysore Resettlement and Development Agency
NABARD	National Bank for Agriculture and Rural Development
NBFC	Non-Banking Financial Company
NCCR-NS	National Centre for Competence in Research—North-South
NGO	Non-government Organisation
OBCs	Other Backward Castes
ODA	Overseas Development Administration
PGB	Pragato Grameen Bank
PGI	Poverty Gap Index
PRA	Participatory Rural Appraisal
PRADAN	Professional Assistance for Development Action
PSI	Pastoral Service Institute
RBI	Reserve Bank of India
RCC	Rural Credit Cooperative
RLS	Rural Livelihood Systems
RMP	Registered Medical Practitioner
RRB	Regional Rural Bank
SAA	Service Area Approach
SAPAP	South Asia Poverty Alleviation Programme

SBH	State Bank of Hyderabad
SBI	State Bank of India
SC	Scheduled Caste
SDC	Swiss Agency for Development and Cooperation
SDMC	School Development and Management Committee
SEWA	Self-Employed Women's Association
SFMC	SIDBI Foundation for Microcredit
SGSY	Swarna Jayanthi Gram Swarozgar Yojana
SHG	Self-help Group
SHPI	Self-help Promoting Institution
SIDBI	Small Industries Development Bank of India
SLF	Sustainable Livelihoods Framework
SNSF	Swiss National Science Foundation
SNRM	Sustainable Natural Resources Management
ST	Scheduled Tribes
TB	Tuberculosis
TBF	The Bridge Foundation
TGB	Tungabhadra Grameen Bank
TN	Tamil Nadu
TRYSEM	Training of Rural Youth for Self-employment
UNDP	United Nations Development Programme
UNOPS	United Nations Office for Project Services
USAID	United States Agency for International Development
UTI	Unit Trust of India
ZP	Zilla Parishad

Preface

This book analyses what microfinance money means to women; in doing so, it focuses on the perspectives of individual women and those of women-only groups. Most microfinance programmes are delivered through women-only groups, which are formed when 15–20 women get together on a voluntary basis to form the group, usually with the encouragement of an external agency (for example, non-government organisation [NGO], government, microfinance institution [MFI]) and are engaged primarily in savings and credit activities. The book explores women's own money management strategies, group dynamics and learning processes in groups and, in this context, discusses the divergence between the perspectives of external intervening agencies and those of women who are members of self-help groups (SHGs).

This book does not consciously follow a feminist methodology; yet, the perspective is feminist, as it questions the benefits and costs arising to women from development programmes. The feminist principles used include a focus on gender, valuing women's experiences, rejecting a split between subject and object and emphasising empowerment, political change and emancipation.[1]

In Sampark, we work as practitioners, advisors and trainers in the field of microfinance and microenterprise and in this sense have multiple roles and therefore have access and sensitivity to multiple perspectives in this sector. As evaluation teams, advisors and trainers, we work with several donor organisations and NGOs at the macro- and meso-levels. The task involves understanding women, and one of our professional habits is to listen to women. Our professional responsibility is to represent women's perspectives in a way that the project implementing agencies and donors hear 'their' voices directly, so as to say. The job involves authenticating women's voices and we are aware that it takes a lot of energy. Somehow, we find that we can be talking 'against' the projects, that 'projects' take on personalities to be respected and feared, they cannot be questioned very easily, much less challenged and changed.

As we worked with microfinance reviews and impact assessments, we became aware that most programmes and projects are drawn on the basis of an assumed understanding of the impact of microfinance programmes and also that the implementers are not comfortable when these assumptions are challenged. Yet, the voices that we hear from the field are certainly not the beautiful musical sounds orchestrated by the microfinance sector, they are actually a jarring cacophony that shocks, and so has been subdued. It is no surprise that women are hardly consulted, and if consulted, not heard. Participatory discussions say exactly what the implementing and donor agencies want to hear. The programmes and projects go on unchallenged, as if everything that is happening is on the right track; to question this is blasphemy, it is seen as turning away from all that is 'advanced' and 'given knowledge' or 'best practice' in the sector.

Smita, as a former banker, reminded us of normal banking lessons again and again and questioned why the microfinance industry was bent upon rediscovering the wheel. We wondered why donors were pouring in so much money to learn what was already known in the lessons of the Indian banking sector about reaching or not reaching the poor. There were times when we wondered why the other external agencies did not hear what we heard from women.

We are all committed to improving the lives of the poor; this is what brought us to the development field and this is what has retained us here. This gives us the courage to represent their views in every project that we take on; to use our professional expertise to guide them to become better entrepreneurs and leaders and to advise donors and implementing agencies to work in ways that would improve the lot of women.

With regard to gender equality, we realise that it is both women and men who are responsible for making the society what it is, and any effort at changing the situation must involve both women and men. And yet, as of now, the world does not provide equal opportunities to women, much less poor women. Our endeavour is to make this world a bit fairer for women—even if it is only a little bit, because we believe that in the long run, every bit counts. In this sense, we are all clearly strong feminists.

A question often asked about representing the issues of the poor is how can you represent poor women when you have yourself never experienced poverty? It is true that we are none of us poor now, but two of us have experienced poverty for certain periods in our lives. The dependence, humiliation and indignity experienced were enough to convince us that no one deserves to be poor. We have spent large portions of our time for the past 15 years living with people who are poor, sharing their life concerns and helping them overcome poverty.[2] We have seen women caught up in very difficult situations arising out of their gender, situations that men are not subjected to, and have felt keenly the injustice of it all. Yet, we are conscious that we are not ourselves caught up in these circumstances. We do not claim our voice to be theirs. Our sole endeavour in this book is to try to represent their true voices, using the nuances of their language wherever possible, even though we realise that no translation can do justice to this. It must be borne in mind that we have tried our best to represent their perspectives, but these perspectives have passed through our individual and collective personalities, and to this end we have shared some part of our backgrounds that may have coloured the pictures we frame.

One of the important aspects of this study is the value attached to women's own experiences. It was in the listening to them and in giving credence to their feelings and opinions that the span of the book expanded to cover macro-, meso- and micro-levels and external/institutional as well as local perspectives. It was while listening to the women that the divergence between their feelings and what the microfinance system provides to them first struck home, and this led to the motivation to 'turn the telescope around', or 'to give voice to women's opinions'.

Through this book, if we manage to communicate women's perspectives, have their life stories read and have their group experiences understood as a first step, and later ensure that some of their needs and preferences get greater consideration in the designing of development programmes and policy formulation, and that at least some implementing NGOs take steps to address these concerns arising from the women, then we would have fulfilled our responsibilities in representing their concerns.

With regard to the detailed case studies, all women were given a choice about their participation; out of the 12 who were contacted, 10 participated. The research was introduced to each woman personally. They already knew that Sampark worked in 20 villages (40 villages in 2007) in Koppal with 120 women's groups (156 by 2007) and provided a range of support for group formation, training in management of groups, skill training, credit linkages and linkages for government grants. They were informed that if Sampark was to make a positive impact on the lives of rural people, it needed to understand rural people better. As it was not possible to work with all the women covered by Sampark for an in-depth understanding of their lives, only a few had been approached for this purpose. It was important that women did not feel obliged to participate because they would need to commit time for discussions.

It was important that our discussions with women were not perceived as merely 'getting information' or the women 'providing information'. The intention was to learn together about their lives through close mutual dialogue. This involved multiple visits to individual homes and farms and extended towards other family members too. If women felt a need to meet other participants, workshops were organised accordingly.

The women who participated are referred to as 'research participants' and as 'women case study participants'. The names of all the women have been changed to protect their real identity. Later, most were more comfortable with their 'real names' and photographs being used; however, given the sensitivity of working with *devadasi*s, the more ethical (and also conventional) option was chosen.

We believe that ethical research must return tangible benefits to the participants, which is aided by our long-term commitment to development and the intention to find ways of providing practical benefits to the local community from the research process. Several benefits accrued to the researchers, women participants and the local community.

During the period when we interviewed them frequently, the women became more emotionally attached to the process of sharing as well as to the researcher, and reportedly missed the 'friendly meetings' when the frequency of interaction reduced after the data collection phase. The researchers consciously found the time to continue meeting the women, despite other work engagements. These processes of sharing emotions and joint learning from life stories of women led to the building of relationships between the researchers and the women and motivated both to take more positive action to improve their own and other women's lives. These relationships and common values provide a foundation for freedom and enabling of women's agency. One striking realisation is that women could benefit from consolidated learning from their own past experiences and discussion of future aspirations. It was evident that despite being marginalised economically, socially, culturally and through religion, none had dedicated their own daughters as *devadasi*s. Their life stories included courageous decisions at different stages of their lives, whether it related to choice of partners, birth control measures or taking financial risks. The incidents in their lives reinforced a belief in the capacity of poor women to bring positive changes not only in their own lives but also in those of others in their community. Researchers and development agents need to take more serious cognisance of the agency of women and their potential for courageous and collective action.

The women claimed that they had benefited in several ways from participating in the research. The charts and diaries collected stayed with the women; the researchers only copied such information.

Not only were the findings shared in workshops but also spreadsheets were brought back and openly discussed. This called for a reciprocal responsibility to ensure tangible benefits to the women research participants, which was later fulfilled by obtaining grants for educating the poorest children, a credit fund for education, local organisation building and linkages for official credit for sustainable management of land and water resources.

Researchers and writers cannot escape from ethics even when applying a supposedly value-free research method. Whether at the moment of setting the research issue or when dealing with participant interactions, certain ethical choices are always present. Taking into account that development research forms part of the development agenda, it is necessary to decide how to balance the different expectations raised by the research process. Experience showed that compensating women individually for their cooperation in participating may have contradicted their own ethics and those of the facilitating NGO and researcher. An ethically acceptable solution to the dilemma could be found due to the NGO's institutional commitment, which allowed it to integrate the process of development research as a means for improving reciprocity between local and external actors through a better mutual understanding and efficient use of the capabilities and resources of all the actors involved. This in turn implies that research must select people and institutional partners who are willing and able to give continuity to the relationships.

Collaborative action between external and local actors is not, however, always synchronous or can be made so: there remained continuing divergences. The researchers used an NGO as a base; and there were emerging divergences in women's perspectives and those of the NGO. One concerned the realisation that the NGO emphasised financial empowerment over other types of empowerment; hence, certain issues were not addressed directly, such as gender differentials in agricultural wages, child marriage practices, health and hygiene or the caste discrimination practices followed in the villages.

The findings raise the question about the limits of microfinance. The NGO heeded this result and introduced education, mental health support and vocational training for women and their children, but encountered some resistance with respect to land-based income generating activities and sustainable agriculture. These raised a dilemma for the NGO: if they were to foster long-term ecological sustainability, this would demand working with the more endowed people in the villages, who controlled land ownership. The poor have a low ability to absorb productive credit and would need long time periods for impact and the development of new pathways. These issues were articulated and discussed within the NGO, which opted to continue to work with the marginalised sections, but also realised that this limited its potential for impact on livelihoods beyond the limited resources it could access for this target group via official and external agencies.

This book spans issues from macro- to micro-level and accords priority to women as agents of change in their own livelihoods. Their participation and cooperation arose over time. These women perceive their situation not as a closed world from which there is no exit but as a limiting situation, which they can nevertheless transform. The discussions with them have had the effect of providing more 'liberating' education, with women expressing their situations of being marginalised and then making efforts to release themselves from the financial and physical dominance that they face in their households.

While we have been writing this book, several studies covering SHGs have been conducted to understand group dynamics better. At the policy level, two of us were invited to examine empowerment impacts of microfinance policy and programmes and to help design microfinance programmes that enhance women's empowerment. We would like to thank the four private foundations who have extended support for livelihood initiatives for women's empowerment in Koppal: the Fondazione Pangea Onlus, Italy; Anuradha Foundation, USA; Volkart Vision India, New Delhi and Canadian High Commission, New Delhi. This helped honour the commitment to meet the expressed needs of poor women: education for children, skills training for employment or enterprise for school dropouts and community-based emotional counselling support through women's SHGs. These linkages have helped us experience trans-disciplinarity, that is, linking research and action in a mutually reinforcing learning cycle.[3]

Smita Premchander
V. Prameela
M. Chidambaranathan
L. Jeyaseelan

NOTES

1. These principles are outlined by Pini (2003) in her feminist research methodology.
2. Smita is a founder member of Sampark, since 1991, and Jeyaseelan, Chidambaranathan and Prameela joined in 1994. So we have worked together for 14 years till now.
3. See Hurni et al., (2004) and Hirsch (2006) for detailed elaboration of the concept of trans-disciplinarity. While inter-disciplinarity refers to working together with different disciplines (for example, social, economic), trans-disciplinarity deals with the blurring and crossing of the researcher–participant boundaries.

Acknowledgements

Our first and deepest commitment is to 10 women in the villages of Koppal district whose lives and livelihoods we studied and all the rural women in various states of India who, despite their poverty, shared with us the wealth of information that we sought. They revealed the details of their poverty, troubles and concerns, coping strategies, ways and preferences about using money and experiences of groups and NGO-delivered credit. Studying the lives of poor women, especially the *devadasis*, who are dedicated to the deity and make sexual alliances with men for economic reasons, has been a depressing journey. Even women who were economically better off had problems; one lost her son, one her husband, while another faced domestic violence. These women were generous enough to share details about their own and their family's lives so that others could learn. Theirs is a debt we can only repay by helping others like them.

Dr Pat Richardson's technical guidance, Dr John Ritchie's insights on the current context of microfinance and the unstinting support of Professor Dr Urs Wiesmann, Professor Dr Hans Hurni and Dr Stephan Rist on livelihoods conceptual frameworks and social learning processes are acknowledged with gratitude.

We thank the Centre for Development and Environment (CDE), Institute of Geography, University of Berne, for providing financial support for the fieldwork through its research programme, Social Learning for Sustainability and National Centre for Competence in Research-North-South (NCCR-NS). The research programmes were funded by the Swiss National Science Foundation (SNSF) and the Swiss Agency for Development and Cooperation (SDC), whom we would like to thank for the financial support for the research and for some of the ensuing needs for development support in the research villages.

We wish to thank all colleagues at CDE and NCCR-NS, particulary Professor Dr Urs Wiesmann and Dr Stephan Rist who provided us with guidance and inputs and feedback on the book for their valuable guidance and suggestions in doing case studies and narrative analysis. We would like to thank them and others.

The Sampark team was open and flexible in providing all the information that the organisation had about the groups and their financial and non-financial operations. Access to the data of Sampark's Koppal office was facilitated by Nirmala, Rajshekhar, Akkamma, Iramma and Uma. We are thankful to each one of them for their assistance during this research. Roshni Menon helped us with the literature survey. Our heartfelt thanks also goes to Raju, Meenakshi, Banu, Saumya and Deepa for all the office assistance.

Language corrections and editing continued to be a major undertaking through the whole process, which were dealt by M. Rajshekhar, Saumya Premchander, Ratan Gopinath, Karuna Sivasailam and Jason Klinck, to whom we remain thankful.

Part of the data in this book was collected during field visits for organisations engaged with supporting microfinance, namely Friends of Women's World Banking, CARE India and United Nations Office of Project Services/International Fund for Agricultural Development. These organisations not only provided us with all the grey data they could but also permitted the use of the information. The staff of NGOs/MFIs shared valuable insights on their experiences, dilemmas and inner conflicts in the implementation of microfinance programmes. We are grateful to all of them for being so open as the book has benefited greatly from their rich insights.

Over the past several years, we have been simultaneously engaged in both research and development work to enable the poor improve their livelihoods. It has changed the 'normal' family way of life. We could do this only because of the emotional encouragement and support from our families and we are immensely grateful to them.

Interpreting Multiple Meanings of Money

India accounts for 15 per cent of the global population and 27 per cent of its 1.3 billion were in the absolute poor category in 2001. Though poverty estimates vary, with up to 360 million in absolute poverty estimated by some, recent official figures put the numbers at about 300 million people.[1] Microfinance has become an important economic improvement strategy in many developing regions of the world, and is widely credited as having a major impact on poverty reduction and women's empowerment. Sustainable microfinance organisations have been established all over the world. These developments have been wide ranging and rapid. Indian microfinance, too, barely recognised as an independent sector in the early 1990s, is now a fast growing industry. The National Bank for Agriculture and Rural Development (NABARD) has recorded 3.47 million self-help groups (SHGs) in India in March 2008, with membership of 45.1 million families. Their total savings are Rs 35.12 billion (just short of $ [conversion rate @ Rs 44 per] 1 billion). The total bank loans accessed by these families are Rs 222.7 million ($0.5 billion). In addition to the banking sector, there are nearly 1,000 microfinance institution (MFI). As on March 2008, Indian MFIs served 14 million households, with outstanding loans of Rs 59.54 billion ($15 billion).

Despite the unprecedented growth of microfinance, scepticism about its impact on poverty has persisted. Microfinance has faced criticism regarding low coverage of the poor and its engagement with poor women entrepreneurs as an instrument to meet the ends of neoliberal capital expansion.[2] Set against these contradictory perspectives, the question arises about the real nature and impact of Indian microfinance. While the sector has grown to accommodate a large number of different types of microfinance organisations, questions still remain about whether money reaches the poor. This question is not easily answered, as the Indian microfinance scenario, with its widely varying models of microfinance delivery, does not lend itself to simplistic impact analysis. Further, the positioning of microfinance as a major poverty reduction and empowerment tool, especially for women, has been challenged by those who see it as an instrument to advance competing capitalist ends. This needs a reference to field realities, so as to be able to deal with these contradictions.

An apparently coherent 'policy model' of microfinance, which mostly privileges positive impacts, is challenged by evidence emerging from the field. It assumes that microfinance alleviates poverty, whereas there is sufficient evidence now to show that it does not. The model would have us believe that it reaches the poor, but now we have evidence from the field that it does not, in fact, do so. It would have us believe that credit demand is so high that one needs only to increase supply.

Field experience shows, however, that demand and supply have a serious mismatch, as the type of microfinance products offered is not what the poor need, and what they need is not offered. It would have us believe that poor people need savings services more than credit and therefore MFI collecting women's savings is good for women. The ground reality is that women clearly prefer to keep their own savings with their groups and borrow from this when in need, opting to take external loans only when additional credit is needed. MFIs want to collect women's savings because it is the cheapest source of funds for them and can be used for building sustainable organisations. The policy model overlooks the difference between 'own' and 'external', whereas for women it is a key distinction determining which money they use and for what purpose. The policy model again overlooks the distinction between one source of credit and another, yet for women, loans from moneylenders, friends, banks and government all carry completely different meanings and elicit completely different financial behaviour. An in-depth exploration of these differing perspectives calls for a better understanding of the differential meanings of money and an appreciation of how these multiple meanings develop.

This book engages precisely in this endeavour. It examines the question of what money means to women, especially poor and marginalised women. It questions the dominant institutional views and studies women's own perspectives regarding the use of money, discusses different livelihood contexts and explores the meaning of money through discussions with rural women, including longitudinal case studies with 10 women participants. It explores how social relationships determine and influence financial relationships. As microfinance is delivered through informal SHGs of women, the book explores group dynamics, money management and the social learning processes in the SHGs. It explores how women use money, how they differentiate money delivered in different ways, highlights models of money management that they consider the most empowering and reveals the multiple meanings of money from women's perspectives.

This chapter first lays out the different models by which microfinance is delivered in India. It then discusses how impact assessments of microfinance have omitted several important facets of money, thereby overlooking the way money is used and impacts rural women whom it seeks to benefit. It reveals that impact approaches privilege a positive framing of microfinance, which is widely divergent from prevailing ground realities.

It then describes the exploration undertaken in this book, taking women's own perspectives into account through wide-ranging discussions with stakeholders across the country followed by in-depth case studies of individuals and groups, and it interprets the meanings they assign to money, and what this reflects about impact of microfinance.

INDIAN MICROFINANCE MODELS AND IMPACTS

Microcredit refers to providing very poor families with very small loans, for productive income generating activities (IGAs) and the expanding of their tiny businesses. Subsequently, a broader range of financial services has been provided to the poor, including credit, savings and insurance, known as microfinance. No specific limit for how 'small' an amount of financial services is envisaged, though an informal upper limit is often understood to be $500.[3] The term 'microfinance' or even 'microcredit' combines several categories of credit that are delivered through different models which need to be differentiated.

India's longstanding experience in banking, early efforts in development banking, widespread banking infrastructure, well developed legal frameworks and strong NGOs enabled it to be experimental and innovate according to rural needs. There are thus different models of microfinance delivery based upon approaches. The variation in impact of these models is not yet established, nor has it been the subject of detailed study. Also, such grassroots diversity defies a standard delivery model and frame for analysing microfinance impact.

In India, microfinance is usually offered to women with the mediation of SHGs. A typical SHG in India is formed by a group of 15–20 people (often women only) meeting once every week/fortnight/month. SHGs usually pledge to some informal rules, then open a bank account in the group's name, select two or three leaders and conduct savings and credit activities. They are characterised by homogeneity and affinity, commonality of interests, voluntarism and self-help and participatory decision making.[4] In most cases, the members pool funds to create a common fund, which may be used to access loans from this fund or from banks. In the latter case, the groups act as a collective guarantor for the loan. This book refers to women-only groups, formed on a voluntary basis, but with the encouragement of an external agency (for example, NGO, government, MFI), which are engaged primarily in savings and credit activities. It explores money management, group dynamics and learning processes in these groups and, in this context, discloses how the perspectives of external intervening agencies and women SHG members often diverge in practice.

Different terms are used to define the ways in which microfinance is offered. The term 'traditional' microfinance is used for subsidised credit (Johnson and Rogaly 1997; Robinson 2001), while microfinance offered on commercial terms is considered as 'sustainable'. These authors refer to subsidised finance as the old paradigm and commercial finance as the new paradigm[5] for providing microfinance services. Others refer to commercial microfinance as 'traditional' and see the needs of pro-poor microfinance as different. The terms 'traditional', 'sustainable', 'old paradigm' and 'new paradigm' have normative orientations inherent in the vocabulary used. If the organisation which is providing microfinance is financially sustainable—it is seen as sustainable microfinance. This distinction between sustainable microfinance and subsidised microfinance is drawn with the point of view of the financial institution and is not considered important here.

Instead, this book adopts the perspectives of recipients and users of funds, which have been influenced by the historical development of microfinance services in India. It therefore adopts the terms on which the credit is offered to select the adjective, of which there are three: subsidised, unsubsidised and commercial. Subsidised microcredit is that which carries a subsidy on principal repayment, such that the clients pay back a percentage of the principal and do not need to pay back the rest. Prior to 2000, the subsidy was pegged at 50 per cent, and more recently government subsidy ranges from 10 to 75 per cent for groups/individuals. Unsubsidised microcredit is that which requires the full principal amount to be paid back with the interest rate being 12–18 per cent, the repayment period being 1–3 years and the instalments at monthly or quarterly intervals. Commercial microcredit is the practice of providing loans with 1-year repayment period and regular repayment instalments per week or per month. The interest on commercial microfinance ranges from 18 to 24 per cent per year, or even higher (Table 1.1).

Table 1.1
Terms and Conditions for Different Types of Loans

	Subsidised	*Unsubsidised*	*Commercial*
Principal to be repaid	Part, normally 50%	Full	Full
Repayment period	3 years	1–3 years	1 year
Instalments	Monthly and half yearly	Monthly	Weekly or monthly
Interest rates	12%	12–18%	18–24%, sometimes higher

Source: Authors.

In India, the banking sector has long targeted the poor and 'subsidised' credit was the first model. As the 'banking sector outreach' of this model was very low, a 'new' model of 'commercial' credit emerged, which provides credit to the poor at the high cost judged necessary for financially viable MFIs to flourish and proliferate. Though the model seeks to meet a perceived gap (that is, in supply of credit), it most suits the 'economically active poor' who can pay the costs and thus bypasses the very poor. Indeed, the latter may opt not to use such credit and thereby exclude themselves. The commercial model approaches the 'economically active poor' via 'savings and credit groups' or SHGs. Thus, where the poor assure the MFI of repayments, they also ensure the viability of the latter. It is between these two extremes that the Indian model of SHG-bank linkage has evolved. It provides 'unsubsidised' credit from the Indian banking sector to women's SHGs, at a relatively low cost, usually at 11–12 per cent per annum. The formal financial institutions (Regional Rural Banks in particular) treat poor women's groups as 'clients' rather than as 'recipients' of money. It thus goes beyond the subsidised/welfare approach of the 'subsidised credit' model and the 'neoliberal' approach of the 'commercial' model to one where poor women, by coming together as 'informal' SHGs, can hope to form new relationships with formal financial institutions.

Microfinance supply through the three models is depicted in Figure 1.1.

Figure 1.1
Spectrum of Credit Supply

Subsidised	Non-subsidised credit, bank rates	Commercial microfinance

Source: Authors.

This book classifies and refers to these three microfinance models. Women's preferences and use of money provided through these delivery models then reveal the meanings they attach to different 'monies'.

A Feminist Critique of Microfinance Impact Studies

A review of impact assessments of microfinance, internationally and in India, reveals issues of both approach and methodology. Two basic approaches have dominated the study of impact: the financial systems approach and the impact assessment approach, also referred to as the institutional and welfarist approaches, respectively. The first assumes that if the microfinance delivery institutions are sustainable then impact must be positive, making further assessment unnecessary. Conversely, the welfarist approach questions the assumption of a direct and positive link between organisational sustainability and poverty impact and recognises tensions between the two factors, thereby necessitating further study of poverty impact. Given the primacy of donor initiatives, impact assessments tend to be top-down, using a methodology developed and approved in line with dominant donor interests. Methodological challenges include the variability of approaches, issues and indicators and a lack of comparability across different studies. Participatory methodologies have gained credibility, as if these might also empower.[6] However, even where participatory approaches have been adopted, they can still conceal certain contradictions and also be used to promote donor-dominated perspectives, by presenting and communicating findings in a way that confirms scenarios already projected by policy models beforehand.[7]

Studies have emphasised the 'proving' motive for conducting impact evaluation, wherein the primary concern is to convince donors about efficient and effective use of funds. This is contrasted with the 'improving' motive, whereby the conduct of impact studies is aimed at enhancing learning, so that programme delivery may be improved to achieve better impact. Thus, literature has characteristically highlighted its most positive impacts, where contrary evidence would have questioned assumptions about self-reliance and drawn attention to other models of empowerment (for example, social movements) that question dominant neoliberal economic and political ideologies. The determination of success or failure is also influenced by interpretations of the complexity and confusion of practice which endorse prevailing policy, irrespective of other difficulties.

The growth and profitability of microfinance is built on the foundation of collective and responsible financial behaviour of women. Yet do we know whether the sector is responsive to women's needs? We need to ask whether what microfinance products and processes offered women is based on their own needs and preferences or is it indeed self-interest that motivates NGOs to engage in microfinance and offer the products and services that they do?

The gender discrimination inherent in microfinance is evident, yet rarely highlighted in current discourse. Large rural development grants are observably routed through male-dominated forums, for example, watershed development programmes, while credit is routed through women on the understanding that they are good repayers. This highlights a deep-rooted bias of donor and other support agencies which holds women responsible for results, whether this is related to population control, environment protection, IGAs or microfinance; while it is men who determined programme implementation, in relation to expenditure and repayment.[8]

Formal policy pronouncements do not recognise the paradoxical gender bias inherent in demanding accountability from women in an arena where they have little or no control—finance and poverty reduction. Even as positive impacts have proved elusive in mainstream government programmes targeted towards poor households (such as integrated rural development and watershed development programmes), women are expected to achieve poverty reduction through small loans to be repaid over short periods. Support to women remains conditional on their taking higher responsibility for positive social outcomes, while projects shy away from addressing their strategic needs, like their asset ownership, organisation building and better access to leadership and decision-making roles with regard to their own as well as public resources. At first, the notions of self-determinacy, autonomy and people's power appear as a counter ideal to neoliberalism, but self-regulation becomes another instrument of control.

Microfinance impact literature offers little reliable evidence of women gaining access to greater control over resources or increased autonomy. Instead, the framing of women as neglected resources, both as labour and as consumers, leads to the marginalisation of radical socialist feminism in gender and development debates. Microfinance has offered a compromise with feminists by adopting its vocabulary, as 'women's empowerment' became a periodic rallying point for feminists, governments, World Bank, commercial banks and NGOs, so much so that not only are women's voices and interests under-represented and underserved but even subverted by the use of language. Further, concepts such as empowerment, stakeholder participation and partnership can be used to interpret problems and solutions in ways that serve sectional interests and need to be linked with larger debates on accountability and democracy. Thus, a lack of accountability in government was first used as the rationale to promote NGOs, then later NGOs themselves were found to be lacking in accountability, and this criticism helped to later create a space for commercial microfinance organisations.

Subsequent studies reveal that while microfinance departs from more conventional development practices, its emphasis on individual entrepreneurship remains. This can detract from redistributive approaches to poverty reduction and makes it less of a departure from past practices, than a reconfiguration in line with power and governance relations of a neoliberal nature. Thus, even rights-based thinking, as elaborated in the concept of 'entitlement', has led to a pursuit of microcredit-led empowerment in ways that contradict its stated goals by marginalising any consideration of class relations and other social mobilisation for the reduction of economic and social inequalities.

The focus on the benign qualities of social capital and on the poor's own entrepreneurship has arguably allowed the state to further minimise its role and responsibilities for poverty reduction. Thus, microcredit accommodates the language of multiple interest groups (feminists and human rights activists), through its claims to simultaneously address both economic and social inequalities. This can be exposed in politically committed analyses of the processes through which impact is claimed to occur, and how the subjectivity of poor women is framed in the very projects that would address gender inequalities. It is indeed difficult to discern the real impact of microfinance on poverty reduction. Discussions with rural women in many states of India show deep divergences between the expectations of external agencies regarding how they expected the money to be received and used and the perspectives of the women users themselves. The dominant assumption is that there is a vast unmet demand for credit which, preferring timely access, takes little consideration of the cost while field evidence (presented later) contradicts this.

Political economists have argued that the impetus for the dominant microcredit policy is strategically oriented to facilitate financial sector liberalisation. Globalisation has imbued capital with the properties of 'financial derivative' by which it carries an 'abstract risk' rather than one 'grounded' in production-based labour, and thus allows it to be autonomous from real socio-economic structural relations.[9] Such literature maintains that spontaneous diffusion of industrial development to backward economies is limited by the unwillingness of leading capitalist economies to allow outsiders any claim upon their wealth. This poses a formidable barrier to authentic development strategies being formulated under a neoliberal context.[10]

Thus, impact studies address aspects of microfinance which may not necessarily concern the poor themselves. Such 'planned' knowledge is mostly donor driven and economically evaluative and often produced by a top-down, formally structured, predetermined research process which draws connections between large-scale inputs into microfinance initiatives set against outputs resulting from those initiatives. The intervening work of microfinance-in-action is not always treated as an independent or relevant variable for evaluation purposes, yet it intermediates both inputs and outputs. In this way, 'planned knowledge' can leave questions of implementation and management unasked and unanswered, unless there is more knowledge of actual microfinance-in-action.

This book seeks to shift the present balance of knowledge about microfinance towards more knowledge of the particular development issues emerging right now, which could have further bearing upon how microfinance might develop differently in the future. It highlights the need to identify other/additional variables, or else change the balance between them, in order to evolve existing knowledge. Emergent knowledge needs to capture these 'other' variables better, in a 'live' (and therefore still changing) situation, through well-chosen/executed methods from which fresh 'findings' should result, which the actual actors concerned would confirm, using language they find meaningful for those in their life situation. This book particularly emphasises the roles of local contexts, livelihoods and the gendered meaning and use of money as necessary variables for explaining actual microfinance-in-action, and elicits the actors' own definition of their situation, which then redefines the way microfinance is perceived.

FROM INSTITUTIONAL TO ACTOR PERSPECTIVES

Microfinance clients are situated in vastly varying livelihoods contexts, with geographical, ecological, economic, socio-cultural and institutional specificities that influence how money is used. However, orthodox impact studies do not always address these contextual factors; instead, they sequentially track the use of money from suppliers to women, into microenterprises and the resulting benefits. In following this impact chain, studies find it difficult to determine the benefits as cash can be taken for one use and applied easily to another without being discovered. Attribution of positive impacts to any one intervention such as microfinance is in any case problematic. Another factor is that poor women first access microfinance through groups, which are used as mechanisms for delivery, but the gender dynamics inherent in such use is not always understood and women's participation in SHGs can be utilised to the benefit of external microfinance-providing agencies. An understanding of how these groups both use and manage money (their own savings as well as external) is necessary to appreciate social relations and learning about the use and management of money.

This study explores how women themselves, especially some of India's poorest and most marginalised women, for example, the *devadasis*, regard microfinance and their perspectives as individual clients and SHGs are likewise analysed. This exploration was done through analysis at three levels, depicted in Figure 1.2, which together help understand the multiple meanings women assign to money.

Figure 1.2
Exploring Meanings of Money

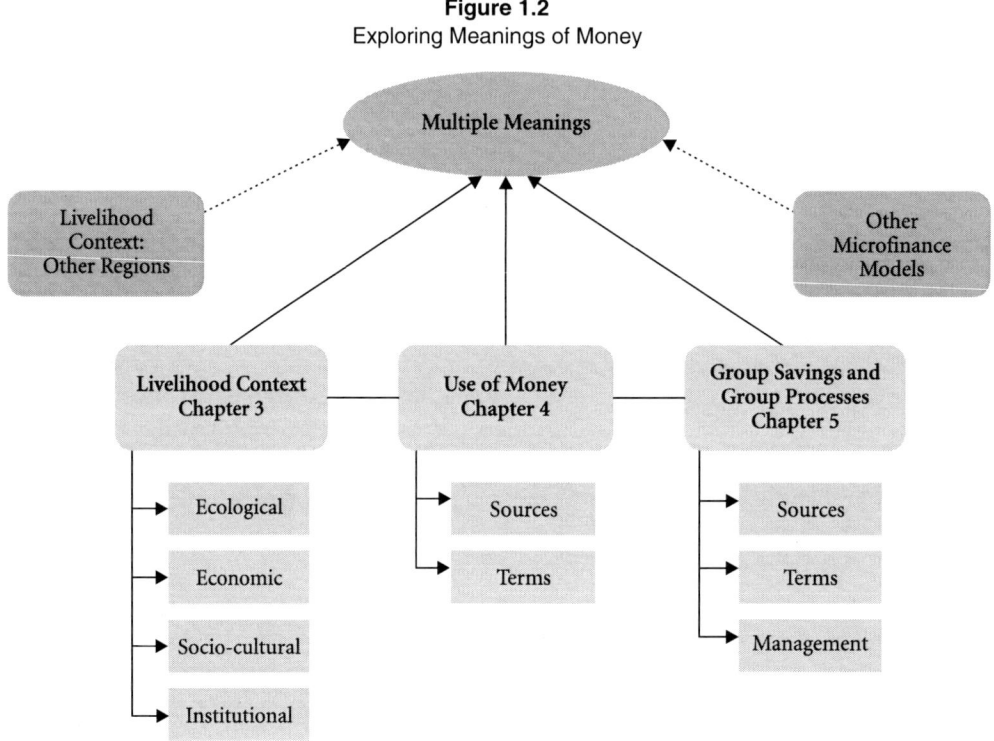

Source: Authors.

The use and impact of microfinance and the differentiated meanings of money are influenced by three factors: the livelihood context in which women live, how women use money and the processes by which groups manage money. Thus, the three critical issues are as follows:

1. How does the livelihood context of women influence their actual use of money? The livelihoods context comprises ecological, economic, socio-cultural and institutional elements. Women's own livelihoods are analysed with respect to their assets, incomes and life histories.

2. When do women access money and how do they use it? Women's perspectives of the different sources from which they access money, the terms on which they take it, the purpose for which they use it and their reasons for repaying or defaulting are analysed.

3. What is the impact of the social learning processes as a result of externally introduced SHGs on the one hand and the internal pre-existing social setting on the other? As women's SHGs are the forums for microfinance delivery, how groups seek and use money is observed. This includes how social learning takes place and how impacts are generated through group processes.

Understanding Livelihoods

Poor women do not see finance in isolation, but as one of the resources they use in order to improve their livelihoods. Women may not regard economic development (or availing microfinance) as a goal, but see it as a limited means of improving their immediate livelihoods. Actors can have different worldviews and assign varying priorities to the different means of improving their livelihoods. There is, thus, a need to go beyond economic, financial or organisational perspectives to understand actors' the perspectives of their livelihoods. Livelihoods are commonly perceived as comprising assets, abilities and strategies by which households make a living and develop the capabilities to protect their income and assets. This book considers the values of actors in designing their respective livelihoods strategies.

One indication of attempts to study livelihoods from people's own perspectives is the development of many frameworks for studying livelihoods systems since the 1990s. Livelihood systems cannot be viewed as the simple sum total of their various components—economic, social and cultural. Rather, they need to be viewed as multidimensional 'wholes', which include all the forces and constraints that determine group life in its entirety. This book uses three livelihood frameworks which are the result of the joint action taken by researchers and development activists to develop a holistic understanding of rural livelihoods.

The Sustainable Livelihoods Framework (SLF) originated from the Department for International Development (DFID), UK, to support policies and actions that promote sustainable livelihoods with the overall aim of poverty elimination. It assumes that the choice of livelihoods and reinvestment in assets is determined by the actors' own preferences and priorities, while recognising the different vulnerabilities they face, including shocks (for example, drought), wider trends (for example, depletion of resource stocks) and other seasonal variations. Weismann (1998) developed the actor-oriented perspectives (AOP) framework in response to the development crisis in South Africa caused by extreme poverty.[11] The SLF and AOP frameworks assume bounded rationality where human beings are often driven by self-interest, a premise that is questioned by those who cite examples of the role of non-economic motivation in development and human action.[12] This underlines the need to recognise 'non-rational behaviour', or behaviour not motivated exclusively by material self-interest, made possible here through the use of the Nine Square Mandala. It combines a rational approach with an intuitive sensing of the situation that increases understanding of rural livelihood systems (RLS).[13] It considers emotional aspects, feelings and orientations of individuals and groups. Högger (2004) conceived the Nine Square Mandala as a tool to undertake holistic research on RLS in India. SLF provided an overall link between the situations of the actors, outlined in terms of assets. When combined with an external set of structures and systems, these links determine livelihoods strategies and their outcomes (see Appendix 2 for the three livelihoods frameworks).

The frameworks were applied primarily at different levels, as indicated in Figure 1.3.

Figure 1.3
Application of Analytical Frameworks

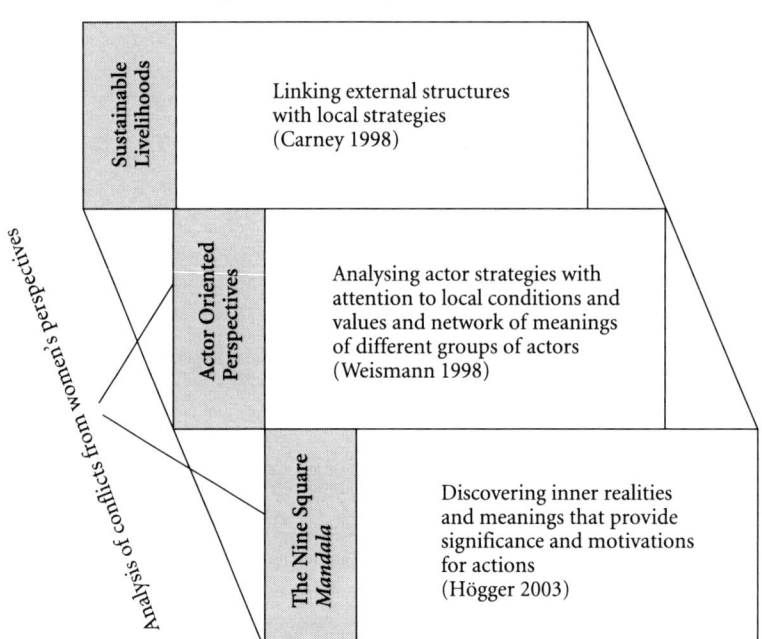

Source: Adapted from Carney 1998; Hogger 2003; Weismann 1998.

The SLF therefore links macro-level structures, conditions and institutions with household assets and strategies. A similar linkage was facilitated by AOP, which also provides the means to study strategies of different groups of actors, by assigning importance to values and meanings. The exploration of values and meanings was deepened further by the use of the Mandala, which accorded significance to emotional orientations. Thus, the three frameworks help to address existing divergence of perspectives regarding use and impact of microfinance. This is not simply a methodological issue of tools and techniques. The differences in understanding arise due to the underpinning philosophy about the sources of knowledge. The attention to actors' experiences and a gender perspective were lacking in earlier studies. The three frameworks address this by linking macro–micro factors, by focusing on women's perspectives and how livelihoods are impacted by microfinance interventions.

Women's own livelihoods are analysed with respect to their assets, incomes and life histories. Their poverty is considered to be geographically, socially, culturally and institutionally embedded and analyses the livelihoods context to understand the use and meaning of microfinance. This book does not adopt any one single definition of poverty such as, for example, income poverty. The finding that socio-cultural placement, that is, caste, is strongly related to the economic positioning in defining poverty is critical for those purposes. Further, certain groups, particularly scheduled caste (SC) and *devadasi* women,[14] who are deprived of basic human rights, experience social exclusion and extreme marginalisation. The intention is to understand the economic, spatial, social, cultural and gendered dimensions, of to both poverty and vulnerabilities as they relate to women.

Case Study Approach and Data Collection Methods

Previous impact studies show that cross-sectional research has highlighted key effects of microfinance delivery, but often overlook how women users, suppliers and intervening agencies all had different perspectives. Moreover, where divergences are identified, they often endorse and validate external perspectives, with less emphasis on women's own perspectives. To understand how women perceive and use money, what money means to them and how this compares with other assets, this book focuses on women's perspectives in various parts of the country and studies ten women's lives to delve deeper into actor perspectives.

The understanding of actors' perspectives and meanings is developed by drawing upon the disciplines of sociology and anthropology as well as development studies. A historical overview of the microenterprise and microfinance sector is supplemented and contrasted with field perspectives. Visits to 99 NGOs in 11 states and discussions in workshops with donors and NGOs provide a meso-level understanding of institutional issues (see Appendix 1). Grassroots perspectives are gained from discussions with over 130 women's groups in the different NGOs visited, and a longitudinal study of women (2001–07) is made, wherein narratives of women's lives supplement the financial and non-financial aspects of their livelihoods. As external microfinance has been introduced to women through SHGs, the mechanism and processes thus generated are important for understanding the women's perspectives.

The case study approach here employs various methods including interviews, participant observation and field studies. The case studies in this book focus on how women at the household level use money over an entire year. In addition, they contain women's life and loan histories over a 7-year perspective. Here, women's life histories have a life-cycle perspective, collected through reflexive and recursive interactions with women, which generated self-consciousness and awareness of their own situations.

The ethics of conducting life stories demand that the researchers be fair, honest, clear and straightforward, and ensure that women's interests, rights and sensitivities are protected. The process of narrating a life story is one of personal meaning-making, as the teller of a story reconstructs earlier experiences and also brings new knowledge while recounting these. Thus, women not only relate financial flows but also explore their attitudes towards money, credit, debt, SHG membership and peer group relations, the emotional content of different money transactions and the power of money as a social obligation.

The case study approach allows for investigation of a contemporary phenomenon within its real-life context, which is highly pertinent to the phenomenon under study. Further, multiple cases allow for the consideration and elaboration of different meanings and strategies, the evidence from which can be considered more compelling. Other economic research classifies rural households on the basis of ownership or lack of physical or human capital and recognises the social embeddedness of poverty as well as the feminisation of poverty. Following this understanding, the women case study participants were selected based on two main criteria: economic and social status, as detailed in Figure 1.4.

Figure 1.4
Socio-economic Positioning

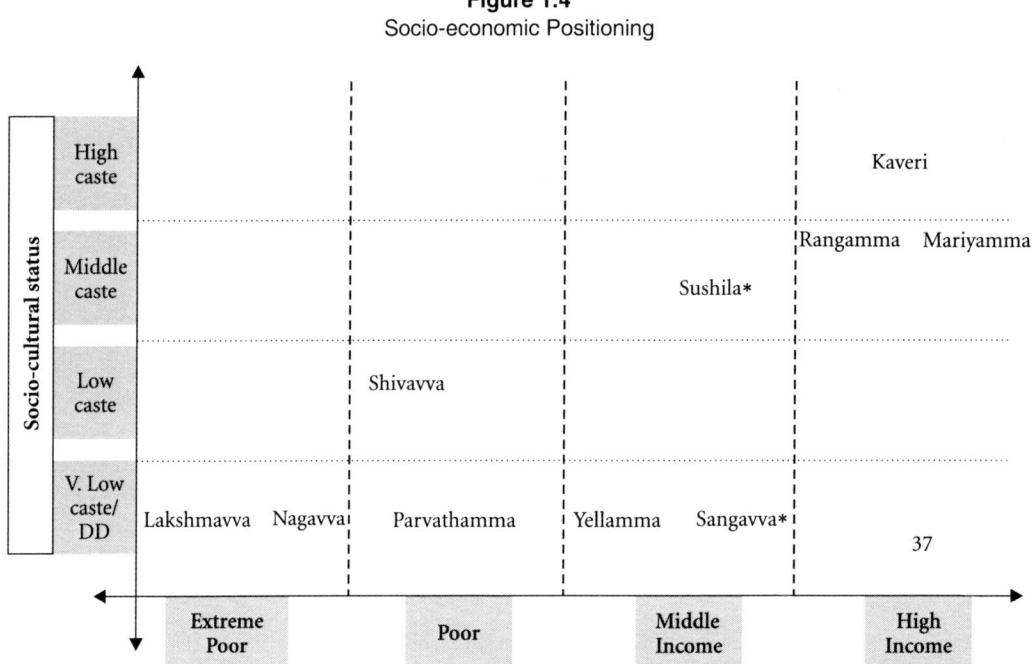

Source: Authors.
Note: *Poor when research started, improved during research period.

There were, however, several variations within these categories, which ensured that each case was different, so that wider insights could be gained. These variations were based on the family composition, whether the women held any land, had taken bank or MFI loans, had exercised leadership in groups/community and were dedicated as *devadasi*s. The selection of women was not guided by the generalisability of their experiences, rather each case study is important for its uniqueness, as each woman had a different family context and offered different interpretations regarding the use of money and group participation.

The *devadasi* practice is prevalent in several states of India. *Devadasi*s are women dedicated to the local deity. Although the reasons were once based on religious ideals, current practice relates to economic insecurity and emanates from the poverty syndrome and lack of other opportunities. Such women are not permitted to marry, but are instead inducted into a life world where they have to forge sexual alliances with men. In return, the men are expected to pay for the household expenses of the *devadasi*s and their children, though research shows that many male partners did not provide much support. It afforded an insight into the perspectives of the socially marginalised, and *devadasi* presence was significant because 23 per cent of the SC households in these villages had *devadasi*s and the average number of *devadasi*s per village was nine.

Some *devadasi* women were very poor, but others did have assets, and differences between them were further reflected in different livelihoods strategies yielding 'within-group' variations. Not only were the economic aspects of poverty important but the social and cultural embeddedness of issues such as gender inequities and lack of entitlements were important too.

Case comparison permits a grounded understanding of each single case, by specifying how, where and why it carries on as it does, and helps to investigate relationships and create constructs. This book considers female diversity and does not treat rural women as just one category. Different life experiences arise from their social (whether *devadasi*s or not) as well as their caste and economic status. In addition, several other factors restricted their choices. They were spread over different age groups from 26 to 50 years and had family sizes varying from 3 to 13. Some were in nuclear and others in joint family households. The diversity of their situations and experiences is difficult to generalise, but it does help to develop an understanding of the socio-economic spectrum that they represent, and also highlights their asset base as a key determinant of the vulnerability/security of their respective livelihoods.

The primary methods of in-depth case studies were semi-structured interviews with women, including questions covering the key issues derived from the three analytical research frameworks (Appendix 2). The case studies included detailed information on seasonality of cash flows over 1 year with each participant, between 2001 and 2003. Women self-recorded several aspects of their daily lives, such as travel, festival celebrations, illnesses and other special events, with a specific focus on collecting detailed financial flows (incomes and expenses) to analyse sources and uses of money within the household over the year. All other information about group transactions, loans, assets and events in women's lives were updated on a 6-monthly basis till 2005 and annually till November 2007. These were done through individual conversations.

Interviewers are necessarily implicated in creating the meanings attributed to money by research participants. As both parties participate in the interview process, meaning is 'communicatively assembled' during the interview, and respondents are seen not as providers of information, but as 'constructors of knowledge in collaboration with interviewers'.[15] Periodical validation meetings with the women participants helped to understand their attitudes towards money, credit, debt, SHG membership, relations with their peers, their means of reckoning fund flows and what is revealed and concealed from NGOs, the emotional content of different money transactions and the power of money as social obligation.

Caste-based practices of untouchability and ostracism were analysed in each village through open-ended group discussions. In addition, data on the socio-economic profile of the villages were collected from Sampark records. This information has been supplemented by means of interviews with key informants and group discussions to focus on topics of interest. Focus group discussions are especially designed to move the discussion towards concepts of interest to the researcher and are therefore useful in understanding the behaviour, customs and insights of the research participants and enable alternate interpretations.[16] The research made use of this methodology regularly over 7 years to validate all the major statements being made in this book on interpreting meaning of money and financial behaviour of women individually and in groups.

This two-stage process of analysis, followed by validation and feedback, enabled seeking alternative views on the data and competing interpretations (Figure 1.5).

Figure 1.5
Data Collection Methods Used

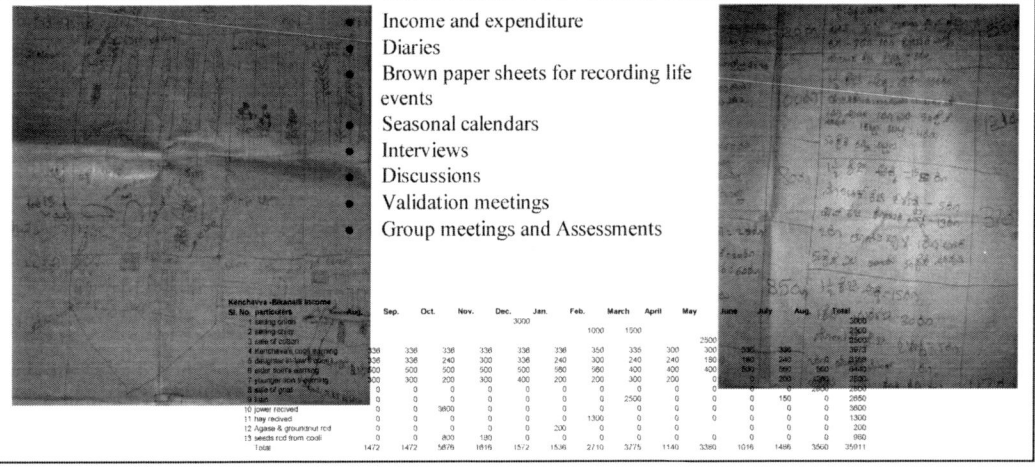

Source: Authors.

In addition to the women participants, discussions were held with family members, SHG members of the seven groups to which these 10 women belonged, villagers from the selected five villages and local NGO staff. There were 15 women's SHGs, and only those groups to which participants belonged were selected.

Benefits and Limits of Participation

An important concern of socially responsible research is tangible benefits for local research participants.

The women case study participants claimed several benefits from the research. The most important benefit was an improved understanding of their own situations and the research process. In most cases, the participation was not confined to the woman; her family members actively participated too. When Yellamma Hosagondabala was out of station, her daughter-in-law took the responsibility of calling the boy who was the scribe, and giving him all the details of income and expenditure to write down. The scribes felt that they had benefited too. The little boys said that they had understood household finances for the first time and also that they had learnt to form letters well, got good practice and improved their handwriting. The most important benefit that women claimed was that they had become aware of, and were therefore able to reduce their expenses. The interviewers learnt more about women's lives, participatory learning methods and seasonal calendars. They stressed that the relationships with women were most important in determining the quality of the information, and that the understanding of rural livelihoods gained from involvement in this research would help them a great deal in their work as field staff of a development organisation.

> *We were not getting an account of earning from coolie work, nor of any of the expenditure. But now we have the accounts of everything, we know the income and expenditure and everyone knows, so there is no fight among us. We know where we spend more, so we have also reduced expenses on beetle leaves, nuts and tea, tobacco, and snuff powder. Instead, we spend more on vegetables.*—Yellamma's daughter-in-law

> *We ourselves understood our life situation.*—Shivavva
>
> *We learnt a lot about our difficulties, expenses, income, food and other things like the way we spend our time and others in the family earn and use their time.*—Rangamma
>
> *It takes time to understand a question clearly.*—Nagavva
>
> *Earlier I could not explain to my son how I spent the money which was given by him, and used to get scolded by him. But now when he asks for details of expenses I do not say anything, I just point my finger towards the brown sheet on the wall where everything is written. He can see how even one paisa is spent and on what item!*—Shivavva

One strong indicator of women's ownership of the information is whether they themselves put it to use. In most cases, women began to use the information soon after they started recording it. It generated conversations within the family. The whole family did an immediate analysis of income and expenditure regularly and discussed where they could reduce expenses, or how they could manage the finances of the household better. Mariyamma's husband wanted to analyse the farming expenses. They were keen on seeing the consolidated figures on the spreadsheets and helped to clean up the anomalies.

Some were able to share emotional experiences. Sushila explained how talking about her life had allowed her to relive and express her pride in the way she had grown and improved her life:

> *I feel my burden is lighter after sharing my bad experiences. When I was a child, there was not enough food at home and I used to go to school with an empty stomach. When I grew up my father arranged my marriage with a person who was already married and did not have any work. At the time of the wedding my husband borrowed a sari from his uncle and told him that he will return it in one year, which he was not able to do because of lack of earnings. One day his uncle came and took away that sari from my body, because I was wearing the same sari that day. From that day onwards, the incident has been in my mind, and always disturbed my concentration on work. Now I feel good after talking about it with you and Sampark staff. Now I have improved financially by working hard, and having two to three businesses, I can say so proudly that I can buy five such saris with my own earning and give to my husband's uncle.*—Sushila

It is important to establish a role that can be assimilated by the society under study, as participatory and longitudinal studies tend to raise expectations of local people sharing their knowledge and experiences, which is problematic if the research is unlikely to link with problem-solving mechanisms.[17] The research was conducted in the field project of an NGO, where women knew and trusted the organisation, and therefore did not hesitate to provide information. The negatives were that there were expectations from the field worker in terms of loans, grants or jobs. In managing these expectations, the skills, sense of humour, personality of the researcher and relationship with the women come into play. The expectations were later fulfilled in a different way by assisting the NGO to initiate new action programmes based on women's common needs and preferences.

> *We feel so proud to be part of these case studies. If our life stories help in making and getting suitable projects to help poor women like us we will definitely try to do our best and share about our livelihoods.*
> —Rangamma

When one has done participatory research with women who are extremely poor, it is not always sufficient just to write about this in research reports and inform other researchers or policy makers. The link to development planning and policy can be difficult and uncertain, and even if some positive changes take place as a result, it may not benefit the participants concerned, as when researchers are asked: 'What will we get out of this research?' Then the only answer is that: 'You may not get anything directly, but poor people like you, somewhere in the country or in other countries, will get the benefit of this research.' The assumption behind this assertion is that new knowledge generated through research leads to changes in policy that positively impacts the poor.

> *In my field experience, I have been involved in many research studies; I never came across even one case where a woman expected money for her time. But definitely there is an expectation among women that this study will help them in some way in the future. Nagavva, Parvathamma, Rangamma and many others want at least one desire that they have for many days to be fulfilled: that they get electricity connections through the Bhagya Jyothi scheme. Rangamma wants a loan for an auto-rickshaw for her son. Sangavva and Nagavva want loans to buy buffaloes.*
>
> *We are working with them regularly, we keep in touch, through our research we understand their concerns and desires, so they want us to attend to fulfil their livelihood needs; they do not want cash from Sampark!*—Jeyaseelan, Manager of Sampark, Koppal

Policy change seemed too distant a promise to make to these actors. Discussions were held with the Sampark team about possible options. The first one was to pay the case study participants for their time. After all, the interviewers would derive benefits, directly (money) and indirectly (through publications, recognition and therefore greater status). This proposal was not acceptable for several reasons. To begin with, the case study women drew a certain pride from participation in this study. Money was not one of the rewards they were looking for; they had originally agreed to contribute their time free. To pay them for their time would have been to devalue their commitment to the research and deny their ownership of it. Second, as a development organisation, Sampark is engaged in many research projects and a practice started on one project would have to be followed by all. A new practice would change the basis of common collaboration, a change viewed by staff as negative. Finally, there could be competition for participating in research activities as compared with other development activities which would give wrong signals at the field level. So, direct compensation to only research participants was impractical while indirect benefits were too remote. Initiators need to plan for how the whole community can derive tangible benefits.

Sampark later reflected on the appropriate response to the question about how research can contribute to improve the livelihoods of local research partners. One of the most revealing explorations of livelihoods of women lies in their expression of their aspirations and hopes for the future. Invariably, these were not related to more money or assets, but to the future and security of their children's livelihoods, for which they perceived education to be a priority. Women in the poorest households, especially *devadasis*, were unable to earn enough through agricultural labour and tended to use the children to help with household chores, child care, sitting in the shop or grazing cattle. Children in these households were engaged in meeting livelihoods needs and tended to drop out of school. For these reasons, women wanted Sampark to invest in the education of their children, which they felt was their most important livelihoods need. Sampark decided to respond to this need, not only for the research participants but also for all the group members in all the villages it worked in. A survey was conducted to identify how many children dropped out of school and why. A full plan of education was prepared for children, whereby grants were to be raised for children of the poorest women and a credit fund for education was created for the group members who needed loans, not grants. Sampark decided to raise funds to educate children, for a period of 5–7 years, until they completed Class 10, that is, secondary education. By 2008, the organisation has extended educational support to 1,400 children.

> *I get Rs. 10–12 ($0.23) as wages. It is not enough for rice for the family. I took a loan and started a petty shop, now I sit there and earn Rs. 25 ($0.57) a day. But when someone is ill, and we need money, I leave my twelve-year-old daughter to sit in the shop and I go for labour work. She is good at studies, and when I make her miss school like this, she gets upset. Her teacher also thinks of her as irresponsible. If she stays with me, she will lose interest in studies. But if you take her away, she can concentrate on studies and I will still somehow manage the rest of the family.*
> —Member of a devadasi group

Another important contribution to the livelihoods of case study participants and others was made through the follow-up of the discussions on natural resources. Sampark engaged in a learning exercise with the villagers about sustainable management of their natural resources, helped to form a farmer's forum and facilitated their access to state funds to implement soil and water conservation measures in the village. This was set up as a credit fund managed by the farmers' forum. It was thus possible to raise issues and give voice to local people, which led development practitioners to consider other local livelihoods issues.

There were, however, instances of the limits to external support. Sushila's 10-year-old daughter has a tumour growing slowly in her brain. Sampark committed the money for her treatment and Sushila brought her husband and child to consult the best specialists in Bangalore. The doctor advised the parents that an operation was essential for the child's survival, but carried a risk of her daughter losing some of her mental faculties. The parents decided against the operation and the researcher and NGO respected this decision. The child now lives with her maternal grandparents, where they ensure that she attends school.

Lakshmavva, Parvathamma, Yellamma and Shivavva's children had dropped out of school. Shivavva still hoped that her child would continue his studies. She said:

> My son studied till the 5th class and stopped going to school. If we had forced him he would probably have continued. He has not gone to school for the past three years; he used to keep his bags and books at home and go to play marbles. He is not at all interested in studies. I had given him a school bag on which I did Kasuti work and look here, the bag and books are lying unused.

When the son was asked, he said: 'My mother took me out of school when I was in Class 3, after which I have not been to school.' When asked if she would send the son to school if someone sponsored his education, she said: 'I will definitely send him if he is interested', but he intervened: 'No, I won't go … I don't know how to read and write, I know how to write my name, that's all.' It was the same with Lakshmavva's children; they are unlikely to join school again. There was a realisation that in these cases there is no way of turning the clock back and that the livelihoods improvements and security for children who have already left school must be approached in other ways, for example, through vocational training for employment or enterprise. Later, Sampark started a programme of sponsoring vocational training with employment or enterprise linkages for school dropouts, which has supported 360 children by 2008. Yet, Lakshmavva's three children have not been able to benefit from this, either.

INTERPRETING MEANINGS OF MONEY

Money is viewed differently in the disciplines of anthropology, economics, sociology and organisational management. These differences evolve around what is considered money, the relation between economy and society, the different uses of money and meanings assigned to it. Individual, institutional and social factors confer different meanings upon money. Money has been analysed first by anthropologists who focus on primitive forms of monies in non-monetised economies. Economists limit money to a medium of exchange, means of payment, a store of value, a unit of account and a standard for deferred payment.[18] They conceptually separate economy and society and then treat economy as an independent autonomous sphere, whereby money supply can be used as a lever. Sociologists question this separation, treating the market as a social institution and the economy as subordinate to society, as if economic action is inherently embedded within given social structures. This book is a sociological endeavour that analyses *what money means to poor women living in backward areas by studying the livelihoods context in which they live, by exploring how they actually use money and how their groups manage both money and their internal group dynamics.* It incorporates the diversity and differences in women's perspectives and actions, as well as those of the intervening agencies. The approach is women centred, where poor rural women are the key actors in demanding and bringing about livelihoods changes, and in assigning meanings to the different monies they choose to access or reject.

The discourse and meanings of development have changed over time, mirroring changing economic and social capacities, priorities and choices. These are ultimately related to the changing relations of power and hegemony. Each development theory either promotes or challenges hegemony, as it is used not only to explain but also to set and promote agendas, mobilise opinions and build coalitions. The prevalent theories reflect currently available social science perspectives, thus highlighting the importance of culturally mediated meanings.

Earlier, in the 1990s, a leading paradigm in development studies and practice credited microfinance with poverty reduction and empowerment impacts. However, the financial systems thinking, which was then applied across microfinance programmes, emphasised modes of delivery that did not necessarily fit into the livelihoods contexts and preferences of the poor in remote and poor regions, although this divergence was not widely acknowledged at the time.[19] The issue of divergence between external perspectives (suppliers of microfinance) and local perspectives (users of microfinance) thus became important for framing further research questions. This meant being aware of 'multiple realities', meaning that various stakeholders may have diverse and incompatible world views.

The world view of the researcher, the ontology, and the understanding of how knowledge is generated, the epistemology, are informed by theoretical perspectives, which in turn influence the choice of methodology. At one end of the spectrum is the constructivist belief that there is no possibility of reflection of external reality. Our approach in this research is less extreme and assumes that the world is in part a construction and in part an interpretation, and that meanings are dependent on their context. This implies some acceptance of subjectivity and relativism. It takes a critical perspective to acknowledge that knowledge production itself can be associated with power and oppression, so that research methodology itself can impose or challenge existing power structures and relationships.

In contemporary research, the value of 'objectivism' as an appealing framework for determining the nature of rationality, knowledge, truth, reality, goodness or rightness has been replaced by relativism, which asserts that as judgements are necessarily based in subjective epistemological and moral positions: no one position could claim privilege over another truth or morality. 'Interpretivism' accepts that any socio-scientific account of social life is restricted in terms of time and space. Access to the past is always mediated by the present. Storytelling, involves 'emplotment', a process by which narrators use their own narratives to create identities.

A tenet of scientific research is its claim to objectivity, which in turn is seen as necessary for wider generalisation and applicability of the results. However, mere use of technology (statistical or analytical packages and use of computers) does not in itself constitute 'objective' research. The way research topics are selected, the research is designed and conducted, who participates and who gets left out may all increase subjectivity in research, and the values applied in these choices need to be recognised and stated. This helps to approach interpretation more cautiously and allows a discovery of deeper meaning. Therefore, it is more ethical to state one's own position in the research than to claim pure objectivity in research. This does not imply that the researchers' own motives, interests, social background, political and religious commitments have no influence over the research process, only that they be made explicit. An ethical concern here in this research has been the rational pursuit of other goals besides knowledge, such as respect to people's agency, social justice and gender equality. The example in Box 1.1 shows how participatory techniques can help find the most underprivileged. It is important to be conscious of this, as even so-called 'participatory research' may reinforce existing donor, project and people's hierarchies and biases.

Box 1.1
Representing the Invisible Women

In the first phase of field visits I met with over sixty groups. As a practice I gifted Rs 500–1000 ($11–22) to a group based on the local need. During a discussion in remote tribal village in Orissa's Kalahandi district, I was aware that all the women were poor and I could not decide whether to offer the money. After the discussion was completed, I asked the leader that if I wanted to give something to the most needy among them, whom could I give it to. She immediately said that the person was absent and asked me to go with her. She took me to an old dilapidated hut where a woman was lying on the floor, with fever and an infected wound on her foot. She had been unable to move for the past three days and was the only one who had not come for the group discussion that day. If I gave cash to her, it would help her to get treated. This underlined the importance of good leaders, and the need to care not only for those who are present for discussions but also for the missing ones.

Source: Authors.

Post-colonial theorists have questioned the ethics of 'giving voice' to others, thus warning that the claim of reflexivity should not be to authorise the writer. Others acknowledge unequal exchanges and argue that empirical research should learn from and not exploit others, and therefore practice greater reflexivity. Several means are suggested for this, which include treating participants fairly, showing them respect at all stages of research, keeping agreed appointments, fulfilling promises and agreed expectations and not compromising their anonymity without their consent.[20] Further, the multiple perspectives people have required 'multiple voices'. This research attempts to counter these biases, by following the precepts of participatory research. It selects rural, poor, remote areas, and most marginalised women of such localities. It involved taking time, being unobtrusive, respecting women's time, listening to and learning from them.

Women were themselves conscious of the responsibility of 'representation'. Some were willing to participate, as they felt that they were representatives of other women like them. Yet others were clear that they only talked about their own lives, which to them were quite unique and not representative of anyone else. Each claimed that she had never talked about herself and her life; no one had ever asked these women before, but they were keen to talk. Some said it would also be an opportunity for them to learn, not only from themselves but also from what the researcher herself was interested in. They were also keen to see the analysis and the conclusions of the research. The five *devadasi* women, who had experienced extreme subjugation, had repressed several emotions which they had never before voiced, and this research provided them an opportunity to do so. They shared their feelings: sorrows, happiness, hopes and dilemmas. Often the women's courage in difficult situations enabled them to learn from relating, sharing, analysing and consolidating their own experiences.

Thus, reality is depicted as multi-layered, with physical, emotional, mental and spiritual dimensions. Reflexivity is used to acknowledge the scholars' role in constituting the narrative text and also entails self-questioning, so it may lead to social learning and social feedback and be politically enabling. It has enabled a dialectical approach especially where local actors have diverging interpretations.

Critical discourse focuses on how language figures in the constitution and reproduction of social relations of power, domination and exploitation, wherein social constructs then tend to become fixed in meaning and implications and resistant to the internalisation of new discourses. This book pays attention to the constitutive role of language in advancing social and political debates in the public sphere through prevailing paradigms.

In selecting a research approach, gender is recognised as an important issue from both the supply and demand perspectives of microfinance. Women are viewed positively as good repayers and good contributors to family welfare, but are also treated as silent, and their voices, views and needs are thereby socially marginalised. It is imperative to develop a new approach that would acknowledge their voices, while also recognising that women are not a homogeneous group, and, like men, speak with different voices. An important feature of new participatory approaches has been the scope they provide for the recognition of the differences between women and men's roles in the production process. When the assumed homogeneity of farm households was deconstructed, space was also created for 'intra-household dynamics'. As the belief that more gender issues should be voiced gained ground, their importance for rural development was further emphasised. With more consultation with disadvantaged groups, the inclusion of women's perspectives gained acceptance. This book incorporates principles of feminist research and takes a post-colonial position in that it questions the hegemony of Western knowledge and models and considers the experience in India and Asia as valid and relevant in its own right.

Here, the meaning of money is being explored by analysing the social relationships created when women use money and explain why they use it as they do, 'earmarking' money from different sources. Human activity is seen as 'text', as a collection of symbols expressing layers of meaning, and interpretations of meaning can be made both by the social actors and by the researcher. This highlights the use of both qualitative and quantitative data for connecting the lived experience of people to meanings they assign.

This book adopts a reflexive and interpretive approach to qualitative inquiry, which emphasises these:

1. Value reflection, which asks whether the researcher is advantaged over the participants.
2. Subjective voice, which asks whether the voice of subjects is heard, legitimised or obliterated by research procedures.
3. Collaborative participation, which asks whether the subjects share the generation of knowledge and the benefits of the research outcomes.
4. Multiplicity of standpoints, which asks whether many different viewpoints and values are represented.

5. Representational creativity, which asks whether the representation and communication of research can be in forms other than formal writing.

It therefore prefers discourse analysis, narrative inquiry and participatory ethnography.

The key to understanding rural livelihoods lies not in the documentation of what actions people take but in their own interpretation of why they acted thus. Such deep probing requires joint exploration with the people themselves, which reveals the concepts and meanings contained in the actors' own accounts of the activities. These accounts are then re-described in social scientific terms and interpreted to answer both the 'what' and the 'why' questions.

This is a longitudinal view, with data collected at different time periods, permitting an analysis that involves the measurement and analysis of change within the same cases, and using the changes women expressed to place money as one of the many resources that they access, use and manage. This longitudinal study also involves creating retrospective data, as when women recall their loan histories.

The research approach emphasises gender and gender relations. It recognises that women-headed households may place an additional obligation on women which is at once physical, material and psychological. Women's agency, that is, what they may or may not do, can be severely restricted by their gendered identity and their formal entitlements, for example, property rights. Women may have unequal access to information and limited control over their own bodies. Gender roles are thus deeply embedded. Values, roles and capacities are all influenced by social and institutional structures, and women and men can negotiate social and institutional structures 'in a different voice'.[21]

Post-structuralist feminism challenges the notion of fixed meanings and moves away from analysing 'categories' to representing the multiplicity and diversity of individuals. This research too recognises the need to understand microfinance impact from the perspectives of different women, analyses their narratives to ground the theory of microfinance, and thus derive a deeper understanding of the meanings that money holds for them. It makes a major paradigm shift in the available understanding of microfinance. Even as it challenges the dominant paradigm, this book does not propose another in its place, instead recognising the multiplicity and complexities of different world views.

Sociologists typically emphasise that money has a social meaning. It is a medium of exchange because of social agreement about its value. It signifies a shift from the kind of personal relationships inherent in barter systems to impersonal relationships, and is even be used as power to maintain or change social relationships. Social relationships are embedded in social structures and are both determined by and determine financial relationships. While some naturalise money, believing that it just 'is', and only the attitudes to money vary, others imbue it with psychological meaning, relating it to self-concepts and identity. Money also has a cultural identity, deriving from the relations between individual and society in different contexts.

Money has always been a deeply gendered concept as well. Patriarchal societies did not consider women 'full', let alone economic citizens for some considerable time: they were among the ranks of those who were originally formally excluded or assigned to the informal finance sector alone. By assuming finance to be a neutral science, this original gender bias has effectively been ignored. The stead-fast (manly) virtue of financial practice was historically contrasted to the wily (female) character of fortune and hence risk. Thus, early depictions of credit portray it as a 'wily woman' to be mastered by the 'financial man'.[22] This could have some bearing upon the possible deep-rooted gender bias of microfinance models. Both the subsidised and commercial models have problems with giving independent agency to poor women themselves, while only the emerging model of unsubsidised bank credit considers them as 'customers' in their own right, and even here such status is only bestowed upon them where they exhibit 'joint liability'.

Multiple meanings of money have been expounded in the American context to analyse how differing perspectives of those who give and receive charity give rise to different 'monies' such as 'charity monies' and 'death monies'.[23] This book highlights the social, cultural and structural embeddedness of the meaning of money, and uses case studies in a particular context to discover differing meanings.

This book therefore seeks to develop a better understanding of money in a given economic ecological, socio-cultural and institutional context. It takes a social and structural perspective by the viewing government, banks, NGOs and SHGs as actor groups who have separate values, interests and behaviour relating to money. It considers values and culture as influencing how SHGs, as financial organisations, manage money. It seeks to integrate structural and cultural perspectives by viewing money both as a cause and as an effect. It examines the role and efficacy of money as a means of poverty alleviation. It emphasises that social and structural aspects define the use and meaning of money for any individual, household or group of people in a given context, not only the economic.

By using an actor-oriented approach, and treating the state, NGOs, banks and SHGs as actor groups, the book specifically endorses the sociological perspective of financial markets. It acknowledges each of these groups to be important actors in the market, along with donors and moneylenders. It brings out several factors of power and control over decisions relating to sanction, use and repayment of loans conducted on the basis of the social relationships formed between the money provider (banks and government), mediator (NGOs) and user (SHGs) organisations. It explores the formation as well as the breakdown of these relations. It shows that inappropriate social relations will not provide the foundation for stable finance, and therefore lead to a form of financial behaviour (non-repayments of loans) that undermines relationships. The book discloses more about when, whether and on what terms the money is borrowed, and also how it is spent. It also considers whether the money is returned, which is related to who is the source of money and what is the relationship with that source. It develops the concept of multiple monies in the context of rural credit for the poor, and a combination of charity and credit (with subsidised credit), and takes a step further by going beyond the use of money to the relationship with the lenders, to differentiate between credit alone and a credit/charity combination. It shows how people label different sources of money and relate differently to them. It also takes the perspectives of different actor groups (women, banks, NGOs and government) into account and therefore explains how they differentiate the external and local meaning of money.

The book follows three important steps for critical management research.[24] It starts with a critical approach, in a context where discourse still privileges dominant perspectives. Other perspectives are then explored with interpretive work focussing primarily on women and with the empirical exploration of meanings from actor perspectives. The third step is to critique Indian microfinance models along the proposed spectrum of 'traditional', 'emerging' and 'new' models without using normative labels such as subsidised, unsubsidised and commercial microfinance. This book goes beyond the 'outputs' and 'outcomes' of microfinance and explores what money means to actors *in situ*, how they opt to use money and how the outcomes are then accounted for. It questions any approach to microfinance impact which only highlights whether the poor 'have been reached' or 'have been left out' as if they do not have any choice. By contrast, it recognises women's agency, and also analyses how they continuously differentiate existing models of delivery, evaluate them according to their social relationships, make specific choices and thus adapt the money available. Thus, it considers problems of local, national and global relevance, and does this by focussing on issues of values and power, so as to use social science for transformative purposes. This discussion of conflict and power deepens social and political enquiry.

NOTES

1. The 11th Plan acknowledges that absolute numbers below poverty line (BPL) have not reduced over the past three decades (GOI 2008). For earlier poverty estimates, see DFID (2004).
2. A state-of-the-sector report on Indian microfinance states that only 30 per cent of MFI members are estimated to be BPL (Ghate 2007). For targeting women in microfinance with essentially supply-led perspectives, see Lingam (2006).
3. See NABARD (1999) for a definition. An informal upper limit was put at Rs 25,000, which is the equivalent of $568 at 2004 rates, which was later raised to Rs 50,000 ($1,036) for enterprises and Rs 1.5 million ($34,090), for housing as per the draft of the Microfinance Development and Regulation Bill (GOI 2007).
4. Early definitions articulated by key agencies working with SHGs included features relating to participatory decision-making (MYRADA 2001; NABARD 1998; PRADAN 1998, 1999).
5. This interpretation of the term paradigm and its application in research frameworks are discussed later.
6. Impact studies so far have not been methodologically sound and too expensive to carry out on a regular basis (Cheston and Reed 1999; Cheston et al. 2001; Sebstad and Chen 1996). The move towards participatory methodologies has been endorsed by many, including Akhter (2003), Blankenberg (1998), Edwards (1998),Johnson and Rogaly (1997), Mayoux (1997) and Rubin (1995).
7. This is highlighted in other large development projects as well (Mosse 2005).
8. Large official programmes implemented with external donor assistance, such as watershed development programmes and tank development programmes, typically form programme implementation groups which primarily consist of men, with women being brought in only in later years, through one or two reserved positions. Women are usually included in these programmes through savings and credit groups. This bias is further institutionalised due to men's ownership of land, keeping men as primary decision makers for spending grant money, while women continue to be responsible for taking and repaying debt. Later studies, such as a review of literature emerging from Asian, African, Latin American and Caribbean countries, show that women bear a disproportionate burden of the impacts of structural adjustments, by taking a higher share of the lower paid and contractual jobs.
9. LiPuma and Lee (2005) outline the process by which global finance becomes independent of traditional constraints, such as information transfers and national regulations and appears context-independent.

10. Patnaik (2006) presents a compelling analysis of this proposition showing growing inequalities despite growth, increasing agrarian distress in countries like India and claims that developed industrialised countries will block diffusion of industrial development to protect their control over their own wealth and overcome natural resource constraints.

11. The historical and conceptual development of the concept and one preliminary application is detailed in an article by Wiesmann (1998).

12. Raju et al., (2000) document a voluntary movement called Swadhyaya as an example of non-economic rationality.

13. A detailed explanation of the development and applications of the concept are found in Baumgartner and Högger (2004).

14. *Devadasi*s are women dedicated to the local deity and not allowed to marry, but stay with their parents and have relationships with men outside of marriage.

15. This is in contrast with a process whereby the participant provides information and the researcher then conducts the analysis without reference to the participant (Holstein and Gubrium 1995).

16. For details see Krueger and Casey (2000).

17. Dexter (1971) accords significance to social assimilation and Gerristen (2003) to understanding and meeting expectations of the participants and the local community.

18. For a discussion on historical insights into the sociology of money, see Baker and Jimerson (1992) and Stookey (2003) and for gaps in understanding of money, see Dos Anjos (1999), Gilbert (2005) and Pixley (1999).

19. A discussion of some divergences is found in Premchander (2004).

20. These principles are elaborated in Brewerton and Millward (2001) and Pini (2003).

21. For discussions on how key gender issues get overlooked in a traditional discussion on poverty and how women's voices, though different, can get subdued, see Jackson (1996, 1998) and Gilligan (1993).

22. See De Goede (2005) for a historical exposition of this thesis.

23. The multiplicity of meanings of money is highlighted in the American context by Zelizer (1989, 1993, 1994, 1998, 2000, 2005).

24. For an elaboration of critical management research see Alvesson and Deetz (2000).

2

Poverty in India and Role of Microfinance

Poverty, especially in rural India, is widespread and women bear the brunt of it. Many rural women are self-employed in very small-scale activities, but their contribution to the economy often goes unrecorded. Further, their income cannot lift them out of poverty, as they lack money, land and property (Agarwal 1994, Bhatt et al. 1998) receive wages that are lower than what men get for similar jobs and too low to pull them out of poverty. Poor women lack work opportunities, and when they have work it is usually casual and keeps them underemployed. They have limited skills and education, feel undervalued and lack access to better technologies, tools and productive assets including credit and other services which could improve their productivity and income.[1]

Officially, there is a multi-pronged approach to poverty reduction, ranging from policy support to agriculture and industry, through to enterprise promotion. Further, high rural indebtedness has long concerned the Indian government and measures have been taken to provide institutional credit to households below poverty line (BPL).[2] This chapter profiles the poverty reduction measures, provides a short history of the microcredit movement and summarises the different partnership models employed, mostly through the group lending method. Debates about these are set against the different behaviours and perspectives observed among users of these loans. These give rise to the key questions debated in this book.

POVERTY REDUCTION INTERVENTIONS IN THE PAST

The estimates of BPL people in India have ranged from 34.7 per cent during the period 1990–2002, and 35 per cent in 1993–94, to 26 per cent (showing that over 260 million lived BPL) in 1999–2000.[3] Historically, social organisations, government and banks have followed different pathways to poverty reduction. Yet, over time, these have converged into one single approach relying heavily on microfinance.

Non-governmental Organisations in Development: The Road to Microfinance

Social reform movements during pre-independence days were largely concerned with educational and cultural matters, as well as 'women's upliftment', albeit with a limited focus on poverty *per se*. In the 1950s and 1960s, a social welfare approach dominated, encompassing education, relief and employment, while the Gandhian approach combined social reform with village development. Inspired by Freire (1970), the 1970s viewed poverty as a structural phenomenon to be tackled through an active mobilisation of the poor. From the mid-1980s, non-governmental organisations (NGOs) emphasised the participation of the poor in integrated development programmes, and development agencies formally recognised the importance of socio-cultural factors. Now there is a convergence of approaches, with more NGOs seeking to combine organisational work among the poor with economic improvement.[4]

With a focus on support for income generating activities (IGAs) and enterprise start-ups since the early 1970s, women not only were targeted as the poorest and most vulnerable segment but also were considered critical to ensuring household welfare. Women researchers like Karl, Jain and Hoskin challenged the assumption made in development programmes that increased incomes for men translate into increased incomes for households.[5] They argued that the contrary holds true: that an increase in women's income contributes directly to a family's food and basic needs, as compared to men's income which is spent on personal consumption. Research further suggested that women's employment also led to reduced fertility rates, and therefore, better population control.[6] Such IGAs were often NGO managed. By the 1980s, with a lack of other employment opportunities for women, support for self-employment and women's enterprise became a viable option for realising their economic potential.[7] Enterprise start-up programmes, entrepreneurship development programmes and microfinance programmes all increasingly targeted women clients. However, most NGOs lacked expertise in business promotion and their programmes became expensive.[8] Thus, even as there was a shift from provision of 'welfare' services (for example, health, education) to a more 'structural' approach, the ideal of economic upliftment with women as the primary clients of projects was common to different approaches. Development programmes in the 1980s were increasingly group based, and savings were encouraged as a way of providing grants of equal amounts (matching grants). Later, programmes providing matching grants were tapered down and merged with microcredit programmes. With the success of microfinance and pressure to cover their costs, NGOs took to 'minimalist' microfinance, which only provided financial services.[9] These shifts are depicted in Figure 2.1.

The emphasis on financially sustainable microfinance institutions (MFIs) increased significantly by the mid-1990s, with NGOs beginning to transform themselves into financially viable microfinance organisations.

Figure 2.1
Changing Focus of Donors and NGOs

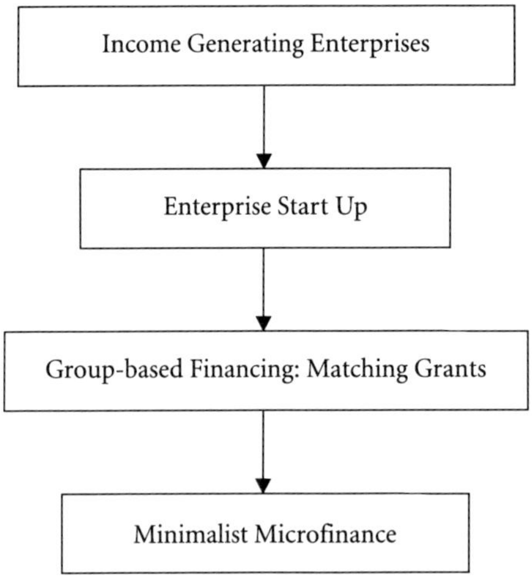

```
┌─────────────────────────────────────┐
│     Income Generating Enterprises    │
└─────────────────────────────────────┘
                   │
                   ▼
        ┌───────────────────────┐
        │    Enterprise Start Up │
        └───────────────────────┘
                   │
                   ▼
   ┌─────────────────────────────────────┐
   │  Group-based Financing: Matching Grants │
   └─────────────────────────────────────┘
                   │
                   ▼
      ┌───────────────────────────┐
      │    Minimalist Microfinance │
      └───────────────────────────┘
```

Source: Authors.

The prevailing Indian microfinance systems are a mix of minimalist, 'credit plus' 'including Business Development Services or other capacity building services' and integrated approaches. Various market-oriented, partially and fully subsidised, credit products are delivered through a range of organisations from professional, private, non-governmental and formal banking institutions. Most NGO/MFIs are fully or partially grant based; there are few examples of poverty-focussed microfinance organisations capable of sustaining themselves without substantial donor support.[10]

Government Attention to Rural Credit

Official planning in India began in 1938, and industrial policies with socialist leanings accorded priority status to agriculture, which supports over 60 per cent of the Indian population. The economic reforms introduced in 1984 were further strengthened in 1991 due to intervention by the World Bank and the International Monetary Fund and have been criticised for increasing the numbers falling BPL.[11]

Banks and Poverty Lending

Policy framers in pre-independence India were of the view that market imperfections led to local monopolies with moneylenders charging exorbitant interest rates. The first estimate of rural debt in India made by McLagan in 1911 placed rural debt at Rs 3 billion ($66.6 million). The Central Banking Enquiry Committee estimated rural debt in 1931 to be Rs 9 billion ($200 million) and the All-India Rural Credit Survey calculated a debt level of Rs 315.8 ($7.01) per family in rural areas, yielding an estimate of Rs 18 billion ($400 million) in 1950–51. Over 90 per cent of the credit was from informal sources, and over 70 per cent from landlords/moneylenders and traders (RBI 1954). The allegedly exorbitant rates led to the loss of land of small cultivators, increasing their debt and overall poverty. The situation deteriorated for peasants as recurrent natural disasters and low productivity compounded the problems of the existing exploitative land revenue system. Land improvement loans were introduced in the late 19th century.[12]

The structure of institutional finance for the poor is depicted in Figure 2.2. The historical development of credit was based on the concept of 'development banking' whereby credit is an instrument for mitigating poverty and promoting agricultural and rural development. The Indian government allowed formation of cooperative credit societies in the early 20th century, with the aim of building an institutional finance system for agriculture and relieving farmers from indebtedness. Later, long-term credit for reclaiming agricultural lands was introduced through cooperatives, and the cooperative credit system was linked to the central banking system. However, local elites could use their position to consolidate their control over the poor.[13] When cooperatives failed to make inroads into informal credit, the Reserve Bank of India (RBI) introduced long-term support for agricultural credit and also revamped the structure to increase state support to cooperatives.

Alongside these cooperative developments, the government also encouraged commercial and other banks to extend credit to priority sectors (agriculture, small and microenterprises). The State Bank of India (SBI) and its eight subsidiaries opened 415 rural branches between 1959 and 1964. On the nationalisation of 14 banks in 1969, the banking sector became more involved in providing rural credit through 'social control' which had three main strategies: promotion of institutional expansion, direct lending to disadvantaged borrowers and priority sectors and subsidised interest rates.

By the 1970s, weak financial management of cooperatives was recognised as a problem and a new experiment to try and meet rural credit needs was conducted through Regional Rural Banks (RRBs). By 1982, the Agricultural Refinance division of the Reserve Bank was constituted as a separate entity—an apex bank—the National Bank for Agriculture and Rural Development (NABARD).

In the 1980s, poverty alleviation programmes were implemented in tandem with district credit plans drawn up by banks and coordinated by NABARD. By 1990, the Service Area Approach was introduced, whereby RBI required banks to estimate and meet the credit needs of defined 'Service Areas'—groups of 20–25 villages, though later abolished—to allow people to access any bank for financial services (RBI 2007a). In this way, a large and expanded structure of financial services through cooperatives, RRBs and commercial banks at local level and support systems at district, state and national levels sought to meet rural credit needs. In 2007, the banking structure appeared as in Figure 2.2.

There were a total of 195,320 branches of formal banking institutions. The total number of commercial bank branches was 68,262 in March 2005, of which, three-fourths were metropolitan and urban and the rest rural.[14] Cooperative banks had over 0.1 million branches, including 92,628 primary agricultural credit societies. There were 196 RRBs, sponsored by 28 commercial banks,

Figure 2.2
Banking Structure

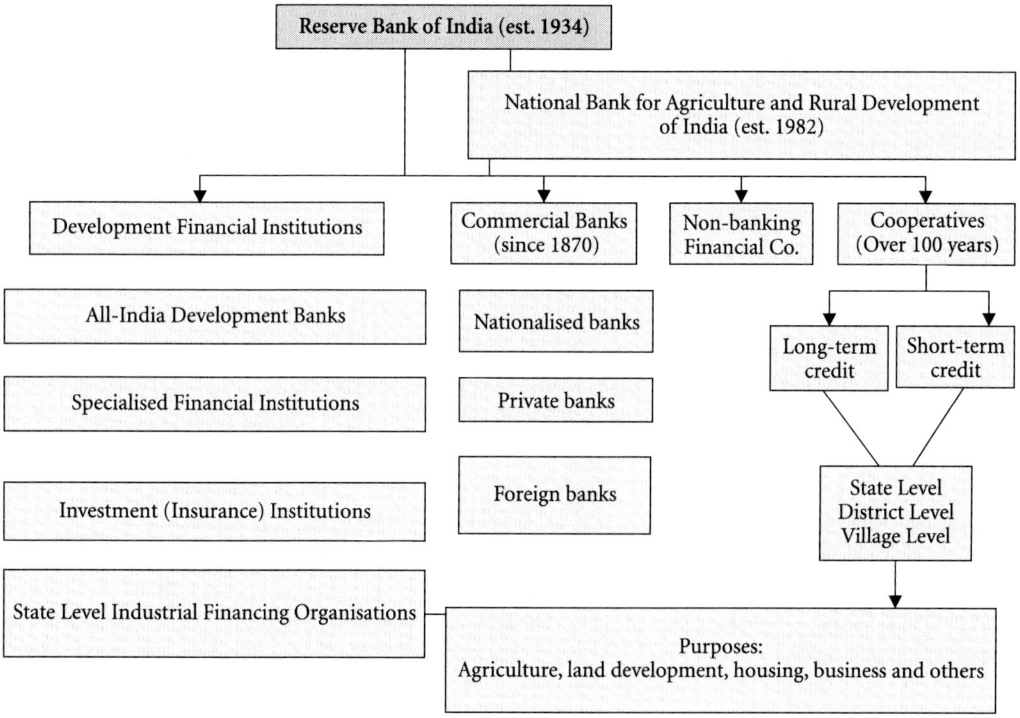

```
                    ┌─────────────────────────────────────┐
                    │  Reserve Bank of India (est. 1934)   │
                    └─────────────────────────────────────┘
                                      │
                          ┌───────────────────────────────────────┐
                          │ National Bank for Agriculture and Rural Development │
                          │             of India (est. 1982)       │
                          └───────────────────────────────────────┘
```

| Development Financial Institutions | Commercial Banks (since 1870) | Non-banking Financial Co. | Cooperatives (Over 100 years) |

| All-India Development Banks | Nationalised banks | | Long-term credit | Short-term credit |

| Specialised Financial Institutions | Private banks |

| Investment (Insurance) Institutions | Foreign banks | | State Level District Level Village Level |

| State Level Industrial Financing Organisations |

Purposes:
Agriculture, land development, housing, business and others

Source: Authors.

with 14,446 branches. There were 403 RBI-approved non-banking financial companies (NBFCs) who could collect public deposits and another 12,209 who were not permitted to accept public deposits (RBI 2007c).[15]

Even with the impressive growth of branches, there is now a widespread recognition of the fact that 30–35 per cent of credit demand is still being met only by informal sources rather than the banking sector, especially moneylenders, at interest rates ranging from 2 to 10 per cent per month, or even higher.[16] Therefore, the government has initiated steps towards financial inclusion, whereby the banking sector is encouraged to extend credit to all households in a district. New initiatives in this direction include the usage of mass media for financial awareness, Kisan Credit Cards, credit counselling and collaboration with the postal services to extend branchless banking. The SBI plans to establish upto 100,000 service centres all over the country and the use of technology is expected to reduce costs and expand outreach.[17]

Government initiatives in microcredit are part of the Integrated Rural Development Programme (IRDP) of the Ministry of Rural Development of the Government of India (GOI). IRDP was launched in October 1980 and involved skills training and subsidised credit support for the poor, which frequently never reached them. The IRDP experienced problems of grant disbursal and was plagued by low rates of repayment and poor quality of assets.

There was a conflict between the logic employed by the government and that of the banking sector with regard to poverty lending. In addition, the government administratively targeted the poor through a system which classified households by issuing of cards as certification of them being BPL. Corruption meant that some never obtained these cards, with others buying them instead. In addition, there were loan *mela*s: loan disbursement events that were politically motivated, wherein loans were given for agricultural and other purposes without due appraisal. This led bankers to believe that the poor were high credit risks.[18] Although banks were expected to extend 40 per cent of their credit to the priority sector, during the first half of 1990s they reached a maximum of 35 per cent .[19]

In the early 1990s, the experiences in subsidised credit to rural areas were not positive and such credit was seen as one of the major reasons for the non-viability of RRBs. In the 1990s, the government sought to reform state-owned banks and many donors (for example, Swiss Agency for Development and Cooperation [SDC]) invested money in the turnaround of the RRBs, which were seen as instrumental in providing rural credit, and open to reform, given the political will.[20] Box 2.1 shows that, by 2003 SHG had become the '*modus operandi*' of almost all government departments.

Box 2.1
Official Acceptance of Women's SHGs

'*The forest department, agriculture department, social welfare department, ICDS and block (a group of 40–80 villages, which form an administration unit of 6–8 panchayats) functionaries, teachers, SC/ST Corporations, in fact all except the Police Department have been asked to form women's groups!*'—Remark by the head of an NGO in Orissa.

Source: Sampark (2003).

Acknowledging the success of self-help groups (SHGs) in channelling benefits to women, the central government then merged most major programmes of the Ministry of Rural Development with a credit component, into a single self-employment programme in 1991. This programme, the Swarna Jayanthi Gram Swarozgar Yojana (SGSY), was delivered through SHGs, at least half of which would be women's SHGs (NABARD 1999). The programme sought to cover 30 per cent of all poor rural families in the 5 years following the reforms.

In addition to the official programmes, private sector banks have also begun taking a keen interest in microfinance in recent years. Those with greater involvement included Industrial Credit and Investment Corporation of India (ICICI), Citibank, Hong Kong and Shanghai Banking Corporation Ltd, Housing Development Finance Corporation, ABN-AMRO and Unit Trust of India, who introduced a range of innovative products and channels to increase outreach. ICICI was the largest private lender in 2006, lending through MFIs as bank correspondents. However, this declined in 2007 due to a confluence of factors internal to ICICI, multiple borrowings by clients and RBI regulations.[21]

Partnership Models

The gradual acceptance of microfinance has led to the emergence of partnerships between donors, government, banks and NGOs. International donors encourage NGOs to enter microfinance as an effective entry point for credit, other development work and livelihoods support.[22] The distinctive character of Indian microfinance, where NGO/MFI interventions coexist with those of the government, paralleled with several multi-partner collaborations, leads to a complexity arising from the different goals of the intervening organisations and the roles they now play. The resulting models, based on inter-institutional partnerships, are characterised as 'relationship' banking or 'linkage' banking and are comparable with the Bangladesh model of 'parallel banking'.[23]

A Typology of Credit Programmes

Classifications can be made according to whether organisations are national or international, whether multi-purpose or minimalist, and are based on the extent of their linkages with external donors. They can also be based on whether the institutions are in the formal or informal sector.[24] The typology of credit programmes, developed here for comparing the models of microfinance in India, refers to the different types of emerging partnerships as depicted in Figure 2.3.

Figure 2.3
Characteristics of Indian Microfinance Models

Institutional form / Role played	Bank	NGO	Cooperative	MFI
Facilitator	**Nature of Partnership:** Combination of institutional form and role played			
Provider				

Source: Authors.

The main differences occur in the following:

1. The form, or constitution, of the institution, which defines its ownership, management and services offered.
2. The nature of delivery, that is, 'provider' of microfinance, or another organisation is used as an intermediary for promoting SHGs and building their capacities, Self-Help Promoting Institution (SHPI), or 'facilitator'.
3. The partnership of different types of organisations and the roles and responsibilities of each.

An application of the three-dimensional typology suggested earlier is presented in Table 2.1.

Table 2.1
Partnership Models for Microfinance Delivery

Institutional Form and Role Played	Bank Linkage Model		Cooperatives	MFI
	Bank	NGO		
Facilitator	Bank as provider (Figure 2.4)	NGO as facilitator	Cooperatives as providers, sometimes they work through SHGs, so are SHPIs too (Figure 2.7)	MFIs as providers, to individuals/SHGs, so many were also SHPIs (Figures 2.8 and 2.9)
Provider	Bank as provider Bank as SHPI (Figure 2.5)	Bank as provider to NGO NGO as provider to SHG (Figure 2.6)		

Source: Authors.

Bank Linkage Model

The mainstream model involves an SHG of 15–20 women, formed for mutual benefit and enables access to basic financial services. Members begin by saving small amounts of money, which are pooled, and these collective savings are converted into credit so that women can borrow from within the group at an interest rate that they agree upon.

After the SHGs are nurtured and trained by the NGO, the local RRB or lead bank can lend directly to these informal groups. As a result, SHGs are seen as grassroots structures to be promoted as channels for lending by the formal banking system. Due to the success of a pilot project launched in 1992 by NABARD and NGOs, the RBI formally established the SHG-bank linkage programme in 1996 as a mainstream lending activity of the banks under priority sector lending. Under its scheme, NABARD provides refinancing to commercial banks at a maximum interest rate of 9.5 per cent. The banks, in turn, lend to SHGs at a rate of 11–12 per cent. The SHGs are free to set their own interest rate when they lend to individual members; they usually set it to around 24–36 per cent.

By 2007, a total of 2,924,973 SHGs had been linked, reaching 41 million households spread over 587 districts. The average first loan per family was Rs 3,167 ($79), increasing to Rs 5,621 ($140) for a repeat loan.[25]

In the most common model of SHG-bank linkage, depicted in Figure 2.4, the bank provides the finance directly to the groups, the facilitator works in the community to promote and train and the NGO is the facilitator, also known as the SHPI. In 2007, this model accounted for 75 per cent of the SHG-bank linkages.

Variations in this model include an RRB, a Farmers' Club in the local area or a local rural volunteer as the SHPI (Figure 2.5). Seventeen per cent of the SHG-bank linkages in 2007 were made this way.

Another type of partnership involved NABARD/Banks providing funds to NGOs who act as intermediaries for lending to groups (Figure 2.6). In 2007, funding provided through NGOs reached 8 per cent.

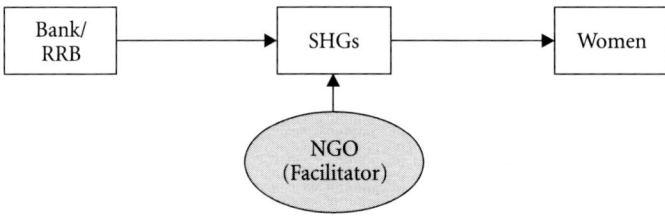

Figure 2.4
SHG-Bank Linkage Model (NGO as 'Facilitator')

Source: Authors.

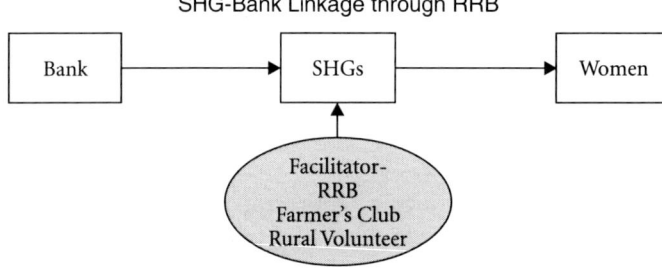

Figure 2.5
SHG-Bank Linkage through RRB

Source: Authors.

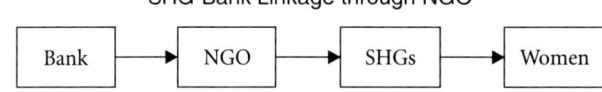

Figure 2.6
SHG-Bank Linkage through NGO

Source: Authors.

In addition to funds and refinance provided through the banking sector, NABARD also provided funds to second-tier institutions to further lend to other NGOs, for example, Friends of Women's World Banking (FWWB). NABARD provided funds to groups or federations of women that function as SHPIs and MFIs, for example, federations of DHAN, Madurai.

In the bank linkage model, the facilitating NGO plays the vital role of strengthening the groups' institutional capacities, with the intention of developing their capabilities to manage resources, including credit, and offering opportunities to acquire new productive skills. It also helps to link SHGs with local banks, markets and/or private sector enterprises. The NGOs thus worked as 'brokers' enabling the poor to become more bankable and the banks to be more poor-friendly. Because SHGs have a record of high repayment rates, the banks only require social collateral—the promise and expectation that group members will pay back on behalf of any defaulters—so the SHGs function as joint liability groups. At the same time, the facilitating NGO may achieve the objective of transforming livelihoods. Organisations such as MYRADA, Professional Assistance for Development Action (PRADAN), League for Education and Development, Outreach and Sampark all follow this framework. These institutions contend that it is not merely the provision of credit which is empowering, leading to a transformation of livelihoods for the better, but that proper self-management will empower as well. However, the relatively slow expansion of SHG-bank linkages in comparison with that of SHGs and the corresponding increased demand for credit necessitated the development of alternative credit delivery methods to fill the 'credit gap'. Commercial banks only dispense subsidised microcredit to fulfil minimum official obligations. NGOs cannot attract enough funding to continue their capacity building and facilitating roles.

Larger NGOs act as facilitators (MYRADA, PRADAN, Centre for Youth and Social Development (CYSD), Outreach, DHAN) or providers (Self-Employed Women's Association [SEWA] Bank, BASIX, SHARE, Spandana, CASHPOR) while still attracting significant donor funding. The medium and small NGOs find it more difficult to attract funding and have to comply with the demands of the more dominant industry models.

Microfinance Cooperatives Model

One alternative to the SHG model is the registered cooperative, which preceded the SHG model in providing short- and long-term agricultural credit in India. The main sources of funds include members' savings and loans from NABARD or RRBs (Figure 2.7).

Figure 2.7
Cooperative Model

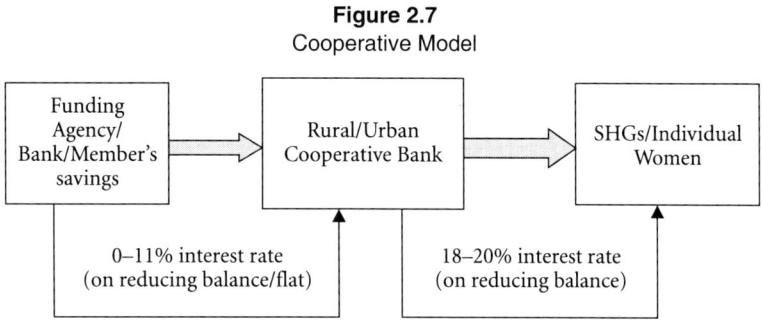

Source: Authors.

A cooperative is an autonomous association of persons united voluntarily to meet their common economic, social and cultural goals and aspirations through a jointly owned and democratically controlled enterprise. Most cooperatives include member-financing and savings activities in their mandate. Historically, while cooperatives were established channels for organising rural producers, they were largely state backed and politicised accordingly. In May 1995, the Mutually Aided Co-operative Societies (MACS) Act was passed in the Andhra Pradesh (AP) state assembly to enable cooperatives to reduce state patronage. Similar acts were subsequently passed in Bihar, Rajasthan, Karnataka, and many other states to this effect; and the Multi-state Cooperative Societies Act was passed by the central government in 2002. More recently, GOI has started a programme for the revival of cooperatives such that they can work as autonomous self-reliant and democratic institutions accountable to their members.[26]

NGO–MFI Model

The bank linkage model was slowly accepted, then proliferated by the early 1990s. As donor interest has grown, more NGOs have become financial intermediaries. NGOs registered as charitable institutions can engage in microcredit, provided they do not collect savings (Figure 2.8).

Figure 2.8
NGO–MFIs as Financial Intermediaries

| Funding Agency/ Bank | → | NGO/ MFI | → | SHGs | → | Women |

| 11–14% interest rate (flat or reducing balance) | 18–21% interest rate (flat or reducing balance) | 24–36% interest rate (flat or reducing balance) |

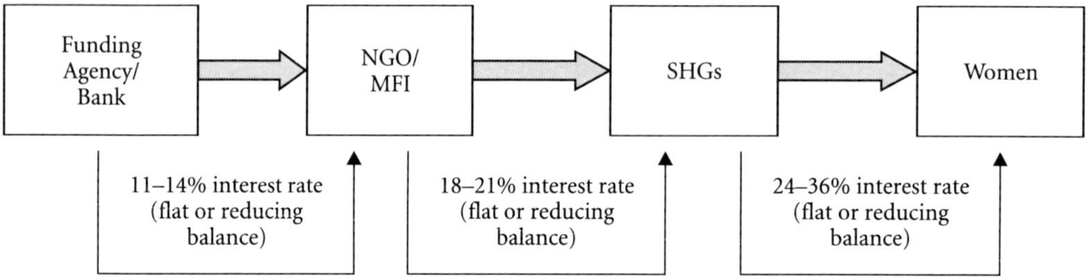

Source: Authors.

Responding to their cost structures, they charge higher interest rates. For instance, while a wholesale lending organisation like FWWB or Small Industries Development Bank of India (SIDBI) Foundation for Microcredit (SFMC) provides bulk finance at 11–14 per cent, NGOs/MFIs in turn on-lend to the SHGs at 18–24 per cent, and the SHGs then charge individual members between 24 and 36 per cent per year. Even with increased interest rates, most MFIs are still not able to reach an optimal scale of operations.

Another institutional form is that of the Section 25 Company, which is a not-for-profit firm registered under the Companies Act. Again, this allows for microcredit activity but not for the collection of deposits. These companies can increase their coverage of the poor only if they can seek large loan funds, which require a large equity base. As few donors invest in not-for-profit organisations, they seek different legal forms, which will ostensibly enable them to reach more borrowers and achieve financial sustainability.

A number of apex refinancing institutions for development converged on lending through NGOs and SHGs to women. Approximately 300–400 NGOs were engaged in financial inter-mediation with Rs 800 million of credit ($17.7 million). However, these institutions had a 'credit first' approach which focused on credit delivery and reduced empowerment to secondary status.[27]

Since the late 1990s, donor-funded projects have encouraged NGOs to become independent MFIs. A few adopted a method by which they established a set of three organisations (Figure 2.9). Women

Figure 2.9
MBT/MACS–NBFC Model

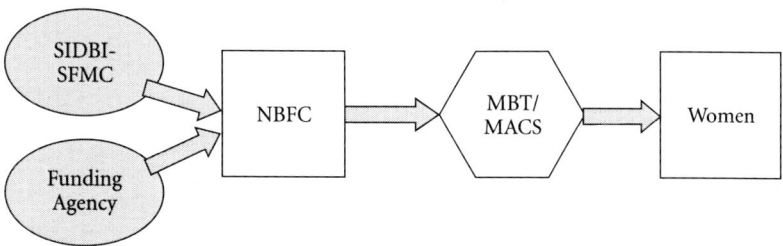

Source: Authors.

members first deposited their money in a Mutual Benefit Trust (MBT) or a MACS—technically a member-owned institution, which is permitted to collect savings from members. Money was then routed to an NBFC, to raise further capital, in the form of both equity and loans. This augmented 'stock' of money was then channelled to women as loans to generate profit for NBFCs. Such NBFCs were not always permitted to take public deposits. The RBI Annual Policy Statement for the year 2004–05 announced that in view of the need to protect the interests of depositors, MFIs would not be permitted to accept public deposits unless they comply with the extant regulatory framework of the Reserve Bank.[28]

In addition to routing the member's savings, some NBFCs also encouraged women to take shares. Members were required to contribute 1 or 2 per cent of the loaned amount to them, at one stage or over 50 instalments in a year, to be taken as equity. This raised legal complications because the law did not then specify whether MBTs and MACS could route their member's money to NBFCs. If NBFCs were not authorised to take deposits, such routing could be interpreted as jeopardising the security of the women's deposits.[29] Women did not necessarily understand the difference between savings and equity, considering equity participation a compulsory charge for taking a loan. Normally, NBFCs would have considered compulsory charges as 'fees' and then book revenues and pay taxes. By booking these charges as women's equity, NBFCs not only avoided tax but also augmented their own equity base, so they could raise more loans. However, the question remained whether it was right to create a stake for women without giving them a voice then. NGO staff and senior management managed these NBFCs and women's direct board representation was nominal at best. These operations were neither covered by deposit insurance nor controlled by bank supervision agencies, and covariant risks were judged high as members were from the same locality and community.[30] As a result, the 'tenuousness of the NGO position was even more dangerous to the saver' (Padhi 2003: 4).

This raises the question of whether ownership and control of their own finances is actually important to women and whether it has an effect on how they manage money. Literature does neither prioritise protection of women's savings in the agenda for building people's own organisations nor recognise that stakes in the organisation must be substantial enough to hold their leaders accountable.[31] This is further explored later in Chapter 5.

APPROACHES TO MICROFINANCE DELIVERY

As regards microfinance delivery, two broad schools of thought have emerged. The first pursues unmet demand for credit through new supply institutions[32] and advocates transformation of NGOs into MFIs, believing that NGOs with little or no previous experience as MFIs reach the poor quicker than the commercial banking network.[33] The second calls for more 'social engineering' as the strength of NGOs and banks in banking.[34] A risk of NGO transformation into MFIs is that the NGO moves away from its development tasks, from investing in human and social capital at the grassroots towards 'pure' financial intermediation.[35]

To the second school, the NGO sector is not yet equipped to become full-fledged MFIs. New MFIs are allegedly slow and expensive to develop, and their success is based on intensive grassroots monitoring, which increased costs, but improved outreach as well as sustainability.[36] Their rationale is not to fill the gap between demand and supply at high cost, but rather to create competition among suppliers that would then resolve the cost of credit, though this may not be an easy option.[37] Those who advocate new MFIs hold that credit needs to be supplied, even at high cost, whereas the second school sees the problem in terms of providing credit to users at reasonable costs.

The move towards minimalist commercial microfinance excludes provision for non-credit services such as entrepreneurship training and linkages, which is variously attributed to the high cost of delivering and measuring these inputs, and the fear of so eroding the financial sustainability of organisations that they lose potential donor funds.[38] Other agencies believe that capacity building of clients is an NGO responsibility (thus externalising of the issue), which they cannot yet meet.[39] Townsend et al., (1999) further attribute the trend towards minimalist microfinance to a situation where southern NGOs have become a transmission channel both for donor fashions and for 'new managerialism', making it more difficult to 'listen' to and prioritise the poor. Townsend et al., (2003) argue that development trends, as evidenced in practice and vocabulary, tend to transfer quickly from donors to NGOs generally creating the phenomenon of 'donorspeak'.

If NGOs wish to develop 'social capital', they should assign priority to people-owned institutions with implementation processes that empower the poor. Such an effort needs long-term partnership approaches.[40] However, in India, while the establishment of financially sustainable MFIs is currently well supported through donor programmes, funding support for microfinance programmes that seek to empower people and build people-owned MFIs is less widespread. Social capital is used to place the financial health of the microcredit programme before the welfare of its members. Holvoet (2005) and Rankin (2002) argue that social capital of women is used as if free of cost, to conduct financial intermediation rather than liberate their transformation potential.

The strategic role of the microfinance sector still needs to be addressed before the questions about its internal structure can be resolved. Berger (1989) conceptualised credit as a system of financial intermediation that allocated/transferred resources over time, and from one household or firm to another. Financial development interventions look towards improving intermediation (through creating institutional structures, mechanisms and policy instruments), with the further goals of development of certain sectors (agriculture or industry), economic diversification, job creation and further political empowerment (ibid.: 1018).

Given its history, a well-developed rural banking infrastructure, with a choice of microfinance delivery models, has produced much debate which has limited connection to its poverty reduction impact.

Although the microfinance sector has grown rapidly, issues about its effectiveness have surfaced. There are challenges to the argument that self-financing is a cost-effective tool for both the delivery agent and client at the same time. Doubts have also been raised about other outcomes for the poor.[41]

Current Approaches to Impact

Impact is hereafter defined as 'the systematic analysis of the lasting or significant changes—positive or negative, intended or not—in people's lives brought about by a given action or a series of actions' (Roche 1999: 21). Figure 2.10 depicts an understanding of impact, with immediate results of activities termed outputs and medium-term effects termed outcomes.

Figure 2.10
Understanding of Impact

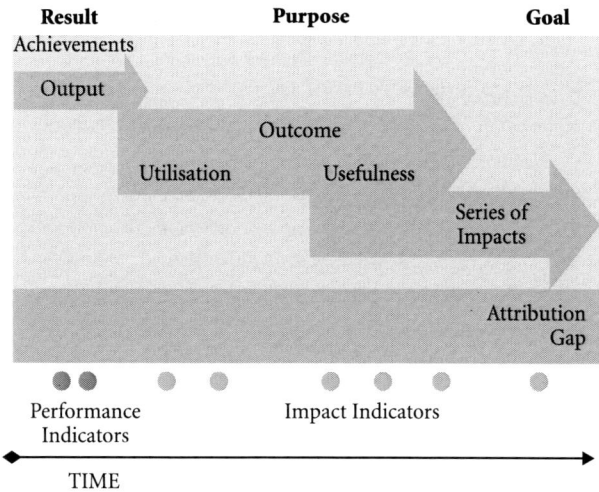

Source: Herweg and Steiner (2002).

Certain studies only focus upon long-term impact but it is difficult to link interventions to specific effects and there maybe more attribution error over time. Donors initiate and fund most impact studies, including those about microfinance, with a perspective of tracking the use of money invested. This supply orientation often results in top-down impact assessments, whereby donors lead the approaches and technology development in this field.[42] Donor-appointed consultants typically conduct the impact assessments.

There are three different perspectives to microfinance impact assessment (Figure 2.11). One debate is polarised between the financial systems and the impact assessment approach. Another questions the rationale of conducting impact assessments just for ensuring effectiveness of money use (proving) and advocates measures to augment it (improving). Yet another contrasts service delivery with its ability to empower.[43]

Figure 2.11
Spectrum of Different Perspectives on MF Impact

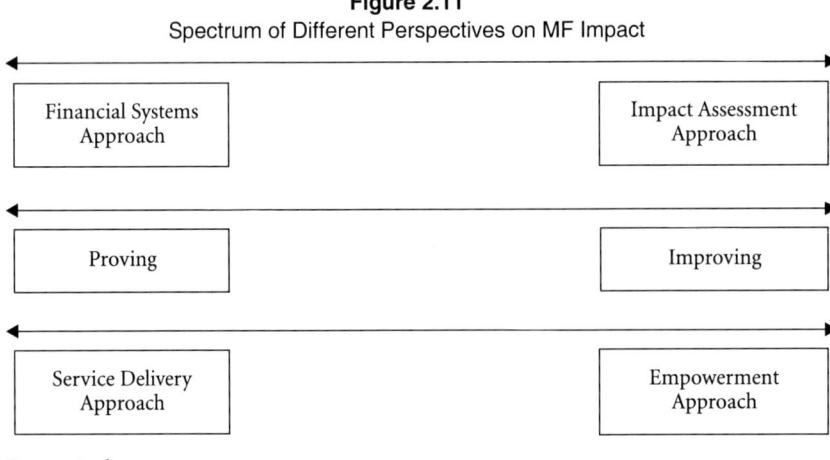

Source: Authors.

In the 1980s, when loan repayments were taken as proxy for good repayment performance, repayment rates was manipulated. By the early 1990s, there was pressure to show real and sustainable returns.[44] The financial systems approach draws upon Yaron's (1992) model, which considers independent financial sustainability of MFIs, in the absence of domestic or foreign aid, as the new benchmark. This holds that if the financial institution delivering the services is financially sustainable, then repayment rates must be high, indicating increased income flows, which makes further impact studies unnecessary. The market provides a proxy for impact, repayment rates being a proxy for client satisfaction and positive impact.[45] The financial health of the MFI is adopted as a proxy indicator of positive change. Hence, the scale and sustainability of the MFI becomes the primary indicator of impact.

Those who challenge the financial systems approach, emphasise the need to audit the MFI users and differentiate them accordingly. In the impact assessment approach, impact on poverty reduction is continually assessed rather than taken-for-granted. Further, while MFIs do not have funds to assess financial sustainability based on indicators like subsidy-dependent index, they do use less formal methods such as participatory rural appraisals instead.[46] The two approaches are depicted in Figure 2.12.

Figure 2.12
Approaches to Impact Assessment

Financial Systems Approach	Impact Assessment Approach
MFO sustainable	Actors can pay from other loans, and become indebted
↓	
Repayments must be high	Loans may not reach the poor at all, but the non-poor
↓	
Businesses must be profitable	Important to verify who is reached, who is excluded and who drops out
↓	
Incomes must have increased	Important to measure what change has taken place
↓	
Impact must be positive in terms of income and assets	

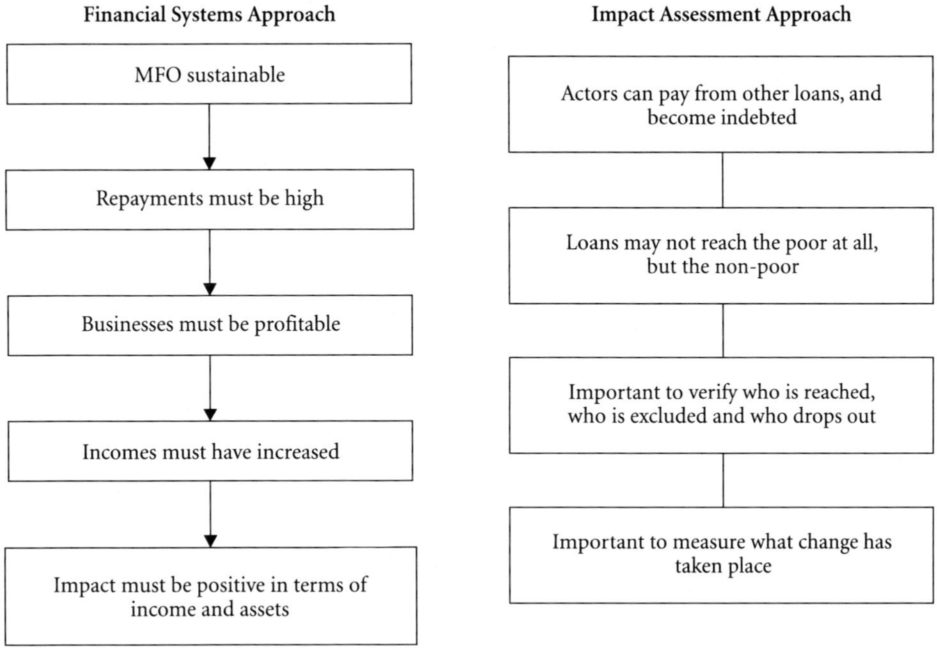

Source: Authors.

The paradigm shift depicted is related to the movement from 'proving' to 'improving', or 'planning' impact,[47] emphasising the role of monitoring and impact audits, client feedback and social performance of microfinance organisations[48] through learning approaches and constructive dialogue.[49] Some experts advocate further dissemination of findings about these improvements. Others recognise that, despite the potential benefits, collaboration is often inhibited by competitive rivalry which reduces genuine information sharing.[50] The change from 'proving' to 'improving' impact can overemphasise short-term projects. As a result 'research on outreach and impact on poor people has not contributed significantly to better product development' (Rutherford 2000; cited in Fisher and Sriram 2002: 109). More recently, a resolution between the two extremes is being sought through 'social performance' measurements of MFIs and other marketing approaches for developing appropriate products for the poor.[51]

The dichotomy between the supply-led financial systems and the demand-led empowerment approach manifests itself first in different beliefs about the best methodologies and approaches to impact assessment. The former emphasising delivery and the latter women's empowerment, therefore assessing different aspects using multiple indicators. This study reviewed several impact studies with regard to their approach, methodology, tools and indicators. These are listed in Appendix 1.

The units of assessment are listed in Table 2.2. The first indicators were related to financial sustainability of the delivery organisation (Yaron 1992). Later, impact for the institution and clients was distinguished and poverty measures were developed, so that donors could check poverty outreach of MFIs.[52] Impact studies usually assess impacts for a subset of six units: individual, household, enterprise, group, community and MFI/NGO. Impact indicators have been classified here using the framework of Chen (1997) and Cohen and Gaile (1997), in terms of whether the change was material, cognitive, perceptual or relational, reflecting the multiple indicators used. The indicators are compiled from a range of impact studies.[53] The classification that emerges, using indicators from a wide range of impact studies, is depicted in Table 2.3.

Table 2.2
Units for Impact Assessment

Client	Institutions
• Individual	MFIs/NGOs
• Household	
• Enterprise	
• Group	
• Community	

Source: Authors.

Some authors expressed concern that integrating women in the development process was 'harnessing women's labour for development', rather than 'development for women' and stated that 'the question of women's participation in credit programmes have a distinctly political light—raising issues of power, not just productivity' (Goetz and Sen Gupta 1996: 47). Women's own leadership and accountability, therefore, do not even appear as a concern:

> Much of the debate around women's financial services organisations is on what 'else' women are doing, apart from the savings and credit—as if the savings and credit activity is strong, and as if women are managing these services well, and as if these services have resulted in their economic betterment. (Rajagopalan 2004b: 3)

Another recent critique of microfinance impact studies alleges that impact studies take a narrow perspective, limiting themselves to households/enterprise (or micro-level) impacts, whereas wider impacts would include meso- and macro-level impacts. The differentiation is thus made between 'types' and 'levels' of impacts, where the types or 'domains' of wider impacts are categorised as cultural, economic, social and political and the 'levels' are categorised as local, regional and national, thereby giving the 'levels' a spatial dimension. Impact studies are also narrow in the sense that they consider impacts of individual programmes or comparisons across them, but do not include impacts arising due to the presence of several MFIs in the same area.[54]

Table 2.3

Aspects and Indicators for Impact Assessment

Aspects of Change	Impact: Client Level (Individual, Household and Enterprise and Community)	Impact: Institution Level (MFIs/NGOs and Groups)
Material	• Income—increased security, reduced poverty and contribution to household (individual, household and enterprise level) • Resources—increased savings, increased access, control over and ownership of assets and income (individual, household level) • Basic needs—improved health care, child care, nutrition, education plus housing, food security or reduced food shortages, reduced infant mortality or school dropouts, paid clinic health subscription, access to fuel, drinking water and toilets drainage (individual, household and community level) • Earning capacity—increased employment opportunity (household and enterprise), community assets creation	• Income: Financial sustainability of MFI/NGOs Resources: increased role of groups in accessing basic needs through state services
Cognitive	• Increased knowledge (individual) • Improved skills (individual) • Increased awareness of wider environment, laws (individual) • Ability to interact in public sphere—increased new contacts and new ideas (enterprise)	
Perceptual	• Self-esteem (individual level) • Self-confidence (individual level) • Vision of future—ability to think ahead and plan for the future (individual level) • Visibility and respect for individual's values (individual level) • Status—increased (household and community level)	• Leadership—increased strength of local organisations and local leadership (group level) Management Capacities—increased leadership and management capacities of groups (group level)
Relational	• Bargaining power (individual, enterprise level) • Participation—in non-family groups, local institutions and government and political process (individual, enterprise, community level) • Self-reliance—reduced dependency for access to resources, markets, public institutions (individual, enterprise and community level) • Decision making—increased (household and community enterprise level) • Solidarity—increased solidarity (community level) • Mobility	

Source: Authors.

Lately, the coverage of impact studies has increased vastly. One example of a behavioural approach emphasises the potential for integrating interests of stakeholders (governments, beneficiaries, donors, MFIs) and argues that MFIs best balance client needs with donor rules.[55] Another approach outlines the need to study not only the physical, social and economic aspects but also the spiritual–social aspects like solidarity, service, cooperation and justice, and espouses the values of unity, development and peace for humanity.[56] Finally, there is greater openness in acknowledging that there are negative impacts.[57] Guèrin (2006) cites several studies with results that show inability of microfinance in reducing inequalities, especially those relating to gender, and in creating over-indebtedness. There have also been incidents of borrower suicides, humiliation faced by microfinance clients and increased indebtedness.[58] However, factors leading to these remain inadequately analysed. Most studies are one-off, annual, mid-term or end-term project reviews, and not longitudinal perspectives. Most have no baseline surveys and have no benchmarks or clarity about the desired impacts or the indicators.

At the same time, there remain the unanswered questions about the selection of appropriate methods, simplistic attributions and the fungibility of cash, which made it difficult to track the use of money from one application to another. Further, even with combined quantitative and qualitative methods, the costs of assessment are high.

Findings of Key Impact Studies

The first landmark study to critique microfinance was Hulme and Mosley (1996) who studied 12 organisations in seven countries (India, Bangladesh, Sri Lanka, Indonesia, Kenya, Malawi and Bolivia), which provided microfinance through private, NGO, formal banking and cooperative institutions. Another impact study (EDA 2003) covered 10 MFIs in India supported by a project implemented by SIDBI and supported by Department for International Development (DFID), UK, and International Fund for Agricultural Development (IFAD), Rome. It was a cross-sectional study intended to serve as a baseline for further work and questioned whether the project was meeting its objectives of 'substantial poverty reduction and reduced vulnerability in India amongst the users of microfinance services, especially women' (ibid.: 4). A third recent study, Burra et al., (2005), presents a set of case studies which specifically examine the extent to which different microfinance initiatives achieve women's empowerment. The programmes/organisations covered included South Asia Poverty Alleviation Programme and SHARE in AP, DHAN Foundation and Activists for Social Action Trust in Tamil Nadu (TN), Swayam Shikshan Prayog and Lokadrushti, Orissa.[59] These three studies covered 28 microfinance programmes, of which 17 were located in different states of India; the first two aimed to measure poverty reduction impacts, while the third one emphasised women's empowerment impacts. In addition, impact studies of four official programmes which have a microfinance component were analysed. These included the Rashtriya Mahila Kosh, SGSY, Swayamsidha and Swashakthi programmes.[60]

Orientations of the Studies

Hulme and Mosley (1996) recognised that microfinance schemes are 'idealised' and 'traditional' state-subsidised finance is denigrated in the then dominant paradigm and sought to go beyond these to seek evidence regarding financial viability, productive impact and poverty impact of micro-finance. An important aspect of this study was the recognition of the role of politics in financial intermediation. They highlighted the tendency of donors (especially in projects supported by United States Agency for International Development, Asian Development Bank and World Bank) to use the money to promote their own ideologies, demonstrate a commitment to poverty reduction and/or simply a pressure to commit and disburse their funds. The NGOs and MFIs in the study, which collaborated in these programmes, did not challenge the donors. The four evaluations of the official programmes also focussed on outputs and outcomes but did not challenge their features.

Poverty Outreach

One case study of microfinance clients (Mosley 1996) found that of the 37 per cent BPL, 75 per cent had never borrowed before, while others had only borrowed from family, friends and traditional moneylenders. RRBs were successful here in expanding savings services and in reaching those hitherto not served by credit institutions, and had survived as organisations despite low repayment rates. Hulme and Mosley (1996) found that impact on borrowers was positive compared to non-borrowers, but benefiting the 'middle' poor more than the 'core' poor. The institutions that pursued their own financial viability had a tendency to concentrate on the former, and the latter needed 'protective' rather than 'productive' credit.

The EDA study did not report poverty outreach by the different organisations, but found that, in total, 30 per cent of the members were from scheduled castes (SCs) and 39 per cent were poor, with others on the borderline or non-poor, and 14 per cent were women-headed households which were particularly vulnerable. Of the four official evaluations, only one reported outreach to the poor.[61] Some assumed high poverty levels, but pointed out limited poverty reduction effects.

Context

Hulme and Mosley (1996) found that loans for agriculture had lower repayment rates. The EDA study showed that microfinance does not adequately cover regions with high poverty. Although the study reveals a supply gap, it does not question or specify how contextual factors affect demand for credit. None of the official studies analysed their findings with reference to economic, ecological, political and socio-cultural contexts.

Women's Use of Money

A study covering impact of microfinance through SHG-bank linkage facilitated by an NGO in Orissa highlights how women did not borrow for productive purposes from their own savings in the bank, keeping them for emergency purposes (Rajagopalan 2005c). It also highlights the risk of women's capital being mobilised and used outside the district. Women's use of credit to reduce indebtedness, increase food security and start small IGAs was evidenced (AFC 2005; Buch 2002).

Group Dynamics and Processes

Another study found how group leaders had taken more loans and had acquired greater access to *panchayat* leadership compared to other group members (IIPO 2005; Parthasarathy 2005). Beyond this, a few studies investigated SHGs in detail, but they did not dwell upon group dynamics. However, they did observe that groups served only as mechanisms of cost and risk reduction for the institutions. 'The most significant political empowerment that our work revealed was not that of borrower or member empowerment, but of the financial institutions and particularly of their leaders and senior managers' (Hulme and Mosley 1996: 153–54).

Caste Discrimination and Further Impacts

Though reduction in caste-based discrimination was not addressed by the studies, they do note that the issue was not addressed by any of the projects. While some occasional anecdotal evidence exists about group members meeting one another, caste continues to be a major determinant of social relationships (Rajivan 2005). Hulme and Mosley (1996) also held out little hope that financial intermediation for the poor would be able to influence local or national socio-economic structures or political relationships.

Gender

Hulme and Mosley (1996) did not cover gender aspects directly, but they did caution that female participation cannot be treated as an indicator of female empowerment, on the basis of other studies. The EDA study found that women were targeted for 'pragmatic reasons', as they were willing to attend group meetings and comply with savings and loan terms, whereas men preferred larger, individual transactions. Sharma (2005) points to negative effects, as new economic enterprises may increase the work burden of children, particularly girl children, through increased enterprise-related work, domestic work and child care responsibilities. The studies do point towards several leakages from microcredit, on alcohol and tobacco consumption, dowry, puberty rites and death ceremonies. Other studies that showed negative gender-related impacts include increased workload, husband's control over the income, lower contribution by men to family income, increased inequalities among women, pressure to repay credit from programme staff and increasing domestic physical and verbal abuse.[62]

Empowerment-related aspects include improvements in leadership and management capacities, the creation of savings and the development of assets linkages with mainstream financial institutions. Many studies showed a large range of empowerment impacts, both for the individual woman and collectively, arising from microfinance interventions. Again, these studies adopt an outcome perspective, offering few insights into processes that inhibit or enhance women's empowerment. In general, the main motivation for delivering credit through women's SHGs remains an instrumental use, as depicted in Figure 2.13.

Figure 2.13
Conflict of Objectives

'It is clear that, despite the rhetorical claims of poverty reduction and empowerment the main motivation for female targeting in many microfinance programmes is higher female repayment rates. The main motivation for group formation is cutting costs through demanding that women contribute their own time and resources for routine programme administration. Microfinance services for men rarely make such demands and where they do so are generally unsuccessful. Changes in products and complementary services currently introduced to increase financial sustainability often have negative impacts on poverty reduction and empowerment objectives. This is not because there is an inherent conflict between sustainability aims and these broader development objectives. It is rather because the gender and poverty implications of the mechanical ways in which sustainability 'Best Practice' has been imposed have not been thought through.'

(Cheston and Kuhn 2002: 6–7).

Cross-model Comparisons

Studies cover outcomes and impacts rather than processes. Although the NGOs and MFIs covered in all the sets of studies earlier examined different microfinance delivery models, many reported impacts of only one model and others did not employ cross-model comparisons or clarify differential impacts. Further, many microfinance initiatives modify products repeatedly, rendering cross-model comparisons difficult.

All these studies take an institutional perspective and largely cover those who take loans. The coverage of those who did not opt to take loans is also from the supply perspective, as a control group to measure outcomes and impacts. They leave a gap in understanding from the perspective of the poor themselves, for instance, in finding out why the latter did not participate in the NGO/MFI microfinance programmes.

MULTIPLE PERSPECTIVES ABOUT MICROFINANCE USE

Our research reveals divergences between institutional (external) and actors' own (local) perspectives about money and its use. These are now discussed.

Use of Money

Early microfinance literature considered loan products—their purpose, interest rate, source and size—but paid less attention to the linkages between financial products and resulting impact.

Role of Savings

The use of savings ranges from supply-oriented (risk coverage) to demand-oriented (emergency needs) uses. For women, SHGs/NGOs/MFJs offer a safe place for savings which husbands cannot access. This can also earn a reasonable return, which helps during lean periods or times of crises. A major reason for saving is to collect significant sums when needed.[63]

The supply perspective highlights that 80 per cent of the world's poor and 90 per cent in developing countries have no access to institutional savings and credit facilities beyond that provided by friends, family and moneylenders.[64] Further, savings options offered by MFIs extend over a spectrum. At one end are fixed sums to be saved compulsorily every week/month, against which loans are given, and which cannot be withdrawn. At the other end are options for flexible savings and withdrawals.[65] This view, that the poor need a safe place to save, has been contested in the Indian context where credit is viewed as the more critical function needed from formal institutions: 'It is quite common to hear people grumble that the bank which willingly keeps their savings is not so forthcoming when it comes to advancing loans; it is rare to hear them grumble that the MFI that gives them loan is not collecting savings' (Fernandez 2005: 2).

MFIs insist on regular savings in order to screen out potential defaulters, build up financial security, augment financial resources for lending and encourage members to appreciate the financial health of the institution. Researchers recognised that MFIs offer savings services to gain a cheap source of funds for further lending, resulting in more sustainable financial operations. Savings are therefore seen as the 'sustaining half of microfinance' (Otero and Rhyne 1994: 9). United Nations Development Programme (UNDP) asserts that savings are not offered as financial services, but rather as a precondition for getting loans; they are blocked without interest and are difficult to reclaim even after full repayment.[66] An additional aspect is the safety of poor women's savings. Deposit-taking institutions are expected to comply with banking regulation and supervision regimes that protect their depositors.[67]

During a visit to an interior village in Orissa, group members claimed that they had been depositing all their savings with the NGO, in the hope of getting loans in multiples of their collective savings.

As a result, there was no cash balance retained at the group level. In one village, a child fell into a well, and needed to be taken to a hospital immediately. The women approached five groups, but none had retained enough cash, and the child died. There were at least three other cases of women needing to take relatives for medical treatment and not being able to get financial support from their groups. The pooling of money with the NGO, which is based on the financial logic of keeping savings as a basis for distributing loans, is clearly at cross-purposes with the need to retain their savings, to cope with emergencies and medical needs.

Further divergence between model and practice of microfinance in relation to savings and loans is given in Table 2.4.

Table 2.4
Divergence in Microfinance Savings: Model and Practice

Claim of Commercial Model	Observed Practice of Microfinance
Supply perspective	
Cost reduction for MFI	Offered nil or low interest on savings
Risk reduction for MFI	Retained control over savings with MFI rather than women, creating low access and high risk for women
Demand perspectives	
Easy Access	Access limited
Returns	Returns nil or low
Safety	Safety risks

Source: Authors.

While models acknowledge that savings help smooth consumption during crisis, impact studies do not cover either the management or the impact of savings. For instance, the amount and impact of savings were not even mapped in the impact study of SEWA Bank.[68] Other literature acknowledges that 'hot money' that comes from women's savings will probably be used better than 'cold' money from external sources (Mask 2000: 23). There are instances where a support institution establishes a revolving fund that makes group loans to collectives (cold money), whereas collectives blend this cold money with their own savings (hot money) to fund loans.

An economic perspective on savings considers it a sacrifice of present consumption for the future, and surmises that savings channelled into productive investment leads to material progress.[69] Desai (1967) elaborates on the role of savings in fulfilling social obligation (for example, education and marriages of children, maintenance of dependent relatives, performance of religious ceremonies and festivals). He thus highlights the use of social and cultural aspects of use of savings. The actuality of access to savings may therefore differ from what many expect, and there is limited research into the value that women's own savings have for them.

Purpose of Loan

Most microfinance organisations visited provided loans for 'productive' rather than 'consumption' purposes. The former included investments in IGAs and businesses, seen as desirable as they led to increased cash flows later used for repayments. The latter, for the same reason, often resulted in further indebtedness instead. The women members of SHGs, especially the poorest who lived in Charbhati, a remote village, in Kalahandi district of Orissa, did not share this perspective. During one field visit, a cluster meeting was observed where over 20 groups came to one central place to deposit their savings and take loans against it from an NGO. Five groups from this cluster, all belonging to the same village, did not attend. A visit was organised to this village to meet the women, and the women members of groups were invited to a discussion in a large open space at the entrance of the village. Only a few were in the village at the time; but nearly 20 joined the discussion. The NGO staff explained that these women were not 'regular' in their savings, were not 'disciplined', and therefore did not 'qualify' for loans. Women who had borrowed from the group savings explained the amount and purpose of their loan thus:

> *'Rs 50 ($1.11) for own fever'*
> *'Rs 40 ($0.88) for child's fever'*
> *'Rs 190 ($4.22) for own medical treatment'*
> *'Rs 60 ($1.33) for own fever'*
> *'Rs 400 ($8.88) for son's fever'*
> *'Rs 100 ($2.22) for son's fever'*
> *'Rs 80 ($1.77) for own visit to hospital during pregnancy'*
> *'Rs 80 ($1.77) for purchase of medicines'*
> *'Rs 200 ($4.44) to cover the shortfall needed to buy a bull'*

They were disappointed that despite saving in the group, the NGO had not given them a group loan. One woman's son complained: 'My mother gave Rs 130 ($2.88) as savings in the group already, but she has not yet got a loan. Why should she continue to contribute more savings?'

The NGO expected women to save and learn the discipline of taking and repaying loans before they 'qualified' for the NGO loans. These women live in a mosquito-infested village where malaria is rampant and most group members are landless, with only agricultural labour to depend on. They need small loans, first to meet their consumption needs, and only as a next step, for small IGAs. The difference in understanding their situation and need for money created a situation where the NGO and women were not able to meet mutual expectations.

In another group in Ganjam district of Orissa, members had regular savings and took loans from savings, but emphatically stated that they would not like NGO loans, because the interest rate of 2 per cent per month was too high and inconvenient to repay in equal monthly instalments spread over a year. They claimed that they could get loans at that interest rate even from local sources, and even gave details of loans they claim to have actually taken (see Table 2.5).

These women explained that the NGO did not offer them money to meet their social needs, for example, marriages and death ceremonies, nor did they offer the size of loans needed. They could get loans according to their needs in the village, at the same cost, and could repay it in a lump sum or in instalments spread over longer periods. They did not wish to take loans from the NGO and would not deposit their savings with the NGO. This example also highlights a mismatch in the perspectives of the users and suppliers of loans, about the sizes, purposes and terms at which loans are dispersed.

Table 2.5
Debts of Women SHG Members in Orissa

No. of Members	Loan (in Rs)	Loan (in $)	Purpose	Source, Repayment
1	2,000	44.44	Agriculture	Cooperative Society
2	250,000	5,556	Truck, medical expenses	40,000 returned, local sources
3	3,000	67	Agriculture	Cooperative Society
4	20,000	444	Agriculture	Cooperative Society
5	200,000	4,444	Daughter's marriage	Local sources
6	30,000	667	Death ceremonies	Local sources
7	100,000	2,223	Daughter's marriage, housing	Local sources
8	200,000	4,444	Marriage of children	Local sources
9	6,000	133	Agriculture	Local sources
10	40,000	889	Agriculture	Bank
11	20,000	444	Agriculture, medical expenses	Cooperative Society, Local sources
12	20,000	444	Agriculture	Local sources
13	40,000	889	Agriculture	Cooperative Society, Local sources
14	22,000	489	Agriculture	Cooperative Society, Local sources
15	10,000	222	Daughter's marriage	Local sources
16	60,000	1,333	Daughter's marriage, housing	Cooperative Society, Local sources
17	30,000	667	Agriculture, daughter's marriage	Bank, Local sources
Total	1.053,000	23,400		

Source: Authors.

Note: All loans from cooperative societies were at 6% per annum, from bank at 6–8% per annum and from local sources and NGO at 24% per annum.

Divergence between 'production' and 'consumption' loans (Premchander 2003a) is summarised in Table 2.6.

Table 2.6
Divergence between Theory and Practice: Purpose of Loans

Topic	Theory of Microfinance	Practice of Microfinance
Supply perspective	Productive loan is less risky	Only production loans permitted
Demand perspective or women's perspectives	Poorer people need consumption loans	Productive loans too small, therefore used for consumption

Source: Authors.

Several observers point that the poor use savings or credit for consumption, as an integral part of their livelihoods strategy. The poorer the target group, the more the emphasis that needs to be placed on financial services contributing to consumption stabilisation.[70] Notwithstanding this, however, MFIs expect their loans to be used immediately for certain purposes, usually productive investments that yield additional incomes out of which repayments can be made. The attitude of MFIs is explained in terms of the fear that if loans are used for consumption purposes, they are less likely to be repaid. The small size of loans makes productive use difficult, so they are used for consumption needs. Women also prefer multi-purpose rather than production-only loans. Certain studies observe differences between supplier and user perspectives. 'If the definition of productive purposes is limited only to income generating activities, then clients who may want access to loans for socially productive purposes such as improving their education or health are likely to be excluded' (FAO 2002: 49). Further, where MFIs provide loans only for 'income generating' productive purposes, poor clients may then propose bogus productive activities as a front for accessing loans.[71] While models recognise that MFI perspectives and poor people's needs differ, this is not always corrected through loan products offered. Impact assessment studies tend to capture increases in loan size (assuming that funds are employed in microenterprises) and use increased participation in borrowing and fund use as a measure of impact. This perspective is limited to 'outputs' and effects, and often does not track long-term impact of use of money for different purposes. In order to reconcile the differences in local and external perspectives, this research examines the purposes for which women take loans and the reasons why different types of loans are used for different purposes.

Interest Rates

There are opposing views about the cost of money. One believes that borrowers are more sensitive to the availability and convenience of taking credit than to the interest rate. This implies that interest rates should be set to cover costs of providing financial services (Berger 1989). If people have a demand for loans, the expectation is that they can also afford to pay high interest rates. Another perspective is that although interest rates should cover costs, NGOs do not want to be seen as 'exploitative moneylenders', so interest is a political issue.[72] Some impact studies show that high interest rates affected repayments.[73] While proponents of commercial microfinance perceive high interest rates as necessary, impact studies show that clients prefer low rates of interest.

The book explores the reasons whether and why women use loans of varying costs, and the repayment ethic related to different loan products.

Amounts and Sources of Loans

MFIs tend to offer small loans in the beginning, increasing the amounts in subsequent loans.[74] Loan sizes are useful indicators of poverty and the risk-taking ability of microfinance clients.[75] The financial perspective prefers small loans as a measure of risk coverage. On the other hand, evidence shows that small loans are not appropriate for productive use.[76]

Models recognise that the source of funds determines the terms of the loan, which can then have a variable impact. Those facing shortages may have only their employers and local moneylenders as sources of credit. The employer may agree to give credit only on the promise of work at lower than market wage rates. Such arrangements can maintain and exacerbate inequalities in power and position. By contrast, user-owned funds maybe more supportive and less exploitative, even though they may widen inequalities between users and non-users of credit. Hence, loan products need to be analysed for suitability to the poor and designed especially to meet their needs.[77] However, impact studies may not differentiate between impact of loans according to the different sources or terms on which loans have been given. This research, therefore, examines the links between the different characteristics of loans: sources, amount, purpose, cost and repayment terms and their repayment and impact.

Poverty Reduction and MFI Sustainability

The debates about provision of financial services question both outreach and impact of microfinance on poverty reduction. While repayment rates attract banks to extend credit to women, actual outreach to the poor is not known,[78] or more recently, acknowledged as low.[79] The lack of attention to the poor in impact studies has been explained away by their being remote, risk averse and heterogeneous, and therefore difficult to study.[80]

One analysis of the size of loans shows that the typical client of subsidised programmes with a clear focus on poverty alleviation had a loan balance of Rs 4,500 ($100). By contrast, the typical borrower from financially self-sufficient programmes had an average loan balance of Rs 19,350 ($430) and even higher loan amounts.[81] Yet another factor is peer monitoring, whereby groups may reject the poorest as members,[82] as this may increase the risk of non-payment and reduce group creditworthiness. It is found that microfinance enables the poor to cope better with seasonal income fluctuations. Such microfinance is increasingly viewed as providing income protection rather than promotion. There is recognition that microfinance programmes, particularly those aiming for financial sustainability, find it difficult to identify, reach and meet the needs of the poor, especially in remote areas, and therefore also have a relatively low impact on the incomes of the poor. Further, the development of successful enterprises or financially sustainable MFIs on the one hand, and improving incomes of the very poor on the other can conflict. However, some maintain that there is little evidence that the poor are left behind as loan sizes grow and that sustainable microfinance organisations are able to reach the poor.[83]

Issues Relating to Groups

An emerging feature of current microfinance practice in India is the introduction of women's SHGs as a medium through which credit is provided. This is a new forum, which did not exist in villages in this form prior to the introduction of microfinance projects. It is therefore useful to understand the role of SHGs in the delivery and impact of microfinance.

Group Processes

SHGs have cost and risk reduction benefits for the credit-supplying organisation. As members have better information on the character and creditworthiness of potential borrowers, they shift loan processing and approval tasks to groups, thereby reducing transaction costs.[84] The expectation about repayment is that, if one member is unable to pay an instalment, others will repay the NGO/MFI, thus creating 'joint liability'.[85] In practice, however, the joint liability characteristic of the group may not occur. Those who do not repay have a demonstration effect, which may lead to increasing non-repayment.[86] Members may not force one another to pay, especially if they fear breaking of social ties. There is also concern about the social costs of group processes, that is, constraints to group borrowing and joint liability approaches. These include coercive peer pressure, loss of trust and the likelihood that the poorest and most vulnerable will be excluded or further stigmatised.[87] Banks also judge their credibility by amount of savings pooled, ability to manage these and solidarity and cohesion among members. The difference in perspectives is also evident here by the finding that women themselves attributed low repayments to drought conditions while external agencies considered it 'lack of systems'.[88] Attention has also been drawn towards 'disciplining' the poor and bringing them under the 'gaze' of new control and productive mechanisms, and thus isolating them in the Foucauldian sense and using them as 'productive mechanisms', and thus in fact reducing the possibility of their making joint representations.[89]

When groups are seen not only as a means of delivering savings and credit services but also as a broader strategy for empowerment, collective action is viewed as an important aspect in bringing about change. Otero and Rhyne (1994) view group methodology as having three main features: means of providing financial services, training and technical assistance and the promotion of organisational and social development. In a context where conventional lenders are seen to neglect poor and minority communities, offer less information and time, charge higher interest rates and deny loans more often than they do to majority communities, they work to maintain social and wealth inequalities.[90] Here, access of low-income families to financial institutions and to financial education, to promote savings is seen as a way out of the distributional outcomes of financial markets.[91] This theory envisages a positive role for SHGs, as forums which facilitate such access. In practice, however, doubts have been raised about whether savings and credit groups promoted by outsiders can achieve long-term independence,[92] thereby cautioning that a forum established through motivation of external agencies may not sustain longer than the external interventions.[93] Rankin (2006) emphasises that when informal credit groups and lending arrangements are documented with a 'cultural' perspective, the term social 'capital' assigned to them is not neutral, but reflects neoliberal economic ideology, which works to 'instrumentalise' women and the poor.[94]

In contrast, there are examples in India from SEWA Bank and Cooperative for Assistance and Relief Everywhere (CARE) India's CREDIT and CASHE projects in Jharkhand, Chhattisgarh, Orissa and AP, where capitalisation of groups is viewed as an important indicator of their sustainability. They recognise the role of own savings as capital, and collective and profitable financial transactions at the group level in sustaining groups as viable local forums.[95] The ability of groups to manage finances, however, can be limited, especially where many are illiterate. Recent studies of SHGs in the state of AP claim that group members have poor book-keeping ability, no leadership rotation and unsound loan management practices, which put the savings of members at risk.[96] Robinson (2001) also observed that groups are liable to collapse when managers are corrupt, members are indisciplined, or when collective shock occurs.

Group cohesion breaks down due to indiscretion or member misfortunes. Grassroots studies in AP attribute the end of money transactions and dissolution of groups to a fundamental lack of trust.[97] Trust is an important element of the relationship between banks and the poor, and Bhagwati (1997) emphasised that national and international NGOs advance values of civil society and democracy. Other studies emphasise role of groups and 'recognise that high repayment rates of SHGs is not an inherent structural feature of SHGs but a commitment to group values' (Padhi 2003: 8). Researchers emphasise the need to go beyond economic reasons to explain the role of groups and processes as embedded in a theory of social relations and highlight networks and norms as factors that enhance social capital through social organisation.[98]

Woolcock draws attention to the 'how' questions, which examine how 'human and material resources are assembled and maintained in the process of trying to attain a goal, exploit an opportunity, or correct a problem' (1999: 2). This contrasts the transactions cost approach to organisational issues with the alternative sociological approach. The former assumes that needs, demands or problems create their own solutions, while the latter regards all organisations as social accomplishments. The evaluations of microfinance programmes have been preoccupied with impact assessments, replication and sustainability issues, and theoretical perspectives have not always been informed about organisational issues, for example, 'the construction of economic institutions to assist the poor' (ibid.: 3). Woolcock takes a socio-economic perspective and case study approach to examine the failures of group-based microfinance programmes which highlight the importance of how human resources are mobilised, assembled and maintained across four key institutional junctures: replication, a branch in crisis, a group in crisis and ineffective guarantors and staff. In the case of a group in crisis, women had indebted themselves to the moneylender to pay the Grameen Bank. This suggests that analyses of impacts have not focussed on how microfinance programmes work. The understanding of process is important to future programmes, because it provides not only financial lessons but calls for more social sustainability as well. Prior to 2000, few studies analysed of role of groups and group processes from Indian and external researchers.[99] More recently, studies on SHGs and federations have highlighted several aspects, for example, the dropout rate of groups can be high because the poorest are most prone to illness, migration and volatile group dynamics.[100] The potentials, challenges and needs of the supportive enabling environment have also been elaborated recently.[101] In general, many impact studies only regard groups as a forum or delivery mechanism without studying their actual processes or the way groups manage money and how social and financial capital can support or contradict each other. The full complexities and dynamics of SHGs are not fully captured any more than the distributional impact of groups, or the impact of their placement in local social structures. In this respect, where the positive impacts of social capital are privileged, this research provides deeper insights into group processes and dynamics and explores these with respect to potential opportunities and constraints within local economies and social organisation. This book highlights how women manage savings and loans in groups and group learning processes; thereby seeks to understand groups as institutional mechanisms for development interventions.

Livelihoods Contexts and Strategies

There is recognition that the place where people live has a definite implication for the potential of IGAs and microenterprise, in terms of both ecological factors and institutions that form the enabling environment.[102]

There is evidence of the link between the geographical context, for example, drought-prone areas, and other dimensions of poverty, namely social and economic exclusion, combined with low literacy, numeracy and other skills of employability, resulting in roughly 1 million Indian households where either parents or the children are engaged in bonded labour.[103] The relation of ecological conditions with poverty and strained livelihoods is thus emphasised. Poverty studies recognise that poverty and calorie and protein deficiency in India vary across states as well as agro-climatic zones.[104] There are risks including seasonality, unfavourable terms of trade, high volatility of prices of agricultural commodities, distorted credit markets, changes in domestic and international policies and a high incidence and depth of poverty in rural areas, especially in those dependent largely on agriculture. Agriculture is recognised as the most important sector supporting the rural population, with strong linkages to the interstate differentials in both growth and poverty reduction.[105] However, agriculturally underdeveloped and poorer environments are too hostile to absorb currently offered microfinance for productive investments in agriculture or other economic activities, without preceding improvements in other sectors.[106] This is not always reflected in the original design of microfinance programmes that apply a single-product model to all the states in which they operate.

> *We walked for three hours crossing two streams, to visit to a group in a remote village in Chhatisgarh. When we reached the hamlet at 3 p.m., women welcomed us and first we joined in a tribal dance with 50 of them. It began to pour, so we huddled into a small hut with 25 women for a discussion. As I glanced around, I felt overdressed in a salwar suit and dupatta, while these women wore only a half sari each. Their groups were 6 months old, they had been saving one rupee every fortnight, and the group had collective savings of Rs 200 ($4.5). I tore pieces of paper from my pad to make serve as currency notes and handed to each different denominations totalling Rs 500 ($11.3) per woman. I explained that this was a loan that an agency was offering them, and asked what they would do with it; it had to be repaid with interest. For some time there was a hushed silence. Then one woman slowly counted and returned Rs 400 ($9) to me. When I asked her what she would do with the hundred retained, she said: 'I will use Rs 50 ($1.1) to buy a sari, and with Rs 50 ($1.1) I will make and sell "Hariya" (liquor from paddy). One by one each woman returned some cash, not even one had considered a loan of more than Rs 100 ($2.3). This group could have absorbed only Rs 2500 ($56.8) as first loan, the project envisaged Rs 50,000 ($1136).'*
> —Extract from field notes, Bastar

In remote villages of the tribal regions of Chhattisgarh and Jharkhand, women group members were able to save Rs 1 or 2 per week, or Rs 5 or 10 per month. Similarly, in the remote coastal regions of Kerala, women organised by an NGO were from families of fishermen and were able to save only Rs 2 ($0.04) per week. By contrast, in Ranchi, Jharkhand, where lands were fertile and markets of Ranchi town were accessible, the women saved amounts varying from Rs 10 to 20 ($0.22–0.44) per week. The regularity of savings differed widely across groups; some groups, for example, those in the economically active regions, had regular savings from all members, while others, for example, those in remote areas and within less monetised economies, stopped savings for a few months during lean periods.

The tribals lived in remote forests, with an average of 2–3 hours to walk to the closest weekly shandies to buy small provisions like salt, oil, kerosene, onions and potatoes. The weekly sale of minor forest produce was about Rs 10 ($0.22) per woman, with which she purchased her weekly ration. In Bastar, typically, each tribal woman walked 6–8 km from her home, carrying a child on her hip and carefully balancing a basket of minor forest products on her head or hip, and maybe even trying to hold a bamboo umbrella to save her child from a drizzle or rain. This journey was taken on slippery paths, usually with two or three streams to cross, with at least knee or waist deep water. Given that the weekly transactions were about Rs 5 ($0.11) or Rs 10 ($0.22), women rarely saw even a note of Rs 50 ($1.11), and few had seen a note of Rs 100 ($2.22). When they began to save money, bringing Rs 1 or 2 ($0.02–0.04) to the group meetings, they did not know who should keep the money in between meetings. When savings reached Rs 100 or 200 ($2.22 or 4.44), they usually divided it between two or three women for safekeeping. Locally women took credit in kind, paying back in kind, with interest. The money equivalence was never established. The economy was highly non-monetised in this region. They could have used credit, but it would be a long-drawn process, requiring increased awareness about the concept of credit, and then providing small amounts of credit for existing micro-businesses that women were already engaged in. It was more important to create the confidence and skills to bargain in the weekly markets for a fair price for the forest produce they brought to prevent exploitation by traders. Credit could have been better utilised if the NGOs also facilitated collective action (in the form of cooperatives, federations, and so on), for trading in non-timber forest produce with the government agencies or external markets. Other ideas that suited the tribal context included grain banks, joint purchase and sale of products and other similar collective economic activities, which could help women, get higher bargaining power and higher returns for the goods they traded in. Other interventions that would have worked related to raising agricultural productivity of the small pieces of land that the tribals cultivated.

Set against this, the credit project of the intervening agency was designed to support the tribals through microfinance. It was a replication of another project in Jharkhand and the assumptions about the latter had been applied in the tribal regions of Bastar, and expected women to take in multiples of $100 (Rs 4,400) as loans, and the NGO to make credit operations sustainable in 3 years. Those assumptions were unrealistic and needed reformulation. The role of money in the local economy was insignificant. Most transactions in the project area were non-monetary, excepting those that took place in weekly markets, and for some large financial outflows. The quality of life in the project area was not linked directly to money alone. The NGO partners saw this dichotomy and resisted a project that would demand financial sustainability of credit operations, in a context where the feasibility of rooting a cash-based credit system was doubtful. The supporting agency was, however, wary of expressing this strongly, as it feared losing the grant for the project and continued to profess compatibility between project objectives and tribal women's needs instead. This demonstrates self-perpetuating policy in action[107] and points to the need to explore the meaning and use of money with reference to a specific livelihoods context.

The socio-cultural embeddedness of poverty and vulnerability is recognised in development literature, which attributes lack of power to social placement, gender, age, caste, ethnicity or wealth. The attitude towards 'low' castes is negative, and women are denied entitlements of equal concern, respect, status and libertarian rights in general, described as constituting 'negative freedom' for these women.[108]

Studies on the Dalit movement in Karnataka provide some evidence of caste, class and gender struggle.[109] The community is not one homogenous whole but is formed of different groups, some of which experience social exclusion in the economic, social, cultural and religious practices, where external agencies (government/NGOs) are unable to make large-scale entry.[110] Other studies also emphasise that because of the trans-disciplinary and political character of the caste and gender struggle, it has not spread among NGOs, who have made the opposite move: from activists to contractors.[111]

There is suspected corruption among government schemes and collusion between bank and government officers.[112] In this scenario, villagers expect NGOs and community leaders to access external resources.[113] In addition to the ecological issues that influence livelihoods, geographical contexts encompass other enabling factors that protect or expose households to vulnerability: socio-economic or political. Similarly, the institutional context, encompassing structures and processes of government, private sector, NGOs and other civil society organisations, creates possible livelihood options or people with disabilities from accessing them (Richardson and Howarth 2002). Thus, the enabling environment or the contexts in which livelihoods are located has an important bearing on the way microfinance is used and the resulting benefit or harm.

Of the impact studies reviewed, none have considered the livelihoods context in which the microfinance programme was situated, except for Hulme and Mosley (1996). While the overall impacts of microfinance programmes were positive, questions were raised about whether gender issues were actually influential.

This research considers how the 'marginalised' live within their society and how their basic human rights were infringed upon in the current context, and considers the institutional relevance of different actors. It examines how relations among different actors influence the supply of money and shape their financial behaviour. It recognises the context embeddedness of poverty, and vulnerabilities arising from geographical, socio-cultural and institutional contexts in which they live. It uses actor-oriented methodologies, which assign priority to agency and embed actions in wider social relations and structural settings.[114] 'The interconnectedness of gender, class, ethnicity and nationality' (Fernando 2006b: 175) also calls for an emphasis on gendered livelihoods context, developed further in the next chapter.

Multiple Meanings of Money

The different uses of money from different sources is internalised differently by women. For instance, women used their 'own' savings differently from the loan provided by the external agencies and they assigned different meanings to the two sources. They experience greater freedom in using their own money for their own needs and preferences. NGO/MFIs, on the other hand, perceive uses differently from women and apply concepts of efficiency, which provide a different basis of thinking as compared to that of women. The tensions between development thinking and financial systems thinking draw attention to a conflicting pecuniary interest, which could be the underlying reason for the differential meaning of money and the language used by the SHGs and the intervening NGO/MFI. The previous instances from the field show how women's perspectives are different, as regards the perception and use of savings, use of money and how women's groups perceive and utilise money. The divergence arises not only from the meaning of money but also from the purpose that microfinance is to serve, for the suppliers and the users, although there are certain commonalities between external and local perspectives.

In analysing use of money given by charities, Zelizer (1994) showed how the institutional notion of 'proper' utilisation of money was quite different from that of those who received the charity money. This phenomenon also appears in the perspectives of agencies that use money as a development tool, and therefore a loan has a different meaning for the suppliers of microfinance. At the same time, the women who receive the loan regard it differently, thereby giving it a different meaning and use. This research explores differential meanings, by analysing uses of money by the different actor groups, and the different rationales that form the basis of such use.

Summary

To begin with, many microfinance project evaluations are not fully accessible. Impact studies available in the public domain provide limited information about their objectives, methodology and assumptions. They mostly present findings related to financial and empowerment indicators which do not provide sufficient detail for understanding the methodology employed.

This reveals important divergences between theory and practice and the difference in local and external perspectives by which microfinance is delivered and assessed. These differences include the role of savings and credit, the size, purpose, costs and sources of savings and loans, and the implications of the different ways in which this money is delivered with the intention to reduce poverty. All these topics are subsumed under the theme of 'use of money'. Women are the main targets of microfinance services and SHGs are the main means of delivery. These groups have been viewed as mechanisms of delivery on the one hand and as agents of empowerment on the other. Economic studies highlight the importance of frameworks of trust involving information on the reputation of others, establishment of long-term relationships and networks based on customer friendship and intermediaries. However, microfinance impact studies do not contain sufficient emphasis on trust, nor do they analyse the processes by which groups manage microfinance and the ensuing impact of these processes. There is a need for analysis of SHGs not only as local institutions through which microfinance services are delivered but also as institutions which have their own character and processes that are relevant to understanding the impact of microfinance. Traditional impact analysis concentrates on the use of money, whereas more insight into group processes, like leadership or group learning processes, is needed for a deeper understanding of how women actually deal with finance. Further, microfinance projects are situated in specific geographical/regional contexts, which have an important bearing on the economic development of that region. The socio-cultural and institutional structures and processes also determine the space within which different groups of people in the community can realise their livelihoods aspirations.[115] Economic studies identify people living in remote, resource poor regions with low infrastructure and belonging to SCs as those for whom poverty is almost a permanent condition. The identification of such groups is considered important, as they are likely to suffer the most in a situation of a community-wide shock.[116] Once more, microfinance impact studies do not give sufficient attention to the livelihoods context and its link with poor and marginalised people.

Hence, the three themes that emerge as important in understanding the perspectives of the users of money are:

1. women's livelihoods,
2. use of resources (money), and
3. groups (learning processes).

The divergence between field observation and discourse analysis (a wide-ranging review of microfinance literature and impact studies, listed in Appendix 1) yields the issues on which this book elaborates. These are organised into three broad themes, as illustrated in Table 2.7.

Table 2.7
Critique of Practice of Impact

Critique	Questions that Reveal Social Meaning
1. Use of Money Outreach to poor inadequately tracked Impact of savings and credit not differentiated Social impacts under-emphasised Impact of different financial models not differentiated Inadequate attention to negative impacts Overemphasis on financial in comparison with other forms of capital	Who takes the credit, what amounts, for what purpose, from which source, on what terms and which type of credit women refuse and why The role of savings and the factors influencing the management of savings The different sources of loans and their social and financial impacts. The impacts of different types of capital and their interrelationships
2. Women's Groups Inadequate emphasis on the impacts of the forums (like SHGs, banks) through which this money is transferred	Role of groups in management of money and the processes involved. The impact of groups in terms of economic, social and ecological and at individual, household and community levels
3. Livelihoods Inadequate attention to the livelihoods context in which the money users are situated	Impact in relation to livelihoods context in which microcredit programmes are implemented and situated

Source: Authors.

Many inconsistencies and differences are a result of the impact being studied from supplier and 'objective' perspectives based on ungrounded assumptions. This has resulted in meanings of external agents getting precedence over those of the users of microfinance, namely poor women. It highlights the need for client-focussed demand perspectives that makes minimal assumptions and tries to map and understand what people do and why. Thus, an actor-oriented approach is required that would enable greater participation of local actors, especially poor women. In giving priority to women's perspectives as users of money, this book focuses not on looking at impact from the point of view of organisations, at macro- or meso-level, but on viewing it from the women-user's point of view, at the micro-level. A longitudinal perspective has helped to gain an in-depth understanding of when and how poor women in rural India utilise microfinance for alleviating their poverty.

NOTES

1. Importance of women's economic contribution, accompanied by low wages and their lack of control over assets, and investments in their capacity building were highlighted by feminist writings (Barry 1995; Bhatt 2006; Bhatt et al., 1988) and acknowledged by international agencies (IFAD 2007; ILO 2007; MHHDC 2002).

2. Rural indebedtedness was recognised much before independence and the first survey after independence was the All-India Rural Credit Survey (RBI 1954), which marked the beginning of development banking in independent India.

3. Poverty estimates by government, international agencies and NGOs have varied in India (McGuire et al. 1998; Planning Commission 2001; UNDP 2004), yet there is broad agreement, even from official sources about the total number of poor being about 300 million (GOI 2008).

4. For a more detailed discussion of the historical evolution of NGOs and their orientations, and their current entry into microfinance, see Kottak (1985), Premchander (1999) and Riddell and Robinson (1995).

5. Karl (1997) compiled a set of essays to outline the economic contributions of women and how to promote women's economic participation.

6. This was part of a larger research conducted by Institute of Social Studies Trust on gender and reproductive health, covering several locations including Karnataka and Delhi (Mukhopadhyay and Savitri 1998).

7. Kraus-Harper (1998) provides evidence that self-employment was hailed as a route towards more economic independence, through wide-ranging field-based studies of women entrepreneurs.

8. In a book that presents lessons from Indian Labour Organization's (ILO) Small Enterprise Development projects, Harper and Finnegan (1998), and show the need for capacity building of the delivery organisations to offer high quality enterprise services as well as attain financial sustainability.

9. Minimalist finance is seen as provision of only microcredit services (often inclusive of savings services, especially when the NGO–MFI collects these as security deposits), exclusive of non-financial services such as education (Premchander 2003a; Quiñones 2000; RBI 2007b).

10. The bias has been acknowledged by many including Hulme and Mosley (1996) and 10 years later, in India by Fernandez (2005). Dunford (1998) questions the bias in favour of MFIs and asks whether it is necessary to build a whole new set of institutions in parallel to the existing banking and credit union systems and warns that this may turn out results no different from those of existing banking institutions, in terms of reaching the poor.

11. After the introduction of the New Economic Policy from 1991 onwards, annual growth rates increased. However, rural poverty declined only marginally, with the head count ratio declining from 39.2 per cent in 1987–88 to 37.5 per cent in 1999–2000 (DANIDA 2004). While earlier official estimates contested this, the 11th Plan accepts that official estimates underestimated poverty, and that post-reform poverty reduction has been limited, with over 300 million people still BPL (GOI 2008).

12. Given the recognition of rural indebtedness, caused by landlessness or small landholding and exploitative land revenue regime inherited from the British period, land reform measures and development banking were both introduced as measures to support poor peasants. For a historical discussion of land reform in India, see Appu (1996) and for rural credit, see Karmakar (1999) and Thorat (2005).

13. Baviskar and Attwood (1995) show how politically powerful people dominated and took control of cooperatives and Woolcock (1999) discusses how group-based microfinance programmes faced similar problems.

14. Leeladhar (2006) showed that by 2005, the average population per branch office had decreased to 16,000 from 64,000 in 1969. However, some states and regions continue to be underbanked, such as Bihar, Orissa, Rajasthan, Uttar Pradesh, Chhattisgarh, Jharkhand, West Bengal and a large number of North-eastern states.

15. Most commercial banks extended credit through SHGs. Apart from NABARD and SIDBI, housing corporations and several private banks considered financing through SHGs. Nearly 100 MFIs have attained the scale and size, so as to be

of interest to over 20 investors looking for microfinance partnerships. CARE and Access (2007) produced a directory of Emerging Microfinance in India to facilitate national and international access to this information. The state of the sector report for microfinance, produced for an annual conference on this issue in India, reports increasing interest of investors, too (Ghate 2007).

16. Among others, high interest rates have been reported by SDC (2007), IIMS Dataworks (2007). The latter also shows that interest rates from moneylenders can be up to 72 per cent.

17. Financial inclusion has been adopted as an integral part of the development and poverty alleviation approach in India recently, with RBI and NABARD leading the move (IIB Vision 2007; Thorat 2007); the Department of Rural Development and other departments adopting several far-reaching measures, and several suggestions by advisors and consultants which require going beyond mere access to financial services to reduction of vulnerabilities (Arunachalam 2008; Mahajan and Regy 2007).

18. Harper (1998) alleges that banks, mobilise savings of the rural poor and lend them in urban areas. The recent 'push' towards rural lending is only due to government pressure back by subsidies.

19. Sinha (2001) quotes these statistics in a political context that seeks to create greater policy space and increased donor support for private and financially sustainable MFIs.

20. The renewed interest in rural and agricultural finance was based on the premise that lessons from earlier failures will result in a new focus on financial systems building, cost-reducing innovations and responding to the demands for financial services from clients (Zeller 2003a, 2003b).

21. The rapid expansion led by ICICI under its 'partnership model' was halted due to two crisis that came in 2006. The first related to suicides by some borrowers in AP where the lenders were ICICI correspondents, followed by RBI raising regulatory concerns about strengthening the Know Your Customer procedures. Thus, new funding under this model was suspended, leading to a shortage of lending funds (Ghate 2007).

22. Joshi (2003) states that the phenomenon of 'funding for current ideas spawns new NGOs' has occurred in the field of education, wastelands development as also in microfinance.

23. Seibel (2000), Banerjee (2002), and Chavan and Ramkumar (2002) discuss features of SHG-bank linkage and Bangladesh models.

24. See Berger (1989), Christen et al. (1994) and Robinson (2001) for different typologies, and though Berger considered institutional forms, none of these considered the nature of partnership between the different types of organisations, which is elaborated here.

25. See NABARD (2007) for statistics of SHG-bank linkage.

26. For a discussion of policy issues faced by cooperatives, see Fisher and Sriram (2002). A National Policy on Cooperatives is now formulated for cooperative reform, to encourage them to have more professional functioning and be more autonomous, democratic and accountable (GOI 2005).

27. An annual review report of an IFAD-supported and DFID-supported project with GOI partnership criticised the prioritisation of financially sustainable microfinance over access and control of own finances by women, and their capacity building to manage own financial organisations (UNOPS 2002).

28. RBI has upheld its firm reinforcement of the policy prioritising depositor safety (RBI 2007a).

29. UNOPS (2002), ibid.

30. Rutherford and Staehle (2002) analysed a fast-growing MFI in West Bengal and warned against this risk, which UNOPS (2002) highlighted as well.

31. This issue has been discussed more recently, with practitioners highlighting the need for 'reclaiming women's leadership in microfinance' (FWWB 2006; Rajagopalan 2003, 2005b).

32. Mahajan et al., (1998) highlight that those who are poor are underserved by the financial sector, yet later (in 2003) he recognised that even though perceived risks are higher, the spreads are greater, thereby making it attractive for banks and private companies to enter the microfinance market.

33. This was claimed as an early lesson from SFMC project funded by IFAD, DFID and the Ministry of Finance (Bose and Ranjani 1998).

34. Dichter (1999) and Dunford (1998) were among the first to question donor support to private microfinance organisations in preference to banking and cooperative organisations. Hendricks (2002) analyses experience of microfinance projects in China to show that instead of thinking of new stand-alone microfinance organisations, it was more effective to work with already established Rural Credit Cooperatives who already were authorised by the People's Bank of China for financial operations. Fernandez states: 'Instead of trying to morph into an MFI, an NGO should promote a separate financial institution' (2003: 17), which then would offer the banks some competition and motivate them to lend to the poor, thus achieving the primary objective of NGO-based microfinance interventions: mainstreaming the poor. However, microfinance organisations who seek to reach the poor do not have sufficient grants forthcoming, to support them for the 4–5 years needed to break even (Gibbons 2002). Gibbons (2003) provides an additional argument that NGOs have chronic capital shortage and dependence on donors and cannot build the funds required to on-lend to a significant number of households.

35. This trend is highlighted by Berbenbach and Churchill (1997), McGuire et al. (1998), Premchander (2003) and Quiñones (2000). Fernandez (2003) points out that in Bangladesh, over 12 years during which the NGO started a major financial programme, Bangladesh Rural Advancement Committee (BRAC) groups moved from discussing issues relating to education, health and religion for 80 per cent of their group meeting time, to discussing financial matters for this time. The RBI also recognised that MFIs tend to be minimalist (RBI 2007b).

36. Harper (2002) acknowledges that starting new MFIs is cost intensive and Nair (2001) explains that this is on account of intensive grassroots monitoring needed by these commercially oriented organisations.

37. Fernandez (2003) holds that private MFIs are needed only to point to an important gap in the market, while Ramanathan (2003) points out that a financial institution or an MFI once established in an area providing services to a client group, may not find it as easy to move away as an NGO, due to the financial considerations involved.

38. Dunford (2001) demands impact evaluations in terms of impact on poor, especially children, rather than be satisfied with just statistics related to performance of MFIs.

39. IFAD, for instance, was concerned about capacity building and inclusion of the poor, and paid attention to this aspect in its review of jointly funded programmes, as evidenced in UNOPS (2002, 2003).

40. Hendricks (2002) finds that bilateral donor projects have short-term lifespan of 4–5 years, whereas sustainability requires long-term support and capacity building. This is supported by Cheston and Kuhn (2002), Dunford (2001), Nissanke (2002) and Wilson (2003) who suggests a longer period of about 7 years.

41. Von Pischke criticised that in microfinance programmes, minimalist strategies are more easily replicable and scalable and that 'transparency is low and hype is high … and while microfinance can reach large numbers of poor people, it is unlikely to be capable of sustainable outreach to the very poor' (1997: 1). Dunford (1998) points out that only few microfinance programmes have integrated a broader educational agenda into their programmes and that these are not representative of most other microfinance programmes across the world.

42. Studies conducted by Cheston et al. (2001), Kamal (1999), Nissanke (2002) and Sebstad and Chen (1996) show evidence of donor-led impact assessments and methodological discussions, including advocating participatory methods like impact audits using internal staff.

43. A key study that analysed motives, methodologies and key aspects of microfinance impacts was by Hulme and Mosley (1996). For a discussion on microfinance, gender and women's empowerment, see Johnson (1999, 2003, 2005) and Mayoux (1997, 2001, 2003a).

44. Woolcock (1999) found evidence of manipulation of repayment rates and such pressure for sustainability is also documented in Bangladesh as well as India (Morduch 1998). The large-scale move towards sustainable microfinance is evidenced in Robinson (1995) who documents best practice lessons from Indonesia.

45. Rhyne argued (Otero and Rhyne 1994) that impact evaluations must move away from impacts on beneficiaries and focus on the quality of financial services and scale and sustainability of financial organisations.

46. An early exposition of participatory research methods for social information gathering is found in Chambers (1991).

47. Elaborated by many economists (Cheston and Reed 1999; Copestake 2000; Goyder 1998; Hulme and Mosley 1999; Simanowitz 2003a, 2003b), who also consider impact assessment and taking actions in response to the emerging perspective as essential for survival of the MFIs.

48. Earlier emphasis in a virtual discussion of Consultative Group for Assisting the Poor (CGAP) partners was summarised by Cohen and Gaile (1997). Garcia (1998) highlights the issue with regard to evaluation of an education programme in Columbia. Coopestake (2003) advocated that in addition to assessing financial performance, micro-finance organisations (MFOs) need to commit to social performance, decide and institutionalise monitoring and assessment of key social performance indicators.

49. Dialogues and learning approaches are widely advocated (Dale 1998) and have become more acceptable post-2000 (Barrientos 2003; Dand et al. 2003; Mayoux 2003a, 2003b, 2003c), both in microfinance as well as in business services and microenterprise (Albu et al., 2003).

50. Even as the demand for greater sharing is articulated (Hulme 1997), reluctance is evident not only among practitioners but also among donors (Mosley 2000).

51. Social performance has since received significant donor support for technical development, as can be seen from CGAP (2007), Thomas (2007).

52. For a review of outreach to the poor by microfinance organisations, see Hatch and Fredrick (1998).

53. The compilation considered several studies from literature in India and other countries (Premchander and Prameela 2007) and also consulted members of a knowledge-sharing forum of the United Nations in India (Solution Exchange 2007a, 2007b).

54. A household-based perspective of impact moved to recognition of 'wider' social impacts with Kabeer (2003), which may occur within the household (for example, reduced domestic violence), effects on non-members (for example, increased investments in education) and participation in collective action (for example, participation in political campaigns). Zohir and Matin (2004) developed the framework further, specifying four domains of wider impacts: cultural, economic, social and political, each of which maybe assessed at three levels: individual, enterprise or household. Later discourse has continued to elaborate on non-financial and wider social impacts (Solution Exchange 2007a).

55. Graziosi (2002) highlights the balance that MFIs make between donor and client priorities, which can pull in different directions.

56. Zahrai (2001) stresses spiritual values and human values as the key motivation that enables the upholding of solidarity, service, cooperation and justice, all of which are considered as enhanced by the microfinance solidarity groups.

57. Recent studies in the Indian context, which mention negative impacts, include Singh (2003), TBF (2002) and Garikipati (2003).

58. Rajshekar (2007) and Shylendra (2006) discuss some of these negative impacts and their causes.

59. Burra et al. (2005) compiled these studies, authored by Murthy et al. (2005), Padia (2005), Parthasarathy (2005), Rajagopalan (2005c), Rajivan (2005) and Sharma (2005).

60. The evaluation studies are unpublished and were accessed through the respective government departments (AFC 2005; Buch 2002; IIHRD 2003; IIPO 2005).

61. This was AFC (2005), which was also the latest study undertaken.

62. These various negative impacts were reported by Goetz and Sen Gupta (1996), IFAD (2007), Mayoux (1997, 2001), Rahman (1999), Sampark (2003) and TBF (2002).

63. For an analysis of role of savings, see Johnson and Rogaly (1997), Rutherford (2000) and Wright and Dondo (2001).

64. See Robinson (1995).

65. See Johnson and Rogaly (1997), MicroSave Africa (1998), Mutesasira (1999), Wright (2006) for evidence from various countries.

66. UNDP (1999) records evidence of such difficulties in accessing own savings.

67. Otero and Rhyne (1994) point out to the need to adhere to these requirements for depositor safety, a concern that has not been voiced in later discourse on microfinance, which has instead sought to change laws to facilitate savings for the microfinance organisations, with no safeguards drawn up yet for depositor safety. In India, though, RBI has held depositor safety as an important consideration in framing regulations and norms for deposit-taking NBFCs, and this has been upheld and recorded in all NABARD discussions as well (NABARD 2002).

68. The study was in fact a baseline study (Chen and Snodgrass 1999), which was expected to be followed up later, but the next stage of the study was never conducted.

69. This was a basic premise of the Keynesian monetary and fiscal theories (Keynes 1936).

70. This is evidenced in India, and elsewhere, such as Bangladesh and Peru (Marr 1999; Pitt and Khandker 2004; Premchander 2003a; UNDP 1997).

71. Empirical evidence of this is found in India and Bangladesh (CARE and FAO 2007; Premchander 2003a; Sampark 2000).

72. Johnson and Rogaly (1997) and Fernandez (2005) indicate this as a reason for some MFIs not raising interest rates.

73. See adversely CETZAM (1999).

74. Impact studies of microfinance programmes in India in the three states of TN, AP and Kerala (FWWB 1997) and in Jharkhand (Sampark 2000) showed a pattern of the first loan typically starting between Rs 1,000 and 2,000, and doubling in subsequent loan cycles.

75. Matin (1998) studied the impact of rapid credit deepening on joint liability contracts and found that the poor opt to take smaller loans, showing their lower credit absorption capacity. Further, rapid pace of credit deepening led towards including the less poor, and also worsened repayment performance.

76. Field-based evidence of demand exceeding the small amounts given by NGOs and MFIs maybe found in UNDP (1997), CETZAM (1999) and Sampark (2003). A study covering households vulnerable to bonded labour, in TN, India, stated that loans given through SHGs were small and sufficed only to meet emergency needs, but not for productive investments (Guérin et al. 2007).

77. Dunford (1998) recommends that microfinance programmes for the poor need to be especially designed to meet their needs, and Mosley's (2000) research in Bolivia indicated the same.

78. The need for further research was highlighted by a group of practitioners from Asia-Pacific countries who discussed their microfinance practices and effectiveness in 1994. Conroy et al. (1998) and Dunford (1998) called for more research on impact too.

79. One recent estimate in India shows that only 30 per cent of MFI clients were BPL (Ghate 2007).

80. See Hulme and Mosley (1996) and Remeneyi (1997).

81. Morduch (1999) highlights this difference to show that either the borrowers of financially self-sufficient programmes are those with higher loan-taking capacities and therefore less poor to begin with or indeed they might have progressively increased their loan sizes.

82. Such rejection in Bangladesh and India is documented by Montgomery (1996) and Tankha (1999).

83. Christen (2000) considered the context of Latin America, where the commercial approach to microfinance dominated, witnessed by new entrants that included NGOs and formal and non-formal banking institutions. He found that the push towards commercialisation could have driven microfinance organisation off their initial mission of serving poorer clients, yet found no compelling evidence towards this and concluded that larger loan sizes could simply have been due to strategic choices of lenders, their period of entry into the market or the natural evolution of a target group. Aguilar (1999) emphasises that though no conclusions can be reached on whether poverty targeting is effective, it is certainly accepted as necessary and points to ways of identifying and attracting the poor and excluding and discouraging the non-poor.

84. Otero and Rhyne (1994) and Stiglitz (1990) also highlight the fact that joint liability mechanisms reduce risks and costs for the microfinance organisations.

85. Stiglitz (1990) highlighted the lenders' need to ensure that borrowers utilised the funds prudently and, such monitoring being costly for themselves, found peer monitoring mechanisms useful. Even as group lending programmes reduced costs for lenders, they transferred the risks from the lenders to the borrowers, which are highlighted by Jain (1996) and Seibel (2000).

86. Matin (1998) documents this in Bangladesh, with Grameen Bank's women's groups. The phenomenon has been referred to as 'borrower run' in a forthcoming article by Bond and Rai (2009).

87. Montgomery (1996) and Montgomery et al. (1996) provide evidence of this from groups in Bangladesh and Marr (1999) from a study of groups in Peru.

88. See Reddy and Prakash (2003) for evidence from SHG federations in AP, India.

89. For an elaborate analysis, see Bhuiyan et al., (2005).

90. Keister (2002) highlights these processes in a sociological analysis of financial markets.

91. A sociological review finds an independent rationale for promotion of savings, as seen in Beverly and Sherraden (1999); Keister (2000).

92. See Rutherford (2000), who emphasises the need for sustainable savings services.

93. Hendricks (2002) warns that exit strategies of microfinance programmes in bilateral projects have not proven successful, thus highlighting the need to plan post-project sustainability at the outset.

94. For an anthropologist's perspective, see Geertz (1962).

95. Rajagopalan (2004a) find evidence of this more generally among SHGs in India.

96. A series of studies conducted in AP showed that leaders could be from the 'higher' caste categories, self-appointed or appointed by officials, and many accessed more loans than other members and sometimes misused savings and revolving loan funds (APMAS 2001, 2003, 2005).

97. Andhra Pradesh Mahila Abhivruddhi Society (APMAS) (2001) find evidence of this from a study of three districts in AP, India.

98. For a sociological perspective of group processes, see Granovetter (1994) and Putnam (1993).

99. Some key studies prior to 2000 include Fernandez (1994), Hulme and Mosley (1996), Rao and Hashmi (1999), Shylendra (1998).

100. Jeyaseelan (2005) studies groups in TN and Malhotra (2006) studies dropouts among SHGs formed by RRBs and NGOs in many locations.

101. APMAS (2007) highlights that as SHG federations model has been scaled up and found effective in AP, policy support should now focus on enabling their registration as cooperatives, charitable societies or corporate entities. Similar concerns about the enabling environment are raised in EDA (2006), Gadenne and Vasudevan (2007), Sahu and Das (2007) and Sampark (2006b).

102. Richardson and Howarth (2002) highlight the importance of enabling environment in women's enterprise development; Edwards, (1998) indicates the need to evaluate NGO performance in the light of local social and political contexts and Schmid (2003) emphasises the natural resource and geographical considerations as well.

103. Parr (2005) links bondage to distress migration. This is supported by Mosse et al., (2004), who highlights that trends towards migration are related to both ecological decline and social relations of dependence and indebtedness.

104. See Gaiha (2000) and Jha and Gaiha (2004) for a spatial analysis of poverty, undernutrition and growth in rural India.

105. Datt and Ravallion (1998) analyse interstate performance in poverty reduction and Osmani (2001) discusses these in the Asian Pacific context and highlights the importance of agriculture in determining growth.

106. Jha (1999) analysed structure and determinants of rural poverty in India in the 1980s and 1990s, and found that the rate of growth of agriculture and food production was lower in areas which experienced higher population growth. Other reasons included lack of formal credit for the poor and their social exclusion. Zeller (2003b) points out that serving rural and agricultural clients is more difficult as production depends on natural conditions and covariant risks are high, with dependence on seasonality of production and prices, thus many rural environments are too hostile without preceding investments in other sectors, for example, infrastructure.

107. A strong example of how policy models are perpetuated is presented by Mosse (2005) through longitudinal analysis of processes at the design and implementation levels of a donor-supported project in India.
108. Narayan et al., (2000) present a multifaceted understanding of poverty.
109. See Batliwala (2001, 2003) for a discussion of women's empowerment, especially Dalit women in Karnataka.
110. De Haan (1999) highlights two major factors leading to social exclusion: that specific groups,including women, get overlooked and also the means by which poverty and deprivation are assessed.
111. Townsend et al., (2003) analyse NGO movements to analyse how women's struggles for power have both been supported and contained by their orientations.
112. Sinha (2001) offers this as an important reason to shun official subsidised credit.
113. Ramaswamy et al., (2004) show evidence of this from AP where popular leaders channel significant official schemes for the village and allocate official benefits to specific political interests.
114. Lyon (1999) finds such an approach useful in conducting an enquiry on cooperation and group formation in the context of marketing of agricultural produce and analysing social and group processes to find their effectiveness.
115. As elaborated by Dreze and Sen (1995) and Sen (1981).
116. Gaiha and Imai (2003) find that those in semi-arid regions are more vulnerable to shocks and therefore persistent poverty.

3

Livelihoods Context

The context in which women live influences the use and impact of money, analysed here through several factors in the macro-economic context, at the district and *taluk* level. The meso-perspective is explored through village level analysis, based on focus group discussions with women's self-help groups (SHGs) and other villagers. The micro-perspective, of individual women's land/livelihoods management, supplements the meso- (village) and macro (district)-level data to provide insights into how women determine their strategies in given livelihoods contexts (Figure 3.1).

Orthodox microfinance studies take a financial perspective and usually track the use and impact of money in a more limited way, with little attention to contextual factors. These factors are all inter-related but, for the ease of discussion, are classified under three broad categories: the ecological and economic context, the socio-cultural context and the institutional context.

ECOLOGICAL AND ECONOMIC CONTEXT

Karnataka stands seventh among 15 major states ranked by their human development indices, yet Koppal is one of the poorest and lowest ranked districts on human development and gender indices,[1] and this can be attributed to certain native constraints. The primary livelihoods constraints affecting demand and supply of credit are imposed by the ecological and economic context, which are now discussed (See also Figure 3.2).

Agriculture in the Drought-prone Region

Koppal district is spread over 5,559 sq. km. and comprises four *taluk*s,[2] with Koppal *taluk* covering 1,375 sq. km., 25 per cent of its total area. The district houses a total population of about 1 million spread over 488 villages. Each *taluk* has varying agricultural potential depending on its access to water from a local dam. In total, 82,702 hectares (60 per cent) is the net area available for farming, amounting to 32,351 landholdings.

Figure 3.1
Exploring Meanings: Livelihoods Context

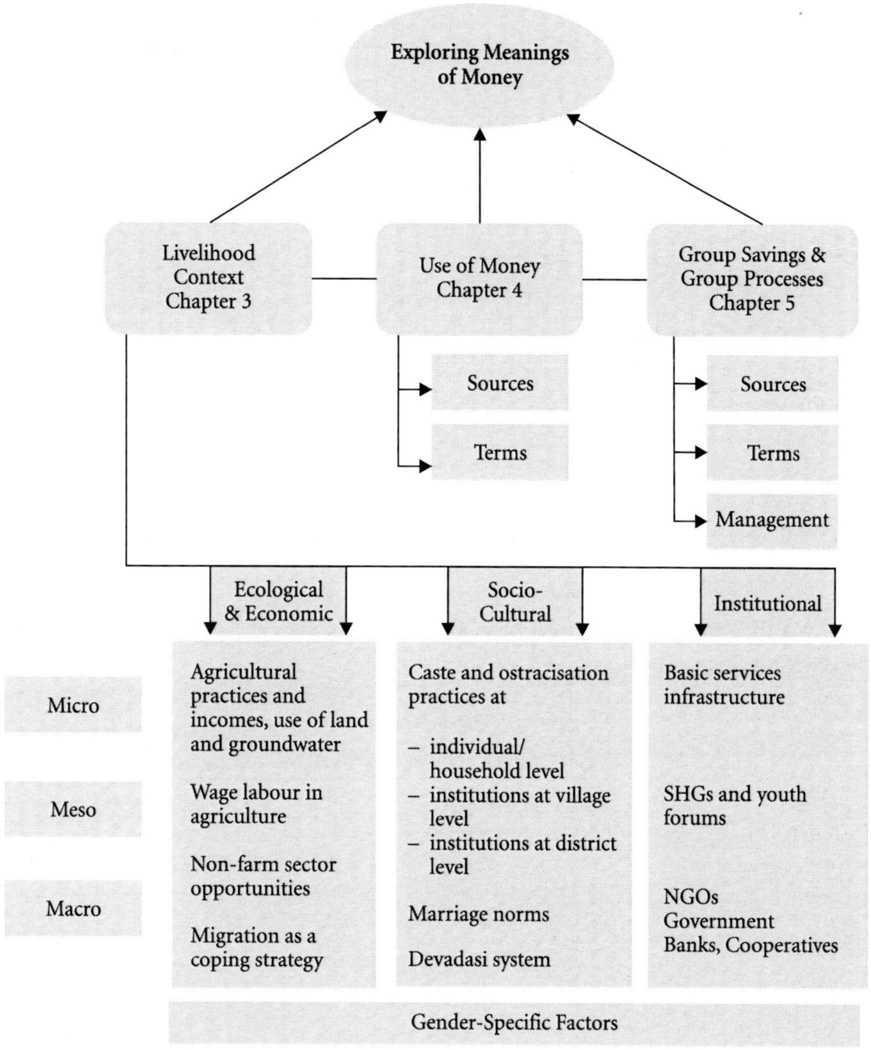

Source: Authors.

Eighty per cent of landholdings are marginal, small or semi-medium, that is, less than 4 hectares. The district level Census data does not disclose how many households are landless. Land is an important asset, though earning from land is primarily rain dependent, with only 24 per cent of all households owning irrigated lands.

I have spent my entire lifetime in search of water. In search of water, my hair has become white.
—Rudrappa, a farmer from Bikanhalli village (Premchander et al., 2003: 21)

Figure 3.2
Research Location

Karnataka State in India

Koppal District in Karnataka

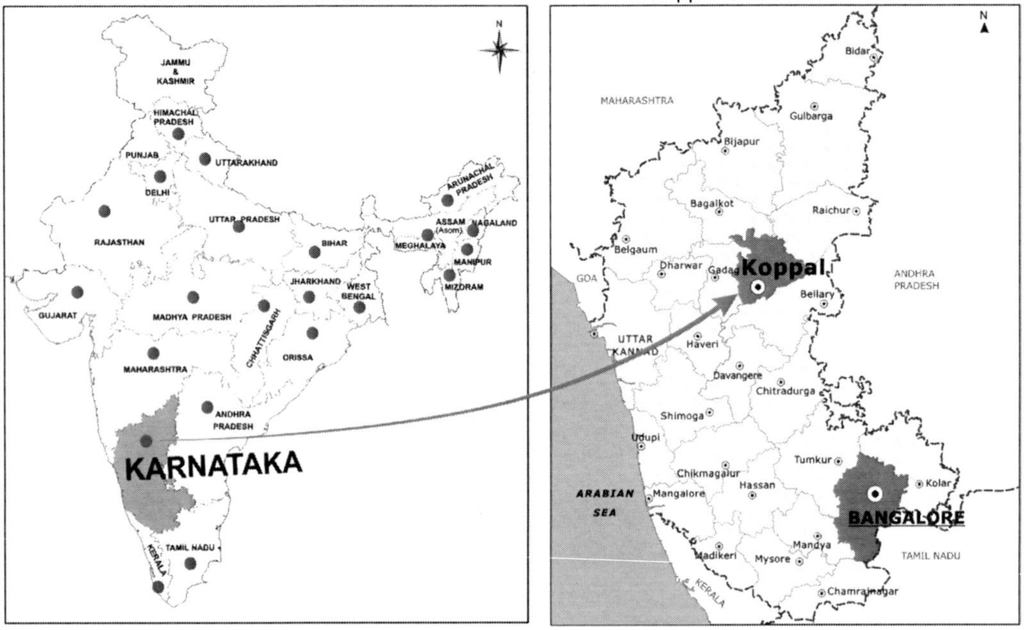

Source: Maps of India, Compare Infobase (2009).

Table 3.1
Distribution of Landholdings

Size of Landholdings	No. of Holdings	%	Area (Hectares)	%
Marginal and small (<2 hectares)	23,770	58	26,816	26.87324
Semi-medium (2–4 hectares)	11,670	28	31,988	32.0562799
Medium sized (4–10 hectares)	5,021	12	29,498	29.5609649
Large holdings (>10 hectares)	804	2	11,485	11.5095153
Total (Koppal *taluk*)	41,265	100	99,787	100

Source: GOK (2006).

Koppal is a semi-arid and drought-prone district. The average normal rainfall in the district is 572 mm per year spread over 28 days; the district experienced drought in the years 2001–03, with an average annual rainfall of 367 mm (GOK 2004). There was good rainfall in 2004, ending a period of 4 years of continuous drought. The years 2005 and 2006 witnessed drought, when agriculture failed due to inadequate rains, and then again 2007 brought good rainfall and high agriculture yield in both dry and irrigated lands.

Low rainfall has led to depletion of ground water, further aggravated by the digging of deeper tube wells, from which only saline water is available. Land conditions in the study

> *There was a forest at that time and I was getting the raw materials (bamboo) for basket weaving from the forest, but now the forest has been cut down and the lands are used for farming.*—Yellamma-D

villages (all belonging to Koppal *taluk*) are thus poor. The fields are
uneven, stony and lack protection from rainwater. Most have no
bunds[3] or any other arrangement to irrigate water. The more fertile
topsoil has been so eroded that farmers use chemical fertilisers
and hybrid seeds to obtain even a moderate yield. Some lands
provided by the government for the *devadasis* are unproductive
because they are rocky with thorny bushes, and need extensive
clearing to be farmed. Others are regularly submerged by the
waters of the nearby Tungabhadra dam for several months every
year. The villagers of Bikanhalli claim that there were 5,000 trees in the 1960s, compared with just
2,500 in 2007, and only 1,000 by 2008. Trees have been depleted not only from private lands but also
from common lands and forests. This has created a deficiency of firewood and biomass availability
in the area and has also accelerated soil erosion from wind and water.[4]

> *I have four acres of land but it is near the river-bank and so it is flooded by the river water for more than half of the year. I cannot grow anything much on that land.*
> —Yellamma-D

Farmers in this region continuously experiment with their cropping pattern, balancing cash
and food crops. Crops are planted in both red and black soils and in irrigated as well as dry lands.
Participatory rural appraisal (PRA) exercises showed that agricultural incomes were subject to
significant seasonal variation and also depended on the type of land. Farmers with irrigation
facility, for example, through borewells, do not keep the land fallow at all, and take three crops in a
year. Those farmers, who have more than one piece of land, use it at different times, always based
on water availability. Cropping on irrigated land is more expensive as it needs regular weeding,
usage of pesticides and fertilizers and also electricity charges. The average expenses of cropping
on irrigated land are Rs 4,000 ($89) per acre to obtain an income of Rs 5,000–6,000 ($111–133).
The average expenses on dry land are Rs 1,500–2,000 ($333–44) per acre and the income
Rs 4,000–5,000 ($89–111) in case of good monsoon.

Detailed analysis of individual farm information shows that the difference between yield on
dry land and irrigated land depends on several factors such as amount and distribution of rainfall,
cropping pattern, incidence of pests, technical management and human labour invested. The micro-
level details highlight that several factors influence earnings from land, which are as much related
to ecological conditions as to economic and management factors. When farmers sow commercial
crops, such as sunflower, groundnut, cotton or maize, they spend about Rs 8,000–10,000 ($178–222)
per acre and on growing foodgrains up to Rs 4,000 ($89) per acre. With good rainfall, the income
is double of what was spent, giving a 100 per cent profit; but if rains fail, the farmer loses even food
security and is indebted. Marginal farmers and the landless take land on lease to grow foodgrains,
cash crops and fodder. The lease varies, ranging from Rs 2,000 to 5,000 ($44–111) per acre for dry
and Rs 5,000 to 8,000 ($111–178) for irrigated land. Cropping pattern and annual returns vary for
every household, making it difficult to generalise about overall earnings. If rains are scanty, which
is often the case in this drought-prone region there is little or no income from dry land cultivation.
Of the 10 women studied, six had land of between 1.5 to 3 acres of irrigated land and 0.5 to 12 acres
of dry land. Income per acre from land is presented in Table 3.2.

In a year of good and evenly distributed rainfall, income from dry land could be equal to that from
irrigated land. Variation in net earnings also depends on the management of the land. Rangamma
managed her dry land such that she earned Rs 3,325 ($73.88), close to Rs 3,375 ($75) per acre

Table 3.2
Income from Land (per acre)

Name	Early Monsoon Season		Late Monsoon Season	
	Irrigated Land	*Dry Land*	*Irrigated Land*	*Dry Land*
1. Mariyamma (3 acres irrigated and 6.5 acres dry land)	Rs 3,375 ($75)	Rs 755 ($16.77)	Rs 3,366 ($74.8)	Rs 899 ($19.9)
2. Rangamma (2 acres of dry land)		Rs 3,325 ($73.88)		
3. Sangavva (0.5 acre of irrigated land)	Rs 2,044 ($45.42)		Rs 10,000 ($222)	
4. Yellamma (4 acres of dry land, near the riverbank)				Rs 733 ($16.28)
5. Kaveri (2 acres of irrigated and 11 acres of dry land)	Rs 2,000 ($44.44)	No data	Rs 4,500 ($100)	Rs 1,209 ($26.86)
6. Parvathamma (0.5 acre of irrigated land)			Rs 3,340 ($74.22)	

Source: Authors.

that Mariyamma earned from her irrigated land. Kaveri was able to earn Rs 2,000 ($44.44) per acre from her irrigated land. Sangavva earned Rs 1,022 ($22.71) on her 0.5-acre plot of land, and could only cultivate it for 4 months when it was not submerged. As she was able to go for *coolie*[5] during the same months, she divided her time between labour work and working on own farm, thereby balancing her earnings from land and labour. However, in the late monsoon season, when there is less demand for labour, she worked on her own land and planted commercial crops like vegetables (which can be plucked more often than food crops like *jowar*[6] and millets, which are harvested only once), earning about Rs 5,000 ($111) on that crop.

Irrespective of the size of land holdings all the women followed a cropping pattern that allowed them to get foodgrains for household consumption and also commercial crops which provided cash to purchase other items like clothes, detergents and meet their medical, travel expenses, and so on.

Kaveri, who had 14 acres, left 9 acres uncultivated over the study period because of no rain. Similarly, Mariyamma cultivated only 2.5 acres of dry land, leaving 4 acres fallow, claiming that she did not have the resources, and would not risk investing in it. Only 24 per cent households have irrigated lands that they can cultivate in dry years. Thus, the earning potential depends, not on the total ownership of land, but on the land where there is irrigation. As irrigation is so critical to production, borewells are considered important and as their numbers multiply, there is further depletion of ground water resources. The following statements of women illustrate this:

> I managed to sink a borewell in this land through the Ganga Kalyan Yojane. I had to spend Rs 1,500 ($33) on this, for the dalal (broker), and getting the relevant papers from the tehsildar (local revenue officer). We had a good crop of groundnut and had some money in hand, so were able to pay for these expenses ourselves (without taking a loan). It used to yield a lot of water, but this has reduced over

the past six months. My neighbour saw the quantity of water I was getting, so he has sunk a borewell very close to mine. (Parvathamma)

Twelve years ago the government provided one borewell for about 50 families in Bikanhalli. It was in Yamunavva's land, who was a member in the Gram Panchayat. All the 50 families took water for cultivation from there. I also got water from this borewell for ten years. For the past two years, Yamunavva has forbidden everyone to take water from this borewell, as her land is getting spoiled by people coming to use the motor. There were now two groups; 20 families supported Yamunavva and others reported to the police but no action was taken. Then an officer from the Agriculture Department came and enquired about the issue. The two groups argued and fought, and the officer went back without solving the issue. The groups then asked for the borewell to be closed. Yamunavva then separated from the group. Eventually the borewell was closed. Then the groups invested Rs 30,000 ($652) each and made separate borewells, one covering 20 and another covering 30 households. Now she is getting water from the new borewell for cultivation. (Sangavva)

The macro-level information thus shows increasing groundwater depletion and salinity of lands. At the household level, farmers have adopted high input agriculture. The availability of water is a critical determinant of earnings, and the sinking of a borewell is the first and single most important investment land-owning households make. There is little evidence that agriculture is profitable,[7] yet, land is a coveted asset and agriculture the main occupation. A Sampark field manager explained:

Although agriculture is risky and appears unprofitable, it is the main occupation. What else do people have to do here? They want at least some land, so that they can cultivate. Farmers have a cultural and psychological attachment to farming; they do not like to leave their lands fallow. In the end, of course, they live on hope: every year, they hope for good rains.

So, while land is important for household food security, it is also important for livelihood purposes. On the other hand, agriculture is risky, and not always profitable. Farmers realise that it does not give satisfactory incomes, as Mariyamma explains: 'By the time we pay off the loans for seeds and fertiliser and pesticides, there is nothing left to carry forward to the next year, and we need to borrow again for the next cycle.'

Many marginal and small farmers, therefore, are only slightly better off than the landless households and also depend on casual farm labour to enhance their meagre incomes.

Agricultural Wage Labour

The landless and small/medium farmers with no irrigation facilities particularly depend on casual labour in the irrigated lands of their own or neighbouring villages, where too work is limited and seasonal. Earlier, wages ranged from Rs 15 to 20 ($0.33–0.44) for women and Rs 25 to 30 ($0.55–0.66) for men till 2005, but have since increased. A typical seasonal calendar in 2007 is presented in Table 3.3.

Women's wages are lower throughout the year. Though men work more for 3 months a year, women do some farm labour all through the year, except between March and May, which are the

Table 3.3

Seasonal Calendar—Agricultural Labour Work

Seasons/Months	Work	Time	Wages
August–October	Women go for weeding	Morning 8 to 2 p.m. Or Morning 10 to 5 p.m.	Get Rs 30 ($0.75) per day Rs 30 ($0.75)
		Extra hours of work; 3–6 p.m. for people who go to work at 8 a.m. and 7–9 p.m. for people who go to work at 10 a.m.	Get Rs 10 ($0.25); in addition, the women get vegetable, pulses, and so on because most of this part-time work need labour in the peak hours like in the early morning/evening. For example, plucking the vegetable for market
November–February	Women go for harvesting work	From 10 a.m. to 6 p.m.	Get Rs 30 ($0.75) per day
March–May	Little work for women in this season	Full day (10 a.m. to 5 p.m.)	In case women are called for work, they are paid Rs 30 ($0.75) per day Men are paid Rs 50 ($1.25) per day Men with bulls/cart earn Rs 100–150 ($2.5–3.75)
	Men get more work: land levelling, spreading manure and cleaning the land		
June–July	Monsoon sowing work begins. Women get seeding and fertilising work	Full day (10 a.m. to 5 p.m.)	During this season they get Rs 35 ($0.88) per day Neem seeds are sold at the rate of Rs 1.5 ($0.04) per kg, the women collect about 15–20 kg per day
	If the monsoon fails in June or July, women can only collect 10 kg *neem* seeds per day		

Source: Authors.

lean months for farm work. Wage labour is paid for in cash and kind. Not having any animals herself, Rangamma allows her workers to take away fodder. The practice of giving fodder for labour (in addition to wages) is common among the villages in the *taluk*, especially during the harvest months when labourers work longer hours. In certain villages, *jowar* is bartered in the grocery store for provisions, and also taken as wages, instead of money. When Rangamma needs *jowar*, she works as an agricultural labour in neighbouring farms, not for cash but to get foodgrain.

Whether in cash or kind, the total earning from wage labour depends on the season, as well as the number of members in the household, and the latter is analysed in detail in Chapter 4.

Non-farm Employment and Skills

Koppal district has a population of 1.193 million and the employment in different sectors is given in Table 3.4.

Table 3.4
Sectoral Distribution of Employment in Koppal District

Sector	Persons Employed	%
Agriculture	348,535	89
Small Business	12,768	3
Professionals	11,822	3
Government	12,428	3
Banks and LIC	761	1
Teachers	3,798	1
Total	390,112	100

Source: Authors.

Industrial development of Koppal *taluk* is particularly low. There are 233 small industrial units,[8] which employ 1,231 people from a population of 313,898 in this *taluk*. Female literacy is particularly low with only 5 per cent of the women being literate (data from group discussions). The only life skills participants and their families have are farm or contract labour, although a few are able to do traditional embroidery and tailoring. There are also several stone cutting units in the informal sector, whereby groups of people blast and cut rocks, convert them into 1-foot cubes or stone jelly, and supply them to contractors. Koppal has over 300 small units where human hair collected from individual homes is brought, sorted, cleaned, sized and exported. The units are in the informal sector, and employ about 3,000 women (Sampark estimate), but there are no recorded statistics. Women are also involved in weaving and making *kowdi*s (local thick bedsheets made from waste cloth). These activities are seasonal and dependent on orders, therefore at best offer small income supplements. Thus, not only is the potential earning from agriculture uncertain but the potential for non-farm activities in Koppal is also limited by low industrial development, and the employability or self-employability of people is further limited by their low skill levels.

Migration as a Means of Survival

As a result of this there is an increasing pressure on people to migrate. Twenty per cent of the households have one or more family members migrating within and outside Koppal district for labour work, as described in Figure 3.3.

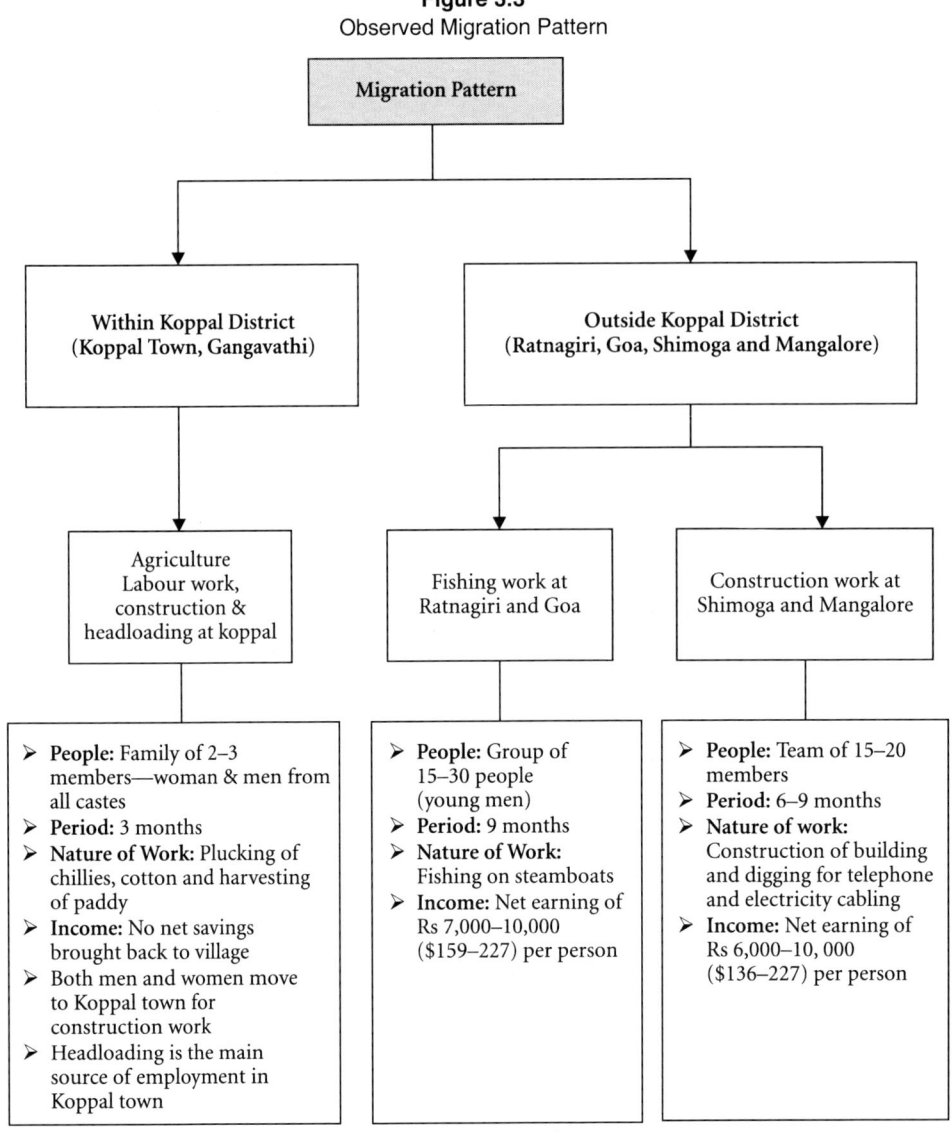

Figure 3.3
Observed Migration Pattern

Source: Authors.

In villages with relatively high irrigation levels, as in Bikanhalli, farmers do not migrate but obtain labour on nearby farms. Nagavva said:

About 10 to 15 people from our village go to Sidhamannahalli near Gangavati for plucking red chilli and cotton. People get a shed to stay from the landlord. They get wages of about Rs 25 to 30 ($0.5–0.6) per day. They stay for about 3 months and come back. The total wages the farmers give meets only the expenses on food and clothes while on migration: *Allige alli, pujege puje* (meaning that they return empty handed, with no savings).

Some go to another village for maintaining coconut trees. Both women and men go together to these farms. Men get daily wages of Rs 30 ($0.6) and women Rs 20 ($0.4) for this work. They also work in brick kilns. This work is available not only to the SCs but also to those from other castes.

By comparison, in Hosagondabala, where lands are submerged for most of the year, there was more out-migration. When migration is to nearby areas for agricultural labour, those who migrate survive the lean months, but do not bring back any savings. When they go for fishing or for high skilled work, they are able to save Rs 6,000–10,000 ($150–250) a year to bring back home. In four cases, sons migrated to the nearest towns for seasonal labour work in construction, cabling and driving. Shivavva's son migrates to a distant place in the neighbouring state of Maharashtra for more than 9 months every year for fishing. Yellamma said:

The money brought back as savings from the fishing work helps a lot. People are able to redeem the lands they mortgaged, repay loans taken for provisions, repair their homes, purchase bullocks or gold, dig bore-wells, and spend for marriages. After they have finished the amount they brought, they go back and work in Ratnagiri.

Migration is thus an important coping strategy followed by several study households. The ecological context of Koppal cannot sustain livelihoods, which depends on unpredictable rainfall, availability of wage labour, and on the quality of the natural resources to which they have access or control. The livelihoods constraints and resulting coping strategies are thus summarised in Figure 3.4.

To summarise, despite degraded land and soils, farmers try to access water through borewells whenever they can afford and adopt to a combination of food and cash crops to earn money. If they get lower yields, they stop growing commercial crops and switch back to foodgrains, as these provide cattle fodder. However, as the soil has already lost its productivity due to salinity, they still do not get good yields, and eventually try to find labour elsewhere. This livelihoods strategy is, however, based on a household perspective and further exacerbates the degradation of natural resources.

In this issue, the overall livelihoods context imposes a natural limit on the demand for credit. In the forest regions of Bastar district in Chhattisgarh, there are

I borrowed Rs 6,000 ($133) from the SHG, I have not yet returned this money. My husband was invited by the forest guard to take wood on the cycle out of the forest at night. There is a ban on this, tribals are not even allowed to collect firewood from the forests these days. But the guard said he would allow on the payment of Rs. 10 ($0.22) every time. One night, when my husband was taking the logs, the guard caught him, and he was taken to jail. I had to borrow from the SHG to get him released.... And now, the guard has allowed him to take the logs again, so our earning has started again, and I will repay SHG money when I can...—Leader of SHG in a remote village in Dantewada district, Chhattisgarh

Figure 3.4
Ecological and Economic Context

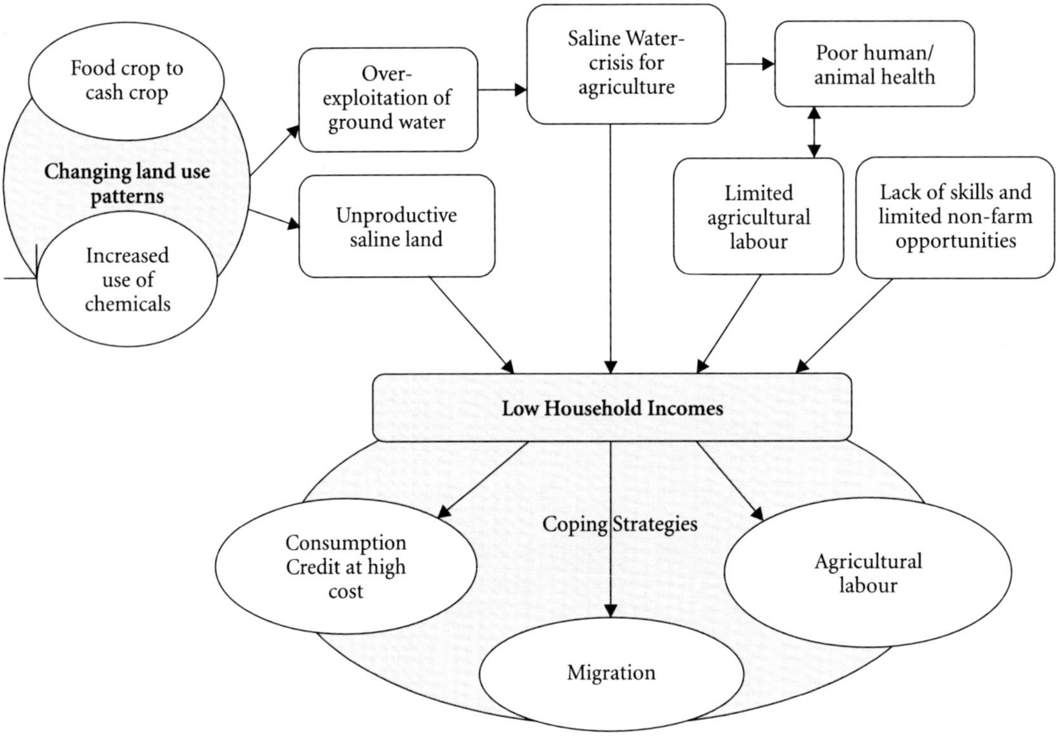

Source: Adapted from Premchander et al., (2003).

sufficient natural resources (that is, forest); however, inadequate infrastructure and markets restrict further economic development. The institutional context is one wherein government, police and traders collude to exploit forest resources without any positive impact for the local tribal people. Low literacy levels, and the differences in tribal and mainstream language privileges urban traders and middlemen over local.[9] One district in Orissa (Kalahandi district) and another in Jharkhand (Lohardaga) are remote and non-monetised and have a similar livelihoods context to that of Chhattisgarh. In another district of Jharkhand (Ranchi), the microfinance project is located close to the city or small town markets, and given the high soil fertility, provides options for women to earn through vegetable and fruit cultivation and trading. In Chhattisgarh, as in Koppal, the local livelihoods context inhibits the use of credit for development purposes. In Ranchi district of Jharkhand, however, where there are market opportunities, there is greater use of credit.[10]

SOCIO-CULTURAL CONTEXT

The main factors include demographic profile, literacy and caste. The norms regarding marriage particularly affect women's lives. The prevalence of the *devadasi* system in Karnataka makes lower caste women singularly vulnerable, as this practice is in tandem with gender, social and cultural norms.

Demographic Profile

The demographic profile of the villages where the longitudinal research was conducted is given in Table 3.5.

Table 3.5
Demographic Profile of the Five Villages Studied

Village Name	Total Households	Population			% of ST Population	% of SC[10] Population	Literacy Level	
		Male	Female	Total			Total Literacy	Female Literacy
Chukkankal	177	514	495	1,009	183 (18%)	273 (27%)	528 (52%)	217 (44%)
Mudhaballi	387	1,044	1,044	2,088	147 (7%)	333 (13%)	1,047 (50%)	392 (38%)
Hosagondabala	700	1,998	1,976	3,974	23 (1%)	347 (7%)	2,261 (57%)	896 (45%)
Bahadurbandi	422	1,300	1,245	2,545	104 (4%)	158 (11%)	1,149 (45%)	388 (31%)
Bikanhalli	131	360	337	697	28 (4%)	197 (39%)	353 (51%)	128 (38%)
Total	1,817	5,216	5,097	10,313	485 (5%)	1,308 (13%)	5,338 (52%)	2,021 (40%)
Average	363	1,043	1,019	2,063	97	262	1,068	404
Data for Koppal *taluk*		159,114	154,784 Sex ratio: 982	313,898	23,800 (7.58%)	8,300 (2.64%)	58.53%	44.76%

Source: Census of India (2001) and GOK (2002).

The village size varies greatly, with the number of households ranging between 131 and 700. The female population is 49 per cent. The overall literacy level is 52 per cent, ranging between 45 and 57 per cent, and female literacy is 31–44 per cent. These census figures may well have been overstated, as group discussions with Sampark staff and in PRAs and SHGs showed that women's literacy levels varied between 5 and 10 per cent in general, and 2 per cent among SHG members belonging to the poorest categories.

A recent study recorded low gender and human development indices in Koppal (see Table 3.6).

Girls, more than boys, drop out of school to help with house work and sibling care, a fact common to women across the world.[11]

Table 3.6
Gender and Human Development Indices (Koppal)

Selected Key Indicator (Koppal District)	%
Female literacy	40.76
Girls married below 18 years	57.10
Current users of FP method	45.40
Birth order 3 and above	52.80
Safe delivery	48.00
Complete immunisation	37.20
Decadal population growth rate	24.57
Composite human and gender development index	53.09

Source: IIPS (2002).

Caste and Economic Levels

Castes, the basis of social stratification in Koppal, are classified as higher, middle and lower. The general castes are venerated as 'higher', while the SCs perceived as the 'lower' castes are often ostracised. About 18 per cent of the village population belong to the SCs and STs in the study villages. Six case study participants are from the SCs, three are other backward castes (OBCs), *Kuruba* and *Marata*, and one is from the general castes, *Reddy*.

Information on Koppal district reveals significant overlap between caste and class categories, whereby the SCs form the majority among the landless and casual wage earning categories as compared to the general castes, and the district average, evidenced by the data from a household survey covering 15,000 households in 56 villages of Koppal district, detailed in Table 3.7.[12]

Table 3.7
Landholdings Distribution in Koppal

Caste Categories	Proportion of All Households (%)	Landless (%)	Casual Wage Earning Households (%)	Owning <5 Acres (Unirrigated Land) (%)	Owning 5 Acres or More (Unirrigated Land) (%)	Owning <5 Acres (Irrigated Land) (%)	Owning 5 Acres or More (Irrigated Land) (%)
Upper castes	28.3	13.3	24.7	28.6	29.1	8.5	20.2
Middle castes	37.8	11.4	36.9	35.2	28.0	9.8	15.6
SCs/STs	26.7	20.9	59.2	45.8	14.3	11.7	7.2
Muslims	4.1	29.6	39.9	31.2	17.1	8.5	13.6
All households	100	15.9	39.8	36.0	24.0	9.8	14.3

Source: GOK (2006).

The PRA exercises also show that in every study village the highest proportion of land holdings belong to the *Reddy* and *Lingayat* communities. Agriculture is the main occupation of the general caste (*Reddys*, *Lingayats* and *Kurubas*) who own on an average, 10–30 acres of land per household, which is partly irrigated by borewells. The OBC households own between 3 and 10 acres each. The SC/STs have the smallest landholdings or are landless. Fifty per cent of the *Madar* community are landless agriculture labourers, while 50 per cent have between 0.5 and 3 acres of land; most are dry lands and some obtain water on a shared basis. The *Oddaru* caste work in stone-cutting, as labourers in house construction and bake the limestone used for whitewashing houses. The traditional occupation of the *Jangamaru* caste is as priests in temples; in addition they graze cattle, and take milk, curd and vegetables to Koppal town to trade. The Harijans and *Talwur*s are engaged in construction, contract and *coolie* work. The *Madar* castes are among the poorest, in each study village.

> *I was 8 years old when I got married. No one took me to coolie work as I was too small, but I used to go and pile cow-dung from roads and fields. I would collect it in one place, and later we would sell it for Rs 25 ($0.55) per cartload. I also used to cut firewood and we would sell this too for Rs 25 ($0.55) per cartload. My parents used to go to coolie work. When I wanted to go to school they did not send me, because nobody is sent to school in our caste (SC Harijan). Even our children are not sent to school because they are born 'to a poor person from a low caste'. Neither I nor my children have had any pleasures in life and till now I am facing difficulties.*
>
> *Both my daughters-in-law and sons are illiterate, even my grandchildren are not willing to go to school. Although we pushed them to school they are not willing to go.*—Shivavva

Social Stratification at the Margins

In the villages, the caste system is followed quite strictly. Discrimination against those from the SCs, especially the *Madar*s, takes diverse forms. In the villages, the SC dwellings are separate from the houses belonging to people of other castes, and are usually huts or *Janatha Mane*.[13] Their houses are located on the village periphery as separate settlements referred to as *SC Keri or SC Oni* (meaning street of the SCs). The higher castes do not allow the SCs inside their own homes. This separation is maintained even in local teashops, which do not serve tea to SCs in their cups, with the latter having to bring their own cups and glasses.

In all the villages, the SCs and STs have separate temples. For instance, there are six temples in Bikanhalli, of which four are located in streets where the general castes live. Temples in the SC streets have *Madar Pujari*s and are open to all from within and outside the village, but the SCs cannot enter the four temples in the non-SC streets, and worshipped from outside.

> *My mother is a Dai, meaning midwife. The general caste people allow her to enter their homes to deliver their babies. Later, usually after three weeks, when she stops going to bathe the mother and child, they offer prayers through a priest, and light a fire, to purify their home because she entered it.* —Sangavva

There are some caste-stratified youth groups, though they do allow friends from other castes to join them. In Mudhaballi, there are four youth groups of this type. Most marriages in the community keep to the norms of caste groupings. SCs and general castes live in separate places, and do not regularly socialise. In Mudhaballi, a Brahmin boy who went to Bangalore fell in love with a Muslim girl, married her and brought her back. In the same village, an ST man fell in love with an SC girl, and she became pregnant with his child; he accepted responsibility at a community meeting, then married her and moved into the SC streets with her. He was widely regarded as an example of how a higher caste person (STs are considered higher than SCs in these villages) was loyal and kept to his commitment. However, by 2008, they were already separated by an order of the village court, which indicates social intolerance of inter-caste marriages. Over the past 9 years, in the five study villages there have been only these two cases of inter-caste marriages involving the lower castes; with this phenomenon totally absent among the higher castes. In fact, one participant from Hosagondabala voiced the majority opinion: 'We don't like inter-caste marriages; it is good to marry within the caste and community.'

During a discussion about practice of untouchability in Bikanhalli village, which included women and men from the SC community, Sangamma *Pujari*, a 60-year-old priest of the village SC temple, refused to question this tradition, saying, 'These "paddhatis"[14] have been coming down from the ages; the ancient people must have had something in mind when they made these practices.' At this point, a younger man, standing near a tree outside the temple, came forward and said, 'In the villages, this chance is not provided: of sitting together, eating together, moving together with the general castes.' When the older man was asked, 'Do you feel that you really are a lesser human being than the higher castes?', he lowered his eyes and said, 'Yes, I am lower than them. I feel that.' The younger man immediately responded to the same question, saying, 'No, I do not feel lower than them. I feel that we are equal. We are the same. I want to do something about it.' When asked, 'Do you discuss it in the Ambedkar Sangha then?', he replied:

> In the *Sangha* we rarely discuss how these caste issues are affecting us, and how to tackle them. We spend more time discussing the different schemes available to us from the different departments, and how to avail of these benefits. We meet once a month to discuss this, and in between if necessary.

The Hosagondabala villagers recalled that two Dalit men were murdered in Hallkeri village of Yelburga *taluk* of Koppal district when they opposed and fought against the local caste system. They said, 'Let the changes come on their own, we wait for that. Demanding and opposing creates fights.' This does not mean that there is total lack of resistance. Ostracisation was challenged in some villages though ironically, with serious adverse consequences for the SCs. In one group discussion in Bahadurbandi, the villagers related:

> Four years ago, some people from the SC community went to a tea shop owned by a muslim, sat where other customers sit, and asked him to serve them tea in the same cups used for serving the other customers. The owner refused, and said that SCs could not sit in the same place and could not use the same cups as those of other castes. That night, some SC people burnt the teashop; the muslims filed a police case, and the police came and arrested many men in the middle of the night. Women came to know of the whole story only the next morning. Twenty SC men and eleven muslim men were arrested. There is no jail in Koppal, so the men were taken to Bellary jail. The muslims were kept for 10 days and then released. The SC people were kept in jail for three months.

One SC man continued:

> When we were in jail, we faced a lot of problems. There was not enough food for the family members as men who were earning were in jail, and we also had to borrow money to come out from the jail. We borrowed nearly Rs 35,000 ($778) from friends, relatives and moneylenders to spend on this police case, and our health was also spoiled due to the bad quality food that was served in the jail. The police case is still continuing and we still have to go to the police station in Bellary from time to time, but there is no 'hearing'; we just go, salute the police officer and come back (we waste bus charges though). After we were released and came back to the village, there have been no problems or fights. We have stopped going to the teashop and to the muslim 'colony'. We used to go to their festivals and death ceremonies earlier, to play drums in front of their homes, but now we do not go.

SCs in Mudhaballi voluntarily keep away from the teashops, restaurants and temples of the general castes, saying, 'What is the use of demanding equal treatment and creating an argument, when we have to line up the next morning in front of their doors looking for *coolie* work?' The SCs are aware that they have few resources, are dependent on the landed farmers of the general castes for work and hence do not resist ostracisation practices.

One old man cited another incidence of ostracisation by the general castes: 'One of us had started a liquor shop. They forced us to close it saying that they would not buy and drink from the hands of SCs.' When asked: 'But you, personally, run a kerosene supply business for 10 years now, don't you? They have allowed that, haven't they?', he replied with bitterness and relief, 'They don't have to eat kerosene!' There is more profit in the liquor business than in selling kerosene, and the general castes have two liquor shops. In this village, in 2001, women's groups had protested and got the liquor shop moved outside the village, but it was moved back into the village 2 years later. In Bikanhalli village too, women protested and got the liquor sales stopped within the village, they stood guard for several months to ensure that the liquor vendor does not enter the SC streets; however, they could not keep it up for too long. In all the study villages, the general castes and OBCs dominate economic activities and restrict the SCs from owning food and provision shops. For the most part, caste discrimination remains unchallenged, as SCs clearly perceive the link between economic deprivation and social discrimination.

This raises the question about the Dalits' organisations that can challenge such norms. Each village has a forum for SCs called the Ambedkar Sangha, comprising mostly of members of the *Madar* community and other SCs. The Ambedkar Sangha meets regularly, usually at least once a month, to discuss how to benefit from official schemes. The village *Sangha*s have links with similar *Sangha*s in neighbouring villages, and with the Dalit Seva Sangha at the district level. The Dalit Sanghas fight from time to time for their legal rights; particularly against harassment, and also to stop the *devadasi* system. The district *Sangha* is also connected with the state level association. The *Sangha* meets twice a month, usually with an agenda to conduct political rallies. The Sampark staff did not expect much from the district level *Sangha*, because, as one of them said,

> The *Sangha* organises events like mass-marriages. One such one-day-event was conducted with the local politician bearing all the expenses of the marriages, 40 marriages were conducted that day, but all the

girls were less than 13 years of age! Politicians just don't question existing norms that should be changed, instead, they perpetuate these. In any case, the politician did not even find out the age of the children before he organised the event.

There are a few leaders among the SCs in the four study villages who resolved conflicts within or among SC households. The most critical issues of ostracisation, and untouchability, are, however, not resolved at the leaders' meetings described earlier.

Discrimination is seen in women's SHGs too. SC women bring their glasses from their homes for tea, even for SHG meetings. When the villagers go outside together (usually only for Sampark meetings and trainings they behaved differently): 'We sit together, eat together, share, touch, make friends.' However, when they are in the village, they do not dare to break the caste system. The

> *When we come out of the village, and we are in Sampark, we follow the rules set by Sampark, where everyone is equal, and we do not mind this. However, when we are in the village, we have to follow the rules set by our religious leaders. There is a priest who comes to the village and who has given a special status to me. We have to follow what he says. If people do not keep the rules of separation between the higher and lower castes, it is my duty to tell him, and then he will ostracise not only them but me as well. See, I wear a 'thali' (pendant) given by him. Every evening women come and touch my feet because he has given me the thali. We have to respect his wishes. So, in the village, we keep to our customs, when we come to Sampark, we follow your customs.*—Neelamma, leader of an SHG

Matangi group in Bikanhalli village, at first, had members from SC and general castes. The meetings were conducted usually inside or in the veranda of someone's house. SC women either had to sit on the floor while others sat on the raised platform or had to sit on the floor of the house across the street, and so after a few meetings, the groups separated on the basis of castes.

Thus, the practice of untouchability continues in these villages, and SCs appear to accept it, with few inter-caste marriages. Informal systems exist in villages, whereby deviations from the norm get reported and deviators are ostracised. The caste institutions do not challenge untouchability practices or are relatively ineffective in doing so, because of economic dependence and fear of strong reactions from the general castes. The Dalit institutions at the district and state level restrict themselves to political rallies and events, and to accessing official resources and benefits for fellow caste members, with less direct concern for social exclusion.

Marriage Norms

Other examples of collective orientations include the child marriage custom arising from the concern that, if girls are not committed to a socially valid sexual partnership soon after puberty, they are at risk. Parvathamma, who got her daughter married in 2000, explained:

> My daughter was given away when she was eight years old. Huligavva from Bhagyanagar brought a match for her. Everything went well so I fixed her marriage. In our custom we do not lose a good opportunity to marry off a girl. Three years after marriage, she attained puberty, and one year after that I sent her to her husband's house. I took a loan of Rs 3,000 ($67) at 10 per cent per month for her marriage, and paid it over four years.

Lakshmavva likewise stated:

> In our community, if the girl stays at home three years after puberty, then it is difficult to get her married and we have to give a lot of dowry and spend more money. We can't give dowry as we live a hand to mouth existence, how can we save? My sons have to work and save, only then I can give her to a better place,[15] else we just have to give (marry) her to a place which matches our own economic conditions.

Similarly, customs of joint marriages arose due to the high social expenses incurred during marriages, which can lead families into either debt or bonded labour, which take several years to resolve. Sangavva recalled:

> When I got the elder son married, I decided to get the second son married too; he was 13 years old. This is the custom among us. Moreover, if I delayed the marriage of the second son, I was not sure that we would be together: if the elder one has separated by then, it would be difficult for my younger son and me to bear the marriage expenses.

Sangavva's younger daughter-in-law was 3 years old at the time of marriage. These customs of child marriage, *devadasi* system[16] and bonded labour persist in many villages despite legal bans and are associated with the social and economic situation of the families.

Though girls from the general castes marry at a higher age (usually after 14 or 16 years), other conventions are still a constraint, for example, norms of widow remarriage. Gangamma, daughter of Rangamma, lost her husband at the age of 16 and returned from her husband's house to her parental home. Even though the law permits remarriage, caste norms do not, and her parents did not challenge these largely because they feared that they may not then get offers for the marriage of their son. Even though the mother was concerned about settling her daughter and looked for vocational training and jobs for her, she would not dare defy caste norms to get her married a second time.[17]

The *Devadasi* System

The old custom of offering young girls to the service of village deities persists in many villages of North Karnataka. These girls were traditionally called *basavis*, or *devadasis*. Originally, female dancers and singers attached to temples; the term *devadasi* literally means 'female "servants" of the deity'. While *devadasis* were dedicated or 'married' to the temple deity and not allowed to marry mortal men, in fact the practice involved sexual partnerships with men outside marriage.

Although the *devadasi* system is illegal, it continues due to a confluence of economic, social and cultural factors. Girls are dedicated as *devadasis* for many reasons. First, because parents see this as a solution to their insecurities, thus ensuring that the girls would live with them and support them and their family. Second, if the family experienced ill-health of a child or adult or if childhood deaths occurred repeatedly in the family, the parents promise to dedicate one girl child to the god in return for an end to the illness or child deaths. Third, families dedicate unmarried girls who have attained puberty, usually due to social pressure or fear for their daughters' continued virginity. Further, girls who belong to *devadasi* families are at a greater risk of being dedicated.[18]

Shivavva and her sister were both made *devadasi*s. When Shivavva asked, 'I do not understand why my parents could not have married at least one of us, I was too young to know at that time', her aunt explained:

> Your parents already had the experience of one of their children dying. Even if one of the girls had died, the other devadasi daughter would still have been with them. Also they wanted grandchildren to be with them, which would not be possible if both of you were married.

Thus, villagers explain *devadasi* dedications on both cultural and economic grounds.

The relationships of a *devadasi* with her children and parents are very deep, as she takes the primary responsibility for their care. The relationship with a partner, though, begins on a transactional basis—he provides economic support to her family and in return has sexual relations with her. When he gives economic and emotional support to her and her children, she then affirms the relationship. However, it is rare for a partner to care both for her and her children's health and also spend time with the children, for example, and giving advice about their work. Most partners nevertheless have long-term relationships with *devadasi*s. When they have a particularly good relationship, the *devadasi* typically feels that they are like husband and wife. When he does not provide support, misbehaves, beats or speaks badly and extracts money from the *devadasi*, she can terminate the relationship, even though few actually do so, despite extreme hardship.

Parvathamma elaborated the difference between *devadasi*s and married women:

> *I don't like this life. If I had got married, I would have been someone's wife, and would have stayed in the husband's house. I have been made a 'basavi' so I have to stay here, it is both husband and mother's house. In husband's house, he would have held the responsibility. Here I am like a man and all the responsibility is with me. I have to invite all my sisters and their family members during festivals and other functions. If I omit any one, that person blames me for denying her and treating others to the family property. They feel they have the right to question me. When my sisters come to my house, they ask me to give gold, silver, clothes, etc. Sometimes when I get new clothes, they take these away, saying 'we are staying at husband's place, you are here, why do you want new clothes?' If I had gone to my husband's place, I could also have come and made demands like this. When they come or send their children, I have to do all the work, and I feel tired. If I had got married, I would also have had a chance to come and stay in my mother's house and get some rest.*—Sangavva

> Devadasis have relationships with many men, so they cannot fight or argue, they have to take a lot of abuse from the partners and cannot retaliate. Married women, on the other hand, may do all this without fear of the man walking away. You know there is a popular saying that 'the quarrel of a man and his wife lasts only till they sleep together'. This is true. They console each other and they do not face the kind of problems that we do. The wife can bravely ask for what she wants and it is the husband's responsibility to fulfil the request. We devadasis have no such rights. Our commitments increase, that is all.
>
> Talking about myself, my father is working hard now, but in the years to come, as he grows older, I will have to look after him. I also have to look after relatives who visit us, however difficult it is to do so; we devadasis have to do these things. Now, when I think of my children, how shall I get them married when they grow up, I wonder. Who will come forward to marry them? People may consider: 'They are after all, children of devadasis, who knows what bad morals the daughters might have picked up from their mother?' When I think of all this, how easy life is for married women!

Sangavva said, with evident sadness:

Very few devadasis get good partners who look after them well. In many cases our lives are very tough, there is no moral or economic support from partners. They doubt us unnecessarily as though they give us everything. We have to stay in our house permanently and the complete responsibility is with us. In married life, even if they have problems, their life is much better as they have status. People know that we are devadasis, so any man can approach us without thinking; we can't fight with them, we simply keep quiet.

Lakshmavva, too, believes that it is important to stay in a long-term relationship with one man:

I had no brothers and sisters, and I had to look after my mother, so from a very small age I knew that my mother would make me a devadasi, and I never thought of marriage. That is why I had the relation with Shivappa. A married girl has to leave her mother's home, listen to mother-in-law and father-in-law; but in devadasi life all the responsibility is with me. I have no fear, for these days parents-in-law give a lot of trouble to a woman. Devadasis live in the same place till they die. I have a relation with only one man, and plan to keep this in future, too. There is no use in having relations with many men, as people look down upon you. The only thing is that when one is old, there is no one to look after a devadasi, while a married woman would be looked after by her husband.

The *devadasi*s feel deprived of the right to have a husband and a traditional home like the married women. *Devadasi*s have several disadvantages: belonging to a lower caste, parents dependent on them, being single parents themselves and having no right to land or property of partners. In 1982, Karnataka banned the dedication of women as *devadasi*s, yet several women were dedicated for the next 15 years. The government does not recognise any *devadasi*s dedicated after 1982.

The women have no recourse to law or to any social forum, as the *devadasi* practice has social sanction. They realise that economic insecurity of their parents combined with caste-related institutions has denied them a right to marriage, and think their situation is unchangeable. Even though some married when an official scheme for marrying *devadasi*s was announced, they are still socially criticised for defying religious oaths. Many believe that their parents, including their mothers, had decided to make them *basavis* in their own self-interest rather than that of their daughters. These women feel strongly about it and thus ensured that their own daughters would get married. The *devadasi* dedication stopped almost completely 9 years ago in the study villages, around 1997–98, when SCs themselves decided to stop it. Many of the women there said: 'It is not good for the girl, and for the houses in the street, if someone just visits her from time to time. It's not a good life. It is better if a woman is married.'

Later, Dalit institutions also took it up as a political issue and held rallies in the districts of northern Karnataka. There was a 'street-order' that in every SC street in a village, every girl should be married and not dedicated as a *devadasi*, and SC households themselves began to monitor this order. The *Sangha* tries to arrange the marriage of girls who have been dedicated despite the order. However, in the two villages of Kavalur and Sindhogi in Koppal, one or two women continue to be dedicated as *devadasi*s every year. An official *devadasi* rehabilitation project, launched in 2005, appointed *devadasi* women as animators, and mandated them to form SHGs, link with subsidised bank loans, and make police complaints in case of any new *devadasi* dedications. Despite this, some dedications continue. The government project, however, supports only women dedicated before 1982; women dedicated later continue their struggle for official recognition.

> *A devadasi woman, appointed as animator under the devadasi rehabilitation project, reported to the government and made a police complaint against a devadasi dedication made in Kavalur village in 2007. While some members of the community supported her, others fought with her, and she left the village for 3 months to escape the quarrels. In Sindhogi village, the community has not permitted the animators to even enter the village to carry on project activities. The official project is considered intrusion, while internally mobilised efforts have succeeded.*

To summarise, the demographic profile of the study villages shows high levels of illiteracy. Eighteen per cent of house-holds belong to lower castes, and caste discrimination is practised in rural homes and temples. Child marriages are a norm and marriages make major calls on household finances. In social terms, *devadasi*s are ranked lowest and suffer the most as they have a low capital base and little support from their partners to meet livelihoods needs. Social, cultural and gender denominations are thus critical to economic and other forms of deprivation and oppression. Often, formal legal frameworks and the enforcement mechanisms, including the police, do not seek to protect the victims of the *devadasi* practice. Microfinance agencies do not address these socio-cultural issues and prefer economic and finance-related interventions instead.

Gender-related Issues

Gender inequities are inherent in the local household and family space. The male contribution to the household cannot be taken for granted. For these case study participants, the situation varied from household to household, but women are usually the primary caregivers, responsible for providing family sustenance.

The *devadasi* partnership is akin to a polygamous situation. If the partner is married, his first responsibility is to his wife and children. He is expected to provide for the *devadasi* and her family, but this obligation is not socially enforced. If the partner is not married or not responsible to his own family or separated, he sometimes retains the partnership with the *devadasi* for a long period and maintains her family. He experiences little social pressure or legal

> *When Reddy's family members started looking out for a girl for him, he came and asked me whether he should get married or not. I said: 'Get married, because you also need children and a wife.' He replied: 'I have three children with you. Why should I marry for children?' My children and I can't be your children and wife. Your caste and family members will not accept that, so you get married. If you don't want to marry, people will think that I told you not to marry. Then they will blame me saying: 'That sulagi got hold of Reddy and won't allow him to marry'. Also, your parents have lots of lands and assets. Only if you marry will you get them; otherwise they will not give you the assets. 'Why give up all this? It is better for you to get married' I told him. Because I forced him to get married, he got angry and fought with me. He said, 'I loved you so much, stayed for more than 10 years with you, and we had three children. Now you are asking me to get married. You are not interested in living with me and are asking me to leave. Maybe you want to have a relationship with somebody else and that is why you are forcing me to marry.' Finally he accepted my suggestion and got married.*—Nagavva

obligation to stay with the *devadasi*; he can terminate the relationship whenever he desires. The risk of a man from the scheduled castes ending a partnership is lower than that of one from the general castes. If a man is single or separated, there is greater probability that he will stay with a *devadasi* woman in a long term partnership (Chidambaranathan 2002).

In general, in the study of villages, the support that *devadasi* women receive from their partners is nil or minimal, barring a few exceptions. Given the relative lack of assets of the *devadasi* households, this absence of support from male partners puts a disproportionate burden on such women.

Nagavva and Lakshmavva formed relationships with their male partners before the latter married. Their relationships were like those of married couples, yet social customs did not acknowledge them as such. Both women permitted, even encouraged, these men to marry other women. They felt that such 'selflessness' was necessary if they did not wish to be admonished as 'prostitutes' who 'cling on' to the men for 'selfish' reasons. After these two men married and had children, the two *devadasi*s lost financial and emotional support, and are now among the poorest in their villages. These two *devadasi*s, still in their early thirties and with small children, depend on their own earnings from wage labour, and struggle very hard to meet their daily needs. Yet, *devadasi* women themselves exonerate their partners from the responsibility of providing support for their households. Nagavva says she feels sad that he does not care for her any more, nor does he provide as much financial support as he did earlier, yet she herself provides an excuse on his behalf: 'Now he has a responsibility to his own wife, I should now earn for my father and children and not expect much from him.' In a similar situation, Lakshmavva says:

> He is a poor man, and his wife is just like me, how can I expect that he cares for me and my children more than for her and her children? After all she is his wife and I am a *devadasi*. I have learnt to earn and care for my mother and my children.

These two women were the poorest among the case study participants. The other three *devadasi* women had more than two partnerships and fortunately at least one of the partners supported them and their children well for long periods of time (15–25 years), even if the children were from an earlier partnership. With support from their male partners, they were able to bring up their children and reached a stage where they could sustain their family. Yet, when asked why she did not marry her long-term partner, Sangavva responded: 'Even if I get married, the label of "devadasi" will remain. Villagers will also accuse me of breaking the promise to God for just a little bit of money and material comfort.'

A related preference is for staying in one long-term relationship, and not to change partners. Parvathamma is practical and also humorous, and said: 'This man who I have taken on lease, let us see how long he stays and how he cares for me,' reflecting the deep-seated fear they have of losing their partners, at the same time evaluating them and keeping a distance so that they can accept a break of the relationship if it should ever become necessary or inevitable. It is this precarious balance which these women deal with all their lives. Such women are not necessarily risk averse, they are just subjected to a constant risk of losing the most important relationship of their lives and face deep impoverishment. The risk of loss of status and dignity is as important to them as risk of material support.

*Devadasi*s know and accept that they 'cannot expect to be treated like a wife'. Such gender inequality is socially sanctioned; the man gets a second wife, without bearing either the expenses or the negative socio-legal consequences.

Among the non-*devadasi* women participants, Mariyamma's husband supports her and the couple work side by side on their own and in other people's farms. Mariyamma has decision-making power and control over money, too. Her husband lets her participate in social forums and the group at the village level. Kaveri, though, in 2000, was dominated by her husband and less independent, as both a member of the family and a leader of the *taluk panchayat*. Men completely dominated the house by controlling cash and decision making. She even felt that her house was 'like a jail', with no freedom to ask or share anything. In one interview she said:

> I cannot even note the expenses and income of the household, if I ask my husband he shouts saying: 'You are not the one to go and buy things so why do you want to know?' I have now just stopped asking, I just cook whatever is there and serve him, and if he takes me anywhere I go with him, then come back and care for the children. I feel scared to talk about anything at home.

The family was politicised in Kaveri's case. Her husband's political ambition dominated the family and she was frustrated as a result. This lowered her confidence, and even though she herself was an elected leader of her SHG and *taluk panchayat*, she could not lead either the group or the *Panchayat*. In one interview, she complained:

> It is impossible to help people, as it leads to a fight at home. I am fed up with all the bickering about whom to recommend for government benefits. My life was much better before becoming a member of the taluk panchayat. Politics is very boring.

However, towards the later months, she became corrupt too, and in her own words, became part of 'the system'. She also became a sales agent of a company selling utensils through an instalment system, achieved good sales and got a mobile phone and some jewellery as incentives. In 2008, she began working as a sub-agent for insurance and investment companies, and continues to support SHGs as a book writer at a payment of Rs 50 ($1.1) per group per month. This enables her to have an income of her own, and she is more confident both at home and in public domains. Similarly, Sushila is the sole earner of her family, her husband does not earn, and earlier used her money to drink and beat her each evening. Later she began to withhold the money from him. She does not send him away as she believes that a woman needs a husband, just to maintain her dignity in society.

The women who are solely responsible for the care of their parents and children particularly feel the burden of such responsibility, especially if they are poor. Rangamma, Sushila, Lakshmavva and Yellamma's stories show that they would in fact benefit from more contribution from their husbands and partners. In fact, Rangamma has been able to organise this and benefit from it. Among the higher castes and classes, women have more support from their parental homes, and their families are closely knit, so they do not suffer the same emotional isolation and exclusion as *devadasi* women. Yet, it is difficult to get men to contribute to family income and expenses when they do not want to as in the case of Sushila, or if the men are not obliged to do so as in the case of the *devadasi* women. The parents of the *devadasi* women take the decisions about dedicating them as *devadasi*s, their first sexual relationship, and even terminating the relationships with partners. The *devadasi*s have little control over their reproductive lives in their formative years. The major responsibility of maintaining the family stays with the *devadasi*s, though the children and other family members contribute their earnings. Those who have been through early sexual relationships, especially the *devadasi*s, recall with rancour the experience of lack of control on their reproductive lives. Lakshmavva said:

> I didn't know about sex at that age, but my mother told me: 'He will have relations with you, obey him and stay together as husband and wife.' My mother talked directly to him and demanded all that he was supposed to give, and asked him to look after me like his wife. I didn't talk to him; I was made to have sexual relations at the age of 13 years, at that age what did I know? I did what my mother told me.

These women do not always see heading a household as a privilege. Sangavva's son was hoping to complete his studies and get a government job; instead he remained unemployed as he did not pass his Class 10 examination. He said:

> Everyone knows that I am the son of a devadasi, children in school did not look at me differently. My mother's name was given as the initial in my school. If I had passed the 10th class, I could have got a job as a clerk in a government office, as the son of a devadasi I would have had priority. I want to complete 10th and try for a job.

Sangavva intervened:

> If I had got married, he would have had a father, who might have been strict and made my son study. The son would have also listened to his father's words and completed his 10th standard. He did not listen as I am only his mother, and he failed.

The privileging of males is thus deep rooted in the individual beliefs of the women themselves. Recent research in Koppal district has found variations in health-seeking behaviour based on caste, class, gender and age. Those who depend on self-employment and casual labour, and have insecure household economic status, are more likely to never treat girls/women for illnesses. Deeply ingrained gender norms are also considered to play a role in this, whereby women imbibe from an early age low self-worth, low recognition of their own needs and 'a value to suffering in silence'.[19] The case studies of women show that this self-denial extends not only to health but also to several other domains, whereby they shoulder responsibilities but do not get the position in society that their work would merit.

Domestic violence is common. In Koppal, a woman said: 'All men beat their wives from time to time. My husband beats only some times, only when I make a mistake.' A tribal woman from Garbutoli, Lohardaga, exclaimed:

> It is our lot to work, work, work provide food for the children and also be beaten up at night. But in return, the assets are owned by men, we do not own land, or house, or anything else, we have a right only to work and to get beaten.

Some women have found ways to influence male behaviour: 'I used to bear all the beating earlier. Now I stop him, and later, when he is sober, I explain to him, always as leg-pulling, so he cannot counter my arguments.' Though few women bring it up as an issue to challenge, when introduced into discussion, they share their frustration, and the change the strategies they employ.

The village society is thus found to be highly caste stratified with significant caste/class overlaps. The SCs, especially *devadasi*s, are among the least resourced households. The SC organisations are oriented towards accessing government grants and do not challenge practices due to economic dependence. Seen in this way, the social capital in the villages appears weak, with high levels of social exclusion of the poor.

INSTITUTIONAL CONTEXT

The institutional context of Koppal district is examined in terms of basic facilities in the villages, government schemes and the presence and activities of non-government organisations (NGOs). The microfinance context is outlined in terms of the number of groups, facilitating NGOs, and the banks and their practices.

Basic Services Provision

The physical infrastructure supporting people's livelihoods in the villages studied is presented in Table 3.8.

Table 3.8
Infrastructure Facilities

Facilities	Chukkankal	Bikanhalli	Hosagondabala	Mudhaballi	Bahadurbandi
School	Primary school	Primary school	Primary, middle and high school with hostel	Primary school	Primary school
Drinking water sources	4 public tanks	3 public tanks, 2 borewells[20]	3 public tanks, 6 borewells, 10 public taps[21]	3 public tanks, 5 borewells, 8 public taps	2 public water tanks, 4 borewells, 11 public taps
Sources of Irrigation	10 borewells	29 borewells	20 borewells nd lift irrigation project from government	30 borewells and lift irrigation project from government	6 borewells
Local health providers	ANM	ANM,[22] RMP[23]	ANM, RMP	ANM, RMP	ANM, RMP
Women's groups	8	6	5	12	8
Men's/mixed groups	—	1 youth group 1 farmers' association	1 (Muslim association)	2	2

Source: Authors.

There are primary schools in each village, and a high school in one. SC children, who pass the Class 4 examination, are eligible for a scholarship of Rs 75 ($1.66) per year at the middle school level and Rs 100 ($2.22) per year at the high school level, with an additional incentive of Rs 500 ($11.11) per year to complete high school. Scholarships of between Rs 90 ($2) and Rs 190 ($4.22) per month are provided to SC children who continue their studies beyond Class 10. SC/ST children living in remote areas have provision of accommodation in residential schools; but as the facilities are limited, the selection is competitive. Such facilities and incentives are provided by the caste institutions for the general castes and OBCs. Koppal district has schools, colleges, hostels and a hospital established and managed by the higher castes. These organisations not only facilitate education but also provide venues for employment.

PRAs and Sampark reports, however, show that the quality of village school education is considered poor, which, combined with local poverty, leads to dropout rates of 37 per cent in pre-middle schools, and 61 per cent in high schools. Sampark statistics about group members' children found 29 per cent in the age group of 6–20 had dropped out of school or pre-university college. Among the SCs, 22 per cent of children did not even enrol in schools, with a further 43 per cent dropout rate at the primary school level. The official schemes, in trying to ensure high enrolment and retention, create pressure on local officials to show that many dropouts are later enrolled back into schools, and therefore they manipulate official records accordingly. The government has established School Development and Management Committees (SDMCS), but these meet only once a year to discuss fund allocation, monitoring of school functioning and education quality. In 2008, five local NGOs have invested their resources in children's education.[24]

The health infrastructure in Koppal district is based on population norms, with fewer health sub-centres in Koppal than suggested by these norms. Each village has an Auxiliary Nurse and Midwife (ANM) visiting them periodically, primarily to attend to pregnant and lactating mothers, and ensure immunisation of children. Official health services are not adequate, making it imperative for citizens to travel to Koppal town to access them. Where villagers have to commute 15–20 km to reach a hospital or clinic, they first depend on local and indigenous treatment, which is both affordable and more accessible, but only effective for common ailments. Four villages have Registered Medical Practitioners (RMPs), private doctors who provide door-to-door medical services every day or every alternate day. Chukkankal, which is close to Koppal town, has good transport connections, so RMPs do not need to visit there. There are drinking water sources in each village, though many still experienced water scarcity in summer months. The government health system in Koppal was judged by the Karnataka Task Force on Health and Family Welfare (GOK 2001) to suffer from problems of corruption, lack of equity and neglect of public and primary health care. The Koppal health care market is dominated by informal providers, of whom many were unqualified men, leading to a 'combination of an unaccountable government health system and an unregulated private health system' (George et al., 2005: 19).

Official Poverty Reduction

Officially, many schemes have been implemented through NGOs with the SHGs as platforms to achieve their goals regarding women's empowerment, credit and income generation and health.

During the research period, the Karnataka State Women's Development Corporation (KSWDC) implemented two microfinance programmes, from 1999 to 2001 (Mahila Arthik Samavrudhi Yojane = MASY) and from 2002 to 2004 (Women's Empowerment and Development Programme-Swashakti). Both were centrally funded, the latter with funds from the World Bank, and both were implemented through NGOs specially contracted for the purpose. The central government is directly involved in promoting groups under a scheme named *Stree Shakti*. Government departments also work on education, drinking water and sanitation, health, housing, electricity and irrigation facilities for agriculture through local government organisations, at the village and block levels, namely *gram panchayat* and *taluk panchayat*. An assessment of these programmes was made based on focus group discussions with case study women, villagers and the staff of Sampark.

The most important government scheme is the Swarna Jayanti Gram Swarojgar Yojana (SGSY), under which the government has merged all its previous self-employment schemes like Integrated Rural Development Programme (IRDP), Training of Rural Youth for Self-employment, Development of Women and Children in Rural Areas (DWCRA), Ganga Kalyan and Ten-lakh Wells programmes. The assistance from the scheme is provided to below the poverty line families through SHGs; therefore, group formation and the link with banks are potentially critical. The former is divided between Anganwadi workers and NGOs, depending on which government department is engaged with the scheme. The credit link is monitored through District Level Committees, as has been the case over the past three decades.

The schemes found to be most beneficial are those that provide housing and electricity, namely the Ashraya and the *Bhagya Jyothi* schemes. Across all the research villages, *devadasi*s, SC/ST people and also the poor families from OBCs could benefit from these schemes. Rangamma, Shivavva, Lakshmavva, Nagavva and Sushila got a house each under the Ashraya scheme and Parvathamma got a house under the *devadasi* rehabilitation project. All of them have got electricity connections under *Bhagya Jyothi* scheme. *Devadasi* women state that the scheme for land distribution for SCs and *devadasi*s has been the most beneficial, as the housing conditions improve the ability for other income generating work, including *coolie*. Other schemes found beneficial are 'Ganga Kalyan' (assistance for digging for borewells) and scholarships for students. The IRDP Scheme is generally known as the 'buffalo scheme', the popular name for this scheme, as assistance under the scheme was given only for purchase of buffaloes.[25] These poverty reduction schemes are based on a target-oriented approach, but targets under these schemes are not always met, as in the case of the District Industries Centre, which could not implement its major vocational training programme for women due to shortage of funds.

*Devadasi*s, particularly, feel left out, and Yellamma narrates several incidents when leaders or brokers of government schemes have cheated her:

> We haven't got any of these government schemes in our village, though the neighbouring villages have benefited. Our elders have done nothing for us though they know that Devadasis live here—if by chance something does come our way, they grab it first.
>
> Recently, a Member of Legislative Assembly (MLA) had come to our village and when we went as a group to meet him he said that he had received information that there were no devadasis in our village. He couldn't do anything himself, he said, as the Congress party had come into power now. He would have to go and meet some people to see what could be done. I have no hopes that anything will come of it.

I know about the devadasis scheme, they get land and house but I don't know whom to contact and ask. Someone said that there is a woman called Swaravva who belongs to our caste, is a member in the municipality and she knows about the devadasis scheme. Then all of us devadasis had a discussion about this and went to see her. When we met her she asked us which village we had come from. I told her that we were all 12 from Hosagondabala, were devadasis, that we did not know about official schemes for us and had not received any schemes or loan facilities because our village elders are not good and if she knew any schemes to tell us. She told us that she needed our documents and that this work would cost money. She said she would inform us when we met next time. So we met her the next week and she said that it would cost Rs 1,500 ($33) per person. We believed her: some sold their 'thali' (pendant) and some their cow and calf. About 20 people gave her money and even I sold my cow for Rs 1,000 ($22), which I gave to her. We have not yet received any benefits. We worry a lot about it; instead of giving her the money, we could have spent it on food. We simply wasted the money. After that, we have not discussed this with anyone; it would be of no use, so we have kept quiet. We won't break our head if anyone tells us about schemes now. No one will come forward to help devadasis. The government and *panchayat* always ignore us. No government scheme is available for us.

In my house, the male members are not responsible, and we don't have many contacts so we have not received any benefits. One year ago, they told me that there was a toilet available in the name of my son so we went to the village head, who is a member of the panchayat, and asked him to build the toilet in front of our house where a little space was available. But the elders and the *panchayat* members told us that it is in the name of some other person and not for us. The one that was sanctioned in our name was given to some other person. What to do in this world where we find more cunning people who value only money? So I felt bad. Though we are devadasis we don't get any benefits. The mother of my daughter-in-law is a devadasi in Bahadurbandi, where three acres of land has been given to devadasis but nothing is available in our village. There is a person named Kapathappa who lives in our Keri, who has taken a loan of Rs. 20,000 ($444) from the bank and has built a house. He has taken a loan even in the name of his wife. Now we have formed a group and if there is any scheme we approach it as a group, so at least we can benefit from the scheme. All government schemes are available only for rich people and panchayat members and not for us. So I feel angry about this scheme, I have nothing much to say about the scheme!

Then Eshappa visited the village and said that there are houses being given for devadasis so we went to him and gave him Rs 50 ($1.1) and 4 photocopies of the bond paper, caste certificate and other documents, but till now, no scheme has come. My son Devappa went to take my photo and the caste certificate. I have wasted a lot of money and till now I have no benefit, so this is the last time I am trying with Eshappa.

These incidents show that information and access to government schemes is mediated by brokers who have privileged access on the basis of family or social relationships, and who often corner the benefits at the expense of those really eligible for official support.

In the water and land management programmes, the Zilla Parishad (ZP) provides 25 per cent of the cost of digging borewells in their lands under the irrigation scheme. The banks sanction this loan and the ZP releases it to the farmers. The government implements a watershed development programme covering certain villages. In the PRAs, villagers judged that:

1. The emphasis is on project implementation, not sustainable management of natural resources (SNRM).
2. The SNRM projects have a limited outreach and were limited to construction of *bunds*.
3. Government is able to implement plans that involved material and labour but they cannot succeed in getting active participation, contribution and creating impact on livelihoods.

Official soil and land conservation and rural development programmes are based on grants and projects executed directly by the departments and NGOs. Even where community level forums are organised for their implementation, the local contribution required ranges from 10 to 30 per cent, based on household landholding, and eligibility to secure the balance as a grant. There are no community level revolving loan funds or credit programmes offered for farmers to collectively ensure soil and water conservation measures on their lands.

Thus, discussions show that official services were inadequate for meeting education and health needs. The local institutions do not demand official accountability, and government support to agriculture is ostensibly through land and water management programmes, which suffer from inefficiencies, as do the poverty reduction schemes of the government. Group discussions in the villages did, however, highlight certain positive changes.

A farmer with 60 acres of land had 30 families of agricultural labourers working for him. On the advice of a local NGO, he sold a portion of it to government, which then granted a housing loan and developed a 'colony' for labourers, which essentially housed the agricultural labour employed on his lands. The NGO also formed a women's SHG with the labourers' wives and in the first and only meeting held by the SHG, a revolving loan fund of Rs 25,000 ($556) was sanctioned under the DWCRA scheme. The money actually went to the landlord, whose brother was a local politician, and not the women who had put thumb impressions for it. The NGO, on the other hand, gained a reputation for its own efforts in this respect, and was assigned the role of a facilitator for the 10 groups targeted under the scheme in Koppal district for the following year. When questioned, the local bank officer explained: 'We have to meet the targets for credit to the priority sector. We also have to pay heed to local politicians. And if an NGO has political links, it will definitely get government recognition too.'

After Koppal was designated a separate district (from Raichur), it acquired the status of the district head quarters. The Deputy Commissioner and Sessions Court are now in Koppal town, while previously they were located in Raichur, 6 hours away by bus or train (190 km). Similarly, several government departments have opened offices in Koppal, for example, Education, the Industries and Health, along with several banks. More credit became available because of a policy shift, which the District Level Review Committee (DLRC) in Koppal had to implement. However, this was mostly channelled in ways that did not benefit genuine SHGs, and benefits were derived by unscrupulous NGOs, as seen in the case illustrated in the accompanying box.

NGOs as Development Organisations

Another factor influencing women's livelihoods concerns local development institutions. The institutions engaged with development or poverty reduction in Koppal include NGOs, government departments/organisations and banks. Local informal organisations include women's SHGs and youth forums. The villages have women's SHGs formed by the government and Sampark, a local NGO. Local youth forums exist in four villages, while Bikanhalli has a farmers' group organised by Sampark.

Between 2000 and 2008, 10 of the 21 NGOs located in the district,[26] have been engaged in microfinance support, implementing various livelihoods activities such as education, skill development, income generation, health, watershed development, empowerment of women, agriculture and forestry development. In 2000, Koppal had about 550 women's SHGs, formed by these NGOs, which increased to about 2,000 SHGs in 2006. However, many of these are non-functional in 2008. All NGOs have worked with official schemes as well as their own small projects. Sampark has the objective of poverty reduction and empowerment, particularly of women, by promoting people-owned and -managed forums, building their capacities and linking them with mainstream institutions for improving livelihoods. Its major focus is upon credit and income generation, education, empowerment of local forums, and agriculture and natural resource management. By 2008, it has promoted over 200 women's SHGs (of which 160 are active) and a farmers' forum to implement further activities. It also works with other organisations to provide training, research and advisory services. Sampark has long-term commitment to work in specific villages. Most other NGOs are engaged in implementing a wide range of time-bound projects for the government or donors. SHGs and other villagers expect NGOs, including Sampark, to make linkages for official support (*Bhagya Jyothi* schemes, subsidised credit, and so on), and to channel resources from external sources.

In this scenario of external agents engaged with rural development, there are very few locally owned and managed organisations. An exception is a porters' union, known locally as the *Hammali Sangha*.[27] The villagers explained that this organisation was registered in 1994 under the Indian Trade Union Act of 1926. The 450 founder members comprised workers who did loading and unloading of goods from lorries and trucks. The original membership fee was Rs 11 ($0.24) and it grew to 1,000 members with a membership fee of Rs 10,000 ($222) in 2005, increased to Rs 25,000 ($625). The previous president of the *Sangha*, who had admitted many members, had absconded with their membership fees, and so from April 2004, the *Sangha* only admitted one new member per month. Its membership fees has been used for members and their families' welfare. The *Sangha* has purchased 9 acres of land, converted into 500 constructions plot and distributed to members at reduced rates. It disperses loans for marriages, festivals and other social functions. It provides Rs 10,000 ($250) on the death of a family member and has linked up with the Life Insurance Corporation of India (LIC) to provide cheap medical insurance. The *Sangha* has an annual earning of Rs 80,000 ($1,778) from the fees it collects from lorries that enter Koppal carrying goods. The *Sangha* is well managed, with its own paid staff, and members posted in agricultural markets in the town to ensure that the members obtain work at the negotiated daily rate. The negotiating partner for the *Sangha* is the Traders' Association in Koppal, which fixes the 'hammali' rate for the porters. All the 1000 members can get work every day, and there is a demand for yet more workers, which strengthens its bargaining position. The *Sangha* is an example of a local member organisation but there are few others. Following this example, in 2007, a new organisation has been formed by those who lease out bullock-carts; only those who are members of the *Sangha* can lease, and the rates are fixed according to the cart-load and distance. In another sector in the informal economy, human hair processing, where Koppal has over 300 units, the employees are mostly women, wages are paid on a piece-rate basis and labour is not organised into a trade union. Most of the NGOs that engaged in the formation of women's groups organised trade unions or strong federations, have only formed groups based on needs of externally funded programmes; most do not supervise SHGs after closure of these programmes and most women's groups continue to be fragmented, unsupported and unregulated.

Microfinance Organisations (Banks, Cooperatives and Cluster Associations)

Cooperatives are a major source of rural credit, and Koppal had 529 of them, of which 94 were credit cooperatives. The total loan to cooperatives was (Rs 510 million [$11.3 million]). However, nearly a quarter of these cooperatives were defunct, and loan recoveries were low (SBH 2004). The second source of rural credit is commercial and regional rural banks (RRBs). Ten NGOs had promoted SHGs here and were involved in savings and credit activities for improving their income. Their groups were linked with banks for loans and also with government schemes. The linkage with subsidised programmes continued to be problematic, as illustrated earlier.

This situation existed in 2002; it changed a little by the next year. In 2003, when the banks and the government sanctioned subsidised loans to 10 groups on political considerations, some Sampark-facilitated women's groups, who had also sent in their applications, protested. They wanted to know why their applications, despite the good financial operations of the groups, had been rejected, and why other newer and less accredited groups had been granted the subsidy. The then district official took cognisance of this complaint, resulting in two of the Sampark-facilitated groups getting subsidised loans in 2004 and 2005. However, as a consequence of the protest by 'Sampark groups', the NGO was dropped summarily from the membership of the DLRC, and this denied it access to crucial information about credit policy intervention.

At this time, the banks offered only government-subsidised credit to the SHGs. Local microfinance was dominated by customary attitudes. Credit coordination was done through the DLRC, where decisions on the targets for priority sector credit were taken. The number of SHGs eligible for subsidised credit was limited, usually 8–10 SHGs per year for the whole district, with 2–3 SHGs for Koppal *taluk*. Later the target increased to 20–30 SHGs for each *taluk*. By 2005, a total of 44 SHGs in Koppal *taluk* had received bank credit, of Rs 4,587,500 ($101,944).

In 2003, the local RRB, Tungabhadra Grameen Bank (TGB),[28] changed its attitude and started extending regular credit to SHGs. It provided non-subsidised credit to 103 groups of Sampark between 2001 and 2007 as shown in Table 3.9.

Table 3.9
SHG-Bank Linkage of Sampark Groups (2007)

Banks	*Sampark SHGs with Bank Accounts*	*Sampark SHGs with Bank Credit*
RRB (TGB)	121	103
Commercial Banks	35	5
Total	156	108

Source: Authors.

By 2006, unsubsidised credit from the RRB had begun to show up in the district statistics, with 364 groups having received bank credit of Rs 6,346,500 ($158,663) (GOK 2006). The other banks continued to be conservative and limited in their reach to SHGs. Thus, commercial banks did not provide non-subsidised credit, leaving the rural poor in Koppal *taluk* with only two SHGs linked for subsidised credit, and except for those who managed to link with TGB, rural credit needs were largely met by local informal sources of credit. The situation of Sampark-promoted groups was particularly difficult, and when official subsidised credit was extended to over 40 groups of Koppal *taluk* in the year 2005–06, none of the Sampark-promoted groups were among those who benefited. By 2008, 18 of Sampark's 170 SHGs received subsidised credit under the SGSY scheme.

By 2008, however, Sampark promoted cluster associations of SHGs, and credit rotation through these is Rs 2,300,000 ($57,500).

High Cost Credit

As their earning opportunities are limited, some people, particularly the *devadasi* families—depend on credit from their landlords. These loans are at high interest rates in exchange for bonded labour. Credit from the moneylenders is also expensive, and can be obtained only with hypothecation of assets. As Lakshmavva said:

> We can get a loan from the 'shavkar' (moneylender) only if we pledge something, land, buffalo, gold or silver ornaments, and if none of these, at least a brass or copper vessel. If we do not pay in time, we lose the asset. He just takes away the animal, or the jewellery, or the vessel. There is no mercy, this is the rule.

I took a loan of Rs 2500 ($57) from our landlord, without interest, for my sons' wedding. My son repaid this loan by working in their house from morning till evening for Rs 20 ($0.45) per day. We have to still repay Rs 1,000 ($23). My elder son is not here so my younger son has to work and repay it, but if he goes to do that work, we will have nothing to eat.—Yellamma

The institutional structures in Koppal district include government departments, NGOs and banks, which implement a wide range of development programmes. However, official programmes do not really meet the basic human needs and poverty reduction. NGOs implement projects for donors or government; yet, they have only a limited outreach and impact. Banks provide microfinance through official schemes that they are obligated to implement and only one bank—the local RRB—has what may be termed a market-led approach to microcredit for the poor. Thus, observed structures and processes are not often conducive to long-term efforts towards poverty reduction or sustainable rural livelihoods.

This reinforces the understanding that ecological, economic, institutional and socio-cultural factors play an important role in determining the vulnerability or security of livelihoods in a specific regional context.

SUMMARY

The study of the livelihoods in Koppal, analysed through three broad categories, is depicted in Figure 3.5.

Figure 3.5
Livelihoods in the Koppal Context

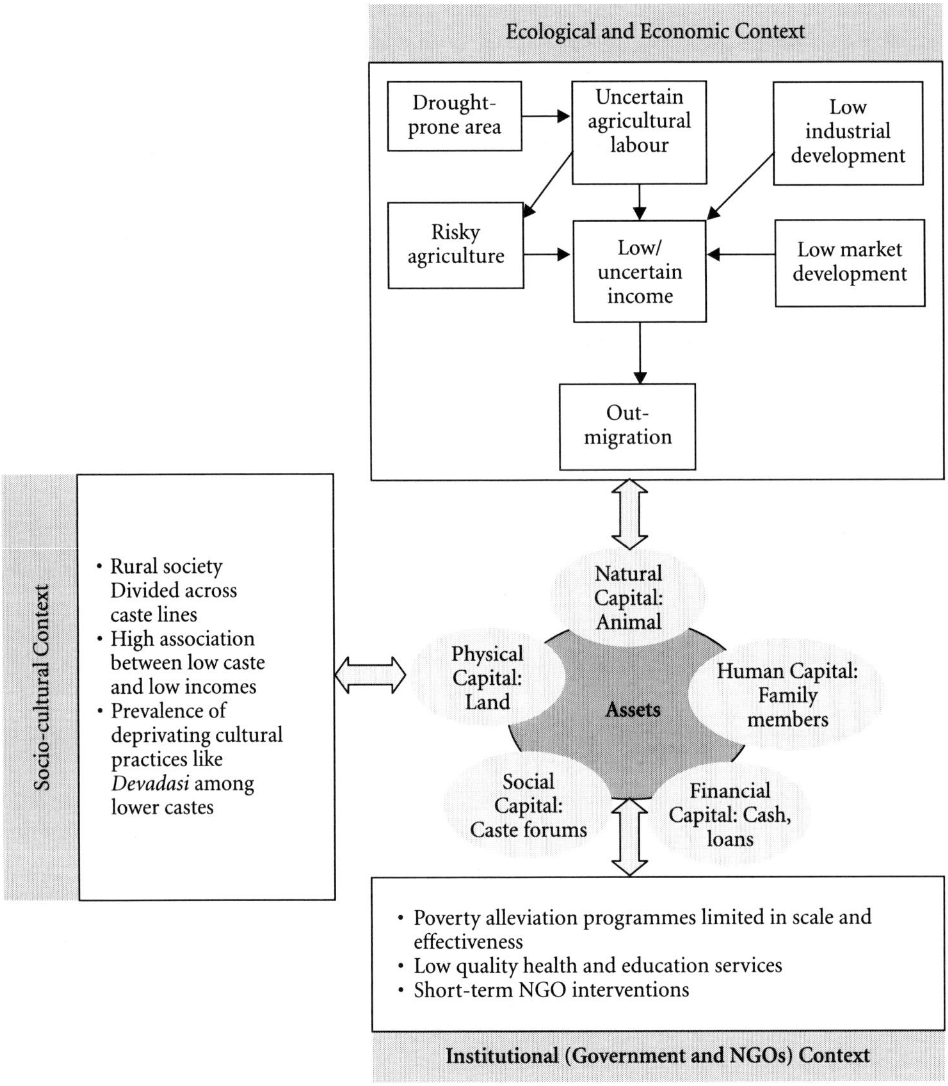

Ecological and Economic Context

| Drought-prone area | Uncertain agricultural labour | Low industrial development |

Risky agriculture

Low/uncertain income

Low market development

Out-migration

Socio-cultural Context

- Rural society Divided across caste lines
- High association between low caste and low incomes
- Prevalence of deprivating cultural practices like *Devadasi* among lower castes

Natural Capital: Animal

Physical Capital: Land

Human Capital: Family members

Assets

Social Capital: Caste forums

Financial Capital: Cash, loans

- Poverty alleviation programmes limited in scale and effectiveness
- Low quality health and education services
- Short-term NGO interventions

Institutional (Government and NGOs) Context

Source: Authors.

In the context of the semi-arid region made inhospitable by a degraded environment, farmers resort to borewell irrigation as a household coping strategy, which results in overall unsustainability of natural resources. There have been no community level efforts to promote sustainable agriculture or sustainable management of natural resources. Those who possessed land have a greater feeling of security as compared to the landless; however, the profitability of agriculture is suspect, though some people do get foodgrains and fodder from their lands. Wage rates have increased, from Rs 8–15 ($0.17–0.33) per day up to 2004 to Rs 20–25 ($0.44–0.55) in 2005, and further to Rs 30–50 ($0.66–1.11) in 2008. Some new opportunities have opened up due to the growth of Koppal town as the district headquarters. Yet, rural activities like animal husbandry and agriculture have little or no scope given their bleak ecological conditions. The relatively low literacy and skill levels, especially of women, are a limitation in using the new opportunities. With the local area not, therefore, providing enough sustenance, there has been large-scale out-migration to other areas for differing periods of time. The type of work can be agriculture or construction labour, fishing or loading and unloading of stones and other products. The major positive changes have come from out-migration and growth of livestock (buffaloes, sheep and goats) among the SC communities, and increasing employment opportunities in Koppal district, and some benefits from official schemes. The caste stratifications shape the interactions among people. They determine family lives of people, as well as their working lives. *Devadasi*s remain among the most marginalised, with deprivation of their human rights. They are kept invisible by a need of government officers not to show their existence, the practice having been banned by law. This has resulted in them being denied the government benefits they were entitled to.

One may reflect on how changes may be initiated in the socio-cultural aspects of a livelihoods context, wherein the tendency is for social and power relations to reproduce themselves. For instance, even women themselves do not question norms about expenditure on marriages. They fear that challenging this practice may result in their children not finding a marriage alliance in a well-off family, is very real for them. This can create family discord where the children may be disappointed that their parents could not even provide basic comforts. The issue is regarded as a household problem, and the inside–outside dichotomy operates to stop them from considering it a community issue, or questioning social conventions. The same analogy is drawn about the financial transactions that occur through corrupt practices among various groups regarding disposition of public resources. Such practices are simply viewed as part of a *system* to be followed rather than challenged.

These insights echo Freire in that the poor need to move away from seeing themselves trapped within structures, and need to start questioning and changing whatever keeps them marginalised.[29] The analysis of the institutional context shows that basic facilities like schools and health are accessible, but statistics about school dropouts do not reflect the true situation. Several government schemes have benefited the villagers, for example, provision of electricity, housing and subsidised loans. There are also corrupt practices, but as awareness has increased over the years, women have begun to question them occasionally. Local NGOs and people have not yet made a serious attempt to question the existing corruption or to seek greater accountability. NGOs mostly work on short-term projects with funding partnerships, and close their offices when these projects end. Local people's dominant expectation about NGOs is related to their obtaining and channelling outside funds.

Microfinance is extended through formal organisations like agricultural cooperatives and banks. The former have become largely defunct and the latter provide credit mainly through programmes subsidised by the government. In these programmes, the assistance is mostly target bound in terms of types of beneficiaries to reach, purposes and amount, and number of such grants to be given. The terms are not negotiable with the organisations administering these schemes. The analysis of livelihoods context first points to several constraints on the demand for credit, namely the ecological and economic contexts, which largely limit the opportunities for productive use of money.[30]

The socio-cultural context highlights the marginalisation and social exclusion of SCs, and of *devadasi* women in particular, which affects asset levels of households. The relation between asset levels and loans will be explored in the following chapter, which details women's own needs, preferences and strategies for the uses of money.

NOTES

1. See George et al., (2005) and GOK (1999) for details of statistics on Koppal district.
2. Each state in India is divided into districts, subdivided into *blocks*, called *taluks*, the next level of administrative units, which comprise between 40 and 80 villages.
3. Soil and water conservation structures, usually 2–3-feet-high walls built of stone and soil.
4. Premchander et al., (2003) present a detailed analysis of the natural resource and water depletion and livelihoods in Koppal and the lack of official attention to key factors in such exploitation.
5. Casual farm labour.
6. Scheduled castes (SCs)/scheduled tribes (STs) are included in Schedule XVI of the Constitution, whereby reservations are granted to these castes for education and government services.
7. Agriculture and non-agriculture expenses were difficult to separate because of fungible monies, labour payments received or agricultural inputs obtained in cash and kind, and produce shared in kind or sold, and even when women faithfully recorded many transactions they did not consider many of these distinctions worth recording.
8. See GOK (2002, 2004) for more details.
9. Women who brought small amounts of minor forest produce to trade in weekly markets in Bastar sold these to traders who, even though they knew the local language, insisted on speaking Hindi, which the women did not know. They did not weigh the minor forest produce (MFP) properly, offered very low prices and the transactions were concluded so fast that women barely had time to evaluate whether they got the right price. With Rs 5 or 10 that they got every week, women bought small amounts of oil, onions, salt and other provisions for the week. While women were so disadvantaged and needed to learn Hindi and how to negotiate better, the microfinance project focussed only on encouraging savings, in a context of low cash incomes, and offering cash loans, for which women had little use (Premchander 2000).
10. By contrast, the microfinance project supported by CARE in Ranchi was close to town and women could grow vegetables to sell them in the urban market (Sampark 2000).
11. For more details, see ILO's report on Global Employment Trends for Women (ILO 2007).
12. See George et al., (2005).
13. A house constructed under a government scheme for the poor, where the walls are made of bricks with an asbestos or tin sheet for a roof.
14. Traditional practices.
15. Implying a family with a better economic position.
16. By 2008, though, dedication of girls as *devadasis* has stopped in many villages in Koppal district.
17. Rangamma's daughter is currently employed in Delhi, and the parents hope that she will find a match, marry and settle down there.
18. Chidambaranathan (2002) in a detailed study covering life histories of 31 *devadasis* found that *devadasis* considered partners from their own caste more comfortable to live with. Unmarried men made better partners, though after marriage they stopped caring for the *devadasis*. Invariably, partner support for the *devadasi*'s parents and children

reduced over time, leaving them the sole carers. Yet, many continued to be loyal to their partners, finding change of partners more difficult to deal with socially, than a lack of money and financial support.

19. George et al., (2005) refer to low self-esteem of women in the context of women not attending to their own health and medical needs.

20. The borewells for drinking water are dug by the government, inside the villages, and are for public use, whereas those on farms are dug by farmers for irrigation.

21. In the three villages with public taps, pipelines have been laid to take water from public tanks to different streets within the village.

22. Auxiliary nurse and midwife.

23. Registered medical practitioner, though the term is also expanded as 'registered' medical practitioner, they were in fact not registered at all.

24. These include Samuha, Gram Shikshana, Sarvodaya, Olekar Education Society and Sampark.

25. The policy changed later and post-2006, women have been permitted to use subsidised credit for other purposes as well, and many have bought goats with this loan.

26. A list of NGOs in Koppal is given in Appendix 1.

27. The tasks of loading and unloading and carrying boxes and sacks.

28. This RRB was later merged with three other profit making RRBs in Karnataka to form the Pragati Grameen Bank.

29. Freire (1970) pointed out that the marginalised and oppressed are not outside the system, but are integrated within oppressive structures, and their struggle to transform the situation begins with an understanding and questioning of these structures, through concscientisation, which libertarian education must facilitate.

30. In the case of Koppal, though, the carving out of a separate district has meant some increased demand due to building up of new infrastructure.

4

Use of Money by Individuals and Groups

Having considered how important a bearing this multiplicity of contexts has upon the supply of finance and its potential use, we now turn to an analysis of women's use of money. The elaboration of the topics discussed is as presented in Figure 4.1.

Women's use of money is revealed by an analysis of the asset base, life and loan histories of individual women, showing how the asset base influences their earnings, which in turn determines their loan taking capacity. The loans women take provide insights regarding sources of credit, which form the second section, and the third section discusses about what influences their use of money.

WOMEN'S STORIES AND LOAN HISTORIES

Women's stories highlight the link between the level of land, human and cattle assets (and the consequent income inflows and expenses), with the ability to take and repay loans. These are discussed in this chapter.

Precarious Livelihoods, Low Loan-taking Ability

The Story of Lakshmavva

Lakshmavva was made a *devadasi* at the age of 12. She explains,

> The devadasi system has come down to us from generations. It should not be practiced, but when parents have only one daughter they dedicate the girl as a devadasi. As I was the only daughter, I was made a devadasi.[1]

Figure 4.1
Exploring Meanings: Women's Use of Money

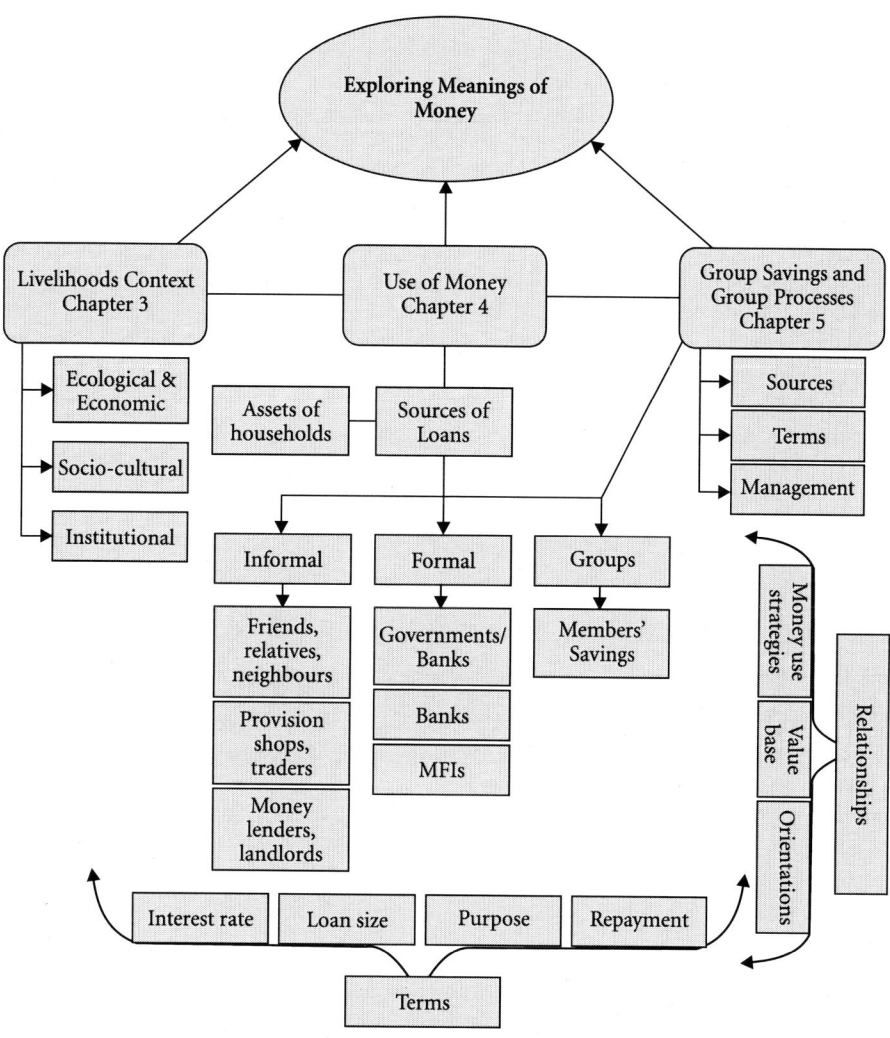

Source: Authors.

I attained puberty at 12 years and within a year I was made into a devadasi. My mother celebrated my reaching puberty with a small function (as was the custom in most communities in the village). I was given a new dress and taken to the temple. My mother offered a new sari to Goddess Durgadevi, and everyone did 'puja' in the temple.

At this time, the high caste villagers suspected that my mother would dedicate me as a devadasi during this function, so as a precautionary measure, the village leader informed the police and they came and took my mother to the police station. Some of our community people went along and explained to the police officers that this was not the case, and the function was only the usual celebration that we have on the 11th or 21st day after a girl attains puberty. The police believed it and let my mother go.[2]

According to our custom, I could not be made a devadasi in my mother's village, so I was taken to my father's village in Betikere. My parents explained to the community that I was the only daughter and that there was no one else to look after them. They then received permission to make me a devadasi.

We hired a tractor and went to Huligi, along with our relatives and others in the community, where I was made a devadasi. The function was celebrated in the temple of Goddess Huligamma, and they tied a 'muthu'—a chain made of white and red beads, interspersed with silver symbols of Huligemma (goddess), her feet and hands. The 'pujari' (priest) did the puja (ritual worship) in the Huligi temple and tied the 'muthu'. He taught me that I must fast every Tuesday and Friday, and also when anyone in the village dies—I still follow this system.

Lakshmavva knew from an early age that she would be dedicated as a *devadasi*. She had made her plans, and this was how she related them:

I liked Shivappa very much even before I matured (meaning, attained puberty). He belongs to the same community (Madar), and my mother knew him too. I don't remember what we spoke about and how our relationship developed, but we had a sexual relationship just two months after I matured. We had the first sexual contact in his house, and his parents came to know, but my mother did not.

After six months, my mother took me to my father's village and made me a devadasi. I was made to stay there for two months as my parents wanted to find me a partner there. I told my mother I would not stay there; I forced her to bring me back to Mudhaballi. After coming back I told Shivappa and my in-laws that since I had already had sexual contact with him, he could ask my mother's permission to have a relationship with me.

Shivappa's parents liked me very much. He was married to a person two years younger than me; she had not yet matured and was with her parents. He was already 26 years old, and his wife was only ten years old. When I matured, they thought that he need not wait for long: he could have a relationship with me, as I was a devadasi, so they were happy to permit him.

Then Shivappa approached my mother. My mother asked him to give clothes and a pair of earrings he gave whatever he had committed to and started visiting me. At this time, my mother did not know about the earlier contact with him; if she had arranged for someone else, I would have told her. As I had already had a relationship with him, it was difficult for me to get along with another man. I have had only one relationship all through my life.

He has three children from his wife—two boys and a girl (one child got aborted), and the same is the case with me. I have two boys and one girl, and I had an abortion. Shivappa was the only son of his parents, and I am the only daughter of mine. He has two acres of land and lives with his parents.

When asked about whether he took good care of her, she said 'yes', but another group member, Bharmavva, contradicted. 'What do you mean by saying he looks after you? He comes till the pregnancy, then he does not turn back and look at her till three or four months after the delivery, then he comes again. This is the habit of man.'

In 2003, Lakshmavva's household included herself (30 years old), her three children (10, 8 and 6 years old, respectively) and her mother (47 years old). Her elder son had already dropped out of school. She was landless and lived in 'Ashraya mane', a house given by the government, consisting of a small hall (10 × 10 feet) with a small partition to mark off the kitchen space. The walls were made of low-cost cement bricks, the roof was a cement sheet and the mud floor was polished with cow dung. She had made a small bathroom outside using woven coconut leaves for walls. The open space in front and back of the house was part of the colony of *devadasis* in the village, located in a low-lying area, often slushy and not clean, especially during monsoons. She tied the cow and calf she owned outside the hut, and gave the unsold milk to her own small children. In 2003–04, her earning was primarily from her own casual farm labour, and sometimes that of her mother's, a meagre amount of Rs 480 ($10.66) per month. She explained the seasonal calendar of wages as follows:

October: In this month we have the festival of Vijayadashmi.[3] We get work on cotton fields and weeding this month, we earn Rs 20 ($0.44) per day for picking cotton. My mother went for this work for 10 days. I went for weeding for 15 days, and earned Rs 12 ($0.26) per day, so totally we earned Rs 250 ($5.55) from cotton-crossing and Rs 300 ($6.66) from weeding. We also celebrate Mahanavami this month, for which we spent Rs 50 ($1.11), using half kg of jaggery, half kg of pulses and 1 kg of rice and oil. We spent Rs 375 ($8.33) for other days of the month; so total expenses this month were Rs 425 ($9.44).

November: We had weeding work this month and the wage was Rs 15 ($0.33) per day. We had work only for 15 days and I have earned Rs 225 ($5) from *coolie* work. My mother worked for 9 days, and has earned Rs 135 ($3) this month. So this month we have earned Rs 360 ($8), we had no income other than this. We spent Rs 100 ($2.22) on Diwali festival this month, buying 1 kg of jaggery, 1 kg pulses, half kg flour and 2 kg of rice, ¼ kg cooking oil, some ginger, cumin seeds, mustard, curry leaf, garlic and coriander. We made holige (sweet chapattis[4]) for this festival. I purchased cloth for children for Rs 100 ($2.22) and paid Rs 40 ($0.88) as stitching charges. The expenses for the rest of the month were Rs 262 ($5.82), so totally this month the expenditure came up to Rs 602 ($13.37), and the income was just Rs 360 ($8) so I took a loan of Rs 300 ($6.66) from the gowda. It is 'kaigada',[5] there is no interest on it, I can pay it back whenever I have money in hand.

December: This month is known as Karthik Amavasya.[6] We did not have regular *coolie* work this month. My mother did *coolie* work for 10 days and I did not go for *coolie* this month,[7] so we had Rs 120 ($2.66) from wages, and I sold one litre of milk per day and earned Rs 235.60 ($5.22). We had Hanumappa fair this month, I spent Rs 50 ($1.11), and for food and ration we spent Rs 370 ($8.2). Apart from this I did not spend on anything else.

January: This month we observe Yellu Amavase. Jowar is grown this month, so we have weeding-work, and harvesting jowar. We had weeding work for 20 days at Rs 12 ($0.26), so that was Rs 240 ($5.33) and 8 days of harvesting jowar at Rs 15 ($0.33), giving Rs 120 ($2.66), so earned a total of Rs 360 ($8) this month. We did not celebrate any festival this month, we had only food expenses and spent all Rs 360 ($8) on food, not on anything else.

February, March, April: February is the month of Amrith Amavase. In this month we do not get *coolie* work so we have difficulty in even getting one meal a day. We didn't have any income this month and for another three months we will not have any work. We take loans from villagers. I took a loan of Rs 250 ($5.55) in February and Rs 300 ($6.66) in March. The entire amount was spent on food expenses and nothing was left. In April we have monsoon, no income in this month, and we have the festival of Ugadi. I took a loan from the gowdaru, of Rs 250 ($5.55) and spent it for Ugadi.

May: May is recognised for Basava Jayanthi. We have *coolie* work for the whole of this month, of removing cow-pea in the land near the river. The daily wage is Rs 15 ($0.33) so this month we have earned Rs 600 ($13.33). We spent only Rs 25 ($0.55) for the feast, spent Rs 250 ($5.55) on food and repaid loan of Rs 300 ($6.66).

June: We went for cow-pea *coolie* work, which was available for just 15 days. My mother and I both went for this work, and earned 600 ($13.33) from plucking cow-pea. They gave Rs 20 ($0.44) on days when we worked from 8.30 am to 6.30 pm. This month we did not spend anything on feast or *jathre*.[8] We spent Rs 260 ($5.77) on food and ration, saved Rs 50 ($1.11) in the Sangha, and did not spend on anything else. Yes, I spent Rs 25 ($0.55) for Amavase.

July: This is the month of Mannethina Amavase. We have weeding and harvesting of *sajje*[9] this month. We got daily wages of Rs 15 ($0.33) for weeding and Rs 12 ($0.26) for harvesting; we earned Rs 500 ($11.11) from weeding and Rs 250 ($5.55) from harvesting *sajje*, a total of Rs 750 ($16.66). This month I did not have any expenses other than household expenses, Rs 280, ($6.22) I saved Rs 40 ($0.88) in the SHG. I also spent on ration, rice, cooking oil, jowar and dal, and only Rs 40 ($0.88) were left.

August: This is the month of Nagara Panchami.[10] We had *coolie* work of cotton-crossing, for which the daily wage is Rs 20 ($0.44). I did not go for work for 4 days this month; as we had the Panchami festival, we had to clean the house, and prepare for the feast. I earned Rs 540 ($12) this month, we had to work from 6 am to 6 pm to be considered *coolie* and get this wage rate. Since we had Panchami festival this month, I spent Rs 400 ($8.88) to get items (groundnut, oil, jaggery, rice, etc.) for preparing sweets (undi-laddoo). Apart from this I spent Rs 280 ($6.22) on household expenses. Adding Rs 40 ($0.88) of savings in the group, this month's expenses were Rs 720 ($16).

September: This month also we have cotton-crossing work. The *coolie* was Rs 20 ($0.44) per day, so I earned Rs 550 ($12.22) this month, in 27 days. We did not celebrate any festival this month so we spent just Rs 280 ($6.22) on ration. I saved Rs 30 ($0.66) in the group, so the total expenses were Rs 310 ($6.88).

Lakshmavva has had one partner since she became a *devadasi*, who made no contribution to her household. She says about him:

He was always the same, he never brought anything to the house, he didn't bring rations (provisions). He only provides clothes for me once a year, and twice for my children. But my parents-'in-law' sent some rations to my house during the delivery. They like me and support me. What can I do? I selected a wrong life, I have no other option, whether he looks after me well or not, I must take care of myself and my mother. How much can she bear? Sometimes we did not have food, and Bharmavva brought *jowar*[11] flour to make *rotti*[12] during my pregnancy. Now I have experience and I can manage my life, but at that time I was young, innocent and inexperienced. He avoided me during my pregnancy and always came back when I started regular work again. But even though I faced very tough situations, I did not look at another man. Whether he gave me anything or not, I could not think of another man. In case a husband does not give enough to the family, a wife does not go to another man; in the same way I have also not bothered whether he supports me or not: I am staying with him.

She took repeated loans from the landlord, four times during the year 2003–04, of Rs 250 ($5.55) to Rs 300 ($6.66) each time, totalling Rs 1,100 ($24). These loans for household expenses were taken during the lean season from March to May, when there was low availability of agricultural labour work, leading her into a perpetual cycle of debt to her landlord. After she joined the self-help group (SHG), she took five loans from the SHG, totalling Rs 887 ($20), on which she paid an interest of Rs 300 ($6.66) but had kept the principal amount outstanding. She acquired a cow under a subsidised loan scheme, which provided small additional income that helped the family survive, but she was not in a position to repay this loan. Even when formal loans were offered by the non-government organisation (NGO), she did not take the option, as she could not afford to be further indebted.

Over a 4-year period from 2000 to 2004, Lakshmavva's elder son left school to graze the buffalo. Later, her second son also left and took over the grazing chore while her elder son graduated to *coolie* work. In 2005, her youngest daughter left school. These children had no time to learn, and their mother had no way to sustain her family except through their earnings. In her case, the asset and income creation from financial capital (that is, buying and caring for the buffalo) was at the expense of her children's development. The loans for consumption helped her to manage difficult periods, and the buffalo taken on subsidised credit helped improve her asset position. By the end of 2007, she had sold the buffalo. Her elder son continued to work, but her second son and daughter rejoined school. Though they absented themselves to do *coolie* work in some months, they attended often enough to stay enrolled and motivated to continue. By 2008, however, all three children have dropped out of school, they were not able to cope with studies, one son grazes the animals and the other son and the daughter go for agricultural labour work.

The Story of Nagavva

Nagavva, a 27-year-old *devadasi* (in 2000), stood thin and tall, with an oval-shaped sensitive face and wheat-coloured skin. She was landless, with a father and three children to care for. Her two sons, aged 10 and 8 years, went to school, and the youngest, a daughter, was 4 years old. She had two houses, one house had tiled roof, walls made of bricks and the floor of mud, polished with cow dung. It had a hall, a part of which she used as the kitchen. She had made another house with a roof moulded with wood and walls of mud, plastered with cement. She had a bathroom and a small kitchen in this house. She had made a small extension to both the houses, where she tied the cattle. She kept all the clothes in one house and cooking vessels in another. She kept her home very clean.

Nagavva was the only child, born after 10 years of her parents' marriage, so her mother cared a lot for her and never allowed her to do any work at home, except for letting her graze the cattle. It was only after she was 12 years old that she went for farm labour with her mother, and if she was unable to finish, her mother completed her portion of the work, too. Nagavva was very close to her mother, and still mourns her mother's death 2 years ago. She has not yet recovered from the loss, and during the interviews, though she speaks with humour, her eyes are full of tears.

Nagavva's maternal uncle had three sons. Her eldest cousin grew up in their home; he was 10 years old when Nagavva was born, and they were very close. He returned to his parents' home after he was 20. Nagavva's parents had decided to get them married. She explains:

> My parents had decided that I would be married to him and we would live with them. Soon after I attained puberty, there was a marriage proposal for me, which they turned down. They thought that they would fix my marriage with my cousin, so they went to my uncle's home and asked if their eldest son could marry me. My aunt and uncle refused saying that they needed his earnings for themselves. My parents were very upset because they were really keen on having him as their son-in-law, and when we were young, my uncle had agreed to let him marry me and stay with my parents, so now they felt slighted.
>
> My uncle's son was also very interested in marrying me; he fought with his parents and came to my house immediately. He also said that he would not marry anyone other than me. I was also interested in him, he had lived for so many years in our home, and we were close then.

My parents wanted to avoid him because my uncle had hurt them. They tried to send him away by telling him some lie. They said: 'We cannot have our daughter married now as we have many loans that need to be repaid. Can you wait till the loans are cleared?' He said: 'Tell me how much, I will clear the whole amount'. Then my parents said: 'Do that first, then we will think of your marriage.' He told my father: 'Give me three months' time, I will go to Ratnagiri for work and will pay off all the loans.[13] Do not give her (in marriage) to anyone till I come back.'

Soon after he left, my parents sounded out some people to look out for a match for me; two or three matches were suggested, but they did not want to let their son live in our home. Then my parents thought: 'Why get her married at all? Let her be a devadasi.'

When my parents started looking out for a match for me, I sent a message to my cousin through a person who works in Ratnagiri, but it took a few months for the message to reach him. This was the first time he worked with the contractor, so he had to complete the mandated nine months before he could take leave. He too sent me a message with someone who came back after a few months: 'I will come back after nine months and marry Nagavva—tell her parents not to give her to anybody'. But before that my parents had already made me into a devadasi and fixed me up with Reddy.

Later someone who went to Ratnagiri told my cousin: 'You are working here, but her parents have made her a devadasi and also started her in a relationship with a partner.' That same day he came to Bikanhalli and clashed with my parents. He told them 'You are big cheats, if I had known you would do this, I would not have left here at all.' He was very angry. Later he calmed down and realised that everything was over; he went back after two days to his home. He did not talk to me, and I could also not talk to him, I was too full of feelings. He was upset and depressed, and did not marry for two years. His relatives told him: 'Now her married life is finished, why are you wasting your life, better marry someone and settle down.' Then he got married. He visited our home only once over the past years, to talk with my mother, and went back the same day. After she died, he never came here at all.

She said about her life:

> My parents wanted me to stay with them and so they made me a devadasi. My mother loved me so much she never let me do anything. Till now I do not know how to cook. If they had let me get married, I would have learnt all these things with my mother-in-law. I would have had land or a husband to care for me, and his family members to share my difficulties; I would not have had the responsibility of the household alone. They did not think what would happen to me after they died, they just made me a devadasi.

Her partner Reddy cared for her until he married, and then the contact became limited to sexual relations and provisions for the house. Even when she was ill, and her children also fell ill in the rainy season, he gave only Rs 100 ($2.22), which had to suffice for the children's treatment. Nagavva claimed her partner had stopped caring. She said:

> Now he comes only in the night, finishes his work (meaning sexual relation) and goes off. I can't even talk to him about my feelings. I was ill for more than 15 days, he did not even turn back to look at me. If I were married, my husband would have stayed with me and looked after me. He is not supporting me properly. My children are small; I don't know how many problems I have to face until they grow big enough. Now I do not have the confidence that he will support me. This is why I stopped with three children; I can earn and look after them. Whatever he can give us, and for whichever period, is fine, but I am clear that without doing *coolie* work my life cannot be, I have to depend fully on *coolie* work. Even later, if my children cannot look after me, I belong to this village, I can take a plate and beg for food for my stomach.[14]

Her earnings were only from her own wages, and sometimes her father went for *coolie* work, too. They took turns to look after the cattle. Her average monthly income was Rs 1,274 ($28.31), to support a five-member household. In 2000, she had one cow, one calf, one goat and two chickens. The cow milk was used for household consumption.

In 1999, prior to joining the self-help group (SHG), her mother was sanctioned a loan of Rs 5,000 ($111) under the IRDP scheme, with a subsidy element of 50 per cent. However, she was told that the subsidy amount would be Rs 1,500 ($33.33) and she would have to pay back Rs 3,500 ($78). The amount released to her was only Rs 3,500 ($78). She bought a buffalo-calf for Rs 1,500 ($33) and used the rest for household expenses. After she reared it for 1 year, she sold it for Rs 700 ($16) and put together some of her own savings to buy an adult buffalo. At this time, her son was ill and had to be taken to the hospital regularly. Being landless and dependent only on *coolie* work, she could not earn enough to repay the loan. She said:

> The buffalo loan was of great use to us. My son had fever since he was two years old; I could feed him with the milk of the buffalo, and sell the extra milk to pay the hospital charges. My son survived because of that buffalo. His health was not good for three years. After that, when we wanted to repay, my mother fell ill; we took her to hospital but she died. Now the buffalo is dead. We could not repay because of all these problems. My son would have been dead without that buffalo. At least now I want to repay because the bank sends me notices. The interest has now become more than 50% of the loan. I don't know when I am going to repay this.

Clearly, the non-repayment of the loan was due more to her inability, than unwillingness to repay. Within the first 2 years of joining the SHG, she had taken five loans, ranging between Rs 250 and 300 ($6.66), a total of Rs 1,932 ($43) twice from the SHG and thrice from the landlord, but made only one repayment to the SHG. Later, she bought two cows, from her savings, and also two hens.

In 2005, her group was offered SGSY loan subsidised by the scheduled castes and scheduled tribes (SC/ST) Corporation, an amount up to Rs 10,000 ($222) per member, for buying a buffalo. She took Rs 5,000 ($111) and spent the money for foodgrains, provisions, education and clothes for the children. Again in 2007, she received Rs 8,000 ($1,778) under the official *devadasi* rehabilitation programme to buy a buffalo. She did not buy one, but showed them the cow which she had already purchased under this scheme. At this time, she had received many notices from the bank to clear the earlier loan outstanding in the name of her mother. She negotiated with the bank through a local politician, got interest waiver, paid up Rs 4,000 ($89) and cleared the loan. She combined the remaining with her accumulated savings in the group, and used it to pay off the balance loan under the SGSY scheme. The group then shared the remaining balances from the SGSY scheme and stopped its operations.

Nagavva acknowledged the support she received in recent years for the education of her children. She said;

> My elder son has completed his school, and now goes to Alavandi village for pre-university college. Sampark pays his fees and my partner pays for his bus pass. My youngest daughter also goes to school. My father is too old to work, he can barely walk inside the house. The children are older now, and expenses have

increased. My second son takes the animals for grazing; the two cows and two goats are his responsibility. I go for *coolie* work, and we can barely manage household expenses. I am happy my children can continue studies.

The Story of Parvathamma

In 2003, Parvathamma's household of three comprised herself (35 years old), her mother (70 years old) and a 13-year-old son; her daughter was 15, married, with a girl child, and living with her husband in another village. She lives in Hosagondabala village, about 15 km from Koppal town. Her son has studied up till Class 3 and works in a tea shop in Bhagya Nagar, near Koppal. Her mother and grandmother were also *devadasi*s, but she broke this custom and got her daughter married at 8.

Parvathamma was dedicated to the goddess at the age of 5. She explained:

> I was very small so I have no memory of this. My mother was also a devadasi and so was her mother. We were only two daughters, my younger sister and I, so at the age of 5, I was made into a devadasi. I was made to wear five pendants, five pearls, five corals and one '*naalige*' (a pendant of a female goddess's tongue). I was called '*basavi*'—My grandmother used to say she did not know the word '*devadasi*' at all, they only used the word '*basavi*'. It was the government that gave us the name *devadasi* and brought the word into our consciousness. The government introduced various schemes for us, using this name.
>
> When I matured, I was 12 years old, and my mother told me that I was a '*basavi*' and could not marry and had to stay home and look after her. For about 4 to 5 years after this, I had no interaction with men at all. I did not like them at all. I was possessed by the Parvathamma goddess—I would go into a trance, my body would shudder and I would break into hysterical talk. I was said to have 'Parvathamma's trouble'.

Her mother wanted her to dedicate herself to this goddess to enable her to become normal again. After 4 years, Parvathamma was convinced to accept this life and relationship; and her hysterical spells declined. Her mother almost pushed her into having *sammandha* that is, forming a relationship with a man. Her reasoning was that Parvathamma had been made into a *devadasi* because there were no males in the house. As a result of *samsara* (sexual relationship), she would conceive and have children who would bring light (*belaku*) into the house. Then Parvatamma agreed to a relationship her mother fixed with a 38-year-old Muslim man from a nearby village. At this time Parvatamma was about 16–17 years old.

He came and 'talked' to Parvathamma's mother (meaning negotiated the terms of the relationship). Parvathamma's mother said that he did not have to live permanently with her daughter, but he had to bring silver anklets and a sari, and clothes. He agreed and brought all this and started living with her. They did not discuss anything and Parvathamma thought that he could stay with her as long as he wished. He was already married and had two children, a boy and a girl. He stayed with her for 10 years; she had two children with him, one boy died after 7 days and another when he was 4 years old.

Parvathamma would not talk about him, and became angry at his mention; for while he maintained the partnership for 10 years, he would also drink, use foul language and abuse her. She felt that he had done nothing but exploit her and her mother by extorting money from them. She had two pregnancies during this period, and both the children died; she returned to work 7 days after delivery, and finally, angry at his neglect, she told him: 'Even if you do not live with me, someone else will, so you do not have to visit us. Please stop coming here,' and when he got drunk and abused her, she said: 'Go and die with your wife.'

Her next *sammandha* was with Yellappa (about 48 years old), also from the same village as Hussain, from the butcher caste. Yellappa used to visit another *devadasi* in the same colony as Parvathamma and came to her of his own accord. She did not want to bargain with a man who had come to her after she had already had a relationship, so she did not ask for anything. He told her that she had the option of not going to *coolie* work as he would provide for her and for her two children.

He trades in sheep and goats, travels from village to village, has a reliable seasonal income and provides whenever her family do not have sufficient earnings. Expressing her loyalty to him she said:

> From the time I started my second relationship, my partner has been providing full support to the children and me. Both the children I have are his. The son fell ill and we took him to several hospitals, he has spent more than Rs 25,000 ($556) over the past seven years for medical expenses. He takes care of all the food, clothes, and hospital expenses. He provided the money for the marriage of my daughter, and the delivery expenses of all her children. He has told me: 'You do not have to do *coolie* work, I will look after you, don't ask anything of anyone else'. He is like my father, husband, and my everything. He also looks after my mother. Even though my son is earning from his job at a hotel, it is only a supplementary income to the family. I never had to take a loan from outside after this man came into my life.

Her mother, Swaravva also spoke about their background and lives. She said that she was a daughter of a *devadasi*, too. Her own parents (mother and steady partner of her mother) died when she was very young, and her relatives looked after her. When she was young, they dedicated her to God and made her a *devadasi*, too. She said:

> I was young, I had to beg for a living. I do not know who made me into a devadasi. I bore two girl children; I got one married and made one into a devadasi. Otherwise, there would have been nobody to look after me. I have grown up without anyone to care for me and faced a lot of difficulties; this must not happen to me again, this is why I made my daughter into a devadasi.
>
> In spite of doing this, the man that my daughter lived with did nothing for her. My daughter stayed with him, but even then the two children that she carried did not survive. After her delivery, I used to labour each day and managed to keep my daughter alive.
>
> I have not been free of doing *coolie* work, from a young age, right up to now. Now, I have been almost blind for the past two years and can hardly see when I go into the fields, so I do not go now. My daughter looks after me very well and so does Yellappa. Now, we have no problems.

Parvathamma supplements:

> From a young age, I had to face many difficulties. When I was made a devadasi, the man who lived with me never went out to work, I had to work and he took the money to drink *sarai* (local alcohol). As soon as I delivered my children I had to work, and now my whole body pains as a result of those experiences. I also suffer from varicose veins. Whenever I asked him to work, he would say that he had a wife and children

to care for. That is why I left him. Now, Yellappa says that I should not go for *coolie* work. We have been together for ten years and I have not worked very much during this time. For the past four years I go for *coolie* work only if I need additional money to spend.

I had myself operated after bearing four children. Actually, I wanted to have this done soon after my first two pregnancies, unfortunately the children died and I waited to have two more. We struggled a lot, my mother and I, at the time that I had my first two boys. My partner was not at all responsible and we had to work even to feed ourselves. I had to go out and work seven days after delivering the children, even my *baananthana* (recovery period after delivery, normally observed for forty days) was very difficult.

Parvathamma considers her male partner as the most important pivot of change in her livelihood. The financial details, though, revealed a different story. The major portion (60 per cent) of her monthly income of Rs 1,027 ($23) was still from the salary of her 14-year-old son, employed in a shop in Koppal. She had 0.5 acre of land, provided by the government, which was often submerged with dam water,[15] and thus provided little additional income. She took two small loans of Rs 100 ($2.22) and Rs 200 ($4.44) from the group for medicines and clothes. As her household needs were met by her son's salary and her partner, and she did not have surplus labour to look after new assets, she did not take any further loans. She also left her group within 2 years and did not join another.

Low Assets, Low Incomes, Small Loans

Lakshmavva and Nagavva lacked human and physical capital, resulting in low incomes. They depended on the labour they committed to specific landlords against small advances of Rs 250–300 ($5.55–6.66). They took loans at festival time to spend on food and recorded them as *festival expenses*. They did not have sufficient cash flows to cover basic survival expenses of the family, and festivals provided a reason for requesting advances from their landlords. Nagavva said:

When my parents were alive they did *coolie* work, my children were small then and we did not have any problems in running (managing) the household. If at all we fell short of money, we used to take an advance from landlords and clear it within 15 to 20 days. If we take loan from outside, we will have the burden of interest, so we don't take any loan of a higher amount than Rs 100 to 200 ($2.22 to 4.44). We have to earn and eat, and we don't have any land; if we take a loan it is difficult for us to repay it. Since we have the group now, we can take and repay the loan to the group. We don't find the need to go to 'outsiders' for loans.

Surviving at the Margins

The Story of Yellamma

I was about 9 years old. Nobody used to call us for *coolie* work at that time, as not enough work was available. My mother used to earn about Rs 1 ($0.022) a day, and if at all anyone took me along, then I might earn half a rupee. Our people never sent us to the school. After I matured, I started doing *coolie* work as well.[16]

I was twelve years old when I was made a devadasi. I thought that I was 'given' or 'promised' to God and that was the reason for wearing the *muthu* (pearl). Afterwards, I started hearing people say that they had tied pearls around my neck, that I was a devadasi or '*basavi*'.

The first Friday after becoming a devadasi, I went to *kari kallu* (black stone) which is kept in an open place in the community. It is a symbol of the Goddess Huligemma (considered a patron goddess of the devadasis) and I prayed. Then, I called and arranged lunch for five *jogamma*s (lady priest) and five children. For the following four weeks, I went asking for alms to complete the rituals associated with becoming a devadasi.

I worked on the field with a neighbour named Yamunavva. Yamunavva had a friend named Badakappa who came to her house regularly. Badakappa told Yamunavva, 'She doesn't have relations with anyone. I want her. Go and ask.' Yamunavva consulted my parents who approved of the proposal after laying down certain conditions: he had to give us a *jamkhane*,[17] a sari, a blouse and Rs 500 ($11). He could stay for only three months at a time. He accepted these conditions, but we continued our relationship for 4 years. I did not have any children with him.

Then Badakappa got married to a woman from Kadhiganur. They have three sons and two daughters together. After these four years I went to my mother's village, Hosagondabala. For two years, I did not have any other relations in Hosagondabala. After two years, Badakappa came to my house and met me. He asked me to go and live with him and promised that he would care for me as his wife. But I didn't want to spoil his marriage, so I didn't accept his proposal. That was my last contact with him. He is still alive, but he never came back.

Then, I had a relationship with a Muslim man, Hussain Sa'b, in the same village. In the same village there was another devadasi called Mailavva who had a good relationship with him. Hussain told Maillavva that he wanted to have relations with me. She said to me 'Husain Sa'b likes you. He'll look after your (household) expenses. You haven't had any relations for the past two years. Let's decide what you want to do.' He had two children, but he didn't have a good relationship with his wife so they were separated and he lived with his mother. I discussed this with my mother and she accepted his proposal.

I continued my relationship with Hussain Sa'b for 25 years and I had five children (2 sons and 3 daughters) with him. He looked after me well. He would care for us in our ill-health and provide for us. He bore all the expenses and never minded. We had relations until my son got married and after that he broke the relationship off with me. He did not take any responsibility during my son's marriage and I took a loan and spent it on my children. He is not my husband to stay with me. Just as Muslims don't keep a corpse in their *Masjid* (mosque), in the same way, he didn't keep up our relationship either—he left me and went. He had left his wife and looked after us like his own family. He would bring *santhe* (goods from the local market) for us and clothes for the children. He would bring me the kind of saris that I asked him for and he never fought with me. Not even a single day.

The third man, Durgappa, lost his wife very early. He has a son who lived with us until recently but now he lives in Mundargi with a family, something like bonded labour. I have had a *sammandha* (relationship) with Durgappa. He belongs to the same scheduled caste (SC). My sister has married into a family from Mundargi; this man is her *maidhana*.[18] He has a Janatha House, (a house built under government scheme) but no land. I had not mentioned Durgappa to you earlier because I was a little scared at that time; I didn't know you very well then but as I am closer to you now I don't mind telling you everything. If you had come earlier today, I could have shown him to you. You have not seen anyone who I have lived with. One of my partners is dead and one is alive. Durgappa and I have had a photograph taken. Tell me, who is better looking, he or I? (She laughed a lot at this).

Durgappa found me after his wife died. He doesn't live in Mundargi for too much of the time; he spends more time here. My children are grown up and they discuss things with Durgappa and they take his advice. He brings things for the house and does whatever work is required. He has even had my children married (*lagna maadidhaane*). During the *Panchami* festival in August, Durgappa's son gave Rs 300 ($7) to me and Rs 100 ($2) to his father, out of the Rs 500 ($11) that he was paid. He calls me *avva* (mother). He asked me to buy things for the festival with this money even though he couldn't come himself. Now, I feel almost as if I have a husband in my home. I live in Mundargi for a week and in Hosagondabala for the rest of the time. Durgappa is a very good man.

First, in Dasanala, Badukappa was not married—he used to come to me every night but I didn't have too much of *sammandha* with him. Hussain Sa'b would also come at night and go away in the morning but Durgappa lives with me for a week and in Mundargi for a week. His wife died three years ago. During my children's marriages, he lived here for three months continuously, but now he just visits.

I have lived with three different men but my children are all from Hussain Sa'b. Durgappa, who is with me now, has performed the marriages of these children and also contributes towards celebrating festivals, etc. He gives them and their children gifts before they leave. He cares about their well-being. He doesn't discriminate against my children. Durgappa's son looks after me like his own mother. My children call Durgappa *appa* (father). He had them all married and it is my wish to do the same for his son—let us see what happens.

In 2001, Yellamma's household comprised six, including two sons, their wives and a daughter, with another two daughters married and living in other villages.

Since my children started earning, I have stopped going for *coolie* work. I don't have house or land so I have to do *coolie* work to eat. This is why I feel that 'health is wealth.' Because of my leg pain; I can't do *coolie* work any more. Maybe I can take loan from the group and do some sort of *vyapara* (trading). I can do dairying now—this is what I want to do. I take the cows for grazing; leave them to graze then sit under a tree for some time so I don't feel the pain much. Earlier, I used to go to bring hay for the cattle, then a boy from the neighbourhood used to bring it, but recently he died of snakebite, so I will have to go and get hay.

There are three landlords: Chanappa, Sharanappa and Shekarappa. If an elderly person passes away they give cattle as a grant in remembrance of them. Since I don't go for *coolie* work, I take these cattle for grazing and bring hay for them. I gave one cow to my daughter, now it is one year old and my daughter takes it for grazing.

There are two big farmers, I work for them, their names are Eshappa and Koiavaru. They give *coolie* wages on the day I work, while other farmers give wages 3 to 4 days after the work has been done. So I get provisions from the petty shop and pay him after I get the *coolie* wage. The landlords also give 16 to 20 kgs of *jowar*, pulses and groundnut when these crops are harvested. I sell them in the Koppal market, and from the money earned I purchase clothes for my children and myself. I also get some provision from the shandy during festivals. This time, two landlords gave me two bags of maize, which I sold in Koppal for Rs 600 ($13), I gave my elder son that money to have an operation for his piles problem.

I am the main earning member in my house. What to do? If one is born in a poor family, one has to think whatever one has is good. When my son Devappa does work of head-loading on the tractor, he earns Rs 50 ($1.11) per day; but he works for one day and stays home for another two days. My daughter Gayathravva goes to work everyday. Her brother told her to go to Koppal *jathre*, but she refused to go, saying that the expense will be Rs 400 ($8.88), and the same is better spent to get provisions for the house i.e. rice for one month. My daughter thinks a lot about the house, she is like goddess Saraswati. Other children demand things, but my daughter's only business is to work, earn, eat and sleep.

My elder son, Nagappa, does not go for *coolie* work, he is sick, so if he wants money for petty expenses he asks me; even when he is sick, I have to bear the cost of his medical expenses. He is the cause of my worry. His wife is also sick, she is suffering from TB. Her parents do not take care of her as they are poor. We are poor too. If she comes here then I have to earn for her medical expenses, and moreover I worry that the disease may spread to my son also, I am very scared about that. Right now she has gone back to her mother's place.

The family could not afford to spend on the treatment of the daughter-in-law, and in one interview, Yellamma said, with frustration: 'We cannot afford to spend on her treatment. Now, she has just gone to her parents, and is taking treatment there, but they are also very poor like us.'
About group loans, she said:

When the group had started, I had taken a loan of Rs 200 ($4.44), paid Rs 10 ($0.22) as interest and Rs 50 ($1.11) towards principal over four months. As my son was ill I took Rs 150 ($3.33) from the group and am now paying the interest but have not yet paid the principal amount. There is no *coolie* work this month, so there is a difficulty in repaying it. I have not taken loan from anyone else because no one helps us when we are in need. That is why it is very rare that I ask for a loan from anybody. When my children got married, I had taken a loan of Rs 1,200 ($27) at 10% per month. They ask us to give something, like gold, to take the loan. That is why I don't take any loans; after the group has been formed I have not taken any loan from outside. Also, nobody is able to give a loan. If anybody in our locality wants to take a loan, they take it from *Baddi Chanappa*. He gives loans to anybody at any time but we have to repay him in the given time else he takes either a cow or a buffalo from the house—that's why his name is *Baddi Chanappa* ('baddi' is the Kannada term for interest).

When I first took a loan it was for my daughter's wedding. Later I took a loan of Rs 2,500 ($56) from our village farmers without interest. My sons repaid this loan by working in their house from morning until night for Rs 20 ($0.44) for a day. That is why I don't take any loans from other people. We still have to repay Rs 1000 ($22) because they had given us a bag of wheat during the wedding. My elder son is not here, and if my younger son goes to do that work to repay it (meaning bonded labour), we will have nothing to eat, even now all of us have to go to work to eat.

I took a loan for my son's marriage, I paid it back within two years by doing *coolie* work, but I still have to pay Rs 2,050 ($46) by doing *coolie* work. I am afraid to take loans. We spend as we earn. We will spend as per our limit. Since we don't have land, gold, silver or a house, who will give us a loan? We are bonded labourers to farmers who have given us a loan. My eldest son works and pays it back. Still, part of the loan is yet to be repaid.

People living in our street are very poor and there are a lot of children so they find it difficult to repay the loan.

I have four acres of land near the river but we can cultivate it only once a year. We grow maize, cowpea, horse-gram and *jowar*. This year even that is not available, as there is no rain, and no water in the river. If we grow crops on our land, there is sufficient hay for the cattle, but as we could not grow hay this year, we will have to get it from outside for Rs 300 ($46) per cartload.

She owned three heads of cattle and one was given to her daughter in Shivapura village. In 2007, she said:

Over the past seven years, there is not much material change in my life. I do not keep well, get tired quickly and cannot work much. Two daughters were married, and the major change is that the two sons, also married, now live separately with their families. Earlier, when we all lived together, the sons did not work much. The expenses for so many people were very high, so my daughter and I worked very hard to earn for the entire family. Last year, I sent Galavva for skill training, and even sold off a goat to buy good clothes that she could wear to Koppal, but her earning has not increased, and she is back to agricultural work. Now we both go to *coolie* work and finish off our wages every day just paying for food. I have only one worry now, to find a suitable boy for Galavva and save for her marriage expenses. She saves Rs 15 ($0.33) in her group every week, and I save Rs 10 ($0.22) in mine. We save Rs 25 ($0.56) every week. I had taken a loan of Rs 500 ($11) for my son's treatment, and he said he would repay it, but he did not. I have repaid some from my wages, but Rs 100 ($2.2) is still due. My sons do not support us at all, but we are happy with whatever the two of us earn, it is enough for us, we do not worry too much about the boys.

The Story of Shivavva

Shivavva shared a small home with her husband, two sons and a daughter-in-law, three daughters (two others were married) and three grandchildren. Between 2000 and 2005 her husband died, her elder son's family separated and went to another house, one daughter got married and left home and her younger son got married and had a child, and also migrated, so the size of the family reduced from eleven to five. She was unhappy with the elder son, and stated:

> If my eldest son works for one day, he may not work for the next two days—his work pattern is extremely irregular. His wife, the eldest daughter-in-law, cares for the children and the home. The younger one does *coolie* work either in the house of the *gowda*, or other people. Each one of us has to work to be able to manage the household.

Regarding education, Shivavva said, 'Both my sons and daughters-in-law are illiterate—even my grandchildren are not willing to go to school. Although we try to send them, they are not interested.'

The income and expenditure pattern of Shivavva is depicted in Figures 4.2, 4.3 and 4.4. The main income came from the agricultural labour of seven members, as her family was landless and uneducated, and only earned an average of Rs 3,500 ($78) to Rs 4,000 ($89) per month during 9 months of the year. Earlier the inflow was lower, but from 2001 there was a lump sum contributed from the migratory income of her son. When the younger son visited home, he brought with him Rs 15,000–20,000 ($333–444). If she needed money in the interim, he sent about Rs 2,000 ($44) or more depending on her need. Shivavva used this to reduce her debts, while the money from the rest of the family's labour paid for regular household expenses. Shivavva had three cows and three calves, producing 2 litres of milk per day, sold at Rs 7 ($0.15) per litre. They collected free *jowar* hay for cows from other people's fields and collected manure from cow dung, sold at

> *I take all the responsibility of the house. My younger son listens to me. I asked my eldest son to take responsibility for the family after my husband died, but he refused. He could not take care of such a large family and he separated. My sons and daughters have all been going for coolie work. The three daughters who were earning are now married, and the younger two have also continued to do farm labour. They earn Rs 15 ($0.33) per day as wages; they get work for about 15 days every month. During the days when they do not get work, they fetch hay for the cows collect firewood, and bring wate.*
>
> *I am happy about being in charge, but I feel bad too. I would have liked my eldest son to take the responsibility. I told my elder daughter-in-law to stay at home and care for the family and children, while I continued to go and work in the fields, and she did so. Some years later, I told my younger daughter-in-law the same. But she told me to be at home instead. Now she goes for coolie work.*
> —Shivavva

Figure 4.2
Shivavva's Inflows Distributions

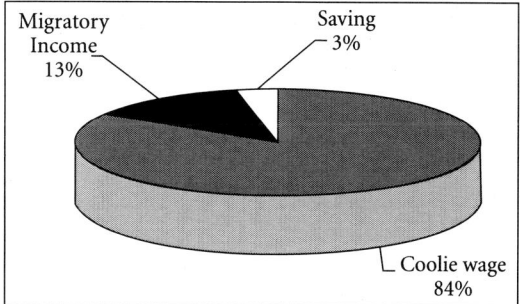

Source: Authors.

Figure 4.3
Shivavva's Distribution of Outflows

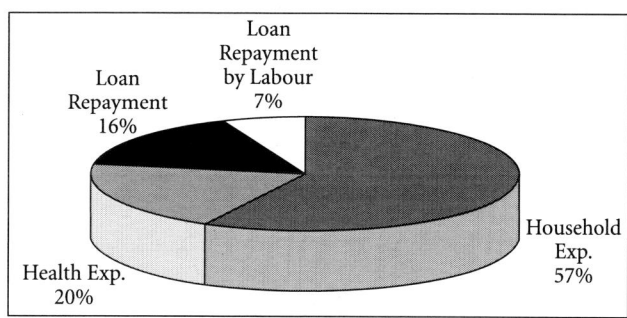

Source: Authors.

Figure 4.4
Total Inflows and Outflows of Shivavva

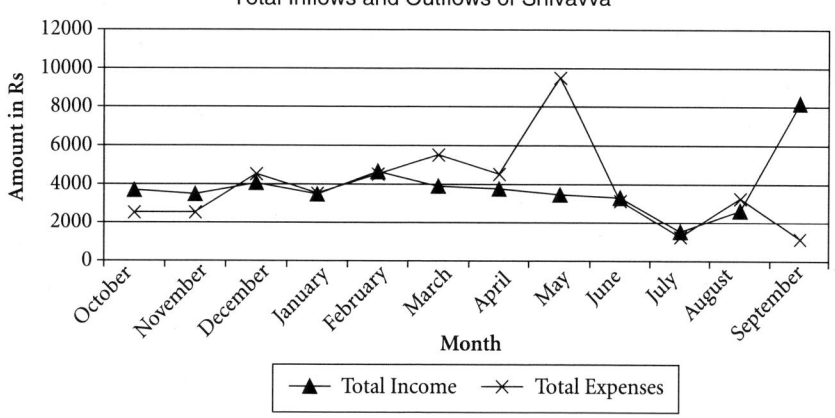

Source: Authors.

Rs 50 ($1.11) per cartload; four times every 6 months. The elder daughter-in-law got as a dowry a 6-month-old female calf 10 years before, from which the rest of the stock was produced.

Household expenses were high because of large family size. Shivavva finally repaid her son's marriage loan in May with her share of savings from the group. The peaks in her expenses were due to her husband's illness and death at a time when her eldest son and his family had also separated from the joint family (he had four girls and a boy). Shivavva regarded this as a sad loss, and a continuation of her responsibility as head of the household.

Shivavva's family had lived in a small hut for 15 years. When her younger son went to Ratnagiri, he gave her Rs 6,000 ($133).[19] She added to this and bought a house for Rs 8,000 ($178), with no electricity. This was remedied when she paid a middleman to become beneficiaries of the government's *Bhagya Jyothi* scheme. She then got a house allotted to them under another government scheme, 5 years ago. When the whole family lived together, they would cook in the old (first) house, and some slept in the new one.

Shivavva's third daughter married 2 years earlier, and a loan of Rs 3,000 ($67) was taken for this marriage at an interest of 5 per cent per month. She made part payments towards this for 2 years. She had taken three loans from group savings ranging from Rs 300 to 400 ($6.66–8.88) each time to meet expenses, visit the temple and to repay the money lender. She had not yet paid the group loans and explained:

> I took loans three times, a total of Rs 900 ($20). I have so far paid interest of Rs 750 ($17). I do not have any loan outside the group. My daughter says that if she gets *coolie* work regularly, then we can repay the principal in monthly instalments. If I take a loan it is from the group not from anyone else. When my husband was earning I had his wages, now I have only the group savings to come to my rescue.

Later, in 2004, she purchased a buffalo through a loan from her SHG; the loan was linked with a subsidy scheme of the SC/ST Corporation, which required her to pay back half of it. The animal stock provided them with some cash inflow, and as family members laboured daily, the household position improved.

About the loans she said:

> I do not get loans from outside. If I get loans from farmers, then I would be bound to them until the amount gets cleared. I do not have land either at my parent's or my husband's place. My sons are my biggest property, like land (Nanna mage nanage hola iddahange). I took a loan of Rs 40,000 ($889) for their marriage expenses from the farmers; it took five years for them to repay the loan, which was deducted part by part from their wages. During this time when my sons were kept as bonded labourers, my husband, my daughters and I went for *coolie* work to manage the expenses of the family.

Despite the fact that Shivavva lost her husband, her elder son moved away, her family was able to survive only because of combined factors like farm labour, the migration earning of her younger son and minor inflows from the sale of milk.

Struggles and Stability

The Story of Sushila

Sushila comes from a family of artisans: her father was a carpenter from Gajanur village in Hangal Block, close to Koppal. He moved from village to village working wherever he found the opportunity. Sushila's parents had three girls and three boys, of which one girl and one boy died.

Sushila narrated:

> We did not have our own house in Gajanur. My uncle's wife did not let us stay with them so we had to live in a rented house. The family had 6 acres of land. When my father requested my uncle to divide the land he did not give us anything. However, my father did not fight with him. He said that we should earn our living through labour. He found it very difficult to earn. My sister was 13 years old and somehow she got married. During that time, we had neither a house nor food to eat. My mother also went out to do farm work and it was a difficult time for us.

> My father used to move about a lot for work, taking us with him. I did my 2nd standard in Kabbur, Haveri Block, 3rd and 4th standard in Maharajpete in Hangal Block and when I was studying in the 5th standard, we came to Somasagar near Haveri, where we stayed for two years. My parents were tired of taking TCs,[20] so they took me out of school. My elder sister's studies were stopped when she was in the 3rd standard. They wanted to take me out of school too when I was in the 3rd standard but I wanted to study so I managed to study up to the 7th standard. When I reached puberty, my father felt it was not good to take a girl when he moved, so he decided to get back from Somasagar to his own native place, Gajanur.

> In 1992, when I was 15 years old, my prospective husband came to see me. My parents discussed everything with him. He said that he was already married but that his wife was mentally ill. He had told people that he would not be keeping her as she was a mad woman and that he would marry another woman. When my parents asked him about his work he told them that he had applied for and hoped to get a job as a 'lines-man' in the electricity department. He said that he worked as an electrician in his village and that he had 7 acres of dry land. My parents thought he was well off and had quite good prospects. They thought they were giving me to a good house and person. I did not want to become the second wife to a man but for the sake of my parents I agreed, got married to him and came to Mudhaballi village.

> After marriage we did not even have enough money to set up a separate home. For three months, we stayed in my mother-in-law's house. The three brothers and my husband fought for the division of their parents, land and the issue was taken to court. My mother-in-law complained that all the daughters-in-law had beaten her to get control of the fields. It was at this time I received a letter from the government that I was selected for training in tailoring under the TRYSEM programme.[21] I was wondering how I would go to the courts and also take up the training but I decided on the training whatever the consequences may have been. During the six-month training, I went to the courts too. After completion of training, I was given a tailoring machine, free.

> By this time, I had decided to start my own business and stand on my own two feet. At home, before marriage, I had worked as a *coolie* to earn and make a living. Fifteen days after my marriage I was sent to the fields to work. When my baby was nine months old I used to tie it on my back and go for *coolie* work.

> When the government allotted us a *Janata* house we moved here. At that time, I had a tailoring machine and when anyone in the village wanted to get a blouse or petticoat tailored, they would come to me. It was with this money that I met all the needs of the household. As soon as I got up every morning, I had to get milk, tea powder and sugar: right from salt, every expense, even my husband's personal expenses were paid from my earnings.

After all these difficulties, my husband's first wife's parents filed a court case complaining about his second marriage. During this time, I had to go to the courts with him. The courts ruled that his first wife's parents had not informed him that she was mentally sick and he did not have a job or income so he could not support her; then the legal notices stopped coming to our house.

At that time, I did not know how to carry on my life. I was very disappointed. I had two daughters, half of my earnings were spent on my husband's drinking and *beedi* (local cigarette), and the remaining half was for food and the children's education expenses, which was not enough. Later, I had my third child, a boy. At that time, I was selected as a tailoring teacher for other women. As I could earn as well as train others, I agreed to this. Then I felt a little satisfaction. I trained women for 8 months. Later, more and more people in the village turned towards me and gave me clothes to stitch and my earnings improved.

I wake up at 5 o clock, clean the house, wash the vessels, store water, cook, feed the children, get them ready and send them to school. Then I stitch from 10 am to 2 pm and have lunch by 3 pm and wash clothes. After 4 pm I train other girls; 3 to 4 girls come for training each day and I earn a fee of Rs 50 ($1) per month from them. When I train them, I also stitch some clothes. Like this, I earn about Rs 100 ($2) per day. I pay for vegetables, fruits, milk, sugar, tea powder, rice, everything. I have to do all the work, right from bringing salt to the house. I spend for the fees of children, for festivals and for school uniforms of children. I give money to my husband for his petty expenses and drinking.

I find it very difficult to get the children ready for school, cook for them, give them food, wash clothes and utensils and after finishing all this, sit down to stitch. If I do not work even for a day, the children will starve. My husband does not take up any responsibility, he does not earn anything. He does not have a job. He knows electrical work but gets some work only once in while and the money he earns is not even enough for his petty expenses. Earlier, he used to get some work from the village but now he does not take up that either. After taking all the responsibility of the household, if I talk in a loud voice, he does not say anything at that time but later he drinks and hits me. If I say that I will not stitch clothes and do any work he fights even more. I allow my husband to do whatever he likes to do.

The responsibility to earn and do all the work is mine, but the 'name' goes to the husband. If there is a man in the house, then villagers consider him to be the head of the family.

For money, Sushila depended on her tailoring skill and a small business, both of which, along with child care, occupied all her time. In 2005, her monthly earning was Rs 3,081 ($68), for a five-member household.

The first bank loan was taken by her husband in 1999 for equipment to repair pump sets. She explained:

> The loan of Rs 10,000 ($222) was sanctioned by Canara Bank Koppal, but only Rs 8,000 ($178) were given to us. The bank manager asked me to make a Fixed Deposit of Rs 2,000 ($44) in the bank. This will be returned to us, with interest, when the full loan is repaid. We have three years to repay the loan. I have repaid Rs 1,700 ($38) over the past two years.

Sushila did not repay the bank loan, did not take further loans till 2004, when she took a loan from the group to buy two goats and expanded her stock to five goats by November 2005.

Sushila was once poor and isolated, with three young children, and subject to domestic violence from an alcoholic husband. Becoming a member of the SHG helped to build her confidence, develop leadership qualities and challenge her husband. She could take risks and diversify her business to earn more for her family.

> Five years back we did not have food security and we used to have only one meal per day. Now I am able to earn more and give my children two meals per day, and clothes. All these changes happened because of my becoming a member in an SHG. After the formation of the group I was able to get the loan and expand the business. Not only the business, but my confidence also increased to such an extent that now I am able to say no to my husband when he demands money for liquor.
>
> I am able to fulfil my dream of giving a good education to my children. I am sending my son to school and paying Rs 50 ($1.11) per month for tuition. I do this so that he can get admitted in the *Navodaya School*,[22] which provides high quality education and also free boarding till 10th standard.
>
> Another good thing that happened during the last five years is that I did not get pregnant, because I decided to have the family planning operation. So I now have time to do businesses (tailoring and selling cosmetics).
>
> Overall, during the last five years my tailoring has improved, my confidence levels increased and my children are studying well. These are all the things that motivate me to work hard and live in this world.

The turnaround in her life arose from NGO support for improving her tailoring and embroidery skills, and using these for income generation. She now has three sewing machines, on which she trains 10 girls and earns Rs 600 ($13.33) per month. She teaches tailoring at Sampark for 6 months and earns Rs 1,500 ($33.33) per month. Sewing orders from customers are many. She saves Rs 20 ($0.44) per week in her group, and Rs 50 ($1.11) per month in the post office. Since May 2007, she has also started monthly saving of Rs 250 ($5.55) with a jewellery shop, intending to buy gold for her elder daughter.

She said:

> I borrowed from the group to repair my house. I covered the open space in front of my house with a tin sheet overhead and black stone on the floor. Now it looks much bigger! I bought a cupboard to keep clothes and important materials. Earlier I used to borrow even to manage living expenses, now I do not take much loan; if at all I need money I borrow from the group. I have no loans due to anyone except to the group.
>
> My husband was not serious enough to support my family. I took loan from the bank, provided him with equipment, still he did not earn well. The Electricity Board offered him a contract job at Rs 1500 ($33.33) per month, for which I paid a deposit of Rs 500 ($11.11): he went to work only for 3 days! Now he is unemployed again.
>
> I am happy because I am educating all my children, and they are studying well. My eldest daughter is now in the 10th class. I had sent her to my parents' home, who looked after her education, clothes and food. But now, for the past two years, I have sent the money to cover all her expenses. I am thinking of sending my son to a private residential school. I am capable of providing good education to all my children.

The Story of Sangavva

Sangavva's household of five included herself (42 years), her mother (55 years), two sons (22 and 18 years) and daughter-in-law (17 years). The elder son and daughter-in-law did *coolie* work, while the younger son studied in secondary school. She had 0.5 acre of land, along with others of her caste, and they had a common borewell for irrigating this land. She could grow two crops per year, of *jowar*, onion, chillies, groundnut and cotton. She kept *jowar* and chillies for home consumption and sold the other crops. She has one house and one small plot of land (the former is in her father's and latter in her name); the walls of the house are made from stones and mud, and the roof with wood and mud. The mud floor is polished with cow dung. The house has a kitchen, a hall and a bathroom and a thatched room to tie cattle.

Sangavva was dedicated as a *devadasi* at the age of 12, as her elder sister had been married, her mother was pregnant and her father died at that time. Her first partner stayed only a month, and she made a second partnership after a few months, with a man of the same *Kuruba* community, which has lasted several years. Her second partner is called *goudar* because he has some land and a house. He queried her expenses every month, and met any shortfall.

Sangavva said about this relationship:

> I was made a devadasi to light my house, like that he needed someone to light his home, so he married. His wife spoke with me earlier, even after she came to know the relation between him and me, but later other people told her 'you are his wife and she is a basavi, why are you talking to her?', so she stopped talking to me. Now they have shifted their family to his wife's village, which is close to the city, he can do business better, and they are managing to live a good life in that place.

Sangavva has two sons, both were delivered by her mother who is a midwife. After having two sons, she had a tubectomy done at the government hospital in Koppal.

> Both my mother and partner wanted me to wait for a female baby, but I did not listen to them. I have the experience of being a woman that is enough; it should not come to my child, so after two boys I did the operation. Of course even if I had a female child, now there is no problem as the *devadasi* system has gone and I could have got her married. Yet, she would have had the identity that she is my daughter, *basavi*'s daughter, so I just took a strong decision I would not even try for a female child.

Sangavva's health has been good; she had two normal deliveries, no abortions or child deaths, and has not had major illnesses other than cold, fever and occasional headaches.

Sangavva's relationship with her partner has been like that of a husband and wife. He took her to Koppal for shopping, watching movies, to the hospital and for festivals to nearby towns and villages. He also visited her relatives and maintained a good relationship with them. Her children like him too.

> *Goudar* first stayed with me, only later he got married, so he has affection for me and my children. He always looked after me, he never fought with me or beat me. But he doubts me a lot; if I talk to anyone else he gets suspicious.[23] If I have even ten rupees extra with me, he asks where did it come from, who gave me? Once we went to Chukkankal village with him to see his sister and her son, and on the way back we bought provisions. Then I requested that we watch a movie in Koppal, we did that, and stayed the night at a relative's place, and next morning he had very little money left, so I gave him Rs 50 ($1.11). He started fighting, who gave you this money. I told him I had saved it from the money he had given me. 'If I tell you I saved, you will not give me money, and then what will I do in an emergency, so I save and keep some money with me,' I told him.
>
> How can he leave me? Earlier he used to come once in 4 to 8 days, now he comes once in 15 days. My son has got married, I have a daughter-in-law at home, so he does not come so often.

Sangavva dislikes the life of a *devadasi*, and feels sad when men insult *devadasi*s by making offers of casual sexual relationships.

Sangavva has worked on land since she grew up and can also rear cows. When she was young, she cared for the younger children at home when her mother went out for labour work. She grazed the goats too. Villagers did not allow her to do labour work before she was 10 years old, fearing that she would work properly; she went for farm labour since she was 13 years old.

Her elder son was a bonded labourer with a farmer for 6 years. She explained:

> They did not pay him wages, just food and clothes, and three lambs every year. They added one lamb each year, so in the last year of work there he got seven lambs. We used to rear those lambs, and sell them from time to time; I used that money for the marriage of my sons. Now my sons go for *coolie* and sometimes my mother goes too. My daughter-in-law has gone to her mother's place for delivery. Women's wages, from morning till afternoon, are Rs 12 ($0.26) and men get Rs 20 ($0.44) for working till 6 pm. We get *coolie* work for about seven to eight months a year, about four to five days a week.

Her annual income was Rs 37,489 ($833) or Rs 7,498 ($167) per person in the household, providing a better standard of living than the other *devadasi*s households discussed earlier, for example, Lakshmavva.

Several years ago in 1999, she had applied for a loan of Rs 5,000 ($111) to purchase a buffalo under the IRDP scheme, whereby 50 per cent of the loan was subsidised, and the loan was repayable without interest over 2 years. Of the loan amount of Rs 2,500 ($56), she received Rs 2,000 ($44) and Rs 1,000 ($22) of the subsidy amount, leaving Rs 2,000 ($22) kept by the middleman. She bought a buffalo for Rs 1,500 ($33) and spent the rest on household needs. She kept the buffalo for 6 months, and because it could not calf, sold it for Rs 600 ($13), again using the money for household expenses. She has not yet repaid the bank, which sent her a notice, and an officer visited her to claim that if she repaid, she would then be eligible to take another loan, which she doubted, claiming: 'Yes, it may be true that if I repay they will give me another loan, but I don't have the money to repay; maybe if my son is able to repay then he will.'

She bought seeds and fertilisers on loan from the local trader and repaid the loan before making the next purchase. She explained her reluctance thus:

> Earlier my mother used to take the responsibility of the house, but now she is unable to travel to town, and I have to do so. My responsibility is to tell my children to go to work, to ensure provisions for the house, to decide upon what to get or not, and see to the consequences. Earlier, my mother used to take the responsibility and I was just cooking, going to *coolie* work and going to our farm. Now I take the responsibility of marketing the crops, getting fertilisers and manure, clothes and shop in the shandy. If there is money in hand, we can give and take easily, but now there is no rain and no *coolie*. It is difficult to maintain my responsibility, and I have to take debt to maintain my family in such situations. Responsibilities mean a hundred and eight worries.

She perceived loans as *debts*, and said: 'When we don't have *coolie* work, when there is some health problem, for household purposes and when we have to travel, we take loans.'

She did, however, take loans from the group. She explained:

> I took three loans in a period of two years, twice to meet household expenses and once to pay the examination fees for my son. The interest rate in the group is low, and when we face problems we can discuss it, and can repay it in instalments, this is the benefit of the group; if we take loan from 'outsiders' we have to pay the principal all at one time and the interest is also high.

In 2001, she did not have any assets, but by November 2005, she had two cows, one calf, five goats and six kids. She bought cartloads of white *jowar* hay and bundles of green hay for the cattle. The cows provided little milk, less than a litre per day, which was kept for home consumption, as was the goat milk. The goats were periodically sold to meet household or medical needs; the rates varied from Rs 800 to 1,500 ($17–33) depending on their weight. While building her house, she sold four goats.

By 2007, Sangavva's livelihood improved significantly. Her sons, now young men, are a source of support and strength. The elder son goes to Koppal town to work on construction sites and earns Rs 110 ($2) per day. He is married and has two young children. Sangavva competed for the Gram Sabha seat, was elected, and is now a member of the *gram panchayat*. She now engages with accessing official schemes for villagers and recommends beneficiaries. As she is completely illiterate, her younger son, who has studied till pre-university, assists her in making visits and doing the paper work needed, and even attending the *Panchayat* meetings along with her. His bride is still too young and is with her parents. Sangavva is perceived as a good and active leader by her community.

Sufficiency and Prosperity

The Story of Rangamma

Rangamma lives in Bahadurbandi village, and belongs to '*marata*' caste, which is one of the backward castes, but not among the SCs.[24] The first two families from this caste came and settled down in Bahadurbandi many years ago (she does not remember how many), at present there are 12 families belonging to this caste in the village. Rangamma belongs to a village Yatnati in a nearby district of Bellary. She got married at the age of 12 to Mailliarappa. When she was newly married, she lived with her parents-in-law in a joint family, which was also shared by two of her husband; brothers and their families. At that time, he had a hotel in the village and did not work on land. When the joint family was divided, this earning was not sufficient for them. Rangamma went for agricultural labour work regularly during this time, and she also received support from her parents by way of rice, *jowar*, chillies, onions and other provisions. She feels that those were the most difficult days; they are much better off now.

In 2001, Rangamma had a household comprising 10 people, with seven earning members pro-viding the household with an average monthly income of Rs 7,881 ($175). The family had 2 acres of land, in two 1-acre pieces, and both the husband and wife worked on the land, but it did not provide enough produce to meet even food needs as the couple had six children. In 1985, as

Rangamma intended starting dairying, her parents gifted her a cow. When the cow had a calf and she could sell the milk, she was prepared to buy another head of cattle. At this time, in 1986–87, she took her first loan from a bank, of Rs 1,500 ($33), which she repaid ahead of time, and got a subsidy of Rs 400 ($8.8). She maintained her cow and buffalo well, which provided three calves, and she sold the buffalo for Rs 1,500 ($33). In this way, she managed to go to the dairy for over 12 years, and the herd grew to seven cows and four buffaloes by 1998. She used to make buttermilk and ghee,[25] go to Koppal town and sell milk and milk products every day. It was from this income that she met the expenses for the marriages of her two daughters and the children's education. Eventually, she grew tired, as she had to travel long distances to collect fodder and as the children grew, they became reluctant to take the cattle to graze *en route* to school, or fetch water and fodder. Her daughters married and left home, one son failed in secondary school, then took up construction work, and others too did not help with cattle care. She gifted five cows to her relatives, and sold all but one. In 2001, her elder daughter's husband faced a serious financial crisis, there were quarrels in their house and he threatened to commit suicide. Instead, her daughter consumed poison, was admitted to the government hospital and Rangamma spent Rs 1,000 ($22) to save her. Now she visits Rangamma's home frequently.

Next she started a hotel in the village, but once again she was tired of being left alone, and cooking and cleaning. Her husband, who used to help her, took up the responsibility of building a temple for their village community; Rangamma fell ill, and closed the hotel. From 2002 onwards, the family erects a food stall during the *deepavali* festival in November each year, and earns Rs 1,500 ($33) to Rs 2,000 ($44) per day, making a profit of Rs 6,000 ($133) during this 1 week.

After joining the SHG, she first took a loan of Rs 1,000 ($22) for meeting expenses of a festival and buying gifts for relatives and another of Rs 2,000 ($44) for construction of her house. At the same time, she also took a loan of Rs 5,000 ($111) for setting up a provision shop for her husband. This loan was taken through the group and was offered by a microfinance institution (MFI) through the NGO. She repaid this loan fully and took another of Rs 5,000 ($111) from the same MFI for house construction. She used a chit fund[26] of Rs 5,000 ($111) for house construction. She also took a short-term loan of Rs 5,000 ($111) from the group, to run a food business during the *deepavali* festival. Her son took a loan of Rs 3,000 ($67) from his employer to fund house construction. The second son, Gururaja, earned Rs 70 ($1.55) per day as a construction worker, the third son migrated out for a week at a time for construction work and the fourth son worked as a driver in a police officer's home. The former two contributed Rs 200–300 ($4.44–6.66) weekly and sometimes brought home mutton or provisions, while the youngest son brought Rs 2,000 ($44) to Rs 3,000 ($67) a year to the household. Rangamma's loan history highlights the fact of her having different sources of income, from the earnings of her sons, from savings made earlier by the household (in the chit fund) and from other businesses. These multiple sources provided her with the ability to borrow continuously from different sources. Her experience with banks and other formal sources was also positive. Her orientation towards taking loans was to return them as quickly as possible, and therefore she was able to take several loans for investing in assets and income generating activities (IGAs).

By 2008, the family has two homes in Koppal, of which one is constructed with assistance from a government programme, the Indira Awas Yojana, as Rangamma's husband managed to secure a BPL (below the poverty line) card for the family. Rangamma has also bought land in Koppal town.

Her daughter, a child widow, is employed in a home in Delhi and plans to start a shop in Koppal in near future, after which she plans to marry again. Rangamma had requested Sampark to find a place for her to work outside Koppal, and her husband supported this, so that now they feel ready to take on objections from their community in case the girl marries again. The youngest son is also married, and Rangamma is contented, except for the loss of her eldest son.

The Story of Kaveri

In 2003 Kaveri belonged to a relatively rich household from the dominant *Reddy* caste, with a good base of human capital, and an economically active father-in-law, husband and two younger brothers-in-law. The family cultivated 14 acres of land (owned 11 acres and leased three) of which five were irrigated, so they could grow crops for sale as well as home consumption. They had two buffaloes and two calves, too bulls and a dog. The entire milk produce of 3 litres a day was consumed at home. Her father-in-law managed the lands the cattle and all family income. Her husband was the vice chairman of the village *panchayat*, had a groundnut trading business and managed household finances along with his father, but was rarely at home. His younger brother worked on the lands and cared for cattle, and the youngest brother worked in a seed company, earning a salary of Rs 2,500 ($56), of which he spent Rs 500 ($11) on bus fares and contributed the rest to the family. Kaveri calculated the household's monthly income as Rs 9,108 ($202), which was probably an underestimation, as she did not know the full earnings of her father-in-law and husband.

Kaveri was encouraged by her family to contest the *panchayat* elections. Kaveri was already a member of a SHG, and once she decided to stand for elections, she approached her own group and other group members and leaders. At this time, the NGO was engaged in promoting women's leadership, and had several meetings of group leaders. With the help of some of the active leaders, she met all the groups in her own village and in other villagers, promising them support from government schemes, tractor-loads of fodder for their cattle, and so on. The women leaders and members of groups actively canvassed for her in the villages. The *Reddy* population in some of the villages is large, and her husband also organised canvassing among men through village youth. Women and youth campaigned in the villages for her, and she became a leader at the *taluk panchayat*.

When Kaveri first got elected, she did not know how the *panchayat* functions. However, she soon developed confidence, came to know of different schemes, how the benefits are allotted and the rules and regulations. Her personality changed, she learnt to fight for getting schemes and learnt to earn as well.

She knew that government benefits are provided to those who are BPL. She formed a group of BPL women, and included two of her family members who were not poor. The government made a new rule that 20 per cent members of an SHG selected for subsidised loans may be above the poverty line, so Kaveri exploited this provision fully by forming SHGs of BPL women, and enrolling herself and her relatives or friends as the BPL members so they could avail of the subsidies. Someone advised her to start a Mahila Mandal as the government was providing money to these, so she registered one, but later found it difficult to manage. She changed her party three times, in an attempt to become the president of the *taluk panchayat*, but she lost every time.

Initially, when Kaveri became a leader at *panchayat* level, she wanted to be honest. She took a list of all the below poverty line (BPL) people in the villages in her *taluk*, and prepared a list for the government benefits to be sanctioned to them. However, her husband cancelled the entire list, and prepared another, with names of people who would give him a bribe. He insisted that he sees the lists. He was a *gram panchayat* member, and she was member of the *taluk panchayat*, so he could, technically, only change the names in the village list. As this resulted in conflicts in the family, Kaveri gave in to her husband. He makes the list and collects the bribes.

As a result, Kaveri said she now found politics very 'boring', meaning quite frustrating, as she says, 'no one will let me do what I want to do'. Here, she refers to two forces to which she has lost. At *panchayat* level she is able to argue and learn about how to get schemes allotted, but not able to take a leadership position. Then again, at home, she is not able to play her leadership role as her family decides (husband and father-in-law) who should get the benefits of these schemes. She has relinquished control to her husband and engages herself in caring for the children and other household chores.

In the initial period of leadership, Kaveri did manage to do some good work, even within these constraints. She got houses for poor women, and also got an *ashram* (home) made for poor women who were homeless. She ensured that no houses were sanctioned to those who had plots in the name of their husbands or sons, but only those who were really homeless. She participated in discussions to select teachers for the local school, and in giving scholarships to disabled students. She asked for a building for a crèche for children and a library, for which government funds are likely to be sanctioned. The water from the water tank of the village was wasted and did not have proper drainage, she got this made. She also got a sign-board made for the local school. Sometimes, she paid for these things on her own and recovered from the government at a later date.

The SC/ST Corporation sanctioned several schemes for the poor in these castes. Assistance was given for the construction of three farm ponds for rain water conservation, a buffalo was gifted to some houses, one borewell and pump-set were sanctioned and one person was allotted a land of 1 acre. A tailoring scheme has been sanctioned for her village. She is one of the members of the committee for selection of beneficiaries; the selected women will be trained for 6 months and then given sewing machines. Another scheme is sanctioned for the construction of a platform with stones, and a drainage scheme. Three people will be selected for training in computer education by the government.

Kaveri knows and learns the criteria of sanctioning these schemes well. However, she is rarely able to select according to these criteria. Usually, her husband takes her list and changes it according to the people he wishes to oblige. When the houses are constructed, he leases them out to others. This has led to many an argument between her and her husband. She has now stopped preparing the list of beneficiaries; he prepares the list and takes her signature. She signs without questioning him. She realises that she is not in a position to answer the questions of those who elected her.

She cried and said that:

> It is impossible to help people. It simply leads to a fight at home. My life was much better before becoming a member of the taluk *panchayat*. After getting into politics, life has become 'boring'. Although they give

33 percent seats to women, this is only on paper, if I try to come forward, the same men who brought me forward try to push me down, and that is the reason that women do not come forward. I feel very bad, if I try to make myself heard the men do not let me.

I cannot even note the expenses and income of the household. If I ask my husband anything, he shouts saying you are not the one to go and buy things so why do you want to know. I have now stopped asking and I just cook whatever is there and serve him, and if he takes me anywhere I go with him, then come back and care for the children. I also feel bad to speak anything inside the home.

Even with all this frustration, Kaveri has ensured that she is able to earn some money on her own. She is a sales agent for a company selling household products/utensils (through a chain system), and as she has done good sales, she has got a mobile phone and some jewellery as an incentive. She also handles some money as a *panchayat* leader and has cash in hand. The women who voted for her are quite disappointed, they see her as corrupt and ineffective, and also believe that sometimes she is not beyond adopting the tactics of her husband, so that she has some money in her own hands.

When she first became a leader, Kaveri was a novice in government, but later, she learnt how the various government schemes operated, and thus became a part of the system. Her progress can be seen in Figure 4.5.

Kaveri took three loans of Rs 1,000 ($22) each from the group, to meet household expenses. When the group got its first bank loan, she took Rs 4,000 ($89) for a poultry unit for her brother-in-law. From the next bank loan to the group, she borrowed Rs 5,000 ($111) for a retail shop, which supplemented a loan of Rs 50,000 ($1,111) that her husband took to open the shop. All these loans were from Tungabhadra Grameen Bank (TGB) and unsubsidised. She wanted to take the next loan to construct a shed for sericulture.

Over time, as her experience as a *panchayat* leader grew, she realised that only 80 per cent of the members of an SHG needed to be BPL to benefit from subsidised schemes, so she left her own group, and formed another with 17 SC women, and two relatives. She then obtained a subsidised loan sanctioned for this group, and when the loan was fully repaid, the group hoped to get a grant that the members would divide among themselves. While Kaveri and her two relatives utilised the loans from the bank, others were expected to benefit from the subsidy later. She promoted and joined five SHGs, and saved Rs 7,540 ($168) in these. She took loans of Rs 8,500 ($189) from these groups, and her share in the subsidy of each.

She started a business of vermicomposting, after being trained by Sampark, and eventually constructed a permanent pit for composting. In 2007, she had sales of Rs 13,000 ($29) through the Department of Agriculture. Government officers invited her as trainer on vermicomposting, accounts maintenance and SHG management to other villages, for which she was paid an honorarium. She felt she had acquired knowledge of official schemes and accounts maintenance.

Kaveri had three life insurance policies, one with a premium of Rs 10,000 ($222) for 3 years, another with a half-yearly premium of Rs 1,500 ($33) and a third with a premium of Rs 35,000 ($778). She bought a mobile phone, table fan, food processor, electric stove and 30 gm of gold jewels. She bought one piece of land in her village and another in Koppal. She was proud that all these assets were created with her own earnings.

Figure 4.5

Dramatic Change in Condition and Position

Year	
1999 (before SHG)	• Housewife; looked after children and household work
	• Husband worked as a partner; good income and very few loans
	• Kaveri did not go out of the home often
2000	• She benefited from SHG, through loans and leadership
	• She took loans for household consumption from the SHG
	• She became a leader, participated in politics (*panchayat*)
	• She started contributing to household income
	• She had to follow directions of her husband, about decisions in the *panchayat*
	• She aspired for better school education for her children
2001	• The family purchased land in Koppal
2002	• Economic change at home, increased earnings
	• Increased visibility due to political involvement
	• Husband started trading business through bank and group loan
2003	• Her brother-in-law left his job, reducing family income, then tried agriculture and failed
	• Main responsibility of the joint household fell on her husband, who incurred losses in trading business
	• Her contribution was 20% of the household income, and she was well recognised by other family members for her efforts
	• Yet, she did not know all the income sources of her husband, father-in-law and brother-in-law
2004	• She gained the capacity and confidence to take larger loans (over Rs 15,000 [$333]) at 2–3% interest from external sources
2005	• She wanted to reinvest in the trading business and get back money lost by her husband
	• She did not want to stand for *Panchayat* elections any more, but aspired for a seat in the State Legislative Assembly
2006	• She left the Sampark-initiated group and formed and joined another BPL group, where she could access government schemes and personally benefit from subsidies
2007	• She felt that the experience in the SHG and later as a politician had given her new entrepreneurial skills

Source: Authors.

Kaveri reported many changes in her life over the past 7 years. As she gained experience as a leader, Kaveri became more ambitious and corrupt, using her position in the *taluk panchayat* to secure resources for the village, but also recommended the non-poor for benefits intended just for the poor alone, and her husband also took commissions from those included in the list of people she recommended. She was able to use the credit and support from the group to set up a business to build up both financial and human capital. She attributed her rise to her exposure to the SHG and credit, but more importantly to politics and the awareness and opportunities that her leadership position opened up for her.

The Story of Mariyamma

Mariyamma belongs to the *Kuruba* caste, who were traditionally shepherds, rearing sheep and goats. Her mother's home was in Bikanhalli and her father's house in Raghunathahalli. Mariyamma was the eldest of five children. She was married at the age of 16 to Siddappa, her mother's brother had came to settle in Bikanhalli, which was also her mother's parental village. Mariyamma is 32 years old and Siddappa 37 (he looks older, but in the village there is a tendency to state that the husband is about 5 years older than the wife). She has a daughter, 14 years old, who studies in Class 8.

Mariyamma experienced major livelihoods changes in the recent years. After marriage, she first lived in a joint family with her husband and his three brothers; they had 18 acres of land and three houses. When they separated from the family 8 years ago, her husband Sidappa got *rathikuli*, the family granary, which was built on a 20 × 30-feet plot. The land was divided according to its quality. There were 6 acres of black soil, of which each brother got 2 acres. From another plot of 4 acres of black soil, they received 1 acre each. In addition, Mariyamma and Siddappa have leased 3 acres of land, so they farmed a total of 8 acres. During the year 2002–03, they constructed a new house on land purchased several years ago.

Mariyamma achieved asset creation by building a new house, digging a borewell for irrigation and purchasing bullocks for agriculture. The assets were financed through various loans from groups, relatives, moneylenders and banks. She explained:

> One major change in my life in the last five years is that I constructed a new house which is big and comfortable enough for both my family and animals to live. I was happy that I could make this big house. After my family separated from the joint family, the household expenses reduced and we were able to save money to spend on the construction of the new house.
>
> Last year I borrowed from several people, like my relatives, my husband's friends and from the group, for house construction. The loan from the group helped me to buy seeds and fertilisers in time.

She thought the turnaround in their life came due to the separation from the joint family, continued access to land and the borewell that enabled an increase in agricultural income. Mariyamma's major income sources were outside loans (60 per cent), agriculture (32 per cent) and animal husbandry (5 per cent). The major expense items were house construction (44 per cent), agriculture (20 per cent), household expenses (15 per cent), travel/transportation (9 per cent) and loan repayment (6 per cent).

The next major project was the building of her home, clearly linking availing outside loans and house construction. Mariyamma also used loans for agriculture and loan repayment. The main sources for meeting the household expenses were incomes derived from agriculture and animal husbandry. The annual income of the household was Rs 96,353 ($2,141), an average of Rs 32,117 ($714) per member. As she had 8 acres of both dry and irrigated land and was growing commercial crops, they were able to generate 32 per cent of the family income from agri-culture. Out of this amount, 80 per cent was from the wetland and from the sale of cash crops such as onion, chillies, cotton and groundnut. The other 20 per cent was from the dry land which produced mostly food crops. Except for the months of September, March and May, when she took 'outside' loans, she got income from agricultural work. There were various reasons why Mariyamma was able to generate a decent and regular income from agriculture. First, she has enough land and could procure irrigation facilities through loans. Her farming strategy is to grow multiple crops every season. She also possesses the ability to travel outside and sell the produce. The most significant of these factors was the availability of a loan that enabled her to sink a borewell and thus ensure irrigation. She said:

> Because we now have a borewell, we can grow two to three crops a year and our income has increased. We don't have any difficulties in the family anymore. If we were not to have this borewell we would have to go to others' farms for work. Now we appoint labour on our field and we work mostly in our land.

In 2006, she took a loan of Rs 10,000 ($222) for agriculture from a commercial MFI, repaid it in weekly instalments of Rs 230 ($5) each, and as she felt that it was very expensive, she did not take the next loan from this source.

Mariyamma has very close relations with her parents. They visit her regularly and she goes over about 10 times a year. Her daughter visits the grandparents once a month. Mariyamma has regular contact with her sisters too. They care for one another and if one of them is ill, one or another accompanies her to the doctor. Mariyamma's father comes to her house often and on these visits participates in the work that is to be done around the house or farm.

Mariyamma leaves Bikanhalli quite often. She goes to the flourmill, to Raghunathahalli to visit her parents, to relatives in other villages where she and Siddappa have relatives and to a village nearby or Koppal for using the bank, buying provisions, jewellery and materials for the house, watching movies and consulting the doctor. She also goes to the water tank to wash clothes, and to fetch hay and fuel wood.

The gender relations within Mariyamma's home are equitable as she has a say in the decision making about agriculture, financial and non-financial matters, enjoys freedom of mobility and has access and control over cash. Her husband works hard and does not drink or waste money in any other way. She is satisfied with her life, looks forward to owning more land and most of all looks forward to educating her daughter well. They will first let her study as much as she wishes to and then think of getting her married.

In 2007, Mariyamma reflected:

> There are no major changes in my life for the past three years. We had a loan of Rs 85,000 ($1889) when we completed our new house, which we have repaid over the years, and now only Rs 15,000 ($333) remains

to be paid. We borrowed for agriculture, but there has been no rain for the past two years, so we still have to repay Rs 6,000 ($133) to the *dhalali* (private lender) and Rs 1,000 ($22) to the group. This year rains have been good and we hope to get some surplus from agriculture.

Lack of rains meant no earning, so most members could not bring savings and stopped coming to group meetings. So all of us decided to share the savings and interest collected so far. Each got Rs 1700 ($38) of savings, and Rs 1504 ($33) by interest earning, I adjusted my loan dues against this. Those who wanted to continue, and some new members have now joined together, and we have a new group. This is now 7 months old and has just started giving loans. We have decided to have only monthly meetings, not weekly or fortnightly, and save Rs 50 ($1) per month.

I supported my daughter to study as much as she would like. She failed in the 10th class, and now after two more attempts she has not been able to pass the exams. Now we are considering marrying her next year to my brother, her maternal uncle.

Linking Assets, Income/Expenditure and Loan Use

The life and loan histories of women show that livelihoods are critically dependent on the level, quality and types of assets that each woman's household possessed, especially landholding, number of people in the household and cattle-holding.

Lakshmavva and Nagavva are the poorest women, with precarious livelihoods, and can barely meet daily family food requirements. Shivavva and Parvathamma just manage to survive. Shivavva is landless, but has six family members with regular *coolie* income, while her younger son migrates for fishing to coastal areas and brings or sends lump sums of money to meet household expenses. Parvathamma has 0.5 acre of land, but it is often uncultivable, and she manages her expenses from the money contributed from her son's salary and her partner's contributions.

Rangamma, Mariyamma and Kaveri are relatively prosperous, with average monthly incomes of Rs 7,881 ($175), 8,029 ($178) and 9,108 ($202), respectively. Mariyamma and Kaveri have large landholdings, with up to 3 acres of irrigated land and 6–12 acres of rain-fed land. In both cases, agricultural income forms much of the family's income. In addition, both Kaveri and her husband hold positions at the *taluk* and *gram panchayat* levels.

Landholding

The size and quality of landholding is a major livelihoods determinant, and is also associated with caste and inheritance. The landless women, Shivavva, Nagavva and Lakshmavva are completely dependent upon unskilled *coolie* work. Six research participants have land varying between 0.5 to a maximum of 3 acres of irrigated land and 0.5–12 acres of dry land. Irrespective of the size of their land holdings, women

> *None of my relatives have helped me. In fact, I give them jumpers (blouses) as gifts when they come to visit me. When my children were married, I didn't even borrow 10 paise from anyone. As they are independent and earn themselves these days, I have stopped going out to do coolie work. But there is one thing—devadasis must have children—only then can they live. Otherwise, they might have to resort to begging.*
> —Yellamma

plan the cropping pattern to ensure foodgrains for household consumption and also commercial crops. This gives them money to purchase other items like clothes, detergents and meet the medical and travel expenses. Agricultural incomes are subject to significant seasonal variation and also depend on the type of land, and all 16 women of the Gallidurgamma group, Hosagondabala (Yellamma and Shivavva's group), belong to the *Madar* (SC) community, and depend on *coolie*. They have 2 acres of government land for each household to rehabilitate, but the lands are flooded from the Tungabhadra dam for up to 8 months a year. In the remaining months, they grow pulses and groundnut. The difference between the yields on dry land and irrigated land depend on several factors like the amount and distribution of rainfall, cropping pattern, incidence of pests, technical management and human labour invested, as shown in Chapter 4 under the section titled 'Precarious Livelihood, Low Loan-taking Ability'.

Cattle Assets

Those with more cattle holding are able to earn more by selling milk, the animals or manure. Smaller animals such as sheep and goats help meet intermittent needs for emergency cash. When animals are ill, non-productive or have died, the household loses both current and future incomes.

Human Capital

The size of the household is an important determinant of household income. Though there is no correspondence between age and earning, those with most earning members can bring higher *coolie* incomes. They can utilise their own labour to save expenditures (for example, labour for own land or building own house). When the family is educated or skilled in some trade, they can take up activities like tailoring (Sushila), driving, trading, jobs that provide salaries (Rangamma, Kaveri) or earn migratory income as in the case of uneducated youth (Shivavva). Even if a household with more members has a lower average income per person, just living together produces economies. In addition, joint families are valued by the women as a source of integration and shared responsibility.

Personal health is critical for determining the earning of the landless, who depend on *coolie* income. Women, particularly *devadasi*s, face health problems including backache, poor eyesight, leg pain, headache, body pain, white discharge and stomach ache. Shivavva's husband had a leg injury, which did not improve for 3 months, after which he died, and her daughter-in-law suffered from tuberculosis. Rangamma's son suffered from chronic stomach ache and anaemia and died (having contracted Human Immunodeficiency Virus/Acquired Immune Deficiency Syndrome). Sushila's 12-year-old daughter had an undiagnosed brain tumour left untreated for over 4 years. Parvathamma had chronic low

Most of my income this year was spent on medical treatment. First I spent Rs 5,000 ($111) on the treatment of my husband in Hospet, for a wound inside his stomach. Then I spent Rs 4,000 ($89) on the treatment of my grand-daughter for a tumour in the neck; she is now cured.
—Shivavva

abdominal pain since child birth, which prevented her from working. She not only suffered physically but also faced stress and humiliation as villagers alluded to her *devadasi* 'profession' as the reason for her illness. Most women, especially *devadasi*s had undergone the family planning operation between the age of 20 and 30 years, despite objections from their partners or parents. These women were the primary income earners for their families and returned to work within a week of delivery. When women and their family members fell ill, they could not earn and medical expenses further drained their incomes, but larger households could pay for the medical expenses. Thus, human capital, seen in terms of number of members, age-profiles, education and health, determines the household's ability to earn, thereby also the capacity to take and return loans.

The average standard of living is critically dependent on the level and types of assets held. The three most important assets identified here were human beings, land and money. In one validation meeting, the group discussed the relative importance of these different types of capital. Even after much discussion, women did not rank them, claiming that they needed both labour and money to cultivate land, and even if one resource was scarce, it too would affect livelihoods. When asked: 'Would you not put money first, could you not manage everything else if you had money?', they replied: 'No. We cannot eat money. Finally we need to eat rice and dal, which comes only from land and labour; money is needed to cultivate.' The diagram they drew is presented in Figure 4.6.

Figure 4.6
Women's Livelihoods Assets

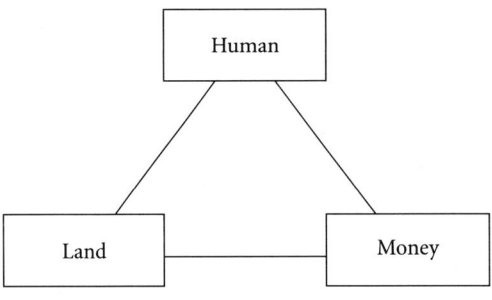

Source: Authors.

The initial asset base determines the expenditures a household could afford, that is, the livelihoods level. The poorer households are short of cash, and therefore have a lower capacity to repay credit. Women with low levels of assets and incomes frequently take small loans to smoothen their household consumption. These loans are usually of Rs 250–300 ($4.44–6.66), taken from the landlord quite regularly, and repaid with farm labour.

Women with higher incomes take relatively larger loans (between Rs 2,000 and 40,000 [$44–889]) often used for asset creation, such as borewells, trading shop and house construction, and crop loans (usually less than Rs 2,000 [$44]) for investment in agriculture. When all types of capital are taken into consideration, the total has to offer a surplus—in terms of a family member's time, cash from an income stream or the possibility of sale of an asset—for women to be able to absorb credit and to enable further capital creation to take place.

The analysis of assets, income and expenses, and loan histories shows that at the individual/household level of impact, the first set of constraints are the economic ones, related to lack of capabilities (literacy, vocational skills), and assets (land and other assets). These create a vicious cycle that keeps the poor deprived, despite outside efforts to break it through income earning activities and assets. The poorest women do not have the capacity to absorb credit. After gaining insight into the capacity for credit absorption, the analysis now moves to a discussion of the perceptions of women and their experiences in use of money from different sources.

ANALYSING SOURCES AND USES OF MONEY

Analysis of the sources of loans, whether formal or informal, has been made on the premise that use and impact of loans may be significantly influenced by the source of money, which in turn influences the terms of lending (cost, repayment period and instalments). The social relationships of women with different lenders influence the give and take of money in a critical way. The use of loans not only depends upon the level of women's own livelihoods and their capital base but is also related to how it is first accessed. The sources of loans have been considered in three broad categories: formal, informal and loans from SHGs, as depicted in Figure 4.7.

Figure 4.7
Spectrum of Loan Sources

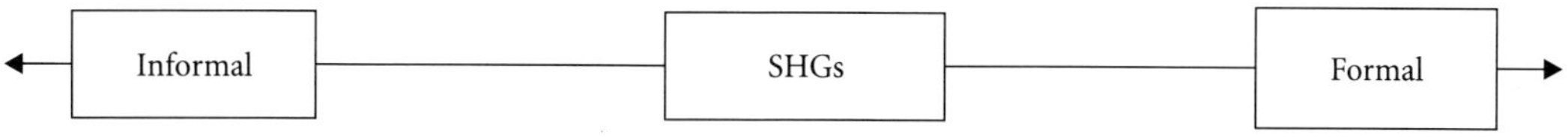

Source: Authors.

Informal sources include friends, neighbours, relatives, local provision shops, local agricultural input traders, local landlords and moneylenders. Formal sources include banks and NGOs MFIs, who offer subsidised or commercial credit. Loans from groups, that is, from women's own savings, comprise a source that may be characterised simultaneously as both formal and informal. The SHG is an informal forum, in that it is an unregistered and unregulated financial institution. However, to the extent that it is initiated, organised and monitored by NGOs, and also maintains books of accounts, which is critical for linkages with formal banking institutions, it also takes on the characteristics of a formal forum.

The loans from different sources each had different characteristics, which are now investigated further.

Informal Loan Sources

These can be clearly delineated into three categories, and money transactions with these three 'actor groups' are based on different socio-cultural relationships and value systems. The first category includes friends and neighbours who provide soft loans. The second category includes local provision shops and agricultural input traders who provided goods/inputs on credit, wherein the cost of credit (that is, interest rate) is ostensibly zero but is possibly subsumed in the cost of the commodity supplied. The third category includes moneylenders and landlords who provide loans on stringent and even usurious terms.

Parvathamma had taken two loans of Rs 5,000 ($111) and Rs 2,000 ($44) from the landlord and a third loan from the group, at 3 per cent per month. She paid the loan from the landlord through *coolie* work on his farm. She explained the repayment patterns:

> I do not get paid for *coolie* work every day. If four days of *coolie* wages are due, i.e. Rs 15 ($0.33) per day, a total of Rs 60 ($1.33), the landlord deducts Rs 10 ($0.22) and gives me Rs 50 ($1.11), with which I buy 2 kilos of rice, vegetables, jowar, and other provisions for a week. It can take me two years to repay a loan in this manner. As there are three or four persons at home who can do *coolie* work, we can manage the household expenses and the loan repayments. When all four of us get *coolie* work, I ask the landlord to adjust my full wages against the loan. We can use two people's wages for household expenses and two people's wages for repaying the loans. Two of us work for the same landlord, but another two work for different ones, so we can take two or three loans at the same time. I prefer to pay off smaller amounts first and then repay the larger loans. I also repay the interest from time to time on unpaid loans, so that the interest does not accumulate.

She had taken these loans in 2001; by 2004, she had repaid all loans to landlords, and had only the group loan to repay. Her management of the loans and their repayments showed how she maintained the financial relations with each lender, through a combination of partial and sequential repayments, along with balancing her household expenses through the overall cash inflows. Other women in the SHGs have similar ways of managing informal loans.

Table 4.1 provides the details of loans from the three categories of informal loan providers, that is, the amount of loan, its use and cost and repayment terms and conditions.

Informal loans are taken to meet household consumption needs. The amounts are small, returned in short periods to friends or neighbours, and no interest is charged. Regular credit transactions with shops include taking provisions and agricultural inputs, and when an earlier loan is repaid, eligibility for further loans is created. Loans from friends and relatives are mostly benign and arise from mutual reciprocity. Regular credit arrangements with provision shops and agri-input traders are regarded as 'no-cost' transactions as no interest is charged. Provisions are provided at the same price, whether on cash or credit, as village shopkeepers consider small credit to be a normal part of sales transactions. However, there is some ambiguity for input traders whereby the cost of credit can be included in the prices of inputs supplied.

Loan relationships with landlords reflect a wide spectrum of features, from mutual dependency to exploitation, as depicted in Figure 4.8. For instance, Lakshmavva and Nagavva borrowed money regularly from their respective landlords for household expenses. Credit from the farmer landlord,

Table 4.1
Informal Loan Sources

Source	Amount: Small <500 ($11); Medium 500–2,000 ($11–45); Large >2000 ($45)	Use	Terms and Conditions
Friends/Neighbours	Small	Emergency/immediate cash needs	Short term/no interest repayment
Relatives	Large (for high-income women)	House construction	With or without interest, flexible/fixed repayment
Local provision shop	Small	Provisions	Repayable before next purchase, no interest charged
Local agri-input traders	Large	Fertilisers, pesticides, seeds	Repayable before next purchase, interest nil or included in price charged
Local landlords	Small	Household consumption	Repayable through own labour or bonded labour of children
	Large	Marriages	
Local moneylenders	Small	Household consumption	High interest (10–15% per month), assets hypothecated
	Large	Marriages	

Source: Authors.

when pledged with labour work, creates a situation wherein he can have labour available when demand is high. On the other hand, the borrower women are assured of labour work in the lean season, even if they do not get paid market rate wages. Another perceived benefit is that the loan against future labour is given without interest. There are also other seemingly benign features to this relationship. The landlord gave Yellamma lambs to rear, in lieu of keeping her son as a bonded labourer on his farm each year. She reared these as if they were her own. Yet, the position was ambiguous, as the asset still belonged to her landlord, who had to be consulted in case of sale to share the proceeds. The landlord also gifted her with a cow after his mother died, and any donations he was required to make as part of religious ceremonies were always given to her. Yellamma used the word 'adopt' with respect to the landlord's relationship with her household. There appeared to be two different understandings working at the same time: that of 'bonded' labour where they felt constrained and tied to the landlord and of 'adoption' where the farmer in fact committed to provide them with *coolie* work and support them. These may be seen as mirror concepts, working at the same time with the same person.

From a market perspective, an agreement to work for a particular landlord may constitute a 'promise of preference' on either side, and an arrangement that contains market forces, which in the agricultural season would mean higher labour cost for the landlord and in the lean season would mean loss of wage labour for the woman. However, these relationships are rarely analysed in such terms, and women do not calculate any opportunity cost in terms such as higher wages. The social embeddedness of these exchanges in caste and religious rituals thus overshadows their simple economic/feudal nature.

Figure 4.8
Nature of Relationship with Landlord

'Exploitative' relationships	'Adoptive' or 'benign' relationships
Bonded labour of children Loss of ornaments, land, animals Fixed wage rates, not increased as market wage changes No opportunity for additional earning	Gift of lambs each year of work with landlord Gift of cows in case of death in landlord's family Fodder/grains/vegetables given sometimes with wage payments Permitted to graze their goats/sheep in employer's land

Source: Authors.

Women do pay a high cost for credit from their landlords. Small loans, usually around Rs 250–300 ($5.55–6.66) as in the cases of Lakshmavva and Nagavva, could be repaid through labour. Even though the financial interest cost is ostensibly minimal, it is often invisible rather than zero, as wage rates considered in lieu of adjusting loans are rarely discussed between borrowers and lenders. A longer term labour commitment is required for larger loans, and when Yellamma and Shivavva's sons had to be committed to bonded labour between 5 and 6 years in order to pay off a loan of Rs 40,000 ($889), there was little discussion of the boys' wage rate as such. Such loans were not taken for *investment in productive assets* like a cow or a small business, but to fulfil immediate consumption needs or other social obligations. From the formal lender's point of view, such social expenditure does not generate any income stream. For many women, however, there is considerable social pressure. They fear that their children may not otherwise find a partner if they do not spend on the marriage. This indicates the limits of these feudal relationships where loans to maintain the 'bonded' or 'adopted' families only prevail on prohibitive terms. Indeed, there were no observed cases of women taking loans for productive assets from local sources on such terms.[27] Confirmation of high cost credit at 36–72 per cent interest per annum, especially for medical treatment and weddings, which creates debt and labour bondage is also found in recent studies.[28]

Short- and medium-term loans of varying size are also taken from moneylenders. Moneylenders provide credit on stringent conditions, higher interest rates, often an asset for security (jewels, vessels, animal and land), even if this security has higher value than the loan. Many require that repayment be made in one single instalment, and if loans are not paid in time, they can confiscate the asset concerned. In this case, there is no ambiguity; moneylenders are regarded as high cost sources of credit, with a risk of loss of hypothecated assets. The reasons cited in literature for local moneylenders charging high interest rates are varied. The financial logic emphasises that in addition to the transaction costs, the risk in lending to the poor is high, especially in ecologically strained areas. The structural rationale emphasises the low bargaining power of the poor and regards moneylenders as high cost and exploitative suppliers of finance.

The findings from Koppal confirm that most of the projects and enterprises that poor borrowers in semi-arid areas can invest in carry high risk of failure. High interest costs combine with other more serious implications of taking loans from local moneylenders and landlords. Those who borrower from moneylenders risk losing their assets (land, animals, jewellery, vessels). Moreover, if the transactions are not in money but other factors (for example, labour), it can create labour bondage (of adults and children, as seen in the case of Shivavva and Yellamma) which deprives the women of the freedom to use their family's labour for better earning possibilities. By contrast, those who have significant assets are able to not only raise loans but are also able to improve the quality of human assets in the household, for example, children could afford to go to school. Thus, the actuality of Koppal represents the financial logic of risk in lending to poor households on the one hand, and also bears out the socially embedded exploitative aspect of rural money lending on the other. This is also borne out by emerging research in other contexts, where money gifts and other reciprocity are seen to conceal the hierarchical nature of social relationships.[29]

Formal Loan Sources

This falls into three different categories: the experience with banks for subsidised loans and that with banks and MFIs for non-subsidised loans, as shown in Figure 4.9.

Figure 4.9
Spectrum of Formal Sources

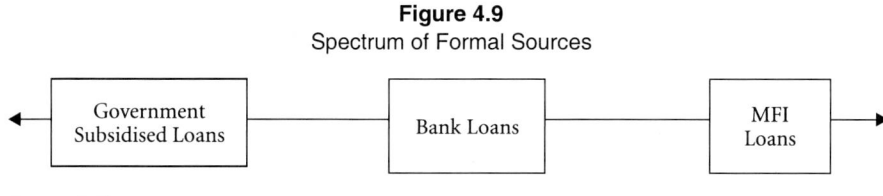

Source: Authors.

At one end are loans provided by banks under government schemes which target the poor and carry a 50 per cent subsidy on loans. Unsubsidised loans by banks carry low interest, being repayable over 3 years, but are not linked to government schemes and carry no subsidy on the repayment of principal. At the other end of the spectrum are loans provided by MFIs on commercial terms, that is, 24 per cent interest, and a 1-year repayment period.

Government-subsidised Loans

In 1998–99, official norms required that banks lend money at subsidised rates to those women who belonged to households below poverty line (BPL) families. Three case study participants had availed subsidised loans before 1999. Nagavva and Sangavva had experiences with the bank that involved giving bribes for taking these subsidised loans. In 1999, when Sangavva took a subsidised IRDP loan, a part of the subsidy was used for bribes; she used part to buy a buffalo and spent the rest on household needs. This buffalo did not yield any calf or milk and seller had apparently cheated her.

She had no income from the buffalo, sold it and used the money for household needs. The total amount of Rs 2,500 ($56) stands as overdue in her name. Nagavva who got a similar amount, could also not repay the money due to insufficient earnings, as explained earlier.

Eligibility for officially subsidised schemes (that is, the BPL card) is often purchased, and households with more information and linkages accessed the schemes best. Further, the assets financed through these loans are purchased from vendors appointed by the middlemen/bankers/government officers and are not of the quality that the women might have bought, if they had purchased the animals themselves. Nagavva and Sangavva did not pay back the loans to the bank. Many women among the 120 SHGs managed by Sampark shared this experience. In several group discussions, women related their experiences with IRDP-subsidised bank loans as involving bribes, low quality of assets purchased by bank-appointed agents, low net additions to income and also frequent defaults on loan repayments. Yet again, later, when banks became more flexible about the purpose of the loan, many women continued to mis-state the purpose of the loan, for instance, when they showed a neighbour's cow instead of their own. Thus, mis-statement and non-repayment of loans with official subsidies has now become a pattern.

Rangamma, however, had a positive experience. The banker, who offered her a loan for a buffalo, asked her to repay the full amount and only then would she qualify for a subsidy. The banker visited her regularly, maintained a good, respectful relationship with her and provided her the guidance she needed to utilise and repay a formal loan. When she repaid well, he gave her the benefit of the subsidy. Rangamma got this loan at a time when she needed to sustain a family of four young children. She expanded the animal stock to six buffalos from this one loan. She had a positive experience of the continued relationship of support, and duly paid her loans.

In 2000, the government merged all the credit programmes under its integrated rural development scheme, the SGSY, and government-subsidised credit thereafter was channelled through women's groups (NABARD 1999). Banks and Regional Rural Banks (RRBs) provided subsidised credit to SHGs only under the SGSY scheme, wherein the government subsidised the loan to the extent of 50 per cent. The SHGs now had to qualify on the BPL criterion for a subsidised loan. This meant that at least 80 per cent members had to be on the BPL list, while two or three could be non-poor. Sometimes NGOs and politicians used the provisions of government schemes to take the grants for themselves, as illustrated in Chapter 3, in the case where an NGO helped a local landlord to form an SHG with his bonded labourers and appropriate government grants and credit. There was also evidence of this from Kaveri, who left her original group, formed a group of SC/STs and ensured that she and her two relatives were members of this new group, so that they could benefit from the subsidised loans for SC/ST people. In the SHGs covered in the study, two groups of SC women received loans under SGSY scheme. The controls exercised by banks and government officers created the combined effect of unproductive assets and high debts for the women as in the case of Durgadevi group. This group in Mudhaballi had only eight members, and another *devadasi* group in the same street had seven members, but the bank needed to support a group with at least 12 members, so the two groups made a joint representation to the bank through Sampark. They were to receive credit, subsidised to the extent of 50 per cent under the SGSY scheme. The loan was to be provided by the bank (State Bank of Hyderabad, which was also the lead bank of the district), and the subsidy by the government organisation.

The women wanted to buy buffaloes with this loan, but they had very small huts, with no shelter for the animals, so they requested the *panchayat,* and obtained sanction for a common shed to keep all the animals. These same women had earlier protested against a liquor shop in the village and had got it removed. This was viewed as an affront against the general castes who owned the liquor shops. So when the SC women needed land for cattle near their homes, the village leaders (from the general castes) refused, and allotted space outside the village, a good 10-minute walk from their homes, which made cattle care difficult. Further, the bankers and government officials did not permit them to buy animals of their own choice from the local area (those would have been more acclimatised and sturdier), insisting that they buy from an outside market instead. The women wanted to buy the animals in September, when there was abundance of green fodder, but the credit was delayed until December, when there was no green fodder left. The bank and government officials went on an appointed day, to an animal-fair where the broker and technical officer had links, certified the animals and bought them. It was only after Sampark's intervention that these women were allowed to accompany them, and influence the selection of animals and their price. When the animals finally arrived, they were found to yield lesser quantities of milk as compared to local breeds. Fodder had to be brought in cart loads from outside the village, at more cost. The animals were sick after relocation and five died. To these women, the animals had to be cared for like family members, hence women lost wages on days they stayed home to do so.

The officials responsible for constructing the shed exceeded the allotted expenditure and in collusion with bank officers booked these costs to the group loan. When the women came to know this, they asserted:

> If we had been allowed to make the shed where we had wanted to, we would have made it to suit our needs, at lower cost, and would have saved the money paid for bringing the fodder. Now, with high costs, low yields, and loss of *coolie* as well, we are not able to pay back the loan to the bank.

They wrote a letter to the bank and government offices, but did not receive a reply from either, and therefore stopped repayments. In such an impasse, the women were listed as defaulters, while the government and bank officers were not held accountable. Moreover, the bank was suspicious of giving loans to the next few SHGs in the village, and other SHGs recommended by the NGO, thereby negatively affecting other women's groups.

This highlights that the subsidised credit scheme was not implemented as originally intended. There were other interesting differences between the original intention of the scheme and actual loan disbursement, repayment and subsidy disbursement practices. The official intention of the scheme is to provide assets to poor families, in units that would provide significant and continuous income streams to pull the household out of poverty. The total loan eligibility for an individual was Rs 25,000 ($556), to enable each household to purchase two cows or buffaloes, so at least one could always provide milk, and increased cash inflows, which would allow for regular loan repayments. In fact, banks only released half of this money: 'the loan portion', releasing 'the subsidy portion' after the loan was fully repaid. Bankers used this method to ensure that the loan would be repaid. They covered their risks in two ways: first, they released only half of the loan, which effectively meant that they only released the money that came as inflow from the government, the grant portion. So in effect, there was no net loan extended by the bank, its loans were fully repaid from the time they were extended! This is also known as a 'back to back subsidy'. Second, the practice of releasing only the loan and holding back the subsidy ostensibly created an incentive for the borrowers to repay; stating that the subsidy would be released after the loan was fully repaid.[30] The original intention of supporting poor households with significant asset building was thus thwarted. Local NGO staff also endorsed the bankers' position, believing that many women first needed to manage one buffalo before acquiring another. The field project manager of Sampark said: 'We are convinced about this strategy because it ensures that the group members will utilise the loan well, and repay it. They will be responsible. There is a risk of misuse if amounts released are too large. And anyway people make their own adjustments.'

The Gallidurgamma group in Yatinatti village had certainly made adjustments. On learning about the Durgadevi group in Mudhaballi, they decided to change. Both the loan and the grant were provided by the SC/ST Corporation, and the women negotiated to take all decisions related to asset purchases. When the Corporation released Rs 15,000 ($333) each for eight BPL women (a total sum of Rs 120,000 or $2,664), the group distributed the money among 13 women. They decided where to purchase the buffaloes from and contacted a veterinarian for insurance purposes. They spent Rs 100,000 ($2,222) and saved Rs 20,000 ($444) for joint purchase of fodder. Two buffaloes died, the insurance was invoked and loan amounts were adjusted. One woman claimed that her buffalo had to be sold so she bought another, which was not yet yielding milk, so she had not started loan repayment. Three other members lacked enough cash for regular repayments. Yet, members collected money whenever women could repay, and the group made regular repayments to the Bank. By allowing such flexibility, the group could make independent decisions, and keep its commitment to repay, even though some individual members faced problems with the assets and income-flows.

A third group of eight in Hosagondabala, Yellamma's group, from among SCs received a loan of Rs 80,000 ($1,778). This was a part of a government scheme, whereby, when the loan was fully repaid, the group would get an equal amount, Rs 80,000 ($1,778) as a grant. (The SGSY scheme is further explained later.) With this loan, four women bought a buffalo each, one a bullock, one bought goats and two women leased land for cultivation. They repaid the bank regularly, usually from wages, and also took short-term loans from local sources so as not to default. The group discussed how to use any subsidy received, as they were likely to use it as revolving fund, or for a collective business. This group, too, was able to use the flexibility to its advantage.

In cases where only part of the groups had BPL cards despite similar income levels, women combined two groups, and took the loan on the names of members with BPL cards and divided the total loan equally. This ingenuity of the groups enabled them to share benefits of external linkages in a more equitable manner, even though the administrative system had anomalies through which such distribution of benefits was not possible. These cases also demonstrate an ability to use innovative strategies to ensure equity, while at the same time fulfilling external conditions for taking loans. When they could exercise control and flexibility over money, they could sustain the group's 'joint liability' character.

Of all the 33 loans taken by the participants and their group members from banks under subsidised schemes, 14 had good repayments, while 19 remained partially or entirely overdue. An analysis of why people did not repay is given in Table 4.2.

Table 4.2
Analysis of Subsidy Loan Defaults

Reason for Non-payment / Women	One-time and not Continuing Relationship	No Link between Repayment of Old Loan and Access to New Loan	Unproductive Investment
Lakshmavva and 14 others	☑ Misunderstanding with banks, government	☑	
Sushila	☑ One-time contact	☑	☑
Yellamma	☑ Bribe paid	☑	☑
Sangavva	☑ Bribe paid	☑	
Mariyamma	☑ One-time contact	☑	

Source: Authors.

When the demand for loans arises from the women, they plan the expenditure, and apply the money to the purpose intended. By contrast, when subsidised loans are 'given', or 'allocated'; they are a windfall and not planned expenditure, and the purpose and application of the money is decided only after the official sanction is conveyed to the women. Therefore, it is rarely applied well, as it is often an unplanned expenditure. Repayment is influenced by both the interest and follow-up by the bankers. When there is a relationship of trust with the banker/corporation, women repay. When people pay bribes to benefit, they consider the bribe a payment for having received the benefit, hence does not care about repayments. In most cases, it is a one-time contact of a transactional nature, between the woman (or her mediator or husband) and the banker/corporation, with no prior relationship with the bank or one formed as a result of this transaction. As subsidised loans are given as part of targeted programmes mandated by the government, they are in fact one-time transactions and banks do not intend to have continuing loan relationships with these debtors. Where the debtors do not perceive the possibility of new credit following the repayment of the old loan they have no incentive to repay. The analysis suggests that labelling of non-repayers as 'defaulters' needs to be questioned. Non-repayment does not imply that women who do not pay the loans have less integrity or less ability to pay or that their investment has failed. No relationships of trust are created and therefore integrity does not come into play, or is even subverted/suppressed by rent-seeking practices of middle-men, bank and government officials. However, even when banks relax some procedures and permit application of loans according to women's own preferences, women do not purchase the asset declared, and a pattern of mistrust is thus confirmed.

Unsubsidised Bank Loan

In the middle of the spectrum of the types of formal loans (Figure 4.9) are unsubsidised loans offered by the RRB in Koppal, the TGB.[31] Typically, these carried an interest rate of 12 per cent per annum and a repayment period of 1–3 years. TGB extended a new loan when the first one was repaid; thereby creating a client relationship that was based on good financial conduct and trust, as illustrated by the experience of Kaveri's SHG, discussed earlier in this chapter.

The Hemareddy Mallamma SHG in Chukkankal was formed in 1999 with 11 members. Its first loan was Rs 12,000 ($267) from TGB. Four members used it for agriculture and business. The group guaranteed the loan, paid interest of 12.5 per cent per annum to the bank, but the four women paid at 24 per cent per annum, thereby creating interest for the group. The women repaid the loan in 10 months instead of the 12 months permitted, which also reduced borrowing costs. The bank then loaned Rs 27,000 ($600), which was used by another four members of the group. This loan was also fully paid and the bank sanctioned a third loan of Rs 50,000 ($1,111). The total savings of the group came to Rs 24,140 ($536), from which they had given loans of Rs 30,800 ($684) with their cumulative interest earning being Rs 12,396 ($275). Even though members could not save regularly, the group still made profits due to the inter-loaning transactions and the margin earned on the bank loan. In the same way, Rangamma's group, the Kasturibai SHG got a loan of Rs 20,000 ($444) from TGB on the same terms, which was also fully repaid on time. Several groups in the village received loans from TGB without subsidy. Two groups got Rs 10,000 ($222) each: one group divided Rs 1,200 ($27) each among eight members and another group divided Rs 1,000 ($22) each among 10 members. They bought one sheep each. The groups paid back these loans in 6 months. They levied interest at 12.5 per cent, which was the interest paid to the bank, and decided not to keep a margin for the group, to make individual profits. The women not only repaid these to the bank but also earned a profit margin for the group or individuals. This resulted in increased sizes of subsequent loans and successful repayments, creating benefits for the banks as well as the SHGs.

While only two of the seven research groups received such loans in 2003, by March 2005 all seven raised a total of Rs 0.157 million ($3,489) from the local RRB, TGB/PGB, of which Rs 0.153 million ($3,400) was repaid by August 2006. Further, in 2003, only 10 of the 120 SHGs promoted by Sampark received loans, but by 2005, a total of 42 groups received unsubsidised loans. The SHGs indeed learnt from each other and started to give loans first to BPL members, with the rest of the group members guaranteeing repayment. Once loans were fully paid, and subsidy received, the group would retain it as revolving loan to be shared by all members, ensuring that benefits were equitably distributed among all. This practice slowly spread to all the villages covered by Sampark, with minor variations from group to group. Only one bank in Koppal *taluk* was able to create such a relationship; all 42 loans given to Sampark groups were by TGB. The other banks in the district continued to follow a targeted approach and loans to SHGs were limited to those mandated under subsidised schemes. Thus, though the RRB realised the market potential of lending to the poor, other banks were slow to offer regular credit and establish client relationships with SHGs.

Unsubsidised MFI Loans

Here, one MFI offered unsecured loans to individuals at an interest rate of 24 per cent (flat) per annum and repayment period of 1 year. Eight women from two SHGs, the Kasturibai SHG and the

Durgadevi SHG opted to take this loan of Rs 5,000 ($111) per woman. The loans were utilised for petty shops, agriculture and purchase of a buffalo and were fully repaid. Overall, among groups managed by Sampark, a total of 120 women opted for loans from the first MFI, The Bridge Foundation (TBF). Another MFI required and charged a higher effective interest rate, and therefore was not utilised at all.

Group Savings Loans

This research analyses savings of groups as an important source of funds for women, and how groups manage and perceive financial transactions from their own savings. This analysis is elaborated in Chapter 5, along with a discussion of group learning processes.

Summary

Traditional microfinance tracks the use of money from an institutional standpoint. This research takes a longitudinal perspective and discusses the major changes in women's lives. The women first described the changes and then identified the factors that they considered critical to these changes, their livelihood and their position in the household or the wider community. Credit just forms one factor among many that can effect positive change in women's livelihoods. Other factors include support from partners, improved skills, access to leadership positions and public resources and family size. There were also women who had limited benefit from microfinance, and some who had none of these possibilities and did not improve their livelihoods significantly during the study period, especially those who had low social positions and asset levels.

FACTORS AFFECTING USE OF MONEY

The loans taken by SHGs in a particular microfinance programme operated by an NGO/MFI depend on several factors. These include demand and supply factors, which are not necessarily in equilibrium. The discussion of factors affecting use of money is also accompanied by the terms women use for money and how they classify it. Women refer to money as *rupai*, a common term for money, as when they say '*nanage ondhu savira rupai sala kodi*', meaning 'give me a loan of Rs 1,000 ($22)'. They use *duddu* and *hana* for household transactions between family members, when they want to buy something, or check with another if they have money. These two words refer to small transactions, for example, coins/notes used for daily needs. The word *rokka* refers to large amounts of money, for example: '*avaralli hechhu rokka ithhu*', meaning 'he has lot of money', or '*hechhu rokka beku*': 'I need a lot of money'. The word *sampattu* refers to sources and assets, and also for money kept in the bank, fixed deposits and jewels. Thus, there exist words in the local language that signify amounts of money, and these words are also related to specific uses of money. Such labelling is evidence of the different meanings that women assign to money, depending on the way it is offered.

Relationship Lending

Informal loans can be classified into three different types. The first—from friends, neighbours and relatives—is the most important and is often provided as interest-free loans. On some loans, however, interest is paid even to these sources. The amounts vary from small to large, Rs 100–40,000 ($2.22–889) and the purposes vary from household consumption and social expenses to agriculture and housing; the repayment period is often flexible. Size and purpose depend upon ability to borrow, and ability of peers to lend. Therefore, the income earning impact of these loans tends to be limited. The second source is the local provisional shops and agriculture input traders. Any loans from them are taken mainly in the form of commodities purchased on credit. These loans are normally repayable before the next purchase, and interest is often included in the price of commodities. These are perceived as normal commercial transactions and have the effect of easing cash flows of the borrowers. Women normally used the word 'Kaigada' for any money or commodity borrowed from friends, family members and relatives. For instance, if 2 kg of *jowar* is borrowed from a neighbour, the same has to be returned, or if Rs 500 ($11.11) is borrowed from a relative, the money has to be returned. The term literally means: hand loan. 'Mungada' is cash advance taken without interest.

The last source of loans includes the local landlords and moneylenders. They often provide credit either on hypothecation of physical assets or on human labour, including bonded labour of children and women. Clearly, these intend to be limited to the borrowing capacity of the women in terms of their holding of physical or human assets. Women perceive these loans to be the most potentially exploitative. They refer to loans given against security of land, jewels, and so on, for a limited period and with high interest, as 'vathi sala', with a clear understanding that if the loan is not paid in time, the 'vathi', or security, would be taken instead of the amount repayable. However, when landlords give gifts to poor families, these blur the perception of the exploitative aspects of the feudal relationships, as women do not fully control the assets so gifted.

Formal loans are also classified into three types: those subsidised by government, unsubsidised bank loans and loans provided through an NGO/MFI. Government-subsidised loans are given only to families qualifying through being BPL. Prior to 1999, individuals were targeted, whereas after 2000 such loans were extended to women SHGs. An analysis of loans from different formal sources to SHGs is done through a consolidation as in Table 4.3.

The findings show that inefficiency and corruption in purchase of assets led to non-repayment. Even though corruption persists in the allocation of the poverty certification, innovative group processes enable poor women to access these loans. By contrast, when the bank provides unsubsidised loans, it does so with apparent recognition of the groups' repayment capacities. The relationship

Table 4.3
Loans from Different Formal Sources (August 2003)

Formal Sources	Banks, Subsidised Loans	RRB (TGB), Unsubsidised Loans	MFI, Commercial Loans	Loans from SHGs
Number of Women	30	18	8	70
Total loan taken, Rs	150,000	59,000	40,000	130,772
	(3,333)	(1,311)	(889)	(2,906)
Repayment record	Poor	Good	Good	Variable

Source: Authors.

that the bank has with the group is that of a service provider. Such loans are found to be paid back in time and sometimes ahead of time. The third type is unsubsidised and from MFI/NGO often with an interest rate of 24 per cent per month and the repayment schedules extending over a year. The processes are more transparent and the relationship is one of equality; however, the terms of these loans are often too stringent for the women to be able to use them. Production in the semi-arid region of Koppal is problematic, and the women are not confident of repaying, so many of them do not opt to take these, more costly, loans.

Sala is the common term used for loans. The women classify three different types of *sala* from formal sources:

1. *Dheerga avadhi sala*—Long-term loan: This is the bank loan given for a period of 4–5 years and repaid in half-yearly instalments, for example, loan for housing, tractor, pump-set, and so on.
2. *Madhyama avadhi sala*—Medium-term loan: refers to borrowing either from a bank or from moneylenders, for a 1- or 2-year period, to be repaid in half-yearly instalments, for example, loans for crops, business, marriage, borewells, and so on.
3. *Finance sala*—Short-term loan: refers to all loans repayable within 1 year and in monthly instalments. People also refer to loans from their SHGs, SHG-bank loans as *finance sala*.

While women prefer the first two, they do not opt for *finance sala* when it is offered on high interest rates.

Demand-related Factors

There are several demand-related factors that influenced women's loan use.

Potential to Take and Repay

If there are many earning members within the family, this provides cash inflows from which the loan instalments can be paid. For instance, a son who has gone out on migration may have access to lump sums of money, which enable the family members in the village to raise loans for an asset. Women consider household capability for cash generation and the needs and capacities of all members of the household, before availing loans, thereby ensuring that use of loans is a household decision.

> *I always remind my children about loan so they try to give their maximum earning to me, otherwise they spend a lot and contribute less to the family. Even my children are concerned about a loan burden. So we take a loan only after a discussion in the family, so that everybody takes the responsibility to repay it.*
> —Rangamma

Purpose

As seen earlier, there are risks associated with investments. Agriculture, for example, carries many uncertainties, and few off-farm opportunities exist for investments that suit the skills of women and their family members. This limits the productive use of credit in this semi-arid region where ecological risks form a definitive constraint to credit off-take. Another mismatch in demand and supply of credit comes from the conditionality of the purpose for which credit is available from formal sources. While women needed the money for household consumption and medical treatment, the credit available in the research area was 'buffalo loans', the only subsidised scheme offered by the IRDP/SGSY prior to 2005.

Loans are also needed to pay off earlier debts. Nagavva's parents asked her cousin and suitor to pay these if he wished to marry her, and he migrated to be able to do so. In this case, indebtedness was a reason for migration, but was also used to separate the two cousins, and retain parental control over their daughter. Thus, the stories also highlight the way money is used to control intimate relationships.

Seasonality and Repayment Schedules

Women prefered to take loans only when they actually needed it, while external agencies interpreted money kept in groups as 'idle funds' during the periods when loan demand was low. The credit off-take is not the same throughout the year. The need for funds varied, and the inflows were seasonal too. Productive credit, usually taken for agriculture and animal husbandry, which have a cyclical nature of earning, demands credit products where repayments are synchronised with the cash generation cycle of the project. Instead, commercial microfinance practice is stringent and expects uniform repayment, as evidenced by their providing loan 3 months late to the Durgadevi group, depriving them of the benefit of green fodder and making the asset more expensive. Thus, many poor women prefer productive credit terms that matched their seasonal cash inflows.

The practice instituted in commercial microfinance, of weekly or monthly repayment instalments, is ostensibly based on the premise that poor women would find it easier to repay small amounts in regular instalments, than find large lump sums at one time. Women's preferences are not so clear. In some situations, they got regular deductions made by the landlord from their weekly wages, as in the case of Yellamma. Yet, they also refused to take loans from TBF on these terms, and explained: 'It is not convenient to repay the landlord and the external loan at the same time. We prefer to repay first one loan fully and then repay another.' The preference to repay one loan first as compared to another is also influenced by the possibility of taking the next loan, by the terms of that loan, especially the interest cost, and whether any labour bondage is attached to the loan.

Cost of Credit

One of the most contentious issues in the microfinance debate is about the interest rate charged on loans. The government introduced low-cost bank credit and subsidies as an alternative to money-lenders soon after independence. Yet, the development sector today offers high-cost credit to the poor. This raises major questions about how, if at all, such credit is an improvement over that of-fered by moneylenders, and whether it is even more exploitative as it comes in the garb of poverty reducing credit.

It is often assumed that poor people need access to credit and that cost of credit is not a con-sideration. Microfinance specialists judge the prevalence of high rates of interest (5–10 per cent per month) in rural areas to be evidence of high demand for credit.[32] Rosenberg claimed that no one could point out a single example of a 'microfinance programme that ran into trouble by driving away clients with interest rates that were too high' (1996: 10).

This research does not support the argument of the financial systems approach that the poor can pay very high rates of interest. The experience of the NGO in Koppal is that when credit is offered at a rate of 2 per cent per month, combined with uniform repayment instalments spread over a year, the poor do not take loans. Poor women take credit for income generation only if they can find good local opportunities for investment, the profitability from the new investment covers the cost of credit, the resulting cash flows permit adherence to externally demanded repayment schedules, and if the risk of delay or default is thought to be low. By contrast, they take loans for household consumption and social needs, even at high costs, from lenders with whom they have long-standing relationships and where there is possibility of repeat loans.

Mismatch of Demand and Supply

We find that women do need productive credit to improve their livelihoods and the credit is needed on terms compatible with the ability of the poor to repay. The demand for loans depends on the perception of risk and opportunities available and terms of supply of credit. Women prefer the repayments to be linked to cash flows generated through the project in which the new loan would be invested. The agencies that supply credit often do not see these risks as they are perceived by others. From their own perspective, they prefer regular and high loan off-take, so that the microfinance project can break even. This was witnessed in the credit models in Bihar and Koppal. Women rejected the loan products that did not factor in the seasonality of their cash flows. Over the period 2005–07, two private MFIs started operations in Koppal. Initially, they attracted some women, but over time women did not take these loans, the Koppal operations of these MFIs did not break even, and they closed shop. This confirms that in dry regions with few economic options, high-cost credit can only be taken by a few, it is difficult to build scale based on high cost commercial credit. This created a demand and supply mismatch.

Microfinance supply is depicted across a continuum of offers, ranging from subsidised to commercial credit, as depicted earlier in Figure 4.9. Subsidised credit in Koppal was limited and offered only under government programmes. Banks provided subsidised credit only to the minimum number of groups that they were required to cover under these targeted programmes. Further, the number of such groups targeted was low compared to the number of groups formed in the district, resulting in inadequate coverage of the poor; therefore, subsidised credit was limited in scale and ridden with inefficiencies as well as other problems like corruption. At the other end of the spectrum of loan possibilities was commercial microfinance, which was offered on terms that women could not afford, given their initially low levels of income and therefore low capacity to pay, and the lack of investment opportunities in the region. The middle range of the spectrum represented the huge market that was created by having women's groups as clients who provided risk coverage as well as cost reductions for the supplier institutions. TGB recognised women's SHGs as a potential market and extended credit to them based on a continuing relationship. The credit was offered on terms that were beneficial to the women, and the fact of good repayments enhanced the sustainability of the bank. The constraints to expansion of such unsubsidised credit in this spectrum were inherent in the government's Service Area Approach,[33] whereby each bank was supposed to service one specific geographical area, usually comprising a few *blocks* in a district. Banks responsible for particular service areas were not always as forthcoming as RRBs and continued their conservative approach, denying normal credit to SHGs. Thus, the supply constraint was overcome only in the service area of the RRB in Koppal, while it continued to persist in those areas serviced by private and conventional banks.

Thus, the amount of loan taken by individuals and groups depends upon several factors, and perceptions of these are different from the point of view of commercial microfinance practices. This is explained in Table 4.4.

Women consider the risks of taking loans from external sources to be high; at the same time, MFIs perceive a high risk in lending to the poor, on terms different from those of commercial microfinance.

Thus, an apparent paradox emerges whereby the credit needs of poor women are unmet by the formal banking system as it is currently organised, while commercial credit offered through NGO/MFIs is at terms that women do not opt to utilise. The mismatch is related to the following aspects:

1. Lack of loans for consumption purposes.
2. Inadequate loans from the banking sector.
3. Incompatibility of terms of commercial microfinance with needs of women in semi-arid regions.

Thus, while unmet demand for credit exists, the 'financial products' available are not suited to women's needs and preferences, thus indicating a gap between what would meet women's livelihoods

Table 4.4

Factors and Perceptions Related to Value of Loan Taken

	Women's Own Perspective	*Commercial Financial Perspective*
Seasonality	Take loan when needed, and repay when cash is surplus	Matching of cash inflows and outflows important for sustainability; therefore, seek uniform flows
Project/enterprise	Agriculture is risky in semi-arid, and few income earning opportunities exist in non-farm sector	Semi-arid and remote regions become high cost regions and therefore not attractive for commercial microfinance
Initial capital base/capacity to pay	Those with higher asset base, steady income flows have higher capacity to pay	Focus on poor gets diluted, services reach the 'economically active poor' instead
Repayment terms	Women prefer 3-year repayment terms and balloon repayments, or quarterly instalments	Preference for weekly or monthly and uniform repayments, of equal instalments
Cost of credit	Preference for 12–24%	Pegged at 24–48% effective rates
Source of credit	Preference for 'own' sources, that is, savings first. Both NGO and banks/MFIs viewed as 'external' sources	Savings viewed as source of finance for the MFI, and women's preference for 'own' sources not recognised or respected, even feared

Source: Authors.

needs and the microfinance that is actually on offer in the rural informal or formal markets. This underscores the importance of women's own savings which they can apply to their own priorities and is discussed later.

Summary

The former analysis highlights certain factors critical in the use of loans: the initial asset base and the source from which the loan was taken. The nature of the source and ensuing relationship with the borrowers determines the terms of credit (costs, repayment schedules) and therefore influences the size and purpose of the loans. This is depicted in Figure 4.10.

Landlords do not charge an interest cost; however, when large loans are taken, higher costs are paid in terms of bonded labour of children. Small advances are adjusted against wages, and blur the view on any exploitation through wage rates. The binding and benefits arising from committed labour appear as two faces of the same coin. Women state a clear preference for freedom rather than committed labour for high season, even if the loans create a certain minimum employment during the lean seasons. Loans from landlords and moneylenders are taken to smoothen consumption or to meet large expenses arising from social obligations (for example, marriages). Loans from these

Figure 4.10
Determining Factors for Use of Loan

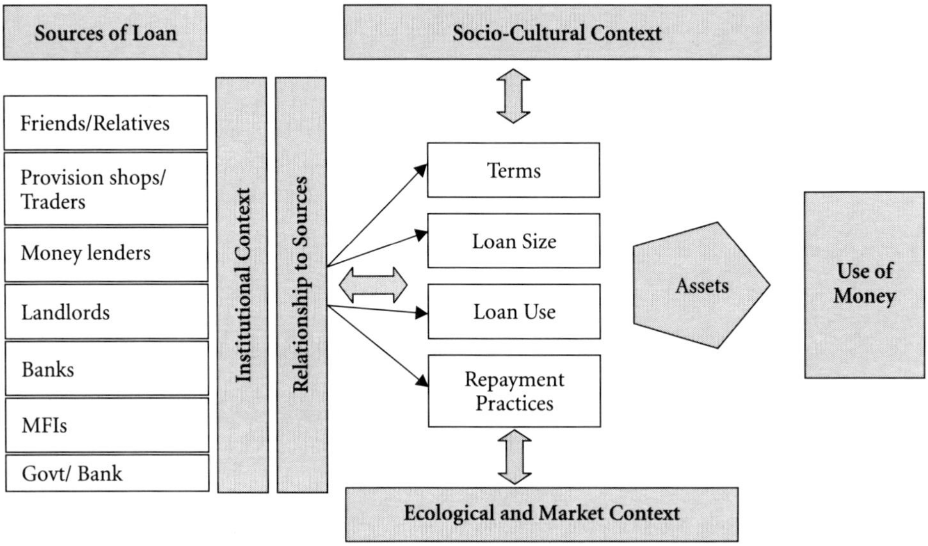

Source: Authors.

sources are not associated with IGAs or enterprise start ups. One reason is the relationship between terms of credit and use of credit for IGA and microenterprise. Women in the seven groups studied consistently denied credit offered on standard 'commercial microfinance' terms, when the projects they envisaged yielded seasonal income flows, a feature that Sampark staff said applied to all its 120 groups. This indicated an association between the following factors:

1. Terms of credit (that is, interest, repayment period, frequency of instalments: supply-related factors)
2. The opportunities available for businesses with steady as against seasonal income streams (that is, feasibility: contextual factors)
3. The credit taking capacity of the women (that is, asset, income stream and other factors determining capital: demand-related factors)

These are depicted in Figure 4.11.

Thus, even if subsidised credit is viewed as a distortion of market forces, the market does not yet provide credit on terms that are acceptable to the rural poor, given the limitation of the external context of application and use of such money. Institutional delivery of microfinance needs to recognise the importance of trust, create long-term relationships before the poor are convinced about sustained access to loans and demand such credit. The study of loans from informal and formal sources shows that factors that influence the use of money are related to both demand and supply, which are influenced by the perceptions of the different actors concerned, creating anomalies in

Figure 4.11
Factors Determining Use of Credit for Enterprise Start-up

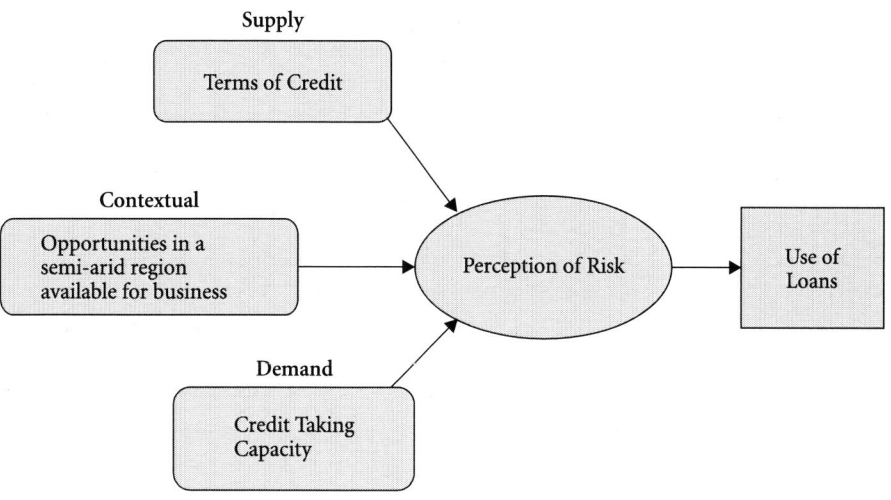

Source: Authors.

the type of credit demanded and supplied. In the spectrum of formal loans, the SHG-bank linkage model that provides credit without subsidy appears as the emerging model with long-term potential for change. It considers women as a market, provides loans without subsidies thereby removing possibilities of corruption, provides loans at cost women can bear (12 per cent per annum) and establishes long-term relationships through repeat loans. This model is specific to the Indian microfinance scenario and has as its foundation women's SHGs who provide the link between poor women and the formal financial institution, the RRB. This highlights the importance of the new source of funds introduced by microfinance programmes, the SHGs. An analysis of savings in SHGs, wherein women have full freedom to utilise the money as per their priorities and SHG group dynamics is discussed.

NOTES

1. Lakshmavva was the only child of her parents, who had separated early in their marriage and lived in different villages. Her father had married another woman. Lakshmavva lived with and was cared for by her mother.
2. This incident took place in 1988–89, when the law banning *devadasi*s had been passed, but dedications continued.
3. *Vijayadashmi, Mahanavami*: Hindu festivals.
4. Chapattis: unleavened whole wheat pancakes roasted on fire.
5. A loan with no interest on it; can be repaid whenever there is money in hand.
6. *Amavasya, Amavase*: Night of the new moon.

7. All members of Durgadevi group got cows this month, from a subsidised loan, the animals needed to be acclimatised to new surroundings, so Lakshmavva stayed home to look after her cow.
8. Local fair, sometimes involving a procession of a god or goddess.
9. *Sajje*: A small millet-type grain.
10. *Panchami*: Fifth day of lunar month.
11. Local grain used as cereal.
12. Local bread made with *jowar*.
13. Men normally go for fishing, and work with contractors. They return after 6–9 months with a lump sum of payment between Rs 10,000 and 20,000, but they can sometimes manage to come home after 3 months, with an advance payment from the contractor.
14. According to the rural custom, *devadasi*s have a right to beg. Should they need to ask for food, the villagers are obligated to feed her.
15. Lands of many families in Hosagondabala village were submerged for 8 months a year with water from the Tungabhadra dam.
16. Villagers refer to attaining puberty as 'maturing', when they begin to look for a marriage alliance for a girl, especially among the SCs.
17. A thick bedsheet or bedcover.
18. Brother-in-law, husband's younger brother is called *maidhana*.
19. These amounts are usually borrowed from labour contractors, creating debt bondage for a 9-month period.
20. Transfer Certificate—required when a child leaves one school and is transferred or admitted to another.
21. Training of Rural Youth for Self-employment, a government scheme for skills training and asset provision to the poor.
22. Subsidised school provided by the government for meritorious children.
23. The allusion here is to her being a *devadasi*, and his suspicion that she takes other partners to earn money.
24. The lowest castes in the social ladder are the SCs, followed by backward castes, and then 'other backward castes'. The higher castes are referred to as 'general' castes in the normal village nomenclature.
25. Clarified butter.
26. Chit funds operate like rotating savings and credit associations, whereby members pool in a fixed amount, and the pooled amount is allotted to one member every month, based on need, bidding or on a draw of lots.
27. This was also observed by Hulme and Mosley (1996).
28. Reported in a recent study on indebtedness and bondage (IIMS Dataworks 2007).
29. See, Guèrin (2006) for an example from Senegal.
30. In effect, as many groups realised that they had to pay back the full loan to get an equivalent subsidy, they opted not to return the loan, and save the interest, too.
31. The bank has since merged with three other profit-making RRBs in Karnataka state and is renamed Pragati Grameen Bank (PGB).
32. Harper (1998) considers that moneylenders charge an even higher rate, so MFIs can afford to charge higher than bank rates. Second, willingness to pay high rates of interest is taken as evidence of demand and ability to pay the cost.
33. This constraint has been removed in 2007, banks can now extend loans to any *block* and people also can exercise a choice about the bank they take a loan from.

5

Use of Money by Groups and Group Dynamics

How women perceive and use borrowed money is determined by their personal experiences. For rural women, self-help groups (SHGs) mediate and create a bridge between individual women and formal institutions like banks/microfinance institutions (MFIs). While being conduits for external funds to individual women, SHGs create the possibility of using another source of money: women's own savings. The analysis of meanings through group processes and dynamics is explained in Figure 5.1.

The basic function of SHGs, namely accumulation and management of savings, is its most important feature for the women, underlying what this new forum means. Women's management of group money in ways to suit their own needs and preferences involves social processes which then lead to women 'owning' these externally introduced organisations.

GENERATION OF SAVINGS

The questions relating to savings include why and how women save, the implications of irregularity while saving and the amount of savings concerned. The amount and regularity of savings is determined as much by non-government organisation (NGO) rules as by women's own capacity to save. The factors which determine savings are the number of family members earning a wage, especially cash wage, whether *coolie* work is available that month and household expenses. The emergency needs for medical and social expenses are the two most important reasons of leakage that diminish women's ability to save, as illustrated in Figure 5.2.

Poor women save from their own or their families' *coolie* wages and many depend on wages from casual agricultural labour to make their savings. Thus, the regularity of savings depends largely on the availability of agricultural labour, and therefore varies between seasons. The women in this study found it difficult to save even very small amounts of Rs 5 ($0.11) on a regular basis and also

Figure 5.1
Exploring Meanings: Group Processes and Dynamics

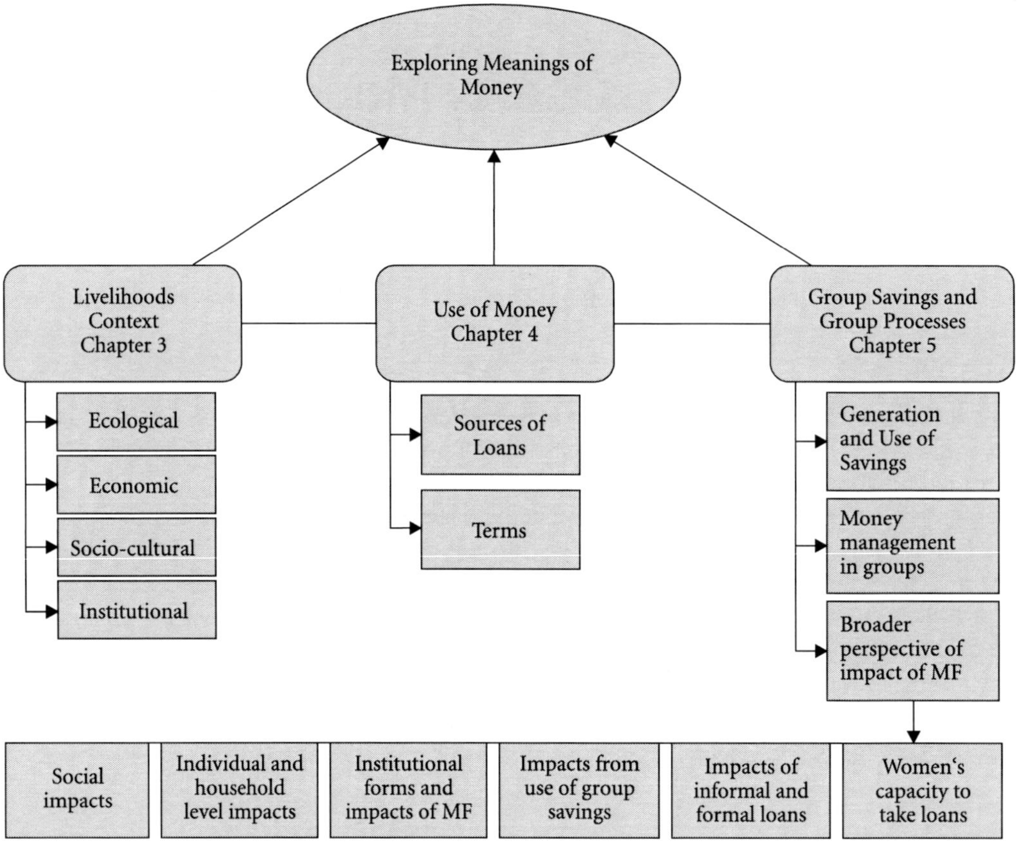

Source: Authors.

faced the problem of alternate demand and use of cash within the household. Typically, they had to choose between several competing uses of money, for instance, illness and other emergencies demanded immediate cash. Yellamma, for example, said:

This year we got one bag of horse-gram from the farm, which we have not yet sold because the rate has fallen. We have sown *jowar*, which is yet to grow. There was less rain, so the yield has been low this year. There is no *coolie* work this year because of low rains, so I go to my landlord's house to work. My daughter-in-law is at home because for the past one month she has been sick. I took her to Koppal twice, I have spent Rs 150 ($3.33) but her fever has not yet reduced. Even my daughter Gayathravva is not well, she has rashes on her body, I took her to Koppal for a check up and spent Rs 100 ($2.22). She is willing to work but there is no *coolie* work. Devappa, my son, is working on a food-for-work programme digging a pipeline. They don't pay cash, but have given one bag of rice instead, which I have used at home. No one in the family other than my son and I are earning, and due to pain in my limbs I stayed at home for four days. Later I went to Koppal and got medicine and the expense was Rs 60 ($1.33). This month I have

Figure 5.2
Livelihoods Perspective of Savings

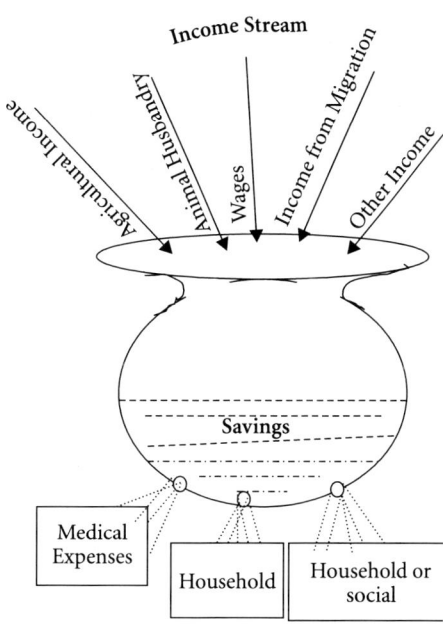

Source: Authors.

had only hospital expenses. I have not saved any money in the group this month. For three weeks no one has gone for *coolie* work; instead I have taken Rs 150 ($3.33) from the group, which I have to repay. Normally, my son, daughter-in-law and daughter also earn, so whatever my daughter earns, I save that money in the group.

Poor women tend to be irregular savers when cash is low, when illness reduces the chances of labour, or these are other emergency or household needs. Conversely, women save more when they have regular inflows, but the overall pattern is erratic. By contrast, women with regular incomes, for example, Mariyamma from agriculture, Sushila from tailoring, Sangavva from agriculture and labour, Rangamma from the provision shop and Kaveri from the trading business or government salary, did not find it difficult to save the mandated amount of Rs 10 ($0.22) on a weekly basis.

Members of Pakiravva's group in Hyati village of Koppal contributed Rs 10 ($0.23) for the group savings as mandated by the NGO and brought an additional sum of Rs 10 ($0.23) to their group meetings. They pooled this latter sum, amounting to Rs 200 ($5) per week and drew lots to allot an amount to each member every week. In this way, each woman got one lump sum, and when each member received the money once, the process was repeated. This was a method different from the savings method mandated by the NGO. Women found their own system of managing savings more efficient than the NGO's. They did not have to return all the additional savings. Instead they managed it as the merry go round described, and there was no interest payment involved.

Among the savings groups in Koppal, many women pegged the savings at a regular amount.[1] Some started their savings with Rs 2 ($0.045) per week, graduated to Rs 5 ($0.11), and stabilised at Rs 10 ($0.23) per week; few saved Rs 20 ($0.45) or more. For instance, saving Rs 1 or 2 ($0.02 or 0.04) per day, and then adding the balance on the last day of the week meant they could save the amount of Rs 10 ($0.23). Gonibasaveshwara SHG, Bikanhalli (Nagavva and Sangavva's group), had 16 scheduled caste (SC) members; of which, five were landless and another 10 were marginal

> *... Now, four members have joined the group; they had been members of our group earlier but they withdrew the membership and took their money back. Their savings were not on par with ours but now they save Rs 10 ($0.23) per week like us.*—Yellamma

farmers. They depended on work on their own lands and *coolie* work on other people's lands. They conducted meetings regularly, but the savings were irregular. In 2000, when there was no rain and little agricultural work, they were unable to make any savings for 3 months, and saved irregularly for another 3 months. Of the three groups that Sampark promotes in Hosagondabala village, the Nulvi Chennaiah group, comprising the Koravar community, migrates for 4–6 months every year to collect material for the baskets that they make and sell. It was observed that they did not follow the SHG methodology of meeting once a week, of bringing in savings regularly and repaying in regular instalments the loans they had taken from the group. The SHG dissolved in 1 year; three members joined another group. The Hemareddy Mallamma group in Chukkankal, Kaveri's group, had 13 members, of which two withdrew because they could not save regularly. Even among those continuing as members, savings were irregular due to health problems, lack of *coolie* work and consequent shortage of money. The attendance at meetings was low where women worked night shifts. When the leader, Manjula, married and left the village, the meetings stopped as there was no literate person to conduct them. Savings were erratic because earnings were erratic and/or meetings irregular. In the Bharmalingeshwara group, Mariyamma stated: 'We have not saved or repaid loans for the past six months. For the past three months we have completely stopped bringing money to the group meetings. There is no rain, no work, and no money to bring.'

However erratic the earnings, women claimed they were serious about savings. Lakshmavva's group comprised the poorest women, hardly able to sustain their families, but they still met regularly and brought savings. Bharmavva said: 'Even if we face difficulties at home, we bring the savings. This way we know for sure that we are building up to an amount that we can use, either to pay off our loans to the group, bank or to someone else.' There were also groups that saved more than the amount mandated and monitored by the promoting NGO/MFI, because they could then use it as they chose, as in an SHG in Hyati village, illustrated in the accompanying box.

The geographical context where the women lived is also important. There was drought in Koppal from 2001 to 2003, which led to low and irregular savings among many women's groups. Among the groups initiated by the local NGO, many members dropped out as they could not save regularly, and due to migration from the area, many groups were forced to dissolve. Of the 130 groups initiated by the NGO between 1998 and 2003, 20 dissolved due to these factors. By external/NGO standards, these groups were judged to have neither regularity nor a good volume of savings, and perhaps even labelled as defunct.[2] NGOs tend to judge groups by the regularity of savings and normally do not make allowances for other factors (seasonality of agricultural income, droughts, ill-health, household needs and emergencies). NGOs also judge total savings to be an important indicator of the financial strength of the credit programme, believing that women should save only in the groups they facilitate, thus regarding use of savings outside NGO-managed groups with suspicion. These judgements arise from the following financial perspective and raise concerns about the management of the financial programme (Figure 5.3).

Figure 5.3
Financial Perspective of Savings

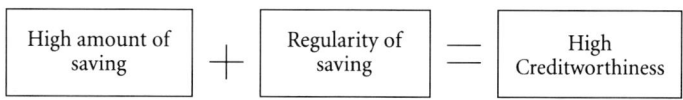

Source: Authors.

While NGOs wish to promote the 'creditworthiness' of SHGs, the SHGs themselves are not similarly motivated. Women do, however, value savings. Even if they cannot save regularly for several months, most groups continue to meet intermittently, as and when they can bring in savings, which keeps the groups operational. This reflects the value they attach to their savings.

Further, once women learn how to form and manage groups, other village women learn from them and form SHGs of their own. For instance, in 2008, Gondabala village alone has 20 SHGs that are not part of Sampark's cluster associations. Women meet every month, save Rs 50–100 ($1–2) and give loans repayable in a year. Similar groups operate in many other villages where Sampark works: Bahadurbandi, Chukkankal, Mudhaballi and Bikanhalli. These groups are completely managed by women with no supervision from any external agency and demonstrate that women have learnt the group savings and loan techniques and use them for their own advantage.

MANAGEMENT OF MONEY AND GROUP DYNAMICS

Clearly, women's management of their own money is directed at maintaining social relations and solving group conflicts with beneficial learning effects, but this sometimes creates financial risks, for instance when money is loaned to non-members and is not repaid.

Use of Savings

Microfinance interventions that operate through SHGs have introduced a new source of loans: the savings of SHGs. The common practice developed earlier by NGOs, when the SHG-based credit methodology was still being tested, was for groups to deposit their savings with the NGOs or local banks. Loans to SHGs were then determined according to the savings deposited by the group (Sampark 2000; Vyas 2003). The ratio of loan to savings was typically 2:1. There was usually an elaborate system by which the ratio of loans to savings would become 4:1, 8:1 and so on over successive loan cycles, reflecting the increased creditworthiness of the SHGs over time.

The groups researched in Koppal had control over their savings and the freedom to decide how to use or distribute these savings. Sampark did not collect women's savings as deposits, instead encouraged women to open bank accounts in the group's name. The intention was to familiarise women with banking operations. The NGO encouraged groups to keep initial savings 'safe', and not loan them out, until 'group discipline' was established (a process which happens normally after 3–6 months), and then begin to rotate their savings in small loans among themselves. Initially (1998–2002), many groups promoted by Sampark did not open bank accounts. They thought the cost of travel to a bank was high, and as they had several livelihoods needs for which they could use small loans, they began to give each other small loans from their savings to meet these. If the group was not planning to take a loan from a bank, it believed that it did not need to prove its creditworthiness, and therefore did not need deposits. For these reasons, groups preferred rotating the savings as loans (the practice of inter-loaning) rather than keeping them as deposits.

As SHG-based credit became more accepted, bankers realised that women might not deposit money in banks, but rather practice inter-loaning, and therefore began to assess inter-loan transactions to determine the loan taking capacity of groups (NABARD 1999). Also, by 2003, some groups believed that they could access credit from the banking sector and opened and operated bank accounts in the expectation of obtaining subsidised loans. This trend was apparent in the Sampark groups by 2005. For instance, Sushila's group, Basaveshwara SHG of Mudhaballi, opened a bank account only in 2005, in the fourth year of its formation, in the hope of obtaining bank loans. A bank account also proves useful when women want to close the transactions, as in the case of Durgadevi group, when the women sought to collect enough money to pay off the bank loan and avoided being 'defaulters', or when they wanted to redistribute the money among themselves.

Groups value savings as a new source of money, as it constitutes 'self-owned' capital, and take loans from group savings on a continuous basis. The details of savings, loans generated from savings and interest earnings accruing to the seven groups to which research participants belonged are given in Table 5.1.

The seven groups studied had given loans amounting to Rs 130,772 ($2,906) and earned a total interest of Rs 46,243 ($1,028), thereby augmenting their capital by 35 per cent, having rotated it as loans 1.14 times over 2–3 years. By November 2007, Sampark's 160 groups had savings of Rs 5.871 million ($146,788) and interest earnings of Rs 1.756 million ($43,916). Their cumulative loans were Rs 14.261 million ($356,514). This shows the collective accumulation of financial capital among the women over the 6-year period when Sampark organised these groups. The financial capital created was impressive, despite low savings due to droughts and irregular earnings; several groups had divided the savings and earnings during these years, and the SHGs also reduced the interest rate charged to individual members. Five groups charged interest rates ranging from 3 to 5 per cent per month; only two charged 2 per cent per month. In the early years of formation of groups, women tended to peg the interest rate at 5–10 per cent per month, the rate at which money was available in the local market. Over time, they realised that high rates prevented them from using credit, and hence reduced these to 2 per cent per month. Some groups retained 5 per cent per month to insure against defaults and to build up their own capital. The loans were typically small, used for

Table 5.1

Details of Loans from SHGs (August 2003)

Group Name	No. of Members	Age of the Group (Years)	Savings, Rs ($)	Interest Earned, Rs ($)	Loan Details		
					Cumulative Loans, Rs ($)	Purpose	Interest, Repayment Schedule
1. Gallidurgamma SHG Hosagondabala (SC group), 2007	10	6.4	23,500 ($588)	4,453 ($112)	137,950 ($3,449)	Household expenses, agriculture, health and travel	Includes the loan received from bank under Swarna Jayanthi Gram Swarozgar Yojana scheme
2. Durgadevi SHG Mudhaballi (SC group), 2007	12	7.8	14,880 ($372)	2,563 ($64)	12,800 ($320)	Household expenses, health and travel	
3. Kasturibai SHG Bahadurbandi (mixed SC and BC), 2007	13	7.8	32,240 ($806)	8,112 ($203)	56,258 ($1,406)	Household expenses, agriculture, health	In 2007 group dissolved savings and reformed
4. Hemareddy Mallamma SHG, Chukkankal (General Castes), 2003	11	3.7	24,140 ($536)	12,396 ($275)	30,800 ($684)	Household expenses, health and travel	Group dissolved in the beginning of 2006
5. Gonibashveswara, Bikanhalli (SC group), 2007	11	7	15,970 ($399)	9,825 ($245)	186,258 ($4,656)	Household expenses, health, festival	The group has dissolved and shared all their savings
6. Basveshwara, (Adhishakti) Mudhaballi (Mixed group), 2007	11	2	9,800 ($218)	2,000 ($44)	3,767 ($84)	Household expenses, health	They shared their savings and profit in 2005 and restarted the group called Adhishakti; the data relates to new group
7. Baramalingeshwara, Bikanhalli (mixed group), 2005	16	6	24,650 ($48)	17,308 ($85)	34,100 ($58)	Household expenses, agriculture, health	In 2007 group dissolved savings and reformed
November 2005: total, Rs ($), 7 SHGs			138,790 ($3,084)		398,890 ($8,864)		
March 2006: total, Rs (USD), 150 SHGs	2,287 members		2,400,693 ($53,349)	602,426 ($13,387)	5,417,574 ($120,390)		
November 2007: total, Rs ($), 156 SHGs	2,835		5,871,508 ($146,788)	1,756,623 ($43,916)	14,260,555 ($356,514)		

Source: Authors.

household, medical, travel, agriculture and festivals. In most cases, members regularly repaid only the interest, whereas the principal was repaid either when the debtors had money or when other members needed to take loans.

The cost of loans had become prohibitive for many members of the SHGs, leading to practices of loaning to non-members, with the objective of earning high interest. Some found that loans extended to non-members were not returned. Yet, most groups, especially those constituted of poor women, tried this alternative and lost money before they could be convinced against it. These are illustrated in a later section. Other factors leading to loans to non-members were the perceived needs of those who could not save in SHGs, and maintenance of social relationships.

Loans to Members

When loans are from group savings, women usually prefer 'balloon' repayments, where part of the principal or interest is paid regularly, but the full repayment is linked to the expected inflow once in 3–6 months, depending on its timing. For instance, women repay agricultural loans at the time of harvest and sale of crops. In case of delays in repayment of interest or principal, groups do not levy a penal interest charge. By contrast, loans taken from NGO/MFIs have to be repaid in equal instalments, either weekly or monthly, and penal interest is levied from members in case of delay. NGOs/MFIs classify as 'defaulters' when in fact women only perceive their act as 'delay' and not as 'default'. In most of them, even if records are incomplete, women know and keep track of the principal and interest amounts payable by themselves and others. These processes and dynamics are now illustrated with reference to the research group's own 'stories' of their experiences.

Gallidurgamma SHG in Hosagondabala had members belonging to the *Madar* (SC) community (Parvatahmma, Yellamma and Shivavva were members of this group). Formed on April 2000, it had 16 women from the SC community, all engaged primarily in agricultural labour. Though the government had provided 2 acres of land to each woman as part of the *devadasi* rehabilitation scheme, these lands were flooded with dam water for 6–8 months a year, and the women cultivated pulses and groundnuts in the remaining months. All group members were illiterate, and none could write accounts. For the first half-year, the group depended on Sampark staff even to attend and conduct meetings, and only one-third of the members attended when the staff were absent. During the following year, Sampark staff visited only once a month and the field officer claimed: 'The members did not understand the objectives of a group, and did not follow rules and regulations. Instead, each one tried to explain her own difficulties and problems.' Later, they found a 13-year-old boy studying in Class 6 who helped them conduct meetings regularly and wrote their books.

In April 2002, their savings and loan transactions were as in Table 5.2.

Yellamma was the group leader. The group had given loans, both to group members and to non-members, that had not been repaid for over a year. The group expected Sampark staff to recall these loans, who complained:

> The group members do not insist on loan repayments, they expected Sampark staff to handle this issue. Even when we facilitate discussions to make a system for loan repayments, they start talking about their

Table 5.2

Savings and Loan Transaction of Gallidurgamma SHG

				Loan Details				Outstanding	
S. No.	Name	Savings	No. of Loan	Total Loan, Rs ($)	Repaid Amount, Rs ($)	Interest Paid, Rs ($)		Principal, Rs ($)	Interest, Rs ($)
1.	Parvathamma*	880 ($20)	3	1,050 ($23)	150 ($3.33)	605 ($13)		900 ($20)	195 ($4.33)
2.	Shivavva*	830 ($18)	1	300 ($6.66)	—	330 ($7.33)		300 ($6.66)	330 ($7.33)
3.	Hanumavva	790 ($18)	1	600 ($13)	450 ($10)	400 ($8.88)		150 ($3.33)	42 ($0.93)
4.	Mallavva	830 ($18)	2	300 ($6.66)	300 ($6.66)	87 ($1.93)		—	—
5.	Yellamma*	890 ($20)	4	500 ($11)	400 ($8.88)	70 ($1.55)		100 ($2.22)	—
6.	Lakshmavva	670 ($15)	3	400 ($8.88)	100 ($2.22)	125 ($2.77)		300 ($6.66)	190 ($4.22)
7.	Huligevva	630 ($14)	1	200 ($4.44)	200 ($4.44)	165 ($3.66)		—	—
8.	Siddamma	860 ($20)	1	300 ($6.66)	—	—		300 ($6.66)	270 ($6)
9.	Lakshumavva	800 ($18)	1	200 ($4.44)	50 ($1.11)	85 ($1.88)		150 ($3.33)	37.5 ($8.33)
10.	Durgamma	730 ($16)	4	700 ($16)	700 ($16)			—	—
	Total	7,930 ($176)	21	4,550 ($101)	2,650 ($59)	1,867 ($41)		2,200 ($49)	734.5 ($16)

Source: Authors.

Note: *Research participants.

difficulties and protect each other. When we are absent from meetings, they do not even discuss loan repayments, they just collect the savings, disburse loans and go home. They are afraid to ask for repayments because each of them has loans to repay. They are also scared of breaking their relationships. They have given loans to non-members and none is willing to collect this money. In fact, to reduce their risks, they have now decided not to give any further loans, and have been saving in the bank. They now have Rs 7,000 ($156) in the bank.

The women felt that, as all had taken loans, no one person had any moral right to ask another to repay, saying: 'Many of us have unpaid loans, so how can we ask another to repay.'

The group had disbursed loans as per the needs of women, without fixing any specific repayment schedules. After April 2002, the group stopped giving loans and asked members to pool money for a full division of cash, and by October 2002, they had collected all the dues and shared the entire money. The group reconvened the very next week, with three members dropping out and five new ones joining. Parvathamma dropped out as she could not save regularly. She had Rs 250 ($5.55) less than other members as savings, and could not repay loans taken. The group did not change its two leaders through the 3 years. Initially, one member, Chanamma, kept the actual cash herself, and her husband compiled the group accounts. He then took Rs 500 ($11) without informing the members. The members quarrelled among each other but could not find an alternative accounts writer or cash keeper, and thus asked Sampark staff to intervene. Then, Chanamma, who had a savings of Rs 500 ($11) in the group adjusted the savings against the cash taken by her husband, repaid another loan, and withdrew her membership. Five other members also left the group. Two had taken loans they found difficult to repay, so they adjusted these against their savings, paid up the balance and found 'release from such issues'. Three others claimed they could not save Rs 10 ($0.22) per week on a regular basis, and withdrew their savings and left. Next, another leader, Shivavva, became keeper of the group's money. She had also taken a loan of Rs 1,050 ($23) and did not repay it for 18 months. Once when she had Rs 700 ($16) in hand, she gave Rs 500 ($11) to her son, and did not inform others for the next three meetings, as they did not check the accounts. The cash shortage was discovered only when the Sampark field officer checked the cash balance. The group members did not blame Shivavva, but the Sampark worker insisted that another person keep the cash, and that the said person bring the money to the group every week to demonstrate the accounts to all members present.

Sampark staff provided training on group management, after which the groups began to conduct regular group meetings and formulated clear working rules. Their savings were also more regular, often because they managed their finances better and also because those who could not save regularly had already dropped out. The remaining 10 members continued to pool savings and take small loans for emergency needs. In the first 2 years of opening the bank account, members had visited the bank only four times, to deposit, but not withdraw their money. Then, with additional bank deposits, they hoped to collect enough (including expected loan repayments) to buy goats and sheep.

The Gonibasaveshawara SHG, Bikanhalli (Nagavva and Sangavva's group), set up in July 2000 with 15 SC members, had similar experiences with leadership and loan repayments. Initially, Sangavva, one of the two group leaders, extended a loan to a non-member, but other members disputed this and made Manjavva, another member, responsible for cash. She too used the common fund without consulting the group, leading to another dispute. The initial experience of lending to non-members was negative, so it stopped such lending and rotated savings regularly as loans among members, keeping very little money in hand and none deposited in the bank for a long period. Members paid interest regularly, but only paid the principal when they got large inflows of cash from sale of agricultural products, or other assets like goats. If they needed to borrow, those with borrowings repaid the principal amount over 2–3 weeks to enable further loans.

The savings amounted to Rs 12,750 ($283) by December 2001, when earnings made through intra-group loans were Rs 7,500 ($167). When women did not repay regularly, the group decided to dissolve and distribute all savings and earnings, each getting Rs 850 ($19) of their savings and Rs 500 ($11) as interest. To some this was a significant earning; they bought jewellery (earrings and nose rings), three bought sheep and others invested in agriculture. When the group dissolved, some dropped out, but others were inducted. Sangavva took a loan from the group and did not repay, she either missed group meetings or picked up disputes when she did, but when certain members supported her, the group split into two. The group did not stabilise in the second round, and had to be reorganised again when Sangavva had five old and 10 new members from the SC community joining her, and another leader, Manjula, formed a group with 10 old members. When the groups split, each member received Rs 900 ($20) as a share of savings. The third time, Sangavvva's group had 15 members, and a savings of Rs 160 ($3.55) each in November 2003, but then held regular meetings and formulated new rules. This showed how the groups shifted and changed over time as they adapted to different conditions.

The Kasturibai SHG, Rangamma's group, was established in June 1999, with 20 members, none of whom were SCs. The group, which usually met at the house of Neelamma, also included her daughter-in-law Savithramma, who was its president. Neelamma, who also controlled the savings, took most of the loan herself, did not maintain accounts and appropriated any interest earned. She claimed religious leadership as she wore a *thali* (pendant) given by the local priest, and therefore declared that the members did not have the authority to demand a written account of the group's finances, but had to accept her word for it. Members questioned this, went to Savithramma's home and asked her to control finances as she was 'educated'. Savithramma came to Bahadurbandi, talked to the members, and at this time, 12 members formed a group with her, the remaining staying with Neelamma. One more woman joined after 6 months, and paid up the additional savings to be on par with the group. Another member joined a year later, saved Rs 20 ($0.44) per week and contributed additional cash whenever she had some 'in hand', until her savings were equal with that of the others. By 2001, each woman had Rs 1,158 ($26), of which Rs 1,060 ($24) was savings and Rs 198 ($4.40) loan interest. Once the groups were split, their worth improved. Ten women took loans from group savings, at 3 per cent per month, with regular repayments in December 2001, the loans taken by members from savings were as in Table 5.3.

By July 2002, savings reached Rs 16,960 ($377), with cumulative loans of Rs 29,435 ($655), and interest earned was Rs 5,589 ($124). Accounts were maintained, and no loans were given to non-members. They took repeated loans from Tungabhadra Grameen Bank (TGB) and were able to keep up bank repayments. The experiences of Noorijan and Neelamma's groups were the first such cases; their stories were widely circulated by both the women and Sampark staff, and later groups were warned accordingly. These experiences showed how some women used social beliefs about 'mantras'

Table 5.3

Loans from Own Savings: Kasturibai SHG

S. No.	Name	Savings	Savings and Loan Details: Kasturibai SHG					
			No. of Loan	Loan (Rs)	Repaid	Interest	Loan	No. of Repayment
1.	Thejaswini	730 ($16)	—	—	—	—	—	—
2.	Nethravathi	730 ($16)	—	—	—	—	—	—
3.	Savithravva	730 ($16)	2	1,400 ($45)	1,000 ($22)	60 ($1.33)	400 ($8.88)	2
4.	Jannathbi	740 ($16)	1	1,000 ($22)	1,000 ($22)	180 ($4.00)	—	1
5.	Husenbi	710 ($16)	1	300 ($6.66)	—	81 ($1.80)	300 ($6.66)	—
6.	Huligemma	740 ($16)	1	500 ($11)	—	133 ($2.95)	500 ($11)	—
7.	Saroja	720 ($16)	1	4,000 ($89)	200 ($4.44)	351 ($7.8)	3,800 ($84)	2
8.	Rangamma*	740 ($16)	1	2,000 ($44)	2,000 ($44)	60 ($1.33)	—	1
9.	Shakunthala	720 ($16)	2	1,700 ($38)	1,000 ($22)	115 ($2.55)	700 ($16)	5
10.	Mabubbi	740 ($16)	2	1,100 ($24)	100 ($2.22)	288 ($6.40)	1,000 ($22)	1
11.	Moulanbi	720 ($16)	1	300 ($6.66)	250 ($5.55)	60 ($1.33)	50 ($1.11)	4
12.	Basamma	740 ($16)	—	—	—	—	—	—
13.	Sharadamma	740 ($16)	1	1,000 ($22)	—	30 ($0.66)	1,000 ($22)	—
14.	Shanthamma	20 ($0.44)	—	—	—	—	—	—
	Total, December 2001	9,520 ($212)	13	13,300 ($296)	5,550 ($123)	1,358 ($30)	7,750 ($172)	16
	Total, July 2002	16,960 ($377)	13	29,435 ($654)		5,589 ($124)		

Source: Group records in December 2001.

Note: *Research participant.

and sanctions, as that given by the *thali*, to exert religious male authority over group members and appropriate their savings and profits.

In the Hemareddy Mallamma group of Chukkankal, primarily constituting of general castes, Kaveri explained that the regularity of repayments had increased once they took bank loans:

> Now we have savings of over Rs 30,000 ($667) in the group, and each member has taken a loan from it at least twice, for household or medical expenses. This loan is returned in instalments, just as bank loans. Earlier, we used to repay over a three to six months period, whenever we had the cash. But now, after taking loans from the bank, we have started the same practice with loans from our savings.

This group had learnt from the discipline banks required, to make their own savings and loans operations more systematised.

Another group, the Baramalingeshwara group in Bikanhalli, with Mariyamma as secretary, was formed in April 2000 with 16 members, only three of whom were SC/ST. Twelve members owned land ranging between 1–6 acres, one owned 14 acres. Most women did *coolie* work. Over 2.5 years, the groups saved Rs 20,790 ($462), extended loans of Rs 29,500 ($655), earning an interest of Rs 8,912 ($198), at 4 per cent per month, later reduced to 2 per cent. Of the loans given, Rs 24,150 ($537) had been repaid. Between members, 65 loans were extended and 45 repaid. The group had fixed a minimum loan of Rs 100 ($2.22), and a maximum of Rs 4,000 ($89). It had an average attendance of 80 per cent for meetings, and all except two members saved regularly. The group did have a bank account in the nearby village of Hiresindhogi, and members said it cost them Rs 10 ($0.22) for each trip. The group was stable, with only one member leaving since its formation, she had a loan of Rs 500 ($11), for which interest repayable was Rs 20 ($0.44); these were deduced from her savings of Rs 650 ($14) and the balance was then paid to her. The president, secretary and bookkeeper of the group were considered open and accountable to the group, and there was no change in its leadership.

Loan repayments from savings were flexible. Members explained:

> We do not have a fixed repayment schedule. We know each other well, and we wait till members repay loans on their own, there is no pressure. Often women pay when they sell their agricultural produce, and if someone has a long-pending loan, then we put pressure on her to repay at harvest time. We do not go to the bank very often, we rotate all our money as loans. Only when we don't have enough money, and a member wants a large amount, we then ask members to repay over the next three to four meetings, and then we collect the amount to meet the larger loan needs.

One Sampark field worker complained:

> There is no repayment system! Even if I discuss setting up a regular system, they give reasons and justifications for one another and do not make timely repayments. Most of the loan from the group is used to pay for agricultural labour, fertilizers and pesticides.

Mariyamma claimed:

> When the group was formed, all our husbands used to come and stand and watch the group operations. Now they have confidence in it. People in the village are also happy as the group savings are useful and

the relationship with Sampark is good. Sampark has provided training in tailoring, agriculture and many other things for the improvement of women, so that we now know how to count and keep accounts and put our signatures.

Three members wanted to take a bank loan for sewing machines and other businesses, but the others wished to have an activity which all of them could start, so they did not agree to take bank loans.

This reluctance was found in other groups, too: when only one or two of the members sought to take external loans, or where other members were unfamiliar or unsure about projects. Rangamma wanted her group to take a loan to buy an auto rickshaw for her son, and Yellamma wanted to start a vegetable business, but their groups could not agree to take external loans for one or two large projects. Thus, extending loans and repayments of loans from own savings were flexible, but sometimes there was internal discord or uncertainty about the proposed businesses, which prevented women from taking external loans for relatively large business ventures.

Loans to Non-members

What the women envisaged as the role of savings differed from what the facilitating agency, the NGO, held to be important. The experiences of two groups here illustrate how loans to non-members were as much to maintain social relationships, which also made recovery difficult, as to fulfil an 'obligation' to 'help' those in need.

Sushila's group formed in 1998, with eight members, all belonging to landless households. The women did not attend the meetings regularly, but sent their family members, with the savings of Rs 10 ($0.22) per week. The group leader lent this out at 5 per cent per month to non-members. In June 2001, their total savings were Rs 4,800 ($107) and interest earned was Rs 1,600 ($36), thus giving each member Rs 800 ($18) as a lump sum, including savings and interest earned, at the end of the year. Some group members had taken loans and had not repaid, which was adjusted at the time of closing the annual accounts. In June 2002, their accumulated savings was Rs 4,000 ($89) and the interest earned was Rs 400 ($8.88). One debtor did not pay the principal, but there was still a profit on their lending operations as they kept the interest rate pegged at 5 per cent per month. Three members dropped out when they started savings for the third time, and six new members joined. As soon as they pooled in Rs 1,000 ($22) they disbursed Rs 700 ($16) as a loan to a non-member on the guarantee of a group member.

By this time, Sampark staff disapproved, and stopped supervising them. The field officer said:

Right from the initial stages of formation, this group did not fully understand the concept of a SHG. The members did not meet regularly, though they sent a family member to contribute the savings. The group did not appoint a President, but was managed by a Secretary who kept the cash and maintained the accounts. They did not discuss any common issues, just did the savings and credit transactions. They sometimes took loans in between the days of the group meetings, and so, many members did not know all the group transactions. They did not open a bank account for nearly three years! Despite our advice, they lend money to non-members and do not even stop after losing money! The group divided and distributed its savings three times in the first three years of its operation. Sushila took loans very often and kept the group's cash, but she never had the time to do the bookkeeping. The members did not attend any of the training organised by Sampark. The accounts of the group were always in a mess. We got fed-up and now I have not gone to their group meetings for three months. The third time they reconstituted in 2005, they asked a young boy to keep their books. Sushila still keeps the cash, but the boy now maintains the accounts, and we have trained him, so the group is now more stable.

The women, however, felt that they were poor, landless and could not afford to take loans at 5 per cent themselves, but would continue to earn interest by lending their collective financial capital to a non-member. Sushila continued to lead the group, and the members believed that they would benefit from it. This group was more interested in profits than in disbursing small loans to group members. Even in 2005, when the group opened a bank account, the members took loans, and if amounts of Rs 1,000 ($22) to Rs 2,000 ($44) were left unused, they sought non-members instead to loan to, so that they would not lose out on potential interest, thus using the group as a surrogate moneylender.

In 2005, the members also took more loans for household consumption and for creating income generating assets. Initially, five members took loans for buying sheep. In the next round of loans, five more members bought two to five sheep each. As the women were engaged in *coolie work*, they did not have the time to graze these sheep. One man with five sheep of his own took the responsibility of grazing the whole flock of 30 sheep, charging Rs 30 ($0.66) per sheep per month. This gave him a reasonable return on his time and gave the women a chance to own sheep as additional assets which they would not otherwise have had.

The Durgadevi (Lakshmavva's) group in Mudhaballi had also extended loans to non-members, primarily because the leader, Bharmavva, believed that as the group had savings, they were 'duty bound to help those in need'. She explained:

> I gave a loan to a person from the neighbouring village who said he wanted to buy an auto-rickshaw. He took six loans of Rs 4,000 ($89) to 6,000 ($133) from different sources, sold the auto-rickshaw, and did not return the loan to any of his creditors. I went with four members of our group, six times, to get the money back. Once I went and stayed in that village for 21 days to recover the money. Finally, I brought back the Rs 4,000 ($89) which I had lent him. I had taken Rs 2,000 ($44) from the group and the same from another person in the village to give him the money. Now the group has kept all the money, saying that they want to recover interest. I want them to return Rs 2,000 ($44) so that I can pay off the other person. You tell me, is the group right, should they not let me clear off both the loans and forgive the interest, or wait for it?

Bharmavva clearly believed that the amount returned should be applied equally towards clearing the principal amounts of two lenders, while the group retained the money to apply it to its own loan and interest due. Village men also used their social contacts with the SHG members to take and not repay loans.

The sharing of labour to graze sheep, in the former case, is an example of how women used human and financial capital to create assets. The second case illustrates how women tried to balance both social and financial relationships.

Flexibility and Problems with Loan Repayments

The flexibility in repayment that women enjoyed because the loans were from their own savings had both benefits and risks, which they dealt with in different ways.

Baramalingeshwara, Mariyamma's group, started in 1998 and accumulated savings of Rs 24,650 ($548) until November 2003. Its cumulative loans were Rs 34,100 ($758). Of these, Rs 15,000 ($333) was outstanding against members, but not regularly repaid. Group members kept these amounts outstanding and did not pressurise one another for repayment. Their savings fluctuated according to the seasonality of earnings, and the group continued to function, knowing that those with outstanding loans also had savings with the group, so that adjustments could be made at any time.

In contrast to the financial perspective outlined earlier, which used amount and regularity of savings to assess the creditworthiness of women, the livelihoods perspective reveals that seasonality of savings and irregularity often arise from uneven income flows and may not be indicative of a 'lack of discipline' *per se*, but rather of the insecure livelihoods of the members of a microfinance programme. In general, women value savings and continue to pool group savings in periods of cash availability.

The Durgadevi group, had 18 SC women as members, mostly *devadasis*, and took a subsidised bank loan, with which 15 members bought buffaloes. Then, one buffalo died. Some were sold as unproductive. As repayment became difficult, there were disputes. Some women repaid the loans. Others did not, using the money for household consumption or other assets. This created tension within the group and resulted in its splitting. The Durgadevi group had seven established old members, of whom only five were willing to repay the loan to the bank. They visited the bank several times to request permission to repay the loans individually, and certify that they were not *defaulters*; as they feared that if they were labelled thus, their children could not draw government benefits. However, the bank officers did not respond to their request. The bankers treated the SHG as one client and did not have a mechanism to recover loans from individuals who wished to repay to *clear their names*, but labelled all of them as defaulters, thus making it difficult for the women to reform their groups and regain access to bank credit.

MULTIPLE MEANINGS

The practices of groups, as seen in this chapter, are different from what NGOs seek and expect. Groups have a different rationale and perspective about microfinance, which leads to the different meanings they attach to savings, accumulation, distribution or even dissolution and reformation of groups themselves.

Differing Meanings, Applications and Competing Interests

Women assign different meanings to loans from their own savings, as compared to loans from NGOs and other external sources. This is evident from the way the women belonging to the research groups labelled their own savings, applied loans from these and managed them.

Application of Own Savings

In most parts of Jharkhand, own savings are referred to as '*baksa*' money or 'box money'. Women believe this money belongs to them, as against their borrowings from the NGO.

To begin with, it is difficult for the poor to save money, as the ill-health of women and their family members is a potential drain on their income and assets. The absence of assets can lead to real hunger and indebtedness. Parvathamma could bear the medical expenses only because her partner supported her. Shivavva took a loan for her husband's illness. Such situations ensured that it would take a long time for the women to build up capital. In this scenario, group savings offer a way for small individual resources to be pooled as a collective resource. And then, once the women learn to save together, they develop their own methods of using this capital.

Groups use NGO loans for what the latter consider 'productive' purposes. Even where women use a large majority of NGO loans for agriculture and small businesses, some are used for children's education, purchasing foodgrains, other household expenses, medical expenses, marriages and loan repayments. By contrast, a majority of women's group savings money is used more for education, health, household expenses in lean periods, marriages and repayment of loans taken at higher rates of interest as compared to group loans. But NGO microfinance projects require that women invest the loan in a business which will augment incomes and improve livelihoods. If money is used for anything except 'income generating' activities, it is considered an 'unproductive investment'. Thus, in the supplier's view, money spent on education, health and food is 'unproductive' and not eligible for loan purposes. From the 'women's' perspective, however, medical expenses incurred today will enable income from farm labour ahead. A child educated now will have enhanced livelihoods opportunities some years hence. These are 'productive' investments for women. The supplier only sees as productive those uses of money that generated cash in a short time cycle, whereby women could repay the short-term loans on the stringent terms established. By contrast, women's own perspective is that investment in human health and welfare is productive use. Evidently, NGO categorisation of money in its regular management processes differs significantly from women's own perceptions.

Some groups calculate the total earnings from intra-group loans and divide the earnings among group members. This involves a division of both the savings and interest earned, after which the groups start saving again. External views on such practices of SHGs are often different. Sampark, for instance, initially viewed this practice as detrimental to the interests of the women, fearing that the group would be evaluated lower in terms of creditworthiness if it were to be assessed by a banker. Therefore, while a facilitator NGO tends to see creditworthiness as important, women may not regard a loan relationship with the bank as either possible or useful in the near future. Thus, women's rationale for savings differs from that of the NGO facilitator.

In contrast, Professional Assistance for Development Action (PRADAN), an NGO facilitator of the groups studied in Lohardaga district (Jharkhand) introduced the practice of calculating and distributing dividends from the profits of the group to women members.

> *My family members and I have acquired the savings habit after I joined the group and learnt to save. I save Rs 10 ($0.22) per week in the SHG, and my daughter saves the same amount in another SHG under a government programme (Streeshakti). My husband saves 20 ($0.44) in a PIGMY scheme of a bank every day, and my son saves Rs 20 per week in a recurring deposit at the post office.*—Rangamma

PRADAN facilitated group formation among tribal women in remote villages of Lohardaga. The staff facilitated a practice of dividing savings, usually along with interest earnings, annually, and the group members looked forward to this annual benefit, which they used to buy food or small assets such as silver earrings. They recognised that the practice of sharing the earnings demonstrated the financial benefits of savings and credit operations and motivated women to keep up their savings.

In both cases, women saved until they collected a reasonably large sum (between Rs 500 and 1,000, that is, $11–22), and then borrowed a similar amount at a time of the year when they could invest it better, either in agriculture or for a child's education. In the cases of both Koppal and Lohardaga, the groups were located in a semi-arid or remote region, with few opportunities for investing in income generating activities (IGAs).

Repayment of Loans from Savings

In Jharkhand as well as in Koppal, women had different repayment practices for 'own money' as compared to 'NGO money' or bank loans. The differences were as in Table 5.4.

The repayment performance varied quite significantly depending on whether the loans were taken from own groups, government or banks, or NGO/MFI. Two primary reasons emerged for this: one concerning terms of credit and the other to the relationships between the different actor groups: women's SHGs, banks, government and NGOs (Figure 5.4).

The actor groups here are placed in two categories: with banks/government organisations engaged in the delivery of subsidised microfinance as one group and those who delivered unsubsidised credit (banks, MFIs and SHGs) as another group. The 'rule of thumb' for the former category appears to be 'Have paid the cost of benefit; no need to repay'. The 'rule of thumb' for loans taken from the NGO/MFIs is 'Take what can be repaid'. Thus, the differences in the value base of the way credit is delivered by these actor groups' results in a different repayment ethic.

> *When my parents were both alive and doing coolie work and my children were small, we did not have any problems in "running" the family. If at all we fell short of money, we used to take an advance from landlords and clear it within 15 to 20 days. If we take loan from outside, we will have the burden of interest, so we don't take any loan of a higher amount than Rs 100 to 200 ($2.22–44.44). We have to earn and eat, and we don't have any land; if we take a loan we find it difficult to repay it .... Since we have the group now, we can take and repay the loan to the group. We don't find the need of going to 'outsiders' for loans.*—Nagavva

Table 5.4

Different Repayment Practices

Practices Introduced by NGO/MFIs	Practices Followed by Groups with Loans from Own Savings
As facilitators, NGOs encouraged opening of bank accounts, as this was a basic criteria on which groups were assessed for loans from banks/external sources NGO/MFIs did not insist on accounts in banks, as they themselves conducted the financial transactions with the groups	Women did not see advantage in opening bank accounts, unless they later planned to take bank loans
Better quality record keeping	Groups did not maintain suitable records for own funds
Repayment instalments fixed by external agency, usually weekly or monthly, very rarely a balloon payment, as in agricultural credit	Usually balloon repayments
External agencies usually did not match loan term with expected repayments	Repayment linked to cash inflow cycle of the IGA, for example, agriculture, animal husbandry
Interest payments and principal payments made as per NGO-determined schedules	Interest paid regularly or periodically, principal repaid only at the end of the loan period
Penal interest levied on anything overdue as per rules set for external loans	Usually no penal interest was levied, member gives reason for non-payment or delay
Second loan may not be given until the first is fully repaid	Groups gave second loans from own savings, even if first had not been repaid, where convinced of member's need or if the member held influence

Source: Authors.

Figure 5.4
Relationships between Women and Formal Sources of Loans

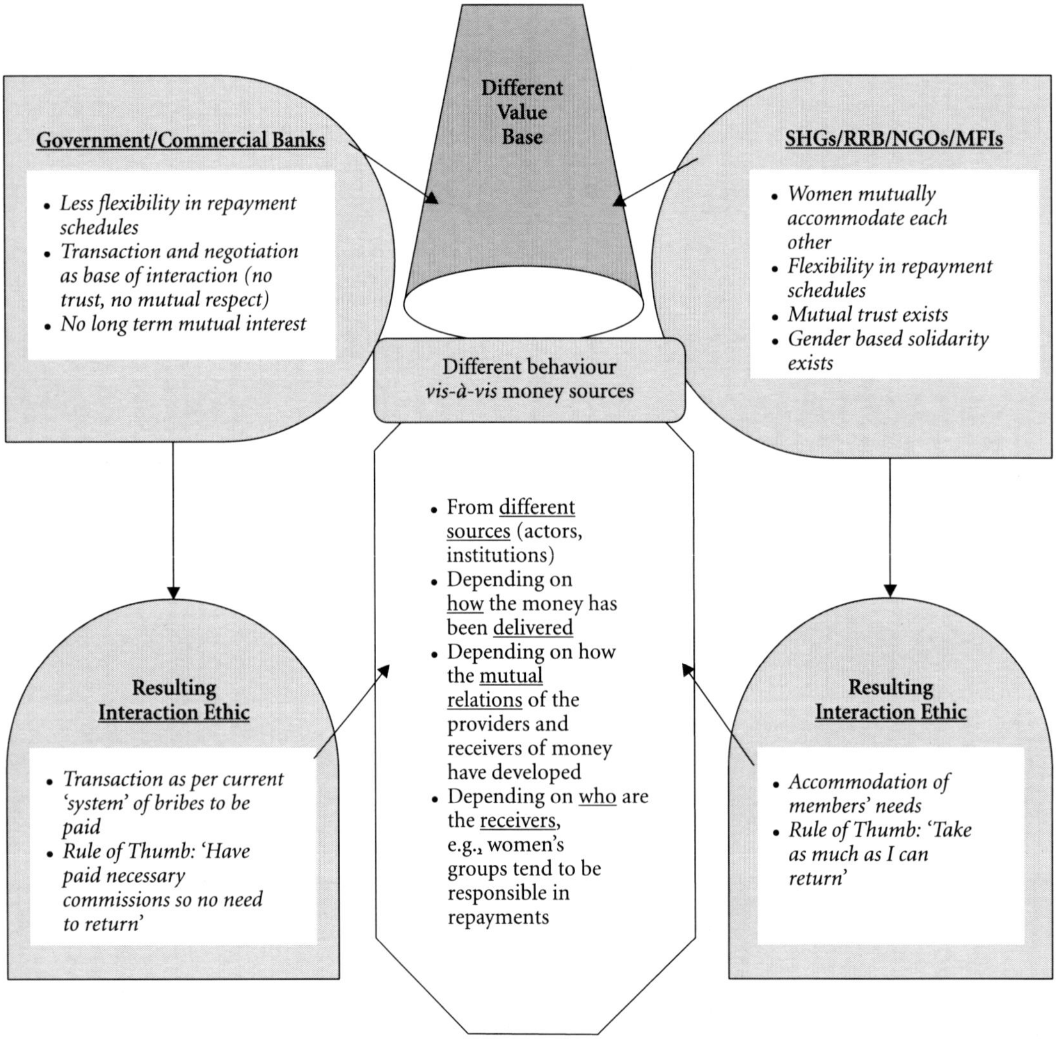

Different Value Base

Government/Commercial Banks

- *Less flexibility in repayment schedules*
- *Transaction and negotiation as base of interaction (no trust, no mutual respect)*
- *No long term mutual interest*

SHGs/RRB/NGOs/MFIs

- *Women mutually accommodate each other*
- *Flexibility in repayment schedules*
- *Mutual trust exists*
- *Gender based solidarity exists*

Different behaviour *vis-à-vis* money sources

- From <u>different sources</u> (actors, institutions)
- Depending on <u>how</u> the money has been <u>delivered</u>
- Depending on how the <u>mutual relations</u> of the providers and receivers of money have developed
- Depending on <u>who</u> are the <u>receivers</u>, e.g., women's groups tend to be responsible in repayments

Resulting Interaction Ethic

- *Transaction as per current 'system' of bribes to be paid*
- *Rule of Thumb: 'Have paid necessary commissions so no need to return'*

Resulting Interaction Ethic

- *Accommodation of members' needs*
- *Rule of Thumb: 'Take as much as I can return'*

Source: Authors (based on AOP framework) [Weismann 1998].

People value relationships based on the other actors they deal with and the nature of the relationship emerging with them. A government-subsidised bank loan is a benefit to be accessed only once, based on their qualifying on a poverty criterion, which can itself be purchased. An one-time transaction and purchased eligibility can create a weak value base for the partnership between people and external agencies. By contrast, loans from NGOs, MFIs or through regular credit transactions with banks are made on the basis of credit-taking ability, transparent processes and the promise of long-term relationships. So, while loans under subsidised schemes of the government are not paid, NGO/MFI and regular bank loans are repaid. Further, when the relationships with the banks provide flexibility, groups return the loan amount, so they can then obtain subsidies. The latter type of relationships involve the value basis and risk of loss of face if they default, encouraging high repayment performance of loans taken from or through NGO/MFIs. Thus, relationships and values determine the loan repayment behaviour of borrowers.

The women in Koppal explained 'own' and 'outside' money thus:

> We have benefited from the group because we can take a loan when we have a difficulty. But if we take loans from others, we have to follow their conditions until we repay them. Instead of asking questions, we believe in others; we don't use our brains, so we are still poor from paying loans and high interest. If we have our own money, it is good for us; there is a lot of difference between group loans and outside loans.
>
> Outside, they give loans at high interest rates, we have to mortgage our gold, land, house and other documents for the sake of the loan and also, we and our children have to be bonded labourers for them. We have to pay the principal amount all at once. That is not the loan for poor people like us, so we find the group loan beneficial. There is no use taking a loan from outside. But the group loan is given for medicines, household expenses, seeds (agriculture) or any other purpose, like functions at home. Our lives have improved after taking loans from the group—*Yellamma*.

In the early stages of group formation, especially among poor and illiterate women, groups typically depend on collective memory, rather than written records. The level of trust is high; there is confidence that members will repay. Women find it difficult to obtain record keeping registers and learn how to maintain them, or get this done by local literate men, girls or boys. However, lack of records does not mean that groups do not 'know' their transactions, which most can recall in detail. Women often know which individual member is expected to pay how much each week, especially when some members are waiting to take credit when others repay. Where such credit demand does not exist, loan monitoring tends to be weaker, and, monitoring systems are also weaker in established groups and with accumulated savings. Such groups see little urgency about repayments and allow individuals to repay at their convenience.

The perception of risk is also socially determined, and differs according to whose money it is. Money taken from friends, relatives and neighbours is seen as a reciprocal facility, safe and flexible and is often taken in amounts that women are most capable of returning. Some poor women are able to take relatively large loans if repayment terms are flexible. Loans from landlords and moneylenders are seen as exploitative because the terms are very high and women take such loans only when forced to do so—for economic needs and social expenditure that women consider obligatory or unavoidable. In contrast; they feel safe and less 'exposed' managing their own money and enough in control to determine terms that are affordable. They feel good about taking loans from own savings when mutual trust has developed among members. Thus, women's SHGs emerge as a *closed* and *safe* place to take loans from. As the women themselves set the rules, they accommodate one another when needed. The rules are flexible and the members are accountable only to one another. If a woman cannot repay, she can always set off her loan against her individual saving, thereby reducing the risk of non-payment (Figure 5.5).

When external loans are offered on terms not preferable to women, they opt not to take it. Clearly, women perceive own money to be less risky than external money and have a marked preference for it.

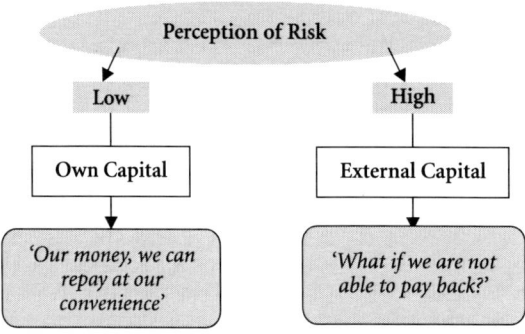

Figure 5.5
Perception of Risk

Source: Authors.

Importance of Social Relationships in the Management of Money

In many of Sampark's groups in Koppal, women divide the full amount of savings as well as earnings, creating a zero cash balance in the group and enabling it to start again. In many cases, groups dissolve and are later formed again. The practice of dividing savings annually is also a feature of many groups promoted by PRADAN in Jharkhand.

In some cases, women take small loans which they do not repay as scheduled. When many group members have outstanding loans and repayments are not made, other members cannot subsequently take loans. Where the loan is given to a non-member and not returned on time, money is accessible to a few people. Therefore, new loans become limited to the new savings being gathered. In order to solve this impasse, members decide that the group will be dissolved so that the money can be divided. All the members bring in money within a specified period and once the division is made, and the balance is put at zero, they start pooling the money again. Often, such a group restarts soon after dissolving. Groups' own development poses further issues, but by bringing back this capital, groups can dissolve without undue financial losses for individual women. Sometimes, one group reformulates into two separate groups, or with one or few members dropping out, and the rest simply continuing their transactions. As common group transactions are related to money, the simplest way by which to disengage the group is also through money. Practices such as dividing the capital and dissolving the group, at least temporarily, are ways in which women resolve social and leadership conflicts.

> *When some members repay regularly and others do not, we fight because only the money of those who repay gets rotated, the others block money. If we fight more, members threaten to sell the buffalo and repay, but we also do not want members to do that. We have no doubt; we have the confidence that everyone will repay.*
>
> *Sometimes the women are struggling, but they will also repay. Two buffaloes of Lakshmavva died, so she is facing a difficult situation, but she will also repay.*—Nagavva

The experiences of these groups highlight the importance of social relationships in the management of money. Sometimes, members hesitate to call for credit discipline, fearing the likely resentment of the member in debt. If the NGO staff insists on loans being returned, the members, however, do not then see this as a disruption of social relationships, as the NGO is perceived as an external agent, and expected to enforce financial discipline. But the groups hesitate to enforce such discipline internally. In some cases, groups change their leaders and continued to save. In case the groups are not able to change leaders, they seek to limit damage and future risk by dissolving the group and changing financial practices as well as leaders when they reform the groups. This dissolution and reformation of groups are important social learning processes from a group dynamics perspective.

> *When a banker comes to assess the group, and their savings are low and depleted, he will rate them low, and use it as a reason to sanction subsidised loan to another group. Sampark groups will get a bad reputation.*
>
> *They do not listen to me, and they do not maintain discipline, but they ask for subsidised loans. It is very difficult to manage these groups and satisfy their expectations.*—Sampark field staff
>
> *It is our money and we accumulated it up to Rs 1,000 ($ 22) each so we can take it as a lumpsum. We need it now so we have to divide it. We have now learnt to save, and will pool it to the same amount again.*—A group member

While external agencies take only a financial perspective, they give little credence to women's own ingenuity in solving leadership and financial management problems. Sampark started with the mindset that dividing savings is unwise as it depletes the capital women create. However, women believe they now have a system through which that capital can be created again, and, therefore, do not see any risk in dividing up the capital. It is more important to them that they have acquired new skills in the management of savings and credit, and learnt a new methodology for creating financial capital. They feel confident about linking up with more like-minded members. What others may see as capital erosion can thus be interpreted as (social) capital creation and a step towards empowerment. Women particularly value the social capital they create, for example, the affinity within the group, the system of savings and the skill in management of savings and credit. The differing perspectives about money management and group dynamics are explained in Table 5.5.

This analysis brings out the relevance of group dynamics and use of money. Through SHG formation, women have gained access to a new source of money—their own small savings—through groups. However, SHGs are not traditional indigenous forums, but a new one introduced by development projects. The internal management processes of these groups are indicative of the way in which the forum has become socially embedded. Thus, quality of leadership, socio-cultural factors, transparency and accountability systems and trust emerge as elements that determine group dynamics and are indicative of the impact of microfinance.

Impact of Savings

The impacts arising from group loans are different from those arising from informal and formal loans, and are depicted in Figure 5.6. For that reason, the use of money by SHGs needs to be linked

Table 5.5

Different Rationales for Money Management

Divergence	External Agents' Perspective	Women's Perspective
Lending to non-members	Risky, as they are not bound by group norms and discipline	Not risky, as they are known to group members Based on mutual support, loans are given when people are in need Profitable, especially when group members are unable to absorb credit
Pooling loans and savings and dividing the capital	Depletion of financial capital	Sharing of benefits Reduced risk of defaults and loss of capital of each member Reduced work on record maintenance, can start fresh accounts every year
Dissolution and reformation of groups	Evidence of lack of group cohesion and stability	Solution to exploitative or ineffective leadership Resolution of conflicts among members Way to resolve old problems and start afresh
Flexible repayments of loans	'Lack of financial discipline' Collusion among group members to delay repayments	Own money less answerable to external agency Allowing more members to repay at their convenience Continued circulation of money until others need it
Opening of bank accounts	Evidence of knowledge and good discipline in microfinance	No cash to deposit in the bank if all savings circulate as loans Loss of a day's wages and transport costs involved in going to the bank No need if there is little expectation or possibility of loan
Joint liability for repayment of group loans	Preparation of future loan from bank All group members can agree to take loans for enterprises of one or two members Group members must pay for the defaulting members	Overexposure to projects of one or two women can be risky for other members All members are equally poor and those who repay must not be penalised for those who do not

Source: Authors.

to the sources of money to which they have access, namely their own savings and external funds (from banks or NGO/MFIs).

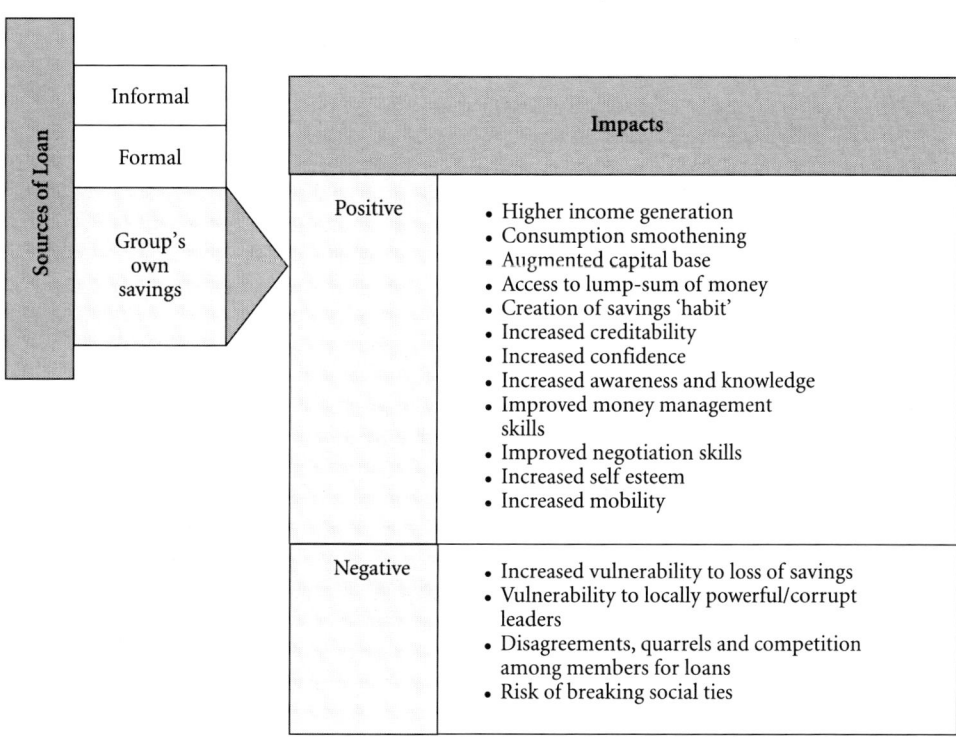

Figure 5.6
Impact from Group Savings

Source: Authors.

The impact of loans from formal sources has been described before; this section will highlight the impacts arising from the use and management of women's own savings.

Women acknowledge that savings are the most important impact generating feature of their participation in SHGs. They categorically state that the greatest impact has been created by the 'savings habit'. It has enabled women to put money aside for their emergency needs, making them less vulnerable and more confident about facing crises. Lakshmavva from Durgadevi group said:

> *Saving is very important to me. 'Hani hani koodidare halla, thene thene koodidare rashi' (small drops of water make a mighty ocean) so small savings is of great use. I have benefited a lot after joining the group.*—Yellamma

> Earlier we used to depend only on *coolie* work for our earnings. If there was no *coolie* work, we did not have any earnings, and used to starve on those days. After the formation of the group we got a loan and

we bought one buffalo each. Now, one family member looks after the buffalo and others go for *coolie* work. The money earned by selling milk is an additional income of our families. Before the formation of groups we used to take loans from the *Shavkar* (landlord), who charges high interest and also asks to keep our children for labour in his house to compensate the loan. Now we borrow money from groups with less interest, which helps us to repay loans quickly.

The positive impact of savings has been felt by members of all Sampark's groups in Koppal. At the NGO level, the Sampark manager explained:

For all the SHGs taken together, savings increase by about Rs 40,000 ($889) to Rs 45,000 ($1,000) per month. Women use group loans for health, house repair, marriages, travel and agriculture. They use external loans for buffalos, sheep and goats, and investment in agriculture, which includes digging borewells, obtaining pumpsets, electricity connection, and purchasing fertilizers and pesticides. They also use external loans for starting petty shops and businesses.

Indeed, several groups across many states and NGOs have reported the practice of saving over and above the level mandated by the NGO, and these savings are used at the women's own discretion.[3] When women take loans from their own savings and the group retains the interest, it augments group capital. In addition to representing the women's equity capital, the savings also indicate the financial strength of a microfinance project itself. The benefits and risks inherent in groups managing their own money are depicted in Figure 5.7.

Figure 5.7
Access and Control Over Savings

Benefits	Risks

• Access to 'own' funds for loans
• Free to decide
   – Purposes of loan
   – Repayment schedules
   – Interest rates
• Can lend to non-members
• Can retain emergency cash
• Can manage seasonal demand
• Capitalisation at group level
• A share in the interest earnings of the group
	• Risk of delay/default by members/leaders
	• Risk of delay/default by non-members
	
	• Risk of members/non-members not repaying properly
	• Risk of social disputes

Source: Authors.

They have more freedom to decide the purpose of loan, interest rates and repayment schedules. They can maintain cash balances, as per their estimation of emergency needs or seasonality of the demand for loan from members. They can loan to non-members and earn interest at 3–5 per cent per month. However, such savings management by groups also carries risks. If non-members do not repay, this leads to disputes among group members. Such loans create the risk of loss of principal, even though they have the potential to earn more interest, and therefore increase the (meagre) capital. When women distribute the savings among themselves as loans, at a reasonable interest rate of less than 2 per cent per month, they can smoothen fluctuations in household consumption. But, if the interest rate is too high, it deters poor women from taking loans. However, groups often provide the flexibility to repay when women find it more convenient to do so. In the groups, this often led to 'suboptimal' credit flows from the 'financial' viewpoint, but as it was their own money, the women viewed this as a valid action. Groups were a new forum, externally initiated, and introduced new activities which were hitherto unfamiliar to these women. It was an experimentative process by which the women learnt, and took decisions that the facilitating NGO may not support, such as lending money to non-members and not making repayments on a regular basis.

Women lose money if there is inequitable distribution of loans among them, if those who borrow do not repay and if they loan money to non-members who default. Women's SHGs handled the collective money of poor women, and just as this created an opportunity to earn, it also created vulnerability. This new forum of groups exposed women to new methodologies of handling money, a task for which they did not have the adequate capacity. This finding raises the question of whether it is ethical to introduce a new methodology that creates new vulnerabilities, without at the same time creating the capacity or potential to cope with the risks accompanying it. In the case of Sampark, the NGO monitored the groups, repeatedly warned them of the problems of lending money to non-members and monitored whenever repayments became irregular. However, as the organisation was a *facilitator* rather than *provider* of microfinance services, it had only an advisory role, and women sometimes chose not to follow their advice, but preferred to prioritise and learn from their own experience.

In a case studied in Ranchi, Jharkhand, the *provider* NGO did not monitor the groups' management of their savings, choosing only to monitor the credit it had given. The NGO was asked by the donor agency to become financially sustainable. The donor had even invested in capacity building of the NGO to do so. Yet, neither the NGO nor the donor had invested in building the capacities of the groups to manage their savings. Similarly, the capacity to manage women's own sav-ings was not created by many *provider* microfinance organisations in Orissa. Instead, the MFIs collected women's savings as security, and also as additional capital for loans. This exposed SHGs to the risk of not being able to deal with local emergencies. When the external agency concentrates on the provision and management of only the credit they deliver, they leave women vulnerable to aspects of local leadership and social dynamics which exposes women to the risk of losing their small savings. The evidence indicates that though *facilitator* NGOs try to build local capacities of groups to manage money, they do not have the *locus standi* to enforce discipline that would safeguard women's savings. Therefore, the safety of women's savings in SHGs continues to be vulnerable to deviant management and processes. *Provider* NGOs, on the other hand, have more interest in their own financial sustainability and tend to focus on aspects of the efficiency of their own operations rather than building groups' capacities for money management.

Competing Interests

The different meanings of money are evident in the understanding of the cash kept by women in the *baksa* (box). Women's SHGs retain cash in the group or in the box. The NGO in Jharkhand considered this to be *idle cash*, believing that this money could get more returns if utilised as a loan.

If money was kept *in the box*, the NGO saw it as a lack of demand for loans. The NGO believed it had the ability to transfer money from *net savers* to *net investors* and sought to transfer such *idle* funds to groups seeking loans. Women kept this money for emergency needs, including medical treatment of malaria, snakebites, accident victims, and so on. They see seasonal fluctuations in the *box cash* as normal, expecting to build it up slowly, so that when the agricultural season began, all women could take loans. If the amount was too small to meet all business needs, they build up the amount to be able to meet large needs by rotation. Sometimes, there was cash left in the box because it was difficult to deposit and withdraw from distant bank branches. Women consequently did not perceive box money as *idle* but as an important *back-up* and a *buffer* when they needed it. Thus, fund retention at the group level enables women to exercise more choices than would be allowed if it is collected together and used by the NGO/MFI.

Four NGOs visited in the first phase of research, in Jharkhand, Orissa, Uttar Pradesh and Tamil Nadu (TN), were known to be under pressure to become sustainable microfinance organisations. This called for more loans to SHGs, and increased access to the savings of SHGs wherever possible. In Jharkhand, once the groups were up to 2–3 years old, their savings were substantial, and the women were confident about handling larger investments into IGAs. So they used their own savings more and reduced their NGO loans. This created a problem for an NGO then poised for 'transformation'. Its head exclaimed:

> If women continue to take more and more loans from their own savings rather than from the NGO, we will have to keep on making new groups and derive all our income from small loans to new groups: a perpetual cycle in which we can never break even. We can become financially sustainable only if we mop up all the savings of the women's groups and rotate them through the organisation.

He clearly recognised that the NGO needed to manage women's savings to make its financial operations viable. Such statements by NGO heads show how they rationalise control of women's money and sometimes unintentionally, subvert the very intention of women's development towards that of the institution.

Another rationale extended by an NGO/MFI in Orissa was that, as these women were illiterate, they did not understand complicated financial matters and could not benefit from the scale, systems and leveraging of funds. It was therefore better *for them* to put their money in the hands of *professionals*, namely NGO/MFIs, and derive the benefits through *access to much larger loans*. As an NGO manager in Kalahandi district of Orissa put it: 'Women are illiterate, they do not understand use of finances, we must make all the decisions for them.' While some NGO heads and staff thus rationalised the move towards transforming themselves into MFIs, others faced internal tensions. A field officer explained:

> We used to sit with women and talk about their issues. After the micro-credit project started, it is only—'Give money, take money; Give loan, take loan'. The only work we do now is related to loans and money. There are no other conversations anymore.

The founder of an NGO in Uttar Pradesh, which was planning transformation into an MFI, referred to another aspect of the tension that arose between the NGO and women's organisations.

'We used to teach women to use their savings. We created federations that learnt to do so. Now we will collect all these savings to create a larger and profitable organisation for ourselves. How will we explain this to the federation members?' Another woman founder of an NGO engaged in microfinance in TN echoed this when she said:

> We created clusters and federations of women; we taught them to retain a larger part of the profit at the local level. We encouraged them to question the NGO's use of money. Now we want to take away more of their savings, and appropriate a greater part of the interest earnings and become financially sustainable ourselves! They will question us about these changes; about the costs. How do you think I can explain this to women in our clusters and federations? They will feel let down. Do the funding agencies not see this, do they not realise they are pushing us in the wrong direction, undoing all we have done in the past in terms of building strong women's clusters and federations?

These statements highlight the competition between MFIs and women-owned organisations to control the flow and profits from money management and provide support for women's classification of money as *own* and *external*.

By contrast, the PRADAN staff viewed the savings collection of tribal women as a positive development. PRADAN lobbied with a local bank to extend cash-credit facilities to the SHGs, whereby each group would be sanctioned a loan, which they could draw on as needed, and repay as and when they had cash, thereby paying interest only on amount outstanding. Few groups drew on this facility, and those who did take loans, repaid these as soon as their savings could substitute the external loans. PRADAN did not consider the non-use of the external facility as a disadvantage, though the donor agency of the project did, and was concerned that PRADAN strategy enabled low credit inflow to the women. PRADAN did not build its own pecuniary interest in the microfinance operation and encouraged self-reliance of tribal women's SHGs instead. When women have to choose between a local bank and their own money, they continue to prioritise use of own money. This is further evidence of women's preference of *own* over *external* money.

Reconciling Women's Perspectives and NGO Decisions

The slow development of groups with 'good discipline', the lack of control over money that women faced due to their illiteracy, the frequent division of group savings and the relatively low demand for external loans across Sampark groups together forced it to rethink microfinance methodologies in Koppal. When the NGO started, the initial plan was to form three levels of financial organisations: SHGs, clusters of 6–10 groups each, based on geographical proximity, and a federation of all the clusters at the district level, as depicted in Figure 5.8

However, the groups soon faced leadership problems and could not establish standard practices for loan making, interest rates and repayment schedules. It was reckoned that creating collaborative organisations at a larger level, when even the basic units were not yet stabilised in terms of accountability and financial transactions, was premature. And, so, Sampark decided against forming a third layer, the *taluk* level federation. Instead, it concentrated on strengthening the groups in 2002–04,

Figure 5.8
Structure of Women's Organisations

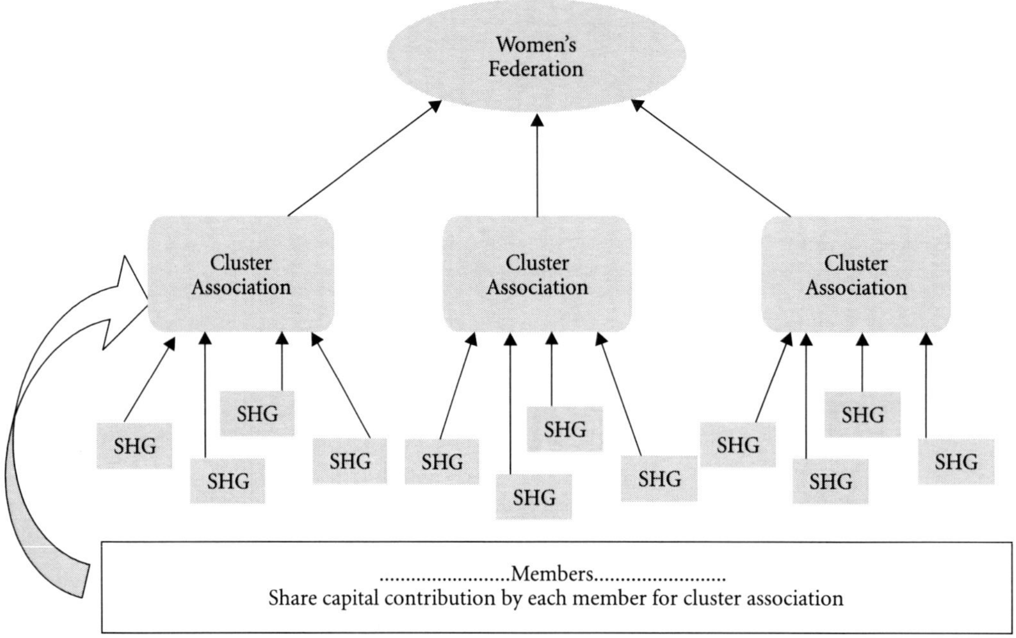

Source: Authors.

and training the groups to form cluster associations in 2004–06. By 2006, 10 cluster associations had been formed, comprising 200–300 women each, with each woman contributing Rs 100 ($2.22) to the share capital. At this time, the NGO found a possibility of raising large loan funds if women came together in one common federation. Women had by then learnt to debate and decide independently about questions raised by the NGO, so they held several discussions about this issue. As they rotated money at the group and cluster level, and they realised that every layer, in terms of a second and third tier organisation, could also add administrative as well as financial costs. They debated the added value of incurring these costs, that is, the benefits that would accrue by having a *taluk* federation, which they would lose with just SHGs and clusters. Savitramma, leader of Rangamma's group and also at the cluster level, articulated their opinion to Sampark as follows:

> Now we give loans from the group and earn interest of 2 per cent per month at group level. When we take loans from the cluster level, we have to share the interest earnings with the cluster association. If we introduce a third layer, the profit at group level cannot be retained. As the group members share the risk of non-repayment, we want to keep the profits at group level. So we do not want to have a federation for micro credit. What we now need from Sampark is to get us more grants and marketing linkages with the government so that we can start more businesses.

The field manager of Sampark explained the dynamic further:

> The women are right and we have stopped promoting the federation idea. We are now concentrating on strengthening the clusters. But it is very difficult to convince external agencies. If we approach them for bulk lending to the groups, they want to deal with the NGO. We have to show scale and volumes to be able to raise loan funds. If we keep hesitating to form a united forum of women at the taluk or district level, we will not become a visible force, and will not be interesting for external agencies.

The pull between external and local perceptions was clearly felt by the NGO manager, who tried to balance the two expectations and to achieve what he felt was 'progress' through the SHG-based microfinance initiative.

These tensions are recognised in democracy and accountability debates which highlight that, over time, NGOs usually confront the problem of role reversal: from demanding of accountability to being targets.[4] For Sampark, this was resolved by December 2007, when these cluster associations were registered as cooperatives, and linked to the Pragati Grameen Bank (PGB) for meeting all their loan needs. In India, Regional Rural Banks (RRBs) have been able to change their attitudes, recognise credit to women's groups and federations as a good business proposition, and move, over time, towards extending formal credit to women's organisations.

Role of Institutional Form

The role of institutional form in the delivery of microfinance has been examined in literature from *supply* (of microfinance) perspective (as discussed in Chapters 1 and 2). The issue of institutional forms, when viewed from the perspective of sustainable *demand* for credit and use of money in ways that empower the members, takes a different dimension.

The research was conducted in a context where the NGO, Sampark, was a *facilitator* of credit linkages. It had limited funds for capacity building, which were spent on technical, leadership and group management training. This had positive effects at individual and group levels, as illustrated in the following cases. The direct impact of training in technical and leadership skills was often positive and significant. For example, Sushila's training in tailoring helped her sustain her family. Kaveri was given training in horticulture, following which she bought plants to put on her farm and homestead and increased the consumption of green leafy vegetables in the household. Sangavva received training from the agricultural department in seed conservation and has applied it to her benefit. Lakshmavva benefited from training in leadership, buffalo rearing and the conservation of hay. A workshop on natural resource management held at the village level benefited not only the participants but also several others in the village. Exposure visits to different groups not only gave the women new clues towards the better management of SHGs but also made them realise that they all faced common problems, for example, alcoholism as a result of liquor shops in their vicinities. Visits by outsiders to the group have brought other opportunities for exchange of opinions and new lessons for everyone. One SHG debated the possibility of augmenting skills of women so they could earn from IGAs like tailoring. On request, Sampark organised tailoring classes for the women and their daughters. While the daughters who were able to stay away from *coolie* attended these classes, the women who were sole earning members of their households could not find the time to acquire new skills.

At the group level, SHG management trainings helped to train groups to manage their own money, to access credit from formal sources. The members had the power to decide whether or not to access loans and on what terms. The use of credit was therefore demand dependent. Traditional impact hypotheses for assessing microfinance impact track its use for microenterprise promotion. Such supply-oriented focus overlooks the possible situation that the primary objective of group formation may not be access to credit. If the objective of women in forming SHGs is to save, not (exclusively) to borrow, a credit focus may eventually be misdirected. There is an empowering impact of retention, management and use of savings by women's groups. This empowerment derives from the financial aspect of creation of capital at the group level as well as social capital created through group processes. Women need to be able to collect and control their own savings, and must at all times know the risks and advantages of a particular deployment of their capital, as well as have control over the expenses of the organisation. This requires an investment in building women's capacity to manage such organisations. Further, while profitability of credit and savings services provided through external agencies can be contingent on scale, women-controlled organisations may benefit from being small or medium size. Thus, the institutional form of the NGO/MFI is important if seen from the perspective of ownership, control and management of finances. The divergence of the two perspectives of external agencies, namely financial services and empowerment perspectives, may be seen as two different paths (Figure 5.9).

If the starting premise is that there is a large demand/supply gap in microfinance which needs to be filled, the solution is to reorganise the supply of these services, often through the creation of sustainable MFIs. In this approach, the role of SHGs is limited to reaching women in an explicitly cost-effective manner. Other empowering impacts of management of the services by women themselves are not considered important. However, if empowerment of the poor and women is the objective, then, women's preferences and priorities for use of their own savings become important. Women prefer SHG-bank linkage to MFIs loans for meeting additional credit needs, as it does not prevent their access to their own savings. Further, the need for building women's capacities also becomes important, both at the group level and at secondary or apex institutions, such as, federations or cooperatives. The empowerment approach calls for long-term investment in building people and NGO's capacities. The conflicts between these two perspectives are not easy to resolve. On the one hand, the supply of microfinance, on reasonable terms, from the formal sector is indeed limited. On the other hand, when NGO/MFIs offer credit on commercial terms, it also becomes too expensive and some women opt not to use it. This highlights that the importance of *unsubsidised* model of credit by RRBs, which women preferred, was based on a long-term relationship and has become more and more popular in Koppal district from 2001 to 2008.

Figure 5.9
Different Perspectives, Divergent Paths

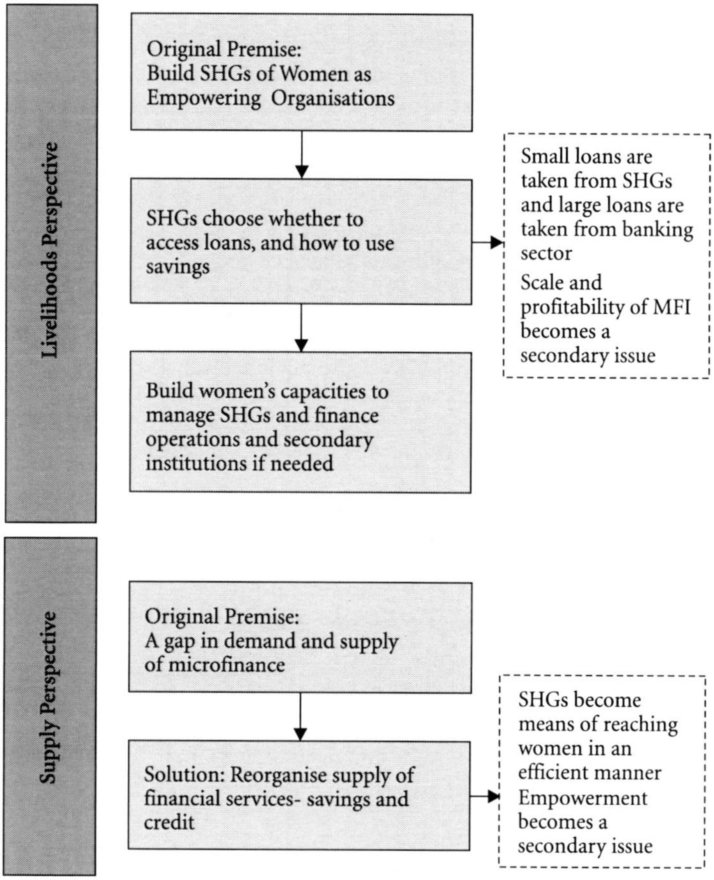

Source: Authors.

IMPLICATIONS FOR EMPOWERMENT IMPACTS

The understanding of women's own management of their saving and their group dynamics shows how social learning processes fostered through SHGs create empowering impacts at the individual, group and community levels. In turn, this has further implications for the type of MFI to be promoted.

Groups Creating Social Capital

Social capital improved by the very process of the women coming together, even in a research context where groups were weak in money management, women did not have the time to attend group meetings and the NGO provided little training. Social impacts of SHGs and their savings and credit activities were wide ranging, as illustrated in Table 5.6. The analysis classifies four types of improving impacts: cognitive, perceptual, relational and community level impacts.[5]

Table 5.6
Social Impacts

Cognitive	• Increased awareness and knowledge
Perceptual	• Confidence in relating to bankers and government officials
Relational	• Status and recognition in family and community
	• Improvements in contacts among peers, through group membership
	• New contacts created, with banks and government officials, local leaders, businesses
Community Level	• Wide range of community activities and influence

Source: Authors.

At the cognitive level, women experienced an increase in awareness and knowledge not only about money and its management but also about their wider world, for example, knowledge of government schemes and how the education or banking systems work. Their own judgements of these organisations changed and they developed more confidence to respond to, approach and represent their needs and preferences to external agencies with whom they had never interacted directly before. They explained:

> *Now we feel comfortable to discuss and communicate with people. When someone visits our houses we are able to discuss why they have come, their projects and plans.*—Mariyamma

> Before joining the group I didn't know anything. I did not have any idea of saving money and did not know how to count. I did not know that the saved money can come to our rescue. Now I have learnt about it and I have the courage to speak; I also participate in group discussions and I can also take decision. —Nagavva.

> I gained knowledge about different aspects of functioning of groups, and about the savings and credit systems. I gained knowledge of banking procedures and bank loans. Now I can teach other new groups about group tasks and activities. I never had any idea about groups before joining one, now I have attended many training programmes in Koppal, Huvinala, Hosahalli, Hyati and Bahadurbandi. I had the chance to speak with and interact with different people. I came to Sampark office at least eight times in the past two years, and gained knowledge about group management, audit, business, etc. Now for some time Sampark has not provided new information and training, they are busy organising more groups. I am not happy to just have group meetings, I want training often.—Rangamma.

> Earlier I did not know anything about a group. When the staff came to our *Keri* (street) they talked about Sampark, SHG and savings. After they left our *keri*, people said that these people have come to take our money so don't pay any heed. I was frightened by this, so I waited a bit. Once when I went to Halegondabala

for *coolie* work, where a few members from another group were discussing about their group and savings. Then I learnt about the group concept and that savings will help us in times of difficulty. Earlier I had to beg my landlords if I needed a hundred-rupee loan, and I also had to leave my sons as bonded labour with these landlords for any loan advance. Now I have escaped all of these since I am in an SHG. The members of the Mudhaballi group and our community have benefited a lot after forming the group, and can also get benefits under the government schemes. I want to come out of my poverty so I joined the group. If women work through SHGs, they can also come forward. If someone falls sick or if there is some function I take money from the group, but if I ask others they do not give in time, so by saving in the group there are lots of benefits and no problems. By becoming a member of a group, we gain knowledge about repaying loans, how to take loans and so on. In this way, I get knowledge about all aspects. After joining the group, I have also learnt to write my name, I have a bank account and I also know how to deal with bankers and do banking transactions.

Every week we have group meetings and we discuss government schemes. Now, they are giving some loans from the SC/ST Corporation for doing dairy farming. The sangha members are thinking of buying goats. For the past three years, after forming the sangha, we have not benefited from any scheme, so now we want to make use of this opportunity. If we get this scheme it will be very helpful for us. Nowadays no schemes come for the village as the elders of the village are not good. We are happy about the Sampark people as they have given us knowledge about the group. They have told us about going to Koppal to discuss issues about loans. Three members from our sangha will go and we will get the information. We have already informed the members to repay the loan in time if they take one. Earlier I did not have any information about bank or bank loan, but now after forming the group, Sampark staff gave us the information about the bank, loan from bank, how to get it by presenting the required papers and for what purpose to take it. Our bank account is in TGB Koppal for the past 1.5 years. We have Rs 8,500 ($189) in it. Since our money is in the bank, we have confidence in it, and also we know about bank officers as we go to the bank. We can get loan from the bank—Yellamma.

Earlier, we did not know how to talk with people like the bank manager and those who work in 'official' places. We used to be scared to talk in public places. Now I am able to talk with group members, non-members, and have learnt how to convince government officers and bank managers. Because of group formation, we have learnt where to go, for which information. For example, when there was a need to get permission to get electricity for our dairy shed we went to the electricity department and got the connection. Now I am able to talk for a Kannada TV program in front of an audience without any hesitation. Earlier, we rarely went out of the village i.e. Koppal. Now we have been to Gulbarga, and big cities like Bangalore.

This was not easy, I faced a lot of problems in the initial stages. I used to go to each house to convince the women to attend literacy classes so we could manage our group better. I used to leave in the evening and come back late at night. My husband punished me, saying that instead of helping the daughter-in-law with the cooking, I had gone visiting, so he did not allow me to enter the house, I had to sleep outside that night. My daughter came later with some food for me, and then she joined me on these rounds. My husband punished us again, and we slept hungry.—Bharmavva, leader, Durgadevi group[6]

She laughed as she related these incidents and was quite convinced that she had done her duty as group leader, despite her husband's objections.

Women also claim that they receive more recognition from their husbands and children for accessing loans and for acquiring new learning. Their own confidence in their abilities increases, as they develop the savings-habit and can now create joint capital for themselves. The confidence building that takes place through groups cannot be easily explained. Women come together slowly, sharing first the money transactions and then discussing other matters. They usually do not talk openly about domestic violence; yet later found the courage to protest against such treatment within the household. For instance, Sushila's husband used 25 per cent of the household income, all of which she earned, for alcohol, and would beat her to extract it from her. She gave it as she lives in a small house in a crowded neighbourhood, and felt ashamed if the neighbours heard their quarrels. But, after forming and leading her SHG, she developed more confidence to stop giving money for alcohol. She says: 'Now I refuse to give him money for drinks. I earn it for the food and education of my children. Let him earn the money he spends on drinks.'

They also become much more assertive regarding control over financial decision making. One group member says:

> If we feel that the loan is for the family, then we take it from the group, but if we feel that it is only for the husband, then we do not even propose it to the group. We also involve the husband and family members in repaying the group loans.

Men leaders in the villages also acknowledge women's needs and desires, who state that women's groups have made them 'realise that women exist'. Sangamma *Pujari*, a leader and the temple priest of the SC community in Bikanhalli elaborates:

> We never really took women into account. We did not really see them, they were around, and that is all! Now at least we see our women as being there. They used to hide their faces, wrap their clothes tightly about them, and move away when they saw us approaching. Now they leave their faces open, and approach us without any hesitation. They have begun to demand equal rights! They actually asked to use soap and coconut oil in their hair like men do. They said, you have to allow us. How is it that men can use soap and coconut oil and we cannot? We had to allow them to use these things! I used to get more respect then, now I hardly get the respect that an elder and leader should get.

He says all this in a seemingly matter-of-fact way, feeling little rancour. It is as if these changes are inevitable and women are right to demand more equality, as male leaders accede.

Women are able to make representations to the government to remove local liquor shops, start bus routes and appoint teachers to the village school. They contribute to the community by donating glasses, water filters and furniture to village schools and cash for celebrations of festivals and cultural events. They plan and carry out community activities like cleaning village roads and the vicinity of the drinking water wells. There are instances of managing conflicts in situations of community resources management. In an SHG in Orissa, Tulsi Jani was a member of an SHG federation. She stood for *panchayat* election and was elected president to the *Palli Sabha* (Gram Sabha). An SHG in her federation bid for and obtained the contract for a pond reconstruction, but the politicians tried to cheat them out of the contract. The women not only confronted the politicians but also managed to get the contract with the help of Tulsa Jani, who

> *We had a discussion about our community problems. We don't have a water facility and also poor people did not get BPL card, so I want to go to the gram panchayat office to talk about these with the secretary.*— Yellamma

declared: 'If women cannot do this work, how am I President here?' There are several other similar incidents of SHG women challenging politicians and government officers.

These activities generate more confidence among women because they are able to influence their immediate living environment and have the collective power to take action, and their status improves both as individuals and as groups. Women, who cannot afford loans for IGAs, can nevertheless take grants and loans for their children's education when the NGO or government offers these.

Such positive actions are limited to household and village domains and do not challenge discrimination on the basis of caste in terms of eating and drinking with the lower castes, except occasionally when attending the NGO's training programmes.

> *All the members come for the meeting every week so I feel happy to go to the meeting.*
> —Yellamma

This brings out the important effect of banking on social capital. The formation of 'homogeneous' groups on the basis of castes and gender reinforces the low status of the group members, for example, *devadasis*. Such homogenous composition has some benefits, but it also has major limitations, that is, it is difficult to break out of the positioning at the lowest rung of the socio-economic cultural ladder. Microfinance organisations can create new opportunities for women to relate to one another beyond their SHGs, which could result in new social and economic linkages, which in turn could enable a break from traditional caste groupings, thus creating new forms of emergent social capital. NGOs enable such augmentation of social capital by conducting capacity building workshops for women, and by linking the groups to banks. Education of children also helps improve the human capital and asset base of the household and therefore bolster its future capacity to absorb credit.

Introduction of SHGs as forums for women creates new socio-economic spaces that allow for more individual aspirations to be met, emotions to be expressed and self-esteem improved. The positive impacts evident at the individual, family and community level are proof of the SHGs' role in creating local capital. This building of social capital takes place through social learning processes in SHGs. It is a trial-and-error process through which women learn. These processes need to be supported, monitored, evaluated and enhanced with a learning perspective. The system evolved should be suited to women's context-specific needs and preferences, rather than the general application of externally devised 'best practices'.

> *When I first went to the bank, I did not have the courage to go inside, so I sat outside. Now I have the courage to go to a bank and also understand how people pay money to the bank and get money from there.*—Parvathamma

SUMMARY

Savings is the key financial activity that binds groups together, and its use reflects the needs of women. Group management of savings involves social processes of cooperation as well as conflict resolution. This leaves women open to risk of loss of money if their savings are mismanaged, or if some members, or non-members to whom they have lent money, do not repay. Non-repayment to banks also leads to them being termed as defaulters, which means denial of further subsidised support through government schemes.

The greatest success of the group-based methodology of lending has been the change in orientations it has brought about at the macro-level, in terms of inducing the government as well as banks to adopt it for reaching credit to large numbers of rural people. This change in the collective orientations has led to greater receptivity and enhanced flows of credit from the banking sector to the rural poor. Thus, the 'transforming structures' have changed to accommodate a new methodology for reaching the poor, and this has had cascading positive impacts. While the proliferation of microfinance has positive financial impacts at the individual and collective levels, it has also had negative impacts, such as increased vulnerability through group processes.

Having looked at the three themes that influence the impact of microfinance in the previous three chapters, the next chapter restates and consolidates the conclusions from the research. It takes a broad livelihoods view of impact, discusses the barriers to greater impact, in terms of the orientations and values of different actors, and how these influence meanings and strategies with regard to money as a resource.

NOTES

1. This practice is promoted by facilitating NGOs, who consider varying individual savings difficult for book keeping, especially if illiterate women have to manage their financial transactions on their own.
2. Premchander (2002) discusses the difference between local and external perspectives in money management and group monitoring.
3. See Acharya and Premchander (1999) and Sampark (2000) for confirmation in many states.
4. Goetz and Jenkins (2005) trace how earlier NGOs demanded accountability from the state and later NGO accountability was questioned with regard to their reach and effectiveness in poverty alleviation.
5. Chen's (1997) framework considers the first three types of impacts, and here an additional category has been introduced to identify and emphasise community level positive actions that women had taken through their groups.
6. Bharmavva suffered a paralytic stroke and passed away in 2007.

6

Conclusions and Reflections

This book has attempted to explore the impact of microfinance from women's perspective, by studying how women in semi-arid and tribal contexts use money and what meanings they assign to it, given the different models through which it is offered to them.

The recent trajectories of different pathways to development work have brought the government, banks and non-government organisations (NGOs) to a point where each, for different reasons, converged upon microfinance as critical for poverty reduction. It is now regarded as an improvement over traditional development banking, which targeted the poor with subsidised credit and proved ineffective. This approach had combined various official poverty reduction schemes, which not only had proved costly but also did not reach the target group. Microfinance provided a way out of unsustainable and expensive donor funding, which wanted to involve the poor as 'agents' rather than as 'targets' of development and was keen on proving its impacts. Thus, at a time when the external environment no longer supported the welfare state concept, microfinance provided a means to restore actor agency, improve development investments and demonstrate impact upon poverty even while enhancing social capital and women's empowerment. This dominant policy model led to the unprecedented growth of microfinance in India, as elsewhere, since the mid-1980s.[1]

Field observations of a wide range of NGOs and women self-help group (SHG) members, however, show an increasing divergence between external and local perspectives about the use of money and social relationships that influence it. Microfinance impact studies did not explore meaning; they tracked the use of microfinance institution (MFI) loans and their impacts at the household level. Positive impacts were emphasised in an environment which promoted neoliberal ideologies and used the empowerment discourse to justify the use of women's collective time and responsible loan repayment behaviour to promote organisational objectives. The dominance of policy models was therefore evident in the context of microfinance.[2] In order to check the ground reality of the policy model, this study prioritised women's perspectives and set out to discover what money means to women, as reflected in how they access, use and manage it. The experiences of women provided an understanding of the multiple meanings of money.

EFFECT OF THE LIVELIHOODS CONTEXT

The livelihoods context (ecological, economic, social and institutional) is an important factor in determining the use and impact of credit. The availability, demand and impacts of microfinance are related to the livelihoods context in which people are embedded.

Ecological and Economic Constraints

The ecological conditions of Koppal are compounded by a loss of forest cover, low rainfall, groundwater depletion and increasing salinity of soils, which makes agriculture risky and unprofitable. Unplanned irrigation based on groundwater extraction has aggravated the problems of soil salinity and led to drops in groundwater levels. Formal banking credit to SHGs is limited and only one Regional Rural Bank (RRB) has provided loans to SHGs outside of official subsidies, and some private MFIs have appeared in recent years. The supply of credit does not meet the needs of those poor households who have to migrate to repay their loans as Mosse et al., (2004) also found.

In Koppal, acute concern about household survival results in greater groundwater exploitation. Reduced groundwater levels endanger the sustainability of local livelihoods in the long term, as there are no efforts to replenish it. Thus, integrative strategies at the community level and collective problem solving efforts are needed. Official credit, which is targeted at households, does not address the ecological dimensions of semi-arid livelihoods. Additionally, the gendered nature of land ownership meant that women are excluded from land-based decision making. Official grants and credit for agriculture and watershed development are channelled through farmers' (men's) organisations, reinforcing this exclusion. Thus, the gendered nature of aid and asset allocation ensures that collective efforts cannot be made on natural resource management, in any case not through women's forums.

Other recent research recognises that depressed rural markets limit the scope of microcredit as an income generating strategy.[3] NGOs typically concentrate credit activities in those areas where the social and physical infrastructure is relatively well developed, and thus provide credit to better placed and better-off groups compared to the poor located in interior and less developed areas (Fernandez 2005). Indian banking experience also recognises that financial services, through banking and micro-finance organisations (MFOs), have favoured better-off regions rather than less affluent ones.[4] Those living in remote areas are more reluctant to participate in credit programmes.[5] While earlier microfinance impact studies do not consider the literature that links agro-ecological considerations with poverty,[6] economic and development literature marks the relationship between poverty, migration and indebtedness.[7]

Further, this study finds that credit directed at households can exacerbate the ecological problem, as the money is used for short-term solutions like borewells which reduce groundwater levels and contribute to increasing salinisation. Thus, current academic debate needs to recognise the context dependence of credit off-take, the limits of household-directed credit and the need for community level solutions and funds to overcome ecological and market constraints. The vicious cycle of degradation of natural resources may only be reversed with different natural resource management practices. These will require long-term subsidies and investments for the regeneration of soil and water before substantial change in livelihoods can occur. And, thus far, while there is some recognition of the need for collaborative approaches for ground water management, both academic literature and development practice are yet to link the current credit methodologies with social relationships for alleviating contextual livelihoods constraints.

It is therefore important to prioritise better returns from the physical asset base. Given the low level of literacy and vocational skills among children, youth and adults, the skill profiles need to be raised as well before the poor can earn better. The economic arguments for augmenting the physical, human or natural capital of an area and providing safety nets for the most vulnerable and poor become relevant to creating sustainable livelihoods in these marginalised areas.[8]

Institutional Orientations and Values

People's financial behaviour is based on their values and orientations, which are influenced by those of the external agencies that bring these finances to them.

The relationship between the government and the people was problematic. For one, there was corruption. The administrative systems in Koppal and the political actors involved (*panchayat* and Legislative Assembly leaders) are often either apathetic or corrupt.[9] Though corruption was challenged by the groups, both rent-seeking behaviour and the claiming of *percentages*[10] by mediators of official grants were viewed as part of the *system* and accepted as such. Then, government officials and local leaders act as intermediaries to distribute such schemes, so that the poor are not equal partners in development. Many NGOs, too, identify such beneficiaries and link them with official schemes, while themselves imposing mediating charges of their own.

Further, government support is not seen as a legitimate right but as a benefit that the state provides. Poverty is among the qualifications for accessing resources from government programmes (BPL cards). Other criteria include social exclusion: caste and religion (SCs, STs, OBCs, minorities), age, widowhood, being a *devadasi* and other disabilities. Actors can show *poverty*, or such eligibility as is needed, to access resources from external agents. When the channelling of external resources depends on showing household *poverty*, it creates competition and a bias towards claiming poverty and the related *benefits* to which it entitles them. It leads to a preference for, and dependence upon, external resources and actors. Thus, the relationship that developed between the government and the poor was that of giver and receiver, or benefactor and beneficiary, often favouring only the benefactor and intermediary.

SHG women and NGOs differ about what NGOs can and should do. Facilitator NGOs view capacity building as important. While women acknowledge that they have learnt how to save and manage in groups, they consider the subsidised financial linkages with banks and governments more important, and expect that NGOs enable them to access free government funds. Here arises a major conflict in the meaning of the 'NGO' itself. Some NGOs channel some benefits to people while appropriating a proportion of the resources. If an NGO seeks, instead, to help the people gain long-term access to unsubsidised and *clean* funds, the latter sees them as more expensive. The general expectation from the NGO is that it will channel external resources into the village, and this shapes much discussion of what is given, and how it is given and received. Thus, actor orientations are adapted to those of the larger administrative and political system, an important factor to be considered for any intervention strategy to improve the livelihoods of the poor.

The inherent weaknesses in the value base show up, as people do not move on from household to wider community-based strategies of resource and property management. Administrative and political actors also do not consider the community but seek to increase their own earnings from the service delivery, and many local actors play safe by following the system of corruption rather than challenging it.

Only a few actors consider sustainability of the natural resource base important, while government efforts do not directly help poverty reduction. The value base of one set of actors is thus corruption oriented and they appropriate benefits meant for the poor. The strategies of the local population, on the other hand, are based on household survival and therefore not oriented towards those community solutions which can be critical for achieving sustainable livelihoods. This is especially true given the prevailing conditions of a semi-arid region, as depicted in Figure 6.1, using the actor-oriented perspectives framework.

Emerging literature about organisational learning and accountability emphasises the importance of integrating the value systems of NGOs, donors and the state,[11] and how social learning processes and communicative action are needed for efficient governance of natural resources.[12] Yet, in practice, such integration is difficult, as seen from the experiences narrated here, where state processes are largely corrupt, an NGO has to choose between aligning with the larger structure to *channel* benefits to the poor or to play an activist role in challenging the structure itself.

Socio-cultural Orientations

Caste-based persistence of poverty is evident in Koppal, with the SCs and STs being among the most marginalised, most poor and asset-less households.[13] The community in Koppal is highly fragmented, with caste-based stratification, ostracisation practices and orientations that marginalise the SCs. Little change has occurred in Koppal, despite the existence of Dalit Sanghas and NGOs, and laws against untouchability. Though microfinance provided some economic support, wider social dignity was still denied to *devadasi* women and to SCs, in general. There are relatively few development interventions in Koppal that have made a real difference to these social norms and practices.

Zohir and Matin (2004) conceptualise wider social impacts such as changes in social relations through mobilising and motivating social organisations to initiate change. Such a process has not been

Figure 6.1
Values of Local and External Actors

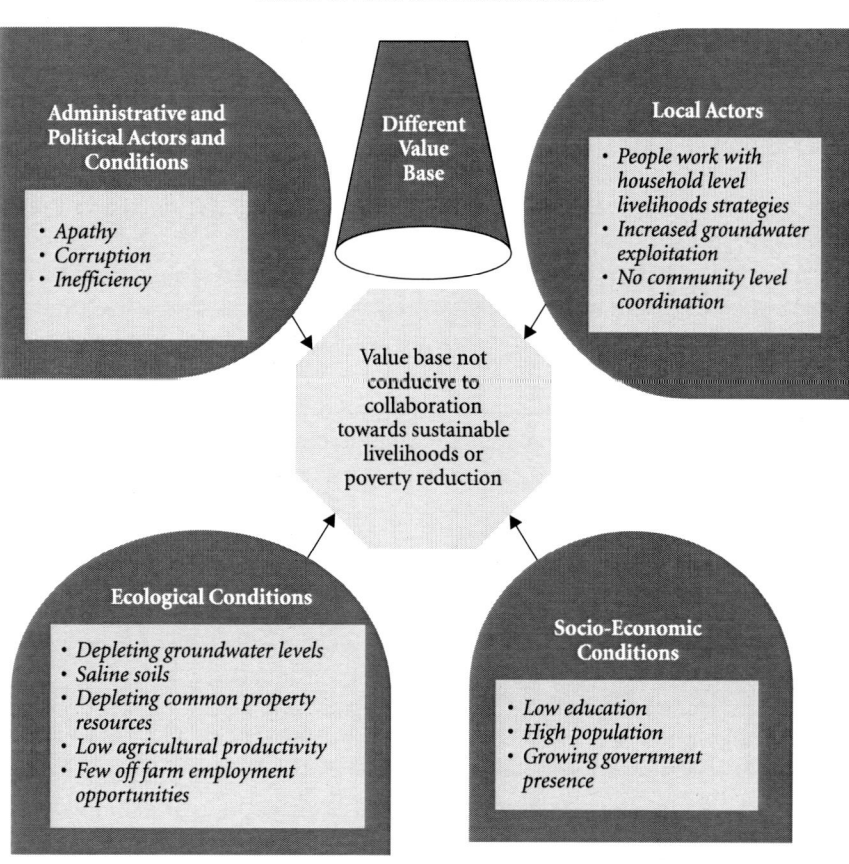

Source: Author.

put forth in any of the groups studied here. Women now borrow less from the landlords individually, yet at the collective, community level; microfinance makes little impact in caste discriminatory practices, with actors stating that they cannot break existing social relations because they are bound to landlords through economic ties.

The question arises whether in this deeply caste-divided society, women's SHGs, as small collectives of women of homogeneous social composition, can lead to wider social impacts. The concept of *affinity* or *neighbourhood* groups indicates a preference for selecting people for building up financial linkages, as there are already existing conditions of trust. Thus, microfinance programmes could even deepen caste affiliations and reduce the incentive for practitioners to ameliorate rural caste discrimination. Indeed, the government may find it easier to channel its benefits through caste-based groups, which deepens caste divides in the name of *affinity*, although there were occasional cases of SHGs bridging caste divisions through NGO initiatives.[14] Thus, affinity-based groups for channelling official support and microfinance are cost efficient in terms of supplying services, yet deepen social divides instead of bridging them.

It is necessary to caution that mainstreaming and treating *devadasi* women as village poor obscures the special issues that they face, (for example, the specific isolation and deprivation of human rights) but having separate groups of SCs, or *devadasi*s can also isolate them, and perpetuate their existing social exclusion. The latter, however, is needed in order to improve access for SC women to state economic support. Thus, strategies that mainstream socially excluded groups can also ignore them, while those that give special attention can further marginalise them. Emerging research recognises this tension. For instance, caste, marriage laws, practice of child marriage and literacy are all factors which determine women's autonomy and social participation[15] and that the balance between enabling women to access benefits, while still enabling greater solidarity can be difficult to achieve.[16]

The expectation of the impact on livelihoods, from a sector-specific intervention like microfinance, has to be tempered with the understanding that significant impact requires more than microfinance alone, and other efforts are needed to make an impact on ecological and social constraints. A change in socio-cultural orientations is essential before socially marginalised groups can attain sustainable livelihoods.

The limits of microfinance in making wider impacts are evident elsewhere. In programmes in Peru, rather than create social structures which will challenge unequal kinship and patron–client relationships, microcredit groups are instead rife with internal competition, corruption by leaders and reinforced existing hierarchies and inequalities.[17] Indeed, most microfinance organisations do not intervene in cases of group conflicts effectively regarding them as an internal social issue. They view financial sustainability as their primary objective, and fear negative publicity. In all, the MFOs lack time, skills and systems for resolving group conflicts. The result is to enforce rather than challenge power relationships in the wider community.[18] Recent ethnographies demonstrate that while microfinance could develop a collective social debates regarding gender and class inequality, a lot hinges on whether such debates are promoted within microfinance programmes, and upon if the MFI institutes a more normative agenda for development and facilitates more transformative interpretations of women's needs.[19]

Fernando (2006b) takes examples from ASA and Grameen Bank to show how donors are apprehensive that an emphasis on microcredit would be at the expense of education, advocacy and structural reforms. He quotes Hashemi of Grameen Bank as warning that any shift of emphasis away from conscientisation and social mobilisation to microlending would cause 'demise of the conscientisation paradigm' (Fernando 2006b: 207). Researchers in the Indian context have also recognised that attention to social issues depends on the emphasis the promoter NGO attaches to this issue. The RBI's fact-finding committee noted recently that microfinance organisations do not engage sufficiently in capacity building and group empowerment.[20] Thus, it is important to emphasise that alongside microfinance services, prioritisation of women's conscentisation and empowerment is needed to address ossified social hierarchies and inequalities.

USE OF MONEY

Microfinance impact literature has mostly addressed institutional concerns, without fully understanding the actors' perspective as the recipients of money. Women's agency or orientations and value base determine their strategies of money management and stewardship of resources such as land, family members, cattle and money, to improve their livelihoods. Here, women demonstrate that the use of money first depends upon the sources of that money, due to the values, like transparency, honesty, mutual support, on which the relationship between women and their creditors is based. These relationships influence the terms on which the money is available, and also determine the size of loans women take. Informal loans help smooth consumption or enable them to meet social or other urgent needs. However, there may be some exploitation inherent in availing loans from some local informal sources. Most women use formal loans for the productive purposes expected by banks and MFIs/NGOs. The poorest cannot afford commercial credit, because they cannot meet the stipulated terms. While some studies show that loans from groups and cooperatives reduce moneylender credit, others show that though nearly 90 per cent women take loans from SHGs, their dependence on moneylenders remains.[21]

Capacity of the Poorest Women to Take Loans

The livelihoods assets analysis demonstrates that women consider three types of assets—land, labour and money—equally important, and that a surplus of human or physical capital is needed to take the new credit terms offered under commercial microfinance. Without surplus income, they cannot take any credit that requires uniform and regular repayments, especially for projects generating seasonal income streams. These are distortions in the credit market working against the poor, who can only access credit from local informal sources at high rates of interest, and at potentially exploitative terms, which make productive use of such credit difficult. Women tend to take loans on these terms to meet their social needs (death ceremonies, marriages), and expenditures that they deem essential, rather than for income generating activities (IGAs). Money for improving livelihoods is important, yet credit does not lead the poorest out of poverty, as they cannot afford the credit offered.

The inability of the poorest to participate in microfinance is now recognised in emerging literature. One recent study found that dropout rates from groups are highest for the very poor, and those who migrate for short or long periods to work accounted for 40 per cent of dropouts in AP and Karnataka. Thirty per cent of women who dropped out of SHGs studied in Orissa and Rajasthan stated their inability to save was the primary reason for doing so.[22]

From a livelihoods perspective, SHGs can help women demand financial and non-financial services on terms better suited to their priorities. Savings help women convert small amounts of money into large sums, but the size of these savings is restricted by their limited ability to save. When women have full access to, and control over, their own savings, as in Koppal, they do not always abide by rules about regularity and use of savings and can prioritise their own particular needs. For instance, they sometimes divide their savings and distribute the accumulated amount rather than take fresh loans and pay interest. Decision making about use of money creates social learning processes that are important in building social capital.[23]

Impacts of Loans

The impact of loans was analysed according to whether they were taken from informal or formal sources, and a third source identified separately was from women's own savings, or group loans. The impacts identified were both economic and social and were also both positive and negative. This framework is depicted in Figure 6.2 and is used for analysing microfinance impacts.

The use of the money borrowed depends on several factors. For instance, the risk is related to the source of money; women's own capital is considered less risky than loans taken from external

Figure 6.2
Framework for Impact Assessment

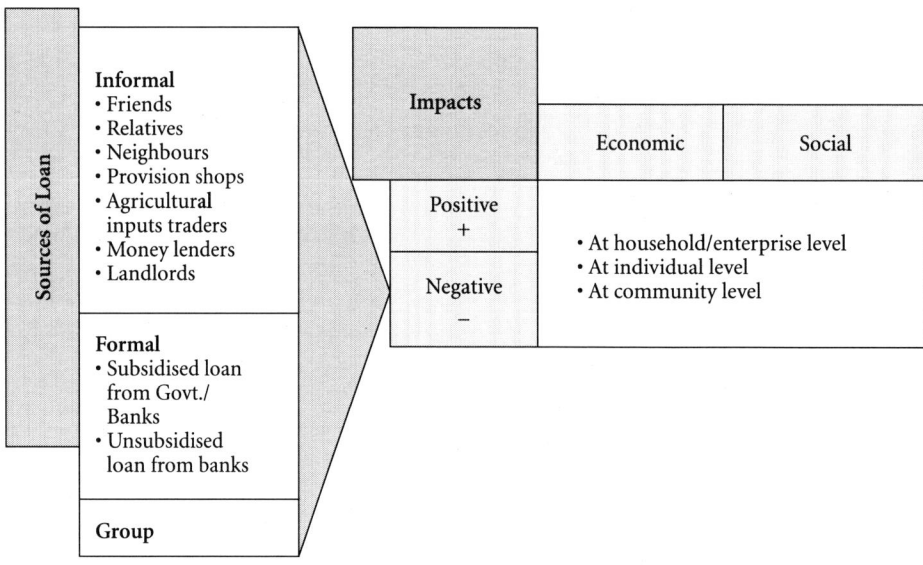

Source: Authors.

sources, whether formal or informal. Generally, women take informal (*kaigada*, handloans) loans from neighbours, friends and relatives, to cope with short-term financial difficulties. Provision shops and agricultural input traders extend credit in kind. These facilitate household consumption and small investments in agriculture, leading to income generating impacts through agricultural produce or *coolie* wages. These transactions are based on socially embedded local ties, as they are from neighbours, friends and relatives and therefore created positive reciprocity. However, they also tend to be limited by the capacity of providers. Financial transactions are socially embedded and existing social networks do not offer the financial capital to lift the poor out of poverty.

Similarly, the seasonality of cash flows in a primarily agricultural economy makes it difficult for women to follow uniform repayment schedules. Their capacity to repay loans is linked to the human capital of their family, which depends upon the number of its members and their earning capacities (that is, education, skills and migration). Thus, capital base is a good indicator for forming the baseline and measuring the impact of credit against it. On the issue of purpose of loans, it is found that women need consumption loans and take these from their groups on a regular basis. They are also tied into constraining labour arrangements with the landlord due to loans taken for consumption or social needs. Finally, the costs of credit and repayment terms are often too stringent to allow any margin on small, local and uncertain IGAs. Therefore, the credit offered and the credit actually needed by poor women does not match, resulting in reduced credit usage from external sources.

Recent evidence shows that improved access to cheaper credit over a long period provides means for women to invest in IGAs and human capital as well as consumption smoothening and asset building.[24]

The impacts of formal loans are presented in Figure 6.3.

The positive impacts of formal loans include income generation and asset creation. In cases where loans are given through honest and transparent processes, which is often not the case, the poor gain mainstream benefits and continued access to reasonably priced credit through banks. Negative impacts ensue when subsidised loans are provided through corrupt government staff, bankers, technical personnel and local leaders. People risk loss of assets, which creates a debt burden if they are not then able to repay the outstanding bank loans in their own names, with consequent loss of access to formal credit in future. By contrast, when banks provide unsubsidised and repeated loans to groups, they view SHGs as regular clients. In these cases, women can start more than one enterprise that would improve their household income and boost employment of family members.

The current discourse on microfinance has been dominated by discussions on financial and organisational sustainability of services, profitability and risk coverage. The emphasis on understanding people's perspectives has been secondary, and where considered, is motivated by the marketing rationale, which aims to design and deliver different microfinance products, always within the *sustainable MFO* framework. This orientation renders the exploration of meaning unnecessary. Microfinance has been approached as a mechanism of service delivery, rather than a process that has empowering and disempowering effects. The former, empowering effects, can be acknowledged, as it has a use for legitimisation of the funding support to microfinance services.

Figure 6.3
Impact of Formal Loans

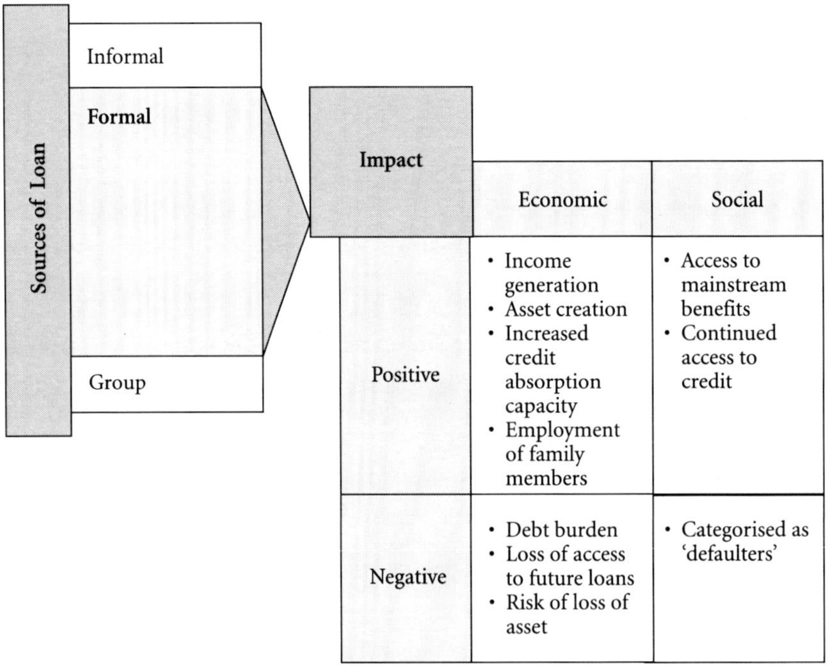

Sources of Loan		Impact		Economic	Social
Informal					
Formal			Positive	• Income generation • Asset creation • Increased credit absorption capacity • Employment of family members	• Access to mainstream benefits • Continued access to credit
Group			Negative	• Debt burden • Loss of access to future loans • Risk of loss of asset	• Categorised as 'defaulters'

Source: Authors.

But the latter, disempowering effects, is an unwelcome intruder to be avoided rather than accepted and dealt with. Even when the term *relationship banking* is used, it relates to banking on women's relationships with one another which, through the SHG mechanism, reduces the cost and riska to the MFO. Social relationships among women members of SHGs are not analysed beyond assumptions of homogeneity and affinity leading to trust, so that any conflicts of leadership and power within groups are ignored. The relationships between SHGs and banks, government and NGOs are not analysed to show whether and why loans are availed of, used and repaid, and therefore how they create positive or negative impacts.

The values of external and local people and their social relationships shape financial relationships. These relationships can be beneficial, neutral (transactional) or harmful (for example, when they lead to bonded labour or to women defaulting on bank loans) depending on the interaction between lenders and borrowers (that is, whether it is rooted in feudal or agrarian relationships, whether money transactions are settled with labour or other goods given as security, and whether the relationships have a long- or short-term perspective). These women reveal a preference for a stable borrower–lender relationship, namely the informal relationships with friends and relatives, landlords and local money lenders, and they preserve this for their most critical credit needs: household consumption and unavoidable social expenditure. Studies in other parts of the world echo the same: the terms and conditions attached to loans vary according to the relationship between borrowers and lenders, the urgency and amount needed and availability of alternate sources.[25] Thus, an improved understanding of the meaning of money may be derived from an integration of structural and cultural perspectives. It highlights the importance of continuing relationships in determining the financial behaviour of both actors and their institutions.

In demonstrating the predominance of social relations, this book contributes to post-development thinking which challenges the centrality of economic relations. It highlights the ideas which the women have about use of money and the management of groups, thus contrasting an anthropological view (women's own), with a more economic (external agencies') perspective about money. Taking a women's perspective gives different insights from the traditional supply side views of microfinance and challenges the assumption that the answer to lack of capital lies in the supply of money through loans, which will then be converted into capital ultimately leading to poverty reduction.

Every microfinance delivery mechanism is not inherently benign. There are devils in the detail, which, if not understood and cared for, may detract from achieving the policy goal of financial inclusion. Impacts of microfinance can only be envisaged once meaning of money is understood in a given context, for a given community, which also depends on social and financial relationships, and the way in which money is offered and delivered to the borrowers.

GROUP DYNAMICS

Women's SHGs have been idealised, with the normative model persisting. As explained by Mosse (2005: 152): 'Normative models survive where they find support within organizations, or where they help address demands on organizations from outside (from donors or senior managers).'

Challenges to the normative concept can be unsettling. Therefore, even as emerging research reveals ground realities to be different, it has taken time to challenge the construct of the *ideal* as *normal* SHG. Further, the first ones to speak out are likely to face scepticism from those who believe in the ideal. As a result, much more evidence is needed to question and challenge a prevailing model than is needed to create an initial model in the first place.

Use and Management of Savings

This study explores the use of money by women and how they manage their own money and the money borrowed from external sources. The social learning processes reveal how the women manage group dynamics to maintain both social and financial relationships. Thus, it goes beyond what impacts occur, to how these impacts ensue and how women adapt SHGs to their own preferences and needs.

The amount and regularity of women's savings depend on the stability of their incomes. Those who regularly migrate attend group meetings only seasonally, or else tend to drop out of groups during migration. And hence have lower income and savings. Some groups stop meeting during periods when most women migrate but save again when they return. Loans from group savings are found to be more useful (by way of using money and earning profits) than savings deposits. The money management practices of groups are geared to the financial and social needs of their members (for example, by allowing for flexible repayments and conflict resolution mechanisms), though sometimes negative impacts ensue (for example, loss of money). Women's groups primarily learn from their own experiences, for example, lending to non-members until they lose money. Yet, they also learn from each other, for example, combining BPL members to take subsidised loans and negotiating with banks and government for greater freedom for selecting assets. Thus, social learning processes in SHGs have important potentially empowering impacts.

In the groups studied, leadership and money-related conflicts are managed by pooling loans and savings and dissolving groups. When members or leaders take loans and do not repay, it becomes more difficult for the other women in the group, so they opt to dissolve the group altogether. Such dissolution is typically followed by an immediate reconstitution of the SHG and the exclusion of offending members. This method of handling money is a problem-solving mechanism that group members have developed themselves. Analysis of group processes reveals several such ways in which women are shaping an externally introduced organisational form, namely the SHG, for resolving issues of leadership, distribution of savings and loans and loan repayments.

As most loans are delivered through SHGs, these groups gain significance as forums that create empowering impacts. Loans from both informal and formal sources can strengthen reciprocity and increase the creditworthiness of poor women. What the women themselves judge as more valuable is how the groups help to create the *savings-habit* which increases capital accumulation. Another important factor is women's access and control over their own savings, which not only enables them to apply the money for their own purposes (for example, education and health) but also enables the groups to retain the profits from the loan transactions to further augment financial capital. In this way the social capital (groups) enables the creation of financial capital, which leads to a joint spiral in both. It is therefore not only money *per se* but also group processes, which provide the dynamic forces for this virtuous spiral. For instance, when leaders are not directly accountable, savings are distributed and groups are reformed. Thus, there is depletion in both financial as well as social capital, which is also cautioned by other empirical studies.[26]

SHGs are new forums introduced by external agencies, for example, microfinance delivery organisations, to fulfil their own agenda for 'cost effective delivery' of microfinance services.[27] These agencies would expect SHGs to take a joint liability for credit, meaning that if one member cannot pay, others take the responsibility instead. In the Indian scenario, SHGs may not perform this role, and if one woman is unable to pay, the others often stop repaying as well. However, financial behaviour of groups is highly variable and dependent on group cohesion, social relationships within the groups and their financial accommodation of one another's needs.

Microfinance is perceived to endow women with important empowerment impacts including a greater sense of community, trust and reliance on the group during times of crisis, sharing of valuable social and market information, and adopting more positive social practices.[28] The idea is further extended to conceptualise a change in power relations with higher authorities, brought about through cooperation, strength in numbers, confidence building and coordinating to create change. SHGs for microfinance delivery, based on networks beyond family and kinship groups, are considered to have benefits in terms of expanding social and information networks, which enhance social capital.[29] These are considered to provide greater mobility and greater emotional and advisory support from group members for resolving household disputes and reduced risks for individual and community members.[30]

This study, which covers over 900 women in 60 groups, shows that the *ideal* SHG, with homogenous group members, with similar and not competing interests, cohesive group management, equal access and control over finances, transparent management and accountable leadership, is an idealistic construct that is not encountered in most Indian rural contexts. Groups in rural remote regions, even when formed of women from similarly marginalised, poor women, are more likely to exhibit difficulties in regular meetings and savings, extreme dependence on leaders, differing abilities to save and borrow, internal discord and inability to absorb large amounts of costly credit.

Women rate the savings developed through SHGs as having the greatest impact on their lives. The flexibility of practices relating to savings and loan repayments from savings accommodates specific needs and objectives of members of each group. The process of pooling savings in a group and rotating these as loans allows the women to create and use their own capital. This reduces dependence on external sources, whether formal or informal, and therefore *own saving* is the single most preferred source of loans, with the exception of subsidised loans which they actively seek. Unlike the normal assumption that SHGs can take increased amounts of credit, these women choose to depend on own savings in preference to external borrowings.

Other emerging literature now recognises the external/internal divide in people's minds (earlier categorised as *hot* or *cold* money) by how women prioritise repayment of *external* over *internal* loans.[31] It also emphasises the role of savings in times of distress, as social insurance, for increased creditworthiness, leverage for external funds and earning interest.[32] Fernando (2006b) shows different ways in which women lose access and control over not only their own savings but also household assets and expenditures when they take *external* loans. Longitudinal case studies in Bolivia show that many women were able to pay loans only by reducing household consumption, thus highlighting the pressure of returning what they consider debt.[33] Thus, other emerging research offers support for the findings in the Indian context that social and structural factors affect use of money, and that impact assessment must shift focus from outcomes at the institutional level to those at the household level.

This highlights that meaning is derived from the association of money as *own* or *external* and from the relationships between group members and NGOs. SHGs appear as organisations which women begin to own through processes of managing money and negotiating their way through disputes to arrive at more cohesive groups with better social and financial relationships.

Women strongly negate the assumption that all money is the same. They differentiate among external agencies on the basis of relationships and prospects of a continuing social and financial relationship. They negotiate their way subtly through the range of financial products on offer and accept or reject these according to what they find beneficial. They repay or default on loans depending on whether the organisational relationship is worth maintaining in the long term. They have a sophisticated way of assigning meanings, which can only be understood by going beyond financial analysis into analysing and understanding social relations.

In Koppal, this has been possible through a microfinance model that does not push external credit and a facilitator NGO that seeks to give women a choice—or a menu of financial products to choose from—rather than offer only commercial credit. Other NGOs in India, such as PRADAN and MYRADA, have adopted a similar strategy. Where NGO interests do not compete with those of SHGs, there is little need for control, allowing it to accept women's preferences. Women accept some guidance from the NGO, too, when they refrain from giving loans to non-members or bring down their interest rates to enable poor members to take credit. However, divergent thinking on all issues is not resolved. In this study, the NGO upholds its strategy of non-corruption, while women continue to expect and demand higher flows of official benefits to themselves, leading to ongoing tensions in the relationship.

The potential conflict between the path followed by MFIs under the influence of the neoliberal model and the need to achieve development goals like poverty reduction necessitates further research on the comparative impact of different models of microfinance delivery (UNOPS 2002). This book highlights aspects of group dynamics which are not fully disclosed and also illustrates what money and its management mean to women, in terms of the interplay of social and financial relationships in creating or resolving group conflicts. Groups have the potential for members to take collective action to address their mutual concerns, with greater social impact. It takes time, a protected space and investment in capacity building for poor women's economic organisations to grow, a recent realisation among microfinance practitioners and researchers.

Women's Agency and Institutional Forms

Women's own life stories suggest more active self-development. Women's agency, at individual and collective level, can enable them to negotiate larger spaces for action and reduce the constraints they face. Intra-household gender inequities can be overcome to some extent through microfinance, where it leads to increased self-esteem and confidence. Women participants of this study were empowered to take decisive actions in their individual lives, like making choices of partners even in constrained situations and taking decisions regarding family planning. However, they continued to bear the economic burden and remained emotionally dependent on their parents, partners and the community in general. Women's experiences, particularly those of the *devadasi*s, were often traumatic right from their childhood. Social and gender inequities resulted in debilitating practices like the *devadasi* system, with these women accepting their situation as secondary to the partners' wives, or the mother's inability to get the widowed daughter married. These inequities still persist in social norms and attitudes, indicating low potential impact of microfinance on socio-cultural factors. The negative influence of gender on self-esteem in Koppal is also documented elsewhere. However, this needs to be tempered by the finding that women who are *devadasis* stopped the practice in most of the groups promoted by Sampark.

Women's empowerment, in terms of more equitable relationships, can be aided by social learning processes in groups that enhance social capital. This is evident by how women manage groups, money and conflicts, and in this process give meaning to SHGs other than the one which is assigned externally, namely that of joint liability for external loans. Changing relations among actor groups (SHGs, banks, government, NGOs)and greater equity in these relationships may be an important indicator of empowerment. Empowerment is expected to result from *bonding* social capital, which arises from members' solidarity, *bridging* social capital, which results from working on common agendas like enterprises, and *linking* social capital, which involves forging relationships with external institutions like banks, government and *panchayat*s.[34] The issue of how women's political empowerment demands more than just dealing with poverty reduction has also been confirmed in this research.[35] The implication is that women's strategic needs may be better addressed by creating women-controlled organisations on the foundation of credit rather than just creation of more credit delivery organisations *per se.*

The instrumentalisation and disciplining of women and their households through microcredit can result in less freedom and autonomy for poor women. Microcredit programmes frame women's empowerment 'within the ideological and institutional parameters of capitalism' (Fernando 2006b: 227–29). Many evaluators highlight the need to specially address women's strategic needs better in microfinance programmes. Special importance is also placed on Dalit women's political empowerment.[36] In the microfinance models studied here, women could access their savings, and their experiences need to be supplemented with those of other microfinance models. There are, however, few studies which compare empowerment impacts across models, especially where women control and manage their savings compared with those who do not.

Discussions in the SHGs, in their cluster associations and among Sampark staff all show that a pre-determined structure of women's organisations, comprising two or three levels, could be inappropriate. In the specific case of Koppal, there is little standardisation of money management practices, low credit absorption capacity, and women do not see the need for multi-level structures of credit organisations. Social cohesion and money management practices of SHGs are difficult to establish, so they consider the task of building each new tier of organisations problematic. They also believe that the administrative costs are high, and the corresponding risk and profit sharing low, and so do not want to have more than two tiers, comprising just SHGs and their cluster associations.

Promoters of profit-making MFIs claim that SHGs are too small to be financially sustainable and well-managed organisations, and that their savings are better managed by *sustainable financial organisations.* Others argue that women must have more access to assets and management and control over their own financial institutions, in order to create empowering impacts, both financial and social.[37] Recent research provides evidence that emerging women's self-help cooperative federations, even as they exhibit leadership and caste-based inequities, provide significant opportunities to manage own and external funds, give women a sense of ownership and identity and provide a platform for increased financial participation.[38] Challenging the view that NGOs and MFIs must be prioritised over women's own cooperative institutions, Rajagopalan (2004b: 3–4) asks:

> In whose interest is it to continue to project the savings of rural women as 'micro'? In whose interest is to continue to ensure that the savings do not get paid an interest? That the primary agency in which savings are being made, is kept small, and informal in nature? SHGs, small as they are, cannot offer women long-term savings services. All that they can offer is to try and use the savings as collateral. It will be unforgivable, if we were to aim at women accessing the services of external agents, if this were at the cost of them building strong, inter-generational institutions of their own—and if our efforts contributed to further flight of capital from their areas.

There can be latent competition between those who manage federations and women members and leaders, with the former having a vested interest (continuity of their jobs) in not building capacities of women and in some cases managers consider capacity building tasks as competing with the demands of their projects. Thus, NGOs/MFI who seek to have financially sustainable microfinance operations of their own may compete with the financial interests of women and their SHGs.[39]

In 2005, it seemed that Sampark, as a facilitator NGO, was falling between the cracks of two predominant microfinance models in India. The SHG-bank linkage programme with subsidised credit was limited to a few SHGs. This linkage was possible only through challenging the corrupt linkages with the NGO, then favoured with the official subsidy-linked sanctions. Sampark chose not to take this route. The alternate dominant model was of private finance to SHGs through the commercial model, which was offered, but women opted not to take this high cost credit. As Sampark elected not to compete with women's forums for financial profits from the microfinance operations, its capacity to pass large amounts of credit to SHGs, through funds raised, for instance, from bulk lending organisations, remained limited. Instead, it opted to be a facilitator agency that creates capacities among SHGs to take non-subsidised loans from banks. It also helped SHGs to come together in cluster associations, registering them as cooperatives and motivating the banks to directly lend to these cooperatives. This latter choice meant that it had access to few resources for capacity building. As the unsubsidised credit model was only emerging at the time when Sampark took this path, there was no policy or institutional support for this model. Even in 2008, few donor agencies provide support to build women's own organisations.

There were, however, accompanying changes that took place in the mainstream. First, a commercial microfinance agency opened an office in Koppal district and provided credit to the SHGs. Over a period of 2 years, only the better-off women took credit from the agency, proving again that the poor do not opt for high cost credit. Second, as Sampark organised the cluster associations into cooperatives, the RRBs came forward to provide loans to them. This was due to increased market orientation of the latter. Sampark found support to build capacities of women-owned organisations, from an international women's empowerment agency. By 2008, Sampark has supported the cluster associations to register as cooperatives, with direct access to formal credit. This has enabled women to retain and build financial and social capital, while there has also been renewed interest in India in women's organisations through a re-examination of cooperatives, and an official policy to revive cooperatives as autonomous organisations. The impetus from these investments augurs well for some mainstream attention to a development approach that promotes people's agency.

CONCEPTS AND MEANINGS OF POVERTY AND MONEY

The book begins with a consideration of the various conceptualisations of poverty, regarding literature concerning the overlap between social and economic categorisations—lower castes having greater representation among the economically weak sections. Economic thought also recognises the regional nature of poverty, with greater proportion of the poor living in semi-arid regions. Similarly, the gendered nature of poverty has been well documented. Here, all the four categorisations were used to select poor women in a semi-arid region.

Revisiting Vulnerability and Poverty

The livelihoods analysis revealed vulnerabilities arising out of poverty and the introduction of the new forum, namely SHGs.

The first vulnerability stems from economic deprivation, gender, caste and social categorisation (for example, *devadasi*). This vulnerability is sustained by the apathy of institutional structures—banks, social and religious institutions and the government. The experience of being poor *per se* is not necessarily so stigmatising to the very poorest, especially the *devadasis*, who live among others who are in the same situation, and whose status is not determined by material aspects of poverty alone, but by other parameters as well. For instance, Lakshmavva does not see poverty as a factor determining her status or vulnerability, but instead she resents her inability to be a *wife*. She sees her 'powerlessness' in the social and gender rather than the economic sphere, assigning a different meaning to powerlessness and vulnerability than that considered in most microfinance impact studies, which take economic factors into consideration. Poverty here is closely associated with vulnerability, which has an element of 'powerlessness', and multidimensionality, including ecological, economic, social and gender dimensions, as also elaborated by Sen (1999). The poor experience multiple aspects of poverty (Narayan et al.,2000). Poverty and vulnerability are found to be related to asset levels, with human capital (in terms of the number of people in the household, literacy and skills) important to the asset base and credit-taking ability. Literacy, education and skills have a definite impact on occupation, wages and poverty.[40] The potential for poor agro-ecological regions for greater reductions of poverty has increased attention to its regional dimensions. The continued prevalence of caste-based prejudices and the human rights violation camouflaged in poverty is highlighted in Dalit literature.[41] Exclusive reliance on money to define poverty lines has been criticised as narrow, with the need to include nutritional levels and human capabilities and other fundamental human needs like drinking water, shelter, sanitation and the cost of energy as well.[42] Thus, emerging research endorses the conceptualisation of poverty in this book, as multidimensional, and emphasises the link between gender, social, economic and spatial categorisations as determinants of asset-holding of households, their access to public resources and the consequent impact on credit relationships that women are able to make.

The second type of vulnerability, arising from the introduction of group-based microfinance, is related to the mechanism of collective savings, either in SHGs or with the NGO/MFI concerned. SHGs are a new forum, introduced in traditional settings, and carry a mix of external and local characteristics. Financial and managerial tasks are introduced by the microfinance interventions, and the effectiveness of these depends on capacity building by the intervening agencies, but may prove difficult due to women's low literacy and education levels. Leadership quality and processes, influenced by both local and external factors, also create vulnerability, especially as pooling and common management of funds is a new activity that risks women's sparse savings. There is evidence from both Bangladesh and India that the group leaders can appropriate benefits.

There is a need to understand better the nature of acute poverty, and what it means to those who experience it. Currently, debates include issues of rights, entitlements and experiencing development as a process that frees the poor from several constraints and gives them rights as citizens.[43] However, measurements of poverty by most development agencies continue to be money related.[44]

Is Microfinance 'New Money'?

Money transactions in a traditional rural setting are largely individual, with different meanings assigned to money according to socio-economic relationships that the borrower has with the lender. The introduction of SHGs creates new possibilities for women to come together and to form new relationships between themselves, the banks, the government and the NGO facilitating the group formation. These groups are embedded in village social structures, yet still have the potential to challenge existing norms and thus change relationships—relationships with one another change, as the women meet regularly and conduct informal financial transactions that take on a semi-formal form through NGO monitoring and official recognition. Relationships with village social structures change, as the women begin to work for better school education, health or transport services, closing of liquor shops. Relationships with the informal and formal sources of money, change through erosion of earlier and formation of new relationships.

These are arenas where 'new monies' are being created. These processes validate Zelizer's (1989) view that individuals, institutional and social aspects influence the meaning of money. This research further postulates that new structures and new relationships change meanings of money. The use of such new money, in creating social capital, for instance, creates possibilities for changing institutional structures, by making them more responsive, holding them more accountable and improving their attitudes towards the poor.

Language and Meanings

Reflection on the divergence between external and local perspectives highlights the questions which are critical for the ongoing debates within microfinance and rural development today. For instance, the tension between outreach to the poor and sustainability of the MFI is recognised[45] well enough.

However, official project documents still assume it is possible to achieve such divergent objectives.[46] Such a lack of recognition overlooks the different processes involved in achieving the two objectives. When such divergences between local and external agencies are overlooked, it can obscure problems of practice and also the values of development. The language of empowerment has arguably been appropriated by those who promote the neoliberal model and use microfinance to meet ends of capital expansion. The concept and language of money has also been gender biased.[47]

In order to correct this balance, discourse needs to pay attention to the views of local people. The local and external perspectives of practices in money management can differ quite significantly and are indicative of what meanings are attached to these different terms by women as against meanings attached by external development agencies. These differences are summarised in Table 6.1.

Table 6.1
Financial and Women's Perspectives

Financial Perspective	Attributed Characteristics	Women's Perspective
'Idle' funds	Cash retained with groups	'Emergency' funds
'Consumption'	Expenses on health, education	'Investment'
'Subsidies'	Subsidised credit	'Investment' in asset creation
'Credit' to be recovered	Loans	'Debt' to be repaid
'Joint liability' groups	Groups	'Savings and credit' groups
Sustainability of MFIs	Sustainability of MF services	Sustainability of SHGs

Source: Authors.

Distinction between Money and Credit

The Koppal women make a distinction between money and credit. *Sala* (credit), or external borrowing, is to be repaid. However, loans from own savings are seen as 'our money' (*namma duddu*) and thus there is greater freedom in repayment. Further, the understanding of 'own' has both an individual and collective dimension. To the extent to which any individual woman collects savings in the group, she considers it as her *personal* money and deems it her right to not repay a loan she took from the group, up to the full extent of her individual saving. As women pool their savings, extend loans, repay the group and as the pool continues to grow through savings and accumulated interest, the relationship to this accumulated amount grows as a *collective* sum. By contrast, when subsidised official loans involve commissions (*luncha*), women do not consider it *sala*, as the promise to pay is usually undermined by bribes or other loan conditionalities. This highlights that not all money is credit, as conceptualised by Ingham (2006), who considers all money as constituted by credit and debit relations, having a promise to repay. Here, women differentiate between monies received in many ways.

Emerging research in other countries also shows how *debt is permeated with spiritual, moral and legal meaning* (Ferraro 2004: 77). There is a need to take greater cognisance of the way meanings are derived, and the implications this has on the type of credit that would create most positive impacts.

Cash Retained with Groups

Money kept as cash balance in groups, in excess of that rotated as savings, is termed 'idle funds' in microfinance practice. This is considered a less preferred condition than when in rotation and earning interest. From the women's perspective, however, excess cash balance is referred to as *rashi* (wealth), indicating the significance of that money as a reservoir to be drawn when needed.

Classical economics recognises the liquidity function of savings. However, the financial perspective in current microfinance practice has the goal of financial sustainability of the NGO/MFI and marginalises the preferences of women, privileging instead the goal of institutional sustainability over that of empowerment of women, and provides the rationale for MFIs to access and control *idle* funds of women for their 'better and more effective rotation'.

Expenditure on Health and Education

Investments in health and education continue to be seen as consumptive rather than productive loans, as they may not generate immediate cash flows from which to repay the loan. From the women's point of view, such expenses are not consumption but investment. This was first recognised in literature by Hulme and Mosley (1996), but the relevant financial instruments have only recently been changed. Current studies have also highlighted the protective role of credit, whereby loans for consumption or medical treatment help to protect productive household assets.[48]

Subsidised Credit

Another anomaly concerns subsidised credit. The argument for not providing subsidies has been justified on the assumption that they create market distortions. However, just as debt and credit can be considered as two sides of the same coin, so can subsidy be considered the converse of investment. An initial input in the interest of long-term independence is often seen as investment. This is just as valid in the case of poor households, who need investments in asset creation to become financially sustainable. The focus on improving sustainability of the poor household is shifted to the financial health of the organisation. The same subsidy that is not considered justified for the poor is justified for the MFI, using the rationale of long-term MFI sustainability. Thus, the same argument that enables donors to stop subsidising the poor also enables them to shift the subsidy to delivery organisations. Donors have moved to investing in intermediary organisations rather than investing directly in the poor.

Groups

The term SHG implies self-help, but practitioners may use groups only for savings and credit activities, as evidenced by lack of capacity building support to SHGs. With such changes in the groups' role, there has been no corresponding change in discourse, thus creating a discrepancy between espoused terminology and other practice. External agencies regard women as *recipients* of inputs such as group formation, credit and training. They ignore the agency of poor women and do not incorporate their potential to perceive meanings and act according to their motivations into programme planning and delivery. Concerns have also been raised that women lose leadership space in order to be considered good borrowers, along with opportunities to build personal and joint assets and to manage organisations, thereby rendering them more vulnerable to a larger 'loan adjustment game'.[49]

Emerging literature holds out the potential that when bank linkages become stable and groups mature, they are able to build assets, financial capital and social capital.

Sustainability of Microfinance Services

Most discussion on the concept of sustainability inherently incorporates a normative understanding of what it is. A typical supply-driven perspective assumes that the sustainability of financial services is related to the financial sustainability of the microfinance delivery institution. This contrasts with an approach that accords priority to sustainable management of resources by local actors. Women greatly value their collective ability to augment their own resources, to leverage external resources (banks) and to manage their own finances. Therefore, even though the sustainability of microfinance services has been defined as the continued provision of financial services, the meaning of sustainability for the external and local actors differs. These meanings have different implications for the design and implementation of microfinance programmes. For instance, when supply of credit through sustainable MFIs is prioritised, the programme would invest in the capacity building of MFIs, whereas when women's empowerment through managing own savings and loans is prioritised, programmes would invest in the capacity building of women and their organisation. Lack of monitoring or group formation solely to access subsidised loans affected group operations negatively. When SHGs are closely monitored by the local NGOs, they perform better in the utilisation of microfinance and SHG management, but several SHGs formed as a part of government schemes are formed for taking a one-time benefit of subsidy or loan, and in the absence of regular monitoring, become defunct.[50] Mosse (2005) also offers evidence that capacity building of local institutions requires attention and resources that distract from project delivery and its targets. This reveals how prioritising 'sustainable services' takes attention away from women's decision making and directing the microfinance organisations according to their needs and preferences.

Thus, by assuming that what is important to local actors and to external organisations is one and the same, language can draw attention away from what is important to women. Women are not concerned with institutional/financial sustainability; their immediate concern is having credit on reasonable terms for their priorities. Both the discourse of external agencies and claims about microcredit empowering women obscure the differences between women and the MFIs' external priorities. They hide two facts: one that poor women opt not to take, because they are not able to afford high cost credit, and that external organisation's and women's own money management practices are directed at different objectives. It points to the appropriation of the language of *gender equity* and *empowerment* to further the objectives of external intervening agencies, which has also been alleged in other contexts.[51]

Strong evidence of the need for such obscuring of potential conflicts of interest between women and MFI-owned organisations may be found in recent figures. In 2006–07, SHGs mobilised savings of Rs 25 billion ($625 million),[52] indeed a significant resource that women wish to access for own purposes, as do the MFIs for their own financial sustainability. In that context, it is pertinent to mention that the latter group has mobilised political and administrative will resulting in the presentation of the Microfinance Regulation and Development Bill to the Indian Parliament, which proposed to enable MFIs to accept women's savings (which was not passed).

An appreciation of competing perspectives demands more in-depth research on the comparative impact of different models of microfinance delivery. Further research is also needed on the women's relationship with local moneylenders, on the role of rural credit suppliers, namely the input traders, the provision shop, the landlord and the pawnbroker. There are significant differences among these relationships and a differentiated understanding, incorporating both money and non-money exchanges, can better inform the current thinking and planning of microfinance supply initiatives. Other relevant questions concern the differences between moneylenders and commercial microfinance. The high interest rates charged by commercial microfinance are often viewed as necessary for covering risks on non-repayment. Incidentally, moneylender practices of high interest rates are based on the same logic. They foreclose on securities in case of non-repayment, while MFIs call on joint liability of groups to fulfil the condition of full repayment. Further research is needed to see the ground level impact of such practices imposed by MFIs, as emerging research already highlights collusion between NGOs and moneylenders to the detriment of the poor.[53] The recent incidents of suicides among microfinance borrowers and coercive repayment practices have also raised issues about interest rates and repayment schedules creating difficulties for borrowers, not very different from the erstwhile moneylenders who are claimed to be replaced by the MFIs.

These perspectives need to be complemented by more information in the public domain, and a critical analysis of how much local and external sponsors and donors invest in building sustainable MFIs versus building women-owned financial institutions.

Official/unofficial Blind Spots

The neglect of the government is evident in many instances such as ignoring of *devadasi*s, prevalence of child marriages, not recognising BPL families because the couple were under-age as per law, and not recognising the extent of school dropouts, also evidenced in the current research in Koppal. These examples highlight the lacunae that exist between the process of policy formulation and grassroots realities.

The different meanings assigned to terms can be problematic. For instance, the word *credit* has positive connotations in terms of enabling investment, yet women assign to it a binding connotation of *debt* or a commitment to repay. Ignoring the responsibility to repay that microcredit enjoins upon women, is at the risk of not understanding that what external agencies call credit also carries the meaning of 'debt' for women. This phenomenon has recently been highlighted in the increased number of farmer suicides in the states of AP and Karnataka due to high indebtedness to MFIs.[54]

National credit policies, which place SHGs in the informal sector, do not bring them under any banking regulations, and have not recognised the financial risks that are inherent in these new forms of association, especially for poor women. The banking sector and the government have formally recognised these as channels of credit and permitted them to have informal savings. However, the proliferation of unregulated SHGs also puts poor women's savings at risk, calling for further guidelines and measures. Experiences in this research point to the need for financial literacy and basic literacy for all women, and in processes of transparency and accountability.[55]

In the Indian context, both the subsidised credit and the commercial microfinance models relegate the poor to the margins by making credit too costly for them. However, the emergence of a third model—the SHG-bank linkage—offers a way out by linking traditional development banking with a new market orientation. This model has been made increasingly friendly to the poor, with the RBI issuing guidelines that encourage banks to adopt flexible and easy procedures for SHG financing, to leave the groups free to manage their own money, to take consumption loans if needed (RBI 2007a, 2007b). These developments have strengthened the SHG-bank linkage over time, making it clearly the most adaptable to women's own preferences. It allows women's SHGs to retain their own savings even as the banks extend credit. This scenario is very different from Bangladesh, for instance, where MFIs take and control women's savings. In India, MFIs cannot take away women's deposits unless authorised by banking laws to do so. This has created the potential for further transformation and change among all the actors involved: banks, government, NGOs and community.

A new forum, through which financial services are delivered, namely the SHG, has enabled solidarity among the disadvantaged. Group-based finance appears as a strategy that could deepen or bridge financial and structural inequities (for example, by making caste-based groups) but much depends on the actual interventions themselves. Minimalist credit is based on the neoclassical model, and therein lies the contradiction: how can a forum that is created to exploit the existing social and power relations work to change those structures? Being based on existing social hierarchies and divisions, group-based minimalist microfinance rewards those with higher asset levels, more than the poorest, as the former have larger credit taking capacities.

METHODOLOGICAL REFLECTIONS

The empirical validity of the divergent perspectives of interventionists and local people has lately been endorsed by similar studies in different parts of the world by practitioners and researchers. This book provides insights into group dynamics and how groups resolve conflicts and assign different meanings to different monies. It bridges the gap between the understanding of how women's SHGs operate in reality and the popular beliefs about them in the current context of group-based microfinance delivery.

Livelihoods Frameworks

Multiple research frameworks categorise livelihoods aspects in different ways to provide insights and, given their socio-cultural and political embeddedness, lend prominence to different analytical levels. In this research, these frameworks help to analyse the concerns of the marginalised, especially women, and to assess external and household level factors that affect both supply and demand for money, and determine how money is situated in a specific economic, ecological, institutional and socio-cultural context. Policies are formed at the macro-level, but the process unfolds differently in each specific context, highlighting context-dependent meanings of money. Using the three frameworks leads towards a livelihoods assessment approach for analysing conflicts arising from interface of different life worlds. The questions that arise are: Who will decide which perspective will prevail? Are only local actors responsible for their voices to be heard, or should all development actors ensure that the former have representation and voice? If their voices are already feeble and unheard, can just increased participation enable them to guard their own needs better should there be a normative stand, a value attached to enabling them to empower themselves? If the latter, then a resulting microfinance approach, indeed any development approach, needs to incorporate flexibility, autonomy, self-determination and control of the poor, especially women, over the financial system designed for them. Yet, again it needs to be accompanied by capacity building, so that the space created for agency can be utilised well.

Gender-sensitive Research Methodology

Gender sensitivity is seen in its adherence and commitment to gender equality, as indicated in Figure 6.4. It leads to different political standpoints about the use of development projects as interventions, whereby the intervening agents seek to change the people and context *intervened* upon.

Figure 6.4
From Gender-sensitive Research to Practice

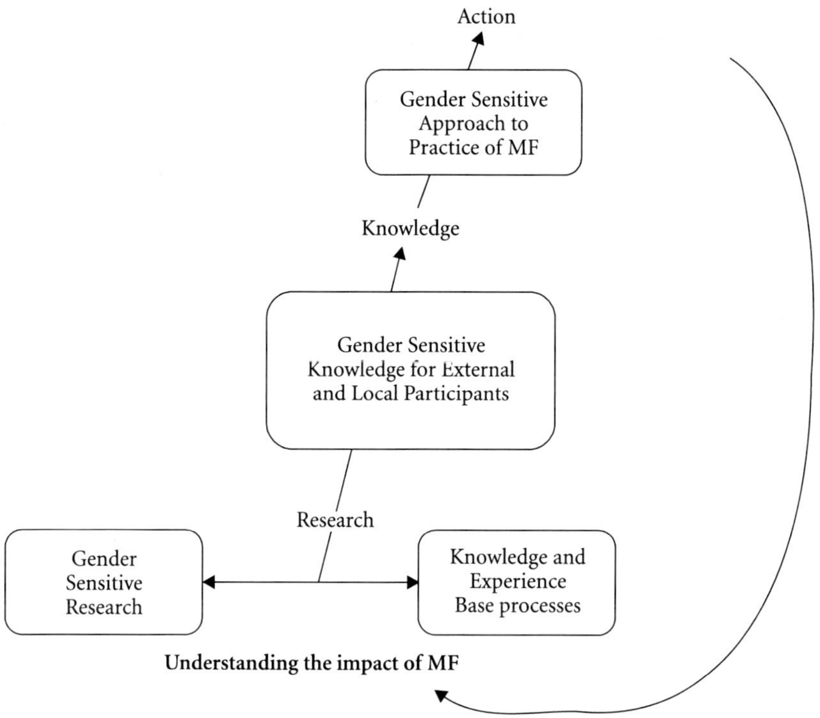

Action

Gender Sensitive
Approach to
Practice of MF

Knowledge

Gender Sensitive
Knowledge for External
and Local Participants

Research

Gender
Sensitive
Research

Knowledge and
Experience
Base processes

Understanding the impact of MF

Source: Authors.

Gender sensitisation is a process of partnership and learning created through interactive processes that change both the intervener and the intervened. Such political agendas need to be recognised and brought into the discourse of both research and practice. This must be done while still dealing with strained livelihoods situations, such as poverty, ill-health, low education and awareness, caste status and domestic violence. This points to the need for creating research processes wherein there is space for women's voices to be heard, as was given priority here.

The participation of women in research is constrained by their acute lack of time, which is taken up by vital life maintenance tasks. These women rarely have the time to participate in research. The question is whether, given this context, research must insist on women's participation, or continue to talk to men as the representatives of the household. Gender sensitivity in research is a value, not a matter of convenience and practicality. If the researcher asks for women's time, which is important to the quality and validity of its results, the responsibility arising from it is to provide a reasonable return for their time. The recommendation here is that time and commitment need to be made to looking for appropriate practical contributions of every research that uses the time and knowledge of women living in poverty.

The actor-oriented approach used here highlights several macro-level issues related to power structures and institutional interactions in the field of microfinance. These issues lend themselves to understanding the emergence and transformation of financial relations in terms of power, competition and institutional forces. Money can be better understood through semiotics, and using the discipline of linguistics in the exploration of the meaning and the use of money.

There is also a need for more in-depth research into the nature of civil society, and its values, livelihoods strategies, negotiation and learning processes. We need to better understand situations of environmental degradation, as that will illuminate the potential for collective and collaborative action towards enhancing sustainability. The need for studying social orientations is paramount as this can break the strongest barrier to equality and human rights, that of inner orientations and beliefs of people. Bhuiyan et al., (2005) endorse this direction when they call for examining theoretical issues about why the process of 'normalisation' is not more challenged or dismantled. Rist et al., (2007) also indicate the need for case studies to explore barriers and potential for communicative action.

The progression of high input agriculture into low returns, the degradation of soils, the depletion of groundwater and the conflicting perspectives between livelihoods sustainability at the household level and sustainability of natural resources at the community level, all need to be tracked over long periods of time.

Impact Assessment Frameworks and Methodologies

The predominance of supply-oriented studies of impact of microfinance has led to an overemphasised concern with causal relationships and to continued engagement with problems of fungibility and attribution. Addressing these problems is difficult using quantitative techniques.[56] There is a need to supplement the causal paradigm with the relational paradigm, and study microfinance with models that explain relationships across structures, organisations, households and individuals. This research suggests a need to move towards more people/women-oriented impact assessment methodologies, with greater attention to their livelihoods needs, and the types of impact they look for and value. Indicators chosen should be relevant for and articulated by them. The research methods which then become relevant are both qualitative and quantitative. Longitudinal studies and life histories are of particular benefit, as these provide further insights into women's lives and better livelihoods choices. Mapping of local contextual factors is needed to study impact of forces changing in the external environment to enable a judgement of cause–effect relationships and processes of the intervention. Yet, attribution of impact to different forces remains problematic. Finally, even if impact of a specialised service like microfinance is to be mapped, the unique methodology followed in this research shows that more holistic studies are needed, and they should take a livelihoods perspective rather than an orthodox financial or organisation management perspective. In viewing how meaning of money derives from and how its use reproduces or changes identities, values and social relations at local and national scale, this book proposes a better formulation of money as a potential change agent.

Microfinance: The Way Forward

Microfinance, as any other development phenomenon (for example, participation), has needed a policy model before it could grow. As it gained acceptance, it could catalyse, lead and provide the momentum for institutional and political change and a paradigm shift resulting in major political support and regulatory changes that helped it gain a prominent place in the country's development plans. This has won microfinance a preferred position in the articulation of the official women's empowerment policy, national plans and in the central bank's financial policy.[57] Microfinance was positioned in the right place when the more recent discourse on financial inclusion emerged as a new concept, allowing it to form an integral part of any official financial inclusion strategy. This could not have been achieved if deep divergences between the policy model and field realities had emerged earlier.

Today, however, there is more tolerance for exposing these divergences. Somewhat paradoxically, as microfinance has already arrived and claimed a prominent position in national and international development policies and debates, some dissenting voices and challenges do not prove a threat, but may even serve to further strengthen the position of microfinance.

Microfinance in India in 2009 is truly at the crossroads; on the one hand, the sector has grown to incorporate a very large number of NGOs, MFIs, banks and other public and private sector organisations providing a wide range of microfinance services. Many believe that sweeping changes in banking regulations are still needed for the development of the sector. Such unprecedented supply should have been fully absorbed given a very large unmet demand. The fact that this has not happened can be explained only by understanding the difference in the money offered and the money demanded. It is also well recognised by now that microfinance does not reach the poorer sections of the population. There is no alternative to providing credit at reasonable cost if the poor have to follow long-term sustainable livelihoods strategies.

Microfinance's achievements are currently recognised more in terms of the privileged models—number of SHGs, amount of loans, loan repayment rates, scale and sustainability of MFOs. The emergent model, of unsubsidised loans from banks, does not yet have full recognition from donors, and therefore does not yet enjoy full backing of policy and donor support.[58] Yet, conditions are fast becoming conducive for policy support to the model, as emphasis on financial inclusion begins to create competition among financing agencies to extend outreach in rural and remote areas.

Over the past 25 years, the most dominant model, that of the Grameen Bank, has been adapted and adopted in several countries. It fits the framework of the neoliberal paradigm, privileging supply side thinking over empowerment perspectives. The India model, of SHG-bank linkage, has emerged since 1981, to offer the biggest challenge to this model, and its very large outreach has now begun to demand official attention and recognition. Over time, this model has been made more and more *poor friendly*, with the RBI issuing guidelines that encourage banks to adopt flexible and easy procedures for SHG financing, leaving SHGs free to manage their own money and take consumption loans if needed.[59] These developments have strengthened the SHG-bank linkage over time, making it clearly the most adaptable to women's own preferences.

The processes in the two microfinance delivery models reveal a tension between two strategies. Providing services, may offer options for participation but not empower. According agency, which empowers, but given that poor and lower caste women are already marginalised, they may not be able to use the opportunity to their full advantage. This raises the dilemma: should the approach be 'participate to empower' or 'empower to participate'.[60] The former may mean some immediate instrumentalisation at the hands of external agencies as is found in commercial microfinance programmes. The latter may lead to empowerment, greater decision making, women's own forums, re-arranged and more equal relationships with mainstream organisations, but may continue to need capacity building and conflict resolution support from facilitating agencies for a long period.

This invites the attention of current microfinance discourse to the choices people make and why they do so. Such attention is important especially when attention needs to be paid to the changes needed in the enabling environment. The Microfinance Regulation and Development Bill was tabled in Parliament, alternately supported and challenged by many in the sector and was finally shelved. Presented as a dichotomy, the divergence of demand and supply perspectives gets problematic. Its solution then lies in going beyond the divergence towards an exploration of the meanings. The divergences can only be sorted out with deference to the experiences and wishes of actors who make the final choice regarding taking, using and repaying loans. It is only by understanding how the users, namely poor women, assign meanings to money, that we can begin to offer microfinance that is truly empowering for them; and even then, the offer will have to heed contextual and capability differences.

Context embeddedness of such exploration is important, and an effort should be made to apply a similar process of understanding meanings in different contexts. It is not possible to disengage any statement about relationships from its context; therefore, any understanding of social and financial relationships must be articulated only within a given socio-economic, cultural and political context. Meanings derived from these embody the context, and therefore to stand independent of context will in fact render them devoid of meaning. The constitutive role of language and meanings also needs recognition. Only then can we design models that are less about proliferation and sustenance of external microfinance organisations, and more about creating spaces for women to have a stronger collective voice, greater control over their own resources, improved access to external resources and leadership and representation that enables them to influence policy—which in turn will lead to better lives, not just for the women themselves but also for the generations that will follow.

Notes

1. Jude Fernando's analysis of post-Cold War microcredit programmes shows how high repayments are predicated on the very institutions and structures that are oppressive to women (2006a, 2006b). Rankin (2006) goes on to analyse how gender relations are nothing but *de facto* class relations, and claims of creating women's solidarity are in fact

not validated by microfinance mechanisms, which are designed more to protect lenders' interests than increasing social capital.

2. Zapata and Townsend (1999: 49) categorically state: 'microcredit, or giving poor people access to small amounts of credit to make a little money ('generate income'), is a leading fashion in the development industry, although no solution to poverty'.

3. Low loan off-take in remote and poor regions has shown up in early impact studies (FWWB 1997) and then again (Sampark 2000) when studies in Tamil Nadu, AP, Kerala and Orissa found that microfinance operations in the remote and dry regions took longer to achieve higher loan sizes and build a larger loan portfolio than irrigated regions which had greater market access.

4. Leeladhar (2006) highlighted that though the number of bank branches had increased, they have not been able to reach the underprivileged sections of the population, and some states and regions continue to be underbanked, such as Bihar, Orissa, Rajasthan, Uttar Pradesh, Chhattisgarh, Jharkhand, West Bengal and a large number of north-eastern states. On all-India level, Thorat (2007) analysed and gives that loan accounts in rural areas are 9.5 per cent and it is 14 per cent in urban areas. Regional distributions show that it is 25 per cent in south and 7 and 8 per cent in north-eastern and eastern central regions, respectively.

5. EDA (2006) provides information from study on SHGs from four states (AP, Karnataka, Orissa and Rajasthan) that regular meetings, savings and loan repayments were barriers for most of the poor people for self-exclusion from the members of SHGs. The field staff also comfortable to work in easy access areas and potential members rather than working with poor people.

6. Jayaram and Srivastava (2003) took an exercise on poverty mapping and monitoring using information technology and found a link between spatial distribution ecological assets and poverty.

7. As illustrated by Mosse (2004).

8. Rosegrant and Hazell (2000) advocate to use more direct policies to encourage human capital formation and improve access to productive assets. Robinson (2001) and Rutherford and Staehle (2002) endorses the emphasis on education and investment in human capital. Sundaram and Tendulkar (2003) advocated safety nets in the form of special employment programmes for households who are vulnerable.

9. The widespread corruption in Indian official schemes is well recognised, Jenkins and Goetz (1999) provide examples regarding combating and increasing public accountability.

10. Words such as 'percentage' and 'system' have become part of the local vocabulary and mean the same in Kannada as they do in English.

11. Lewis and Madon (2004) narrated that NGOs' accountability is assessed in terms of the proper use of financial resources. Instead, they advocate assessment in terms of effective development interventions for meeting clients' need.

12. Rist et al., (2006) give case studies from India and Bolivia to show the need for such social learning processes to move towards more sustainable management of natural resources.

13. This is well accepted in recent poverty literature. Mehta and Shah (2002) also found that in livelihoods contexts with similar characteristics as those described in this book: semi-arid, remote rural or tribal forest regions, social relationships and economic well being is often determined by caste, and poverty of these groups persists through generations. The 11th Five Year Plan recognises that the SCs and STs have higher poverty levels, lower human development index and higher human poverty index as compared to the other castes (GOI 2008).

14. EDA (2006) showed in one of its study on SHGs that there are significant divisions between sub-castes but that may not be cases of strengthening caste division, but rather demonstrate how deep set social divisions can be.

15. DANIDA's (2004) study of four training projects in India found that rights and privileges of women are strongly influenced by the rank of the caste to which they belong. Religion determines marriage laws, such as maintenance rights in case of divorce, property rights of women, and so on. Social interaction and participation of women is also

influenced by caste, religion and the region of the country, as witnessed in practices such as child marriage. Sengupta et al., (2005) advocated rights-based approach to development where the human rights must be integrated into sustainable human development.

16. Illustrated by Premchander and Mueller (2006) through a large number of case studies.

17. See Bebbington and Gomez (2006) for an analysis of these experiences in women's village banks in Peru and Guatamela.

18. Wright find evidence of this in Peru, where group leaders were able to use kinship and other relationships to subordinate the group members' interests to their own, thus 'unequal power relationships in the wider community can be reinforced, rather than challenged by microfinance interventions' (2006: 100).

19. Often microfinance programmes inadvertently suppress such transformative processes. Wright (2006) also found, in her studies in Carjamarca, Peru, that NGOs' processes permitted women leaders to exercise undue influence in defiance of group norms, thereby allowing prevailing power structures to continue rather than challenge them.

20. RBI recognises that NGOs do not go beyond a minimalist approach to financing (RBI 2007b).

21. Sharan (2000), an NGO in Delhi with 69 SHGs clustered into six cooperatives, found that 85.5 per cent of the credit requirement of its members was met earlier by moneylenders, and later 85.5 per cent were met from group savings. However, an impact study of an International Labour Organization (ILO) project which provided microfinance to those vulnerable to bonded labour, found that only 10–15 per cent of the total debt of the poor household was replaced by NGO loans and the dependence on money lenders continued (IFP 2004). The All India Debt and Investment Survey (2002 in GOI 2003) found that moneylenders accounted for 30 per cent of rural household debt.

22. EDA (2006), ibid.

23. This is also endorsed in recent years by other microfinance research (APMAS 2005; Rajagopalan 2004b; Ranadive and Murthy 2005).

24. Gadenne and Vasudevan (2007) analysed that majority of SHGs took loans for income generating purposes and it worked as means to increase their assets in the long run.

25. Fernando (2006b) records that NGO loans are only one of the many sources from which women take loans, others include money lenders and traders. CARE and FAO (2007) quote studies of rural households in India which have at least four different sources of loans: informal local sources, moneylenders, banks and cooperatives and group savings.

26. Montgomery (1996) studied women's groups in Bangladesh, with similar findings about internal group dynamics and their effects.

27. Rankin (2006) and Weber (2004) suggest that features of social disciplining and bearing financial risks are features of this cost reduction and meeting the agendas of external financial agencies.

28. As found in women' groups in Bangladesh (Hashemi et al. 1996).

29. This finds evidence to support the conceptualisations of Granovetter (1994) and Putnam (1993).

30. Peredo and Chrisman (2006) developed the concept of Community-based Enterprise which provides a potential strategy for sustainable local development. They argue that typically rooted in community culture, natural and social capital are integral and inseparable from economic considerations, transforming the community into an entrepreneur and an enterprise.

31. This is also found in recent research by Andhra Pradesh Mahila Abhivruddhi Society (APMAS) in AP (Reddy and Prakash 2003).

32. Rajagopalan (2004a) also highlights this impact.

33. Brett (2006) shows that women prioritised repayment of external loans which caused household stress, borne primarily by women, who reduced household expenditure to honour loan commitments. In India, there have also been cases of women committing suicides when not able to pay loan instalments (Shylendra 2006).

34. This evidence finds support for Woolcock's conceptualisation of 'linking' capital.

35. Mayoux and Johnson have repeatedly drawn attention to these aspects of women's empowerment.

36. In an analysis of decentralised governance, Waghmore (2004) highlights that in a deeply caste-stratified society; Dalits need first to be economically and educationally empowered as well.

37. Bhatt (2005) and Rajagopalan (2003, 2004b, 2005a, 2005b) strongly advocate for creating viable and large women's organisations for them to be empowered.

38. A study of cooperatives from two regions of Orissa, covering six cooperatives promoted by the NGOs—ADHIKAR and FARR, showed that the cooperative processes followed in mobilising deposits, disbursing credit and decision making enabled effective financial and social intermediation (Sahu and Das 2007).

39. Mosse (2004) and Rajagopalan (2005a) also found evidence of this in other field projects, thus providing support for the findings here.

40. Dreze and Sen (2002) elaborate on a 'freedom-centred' perspective of development, wherein different types of 'un-freedom' are to be eliminated. They perceive that such a change will be catalysed by prioritising human agency for eliminating inequalities. Further, they highlight that such social change is hampered by neglect of education in Indian social policies.

41. Narula and Macwan (2001) presented a paper on Economics of Racism in a Seminar, Geneva, where they pointed that Dalits are denied access to land, forced to work in degrading conditions and routinely abused by the police and higher caste groups.

42. Pogge and Reddy (2006) reject the estimates of poverty in World Bank's World Development Reports for 2001, which estimate world poverty based on an international poverty line of $1 per day per person. They criticise that this method employs an inaccurate measure of purchasing power (for example, it assumes no change in consumption distribution) which creates a misleading impression of 'equivalence' that masks the errors in such calculations. Guruswamy and Abraham (2006) make a similar judgement and recommend defining a poverty line including basic needs such as proper nutrition, drinking water availability, shelter, hygiene, clothing and education.

43. Narayan et al., (2000) explain poverty, using narratives and experiences of the poor and vulnerable. Capabilities and entitlement approaches are elaborated by Sen (1999); Kabeer (2005) explores the concept of inclusive citizenship through expressions of citizens themselves, yet warns that those marginalised may not be able to benefit and may need additional support.

44. Pogge and Reddy (2006) suggest uniform standards across the world, related to income-dependent elementary human capabilities, and the characteristics of commodities needed to achieve them, building in variations across country contexts due to cultural factors beyond control of individuals. Douglas and Ney (1998) bring an anthropological perspective to the conceptualisation of poverty, bringing in the individual, a person's values and emotions and the 'poor person's lack of control over other people' (1998: 20).

45. While earlier studies evaluated and commented on whether microfinance is able to reach the poor, as claimed, there is now a clear statement not only accepting that microfinance does not reach the poor (Berenbach and Churchill 1997; McGuire et al., 1998) but also accepting that the poorest do not need microcredit (or self-employment) and therefore must be helped with a more comprehensive conceptualisation of finance, namely livelihoods finance (Mahajan 2005).

46. For instance, project documents expected the microfinance programmes they supported to reach the poor and remote villagers and become financially viable within a 3-year period (CARE India 1997, 1999). Reviews have an opportunity to point out these anomalies (Sampark 2003).

47. Mosse (2005) elaborates, through a case study, how conflicts are glossed over rather than brought to the fore and dealt with. De Goede (2005) details how historically the language of money has been gender biased.

48. Singhdeo (2006) found that consumption credit has positive protectional impacts. It is only recently that consumption credit has been expressly allowed in many microfinance programmes (Premchander and Prameela 2007).

49. These concerns have been voiced more recently than ever before (Bhatt 2005; FWWB 2006; Rajagopalan 2005b), though mostly by women leaders in microfinance sector.

50. Premchander and Prameela (2007) conducted a programme and policy review and found that some of the SHGs have been dormant after getting loan under SGSY Yojana scheme. They have not taken up economic activity despite receiving skill training under the scheme. Dasgupta (2007) finds similar evidence in West Bengal, indicating the importance of facilitation and monitoring.

51. Critics of microfinance consider its historical development in a context wherein state subsidies were considered market distortions and NGO efforts unsustainable and ineffective in reaching the poor, but microcredit was accepted, as it allowed the use of private 'entrepreneurship' and women's willingness to be disciplined and repay to serve the interests of financial institutions, which offered a rationale for using the gender and empowerment language for capitalist expansion (Brigg 2006; Fernando 2006a; Rankin 2006; Weber 2004).

52. IIMS Dataworks (2007) in a recent survey of savings and membership among SHGs.

53. Fernando (2006b) showed evidence from Bangladesh that loans given to women, and their incomes, are appropriated by moneylenders who support the women to use and repay loans, thereby maintaining the women's creditworthiness for the MFI. Thus, microfinance strengthens the existing power relationships while in fact claiming women's empowerment. Brett's (2006) study also found that women reduced household consumption to repay loans.

54. In 2006, district authorities in AP closed down 50 branches of two major microfinance organisations due to allegations about charging usurious interest rates, lack of transparency about these and creating undue pressure for loan repayments such as confiscating title deeds of debtors' assets and using abusive language (Shylendra 2006).

55. These needs are also highlighted based on the experience of four large official programmes (Premchander and Prameela 2007).

56. The need for qualitative studies is highlighted by Cohen and Gaile (1997); Sebstad and Chen (1996), who compile recommendations about impact assessment methodologies from a wide range of practitioners and researchers.

57. For the policy statements and perspectives, see GOI (2001, 2002) and Reddy (2006).

58. One exception to this has been Swiss donors, who have consistently financed capacity building and revival of RRBs in India. Along with this they have also grant funded privately owned and profit making MFIs, so as not to be left behind in supporting private initiative, which has been the more recent fashion.

59. The banking regulations pertaining to these are contained in RBI circulars (RBI 2007a, 2007b).

60. The distinction is drawn by Waghmore (2004) in relation to empowerment of Dalits and their participation in politics through decentralised organisations.

Appendix 1

Non-governmental Organisations (NGOs): Details and Impact Literature

During the research period, several non-government organisations (NGOs) were visited for conducting impact studies, reviews and livelihoods and group assessments. The details are listed in Table A1.1.

Table A1.1
Overview of Field Visits

Organisations, Year	Focus of Discussion and Remarks
Milk unions in Valsad district (Gujarat) and Malabar district (Kerala) (1998–99)	• Women's savings and credit groups have been accepted as the channel for women's empowerment • Impact indicators are different from the perspective of the NGO and the groups/women
NGOs in Orissa, Andhra Pradesh (AP), Kerala (6) Coverage: six NGOs, six groups (1998)	• Supply and demand side issues were different • The group was seen as a means to an end. Group and NGO processes determined many aspects that influenced impact. Yet, impact *per se* was traced at individual and household levels
Workshop with 25 NGOs and 2 funding agencies (FWWB and United States Agency for International Development) on microcredit (1999)	• NGOs and funding organisations discussed issues of financial sustainability, interest rates, impact and ownership of institutions • NGOs related tensions at field level, especially the pressures of government programmes vitiating the atmosphere. A donor representative opined that women's ownership and management was not relevant to delivery of financial services
30 groups in Ranchi district of Bihar (now Jharkhand, a separate state), through two NGOs (1999)	• Indicators of impact were sustainability of credit operations at NGO level, group savings, attendance, women's contribution to income and financial decision making
Four groups and three NGOs visited in Bastar, Madhya Pradesh (2000)	• Tribal area, very poor people in remote areas where microcredit had limited relevance

(*Table A1.1 continued*)

(Table A1.1 continued)

Organisations, Year	Focus of Discussion and Remarks
Workshop in Koppal, Bikanhalli village, one NGO, one village, 25 participants (2001)	• Natural resource management was the focus of the programme
Case studies of 10 women, in-depth case studies from 5 villages in Koppal district (2001–03, with follow-up till 2007)	• Exploratory work, spanning family and work life, income and expenditure analysis. Study at group level also • Quality of data varies for each woman, non-standardised but good in-depth information given by women, validated also through intermittent workshops with them
Four workshops with villagers in Bikanhalli, Gondabala, follow-up of livelihoods workshop (2001–06)	• NGO, group and family level observations • Observed role of NGO, group members and villagers action with regard to resource management
2 NGOs, 2 federations and four groups (2002)	• Discussions with funding and apex agencies, NGOs, federations, groups, individual women
3 NGOs, 6 self-help groups (SHGs) in Uttar Pradesh (2002) Manipur, Meghalaya and Arunachal Pradesh (2003) 3 NGOs in Orissa, 10 groups in 2 districts (2003)	• Understanding role of groups and federations in savings and credit • Tensions between NGO staff and management clearly discernible and pressure of transformation on NGO quite clear
6 NGOs in Orissa, 12 groups in 2 districts (2004) 6 NGOs in Rajasthan, two groups in 2 districts (2004) 9 NGOs, 15 groups in Vishakhapatnam, AP 3 NGOs in Gujarat, six groups in 2 districts (2004)	• Discussions with NGOs in workshops • Groups felt commercial credit was too expensive • Own savings was most important felt benefit of SHG • NGOs worked on projects, and when projects closed, SHGs were not supported • Women requested more guidance to use collected savings
1 NGO in AP, 10 groups in 2 districts (2005)	• Well-connected villages had more income generating opportunities • Those with larger loans had earlier assets, sometimes they had not informed these to NGOs, who listed them as poor
Two NGOs in Tamil Nadu (TN), 10 SHGs, 1 NGO in AP, 4 groups in two districts (2006)	• Women's groups lent money to release children from bondage • Good enterprise training and linkages helped even the poorest • NGO support and training to SHGs was the deciding factor in group strength and operations
10 NGOs, 6 groups in Madhya Pradesh 2 NGOs in Rajasthan, three groups in two districts (2007)	• NGOs had a range of microfinance products, these had to be especially tailored to the poor • Women's group leaders tend to appropriate benefits and only close supervision could establish equitable group processes • Low investments were made in group capacity building

Source: Authors.

The details of several visits made to groups, women and NGOs outside the study area, through conferences, workshops and group settings, is listed in Table A1.2.

These reviews of impact studies and field level discussions with a wide range of institutional and local stakeholders in microfinance helped clarify the divergences that existed in perceptions and perspectives, and thus formed the basis of the delineation of the research themes as outlined in Chapter 2.

Table A1.2
Number of NGOs, Groups and Women Visited

	NGOs	*Groups*	*Women*
AP	14	29	621
Rajasthan	8	5	100
Madhya Pradesh	10	6	120
North East (Manipur, Meghalaya, Mizoram)	6	10	200
Uttar Pradesh	3	6	180
Chhatisgarh	3	4	80
Kerala	11	8	210
Jharkhand	2	30	400
Orissa	5	16	400
TN	2	4	60
Gujarat	4	12	280
Workshops	31		
Total	99	130	2,651

Source: Authors.

LITERATURE-REVIEWED INDICATORS AND TOOLS

During the research period, several impact studies were reviewed to get an overview of the aspects studied, the methodologies, tools and the indicators used by them for impact assessments. 20 impact studies, of which 18 were donor initiated, are listed in Table A1.3.

Table A1.3
Review of Selected Microfinance Impact Assessment Studies

Organisation/Programmes Studied	*Year*	*Country*	*Donor Agency*
SHARE, Mysore Resettlement and Development Agency (MYRADA), PRERANA	1999	India	Friends of Women's World Banking (FWWB), as funding agency
South Asia Poverty Alleviation Programme (SAPAP)	2002	India, AP	United Nations Development Programme (UNDP)
Centre for Youth and Social Development (CYSD 1)	1996	India, Bhubaneshwar	NOVIB, OXFAM
CYSD 2	2001	India, Bhubaneshwar	Ford Foundation sponsored Action Research Project with Universities of Bath, Sussex and Reading, UK
SHARE	2000	India, AP	
Professional Assistance for Development Action (PRADAN) (Dhan)		India, Madurai	
Activists for Social Action (ASA)	1999	India, Trichy	Chairman, ASA initiated
ASA	2000	Bangladesh	ASA, donor supported
The Bridge Foundation (TBF)	1990	India	TBF initiated

(Table A1.3 continued)

(*Table A1.3 continued*)

Organisation/Programmes Studied	Year	Country	Donor Agency
China Women's Income Generating Project	2000	Canada	Canadian Cooperative Association
UNICEF (FDP)	1998	Egypt	SEEP, AIMS studies
KATALYSIS	1998	Honduras	Freedom from Hunger
Reseau des Caisses Populaires du Burkina (RCPB)	1997	Mali	Freedom from Hunger
Workers' Bank	1998	Jamaica	AIMS
Self-employed Women's Association Bank	2000	Gujarat, India	AIMS
Grameen Bank, Bangladesh	1998	Bangladesh	Grameen Bank
Bangladesh Rural Advancement Committee (BRAC) I	1997	Bangladesh	BRAC, donor supported
BRAC II	1999		
Proshika, two studies	1998 2002	Bangladesh	Proshika, donor supported
CETZAM	1999 2000	Zambia	Department for International Development
CARE Manual	1995	Bangladesh	Only manual made, no information on its implementation
Swashakti	2005	India, Bihar, Gujarat, Haryana, Karnataka, Madhya Pradesh and Uttar Pradesh	Government of India (GOI)
Swayamsidha	2005	India, 33 states and union territories	GOI, State Department of Women and Child Development
Rashtriya Mahila Kosh	2002	India, Delhi, Haryana, Himachal Pradesh, Jammu and Kashmir, Madhya Pradesh, Rajasthan, Uttar Pradesh, Gujarat, Bihar, Manipur, Nagaland, Orissa, West Bengal, AP, Karnataka, Kerala, TN	GOI, State Department of Women and Child Development
Swarna Jayanti Gram Swarozgar Yojana	2003	India, TN	GOI, Ministry of Rural Development
National Finance Support Project	2004	India	Small Industries Development Bank of India
AP Rural Livelihood Project	2005	AP	GOI and AP state
SAPAP	2005	AP	UNDP and GOI

Source: Authors.

Many of the earlier studies used several participatory tools that helped to analyse one or more aspects of microfinance impact. A listing of the major tools is given in Table A1.4.

Table A1.4
Tools

• Internal learning systems	• Loan and savings use
• Action learning workshops	• Decision-making matrix
• Means test	• Gender division of labour and resources mapping
• Impact survey	• Mobility mapping
• Exit survey	• Happiness mapping
• Focus group discussions	• Caste discrimination mapping
• In-depth interviews	• Chapatti diagramming
• Impact survey	• Wealth ranking
• Client exit survey	• Pictorial diary
• Client satisfaction survey	• Diagrams
• Client empowerment survey	• Life story interview

Source: Authors.

These tools were compiled from 69 studies, which ranged from impact studies of specific projects to methodological reviews. They included AFC (2005), AIMS (1998, 2001), Andharia et al. (2003), ASA (1999, 2000), Atkinson (2004), Baumgartner et al., (2000), Bayes (1999), Blank (1998), BRAC (1997, 1999), Burra et al. (2005), CASHPOR (2001), CCA (2000), Centre for Management Development (2003), CETZAM (1999, 2000), Chen and Snodgrass (1999), Cheston and Khun (2001), Cheston and Reed (1999), CMF (2001), Copestake (1996, 2003), CYSD (1996), Dasgupta (2007), Deshpande et al., (2003), FWWB (2001), Grameen Bank (1998), Guijit and Cornwall (1995), Harper (1998), ICMC and PRIZMA (2000), Jeyaseelan (2005), Johnson (2003), Malhotra (2006), Mayoux (1997, 1999, 2001, 2003a, 2003b, 2003c), Menon (2003), Murthy et al., (2002), MYRADA (2001), National Labour Academy-Nepal (2006), Nigam and Manowar (1998), Noponen (2003), Padia (2005), PRADAN (1997, 2006), Premchander (2003b, 2005, 2006) , Premchander and Prameela (2007), Proshika (1998, 2002) , Rajshekar (2007), Roche (1999), Sampark (2000, 2006a), Schürmann (2002), SHARE (2001), Singh (2006), Sinha and Patole (2003), Solution Exchange (2006), Srinivasan (2004), Srinivasan and Castro (2003), TBF (2002), UNDP (1997, 2002), Wilson (2004).

NGOs in Koppal District

The NGOs working in Koppal district are listed in Table A1.5.

The last four NGOs started operations in Koppal in 2007. Two (Ekalavya and VIKASA) have closed their office in Koppal after the completion of Swashakti, a World Bank programme. Out of 21, seven NGOs (BAIF, Outreach, Manju Shree, Mahila Samakya, Amma, Bimarao Grameen Abivirti Seva Sangha and Minority Rural Development Society) work at district level and they do not have office in Koppal, the remaining 14 NGOs are working only in Koppal *taluk*.

Table A1.5

List of NGOs in Koppal District

S. No.	Name of the NGO
1	Bharatiya Agro Industries Foundation (BAIF)
2	Chetana Foundation
3	Ekalavya
4	Guru Shikashana
5	Institute for Rural Development and Education Society
6	Jnana Bharati Education Society
7	Mahila Samakya
8	Manju Shree
9	Olekar Education Society
10	Outreach
11	Pastoral Service Institute
12	Sampark
13	Samuha
14	Sarvodaya
15	SHARE
16	Swayam Krutha Sangha
17	VIKASA
18	Amma
19	Bimarao Grameen Abivirti Seva Sangha
20	Bapuji Grameen Abivirti Seva Sangha
21	Minority Rural Development Society

Source: Authors.

Appendix 2
Livelihoods Frameworks

Sustainable Livelihoods Frameworks

A study of any intervention's impact on people's livelihoods needs to recognize the broader context in which actors develop their livelihoods strategies. The Sustainable Livelihoods Framework (SLF) defines secure livelihoods as the existence of sufficient stocks and flows of food and cash to meet basic needs (Chambers and Conway 1992). It was developed through Department for International Development's (DFID's) field-based work at both the macro- and household-level of livelihoods. It has since been utilised in planning several development projects and for assessing development impacts (Farrington et al., 1999). Its key assumptions are that actors pursue a range of different livelihoods outcomes (for example, health, income, reduced vulnerability) by drawing on a range of assets as they pursue a variety of activities.

The approach identifies five types of capital assets: financial, human, natural, physical and social. It conceptualises improved livelihoods outcomes in terms of increased income, increased well being, reduced vulnerability, improved food security and/or more sustainable use of the natural resource base of an area. A diagrammatic presentation is given in Figure A2.1.

However, this framework does not explain the perspectives of the actors and why they follow the strategies they do, which is aided by the actor-oriented perspective (AOP) framework.

The AOP framework has its origins in peasant and actor network theories, and uses rational economic theory as an entry point. It assumes that actors always try to do something that fulfils their livelihoods aims. This approach perceives actors as:

> Actors in an arena of interdependent and interacting individuals or categories of actors. They interpret specific features of the ecosystem and the socio-economic and socio-cultural systems, and they act competently and rationally on the basis of their specific knowledge, as a function of their values, motives and expectations of utility. An understanding of regional dynamics and potential conflicts in rural development and environmental care must consequently be approached in connection with divergent strategies, perceptions and assessments of the respective individuals and collectives. (Kuenzi et al.,1998: 54)

It considers actors as individual households and also as groups within economic, socio-cultural, legal and ecological systems and their livelihoods strategies arising from their knowledge of these contexts as also from their value base and aspirations.[1] Figure A2.2 depicts this framework:

Figure A2.1
Sustainable Livelihoods Framework

Livelihoods Assets

Transforming
Structures and
Processes

Livelihoods
Strategies

To
Achieve

Vulnerability
Context

H

S   N

Influence
& Access

P   F

Structures
• Levels of
  Government
• Private
  Sector

• Laws
• Policies
• Culture
• Institutions
Processes

• Shocks
• Trends
• Seasonality

Livelihood
Outcomes

H represents Human Capital
P represents Physical Capital
S represents Social Capital
F represents Financial Capital
N represents Natural Capital

• More Income
• Increased well-being
• Reduced vulnerability
• Improved food security
• More Sustainable use of
• NR base

Source: Carney (1998).

Figure A2.2
AOP Framework

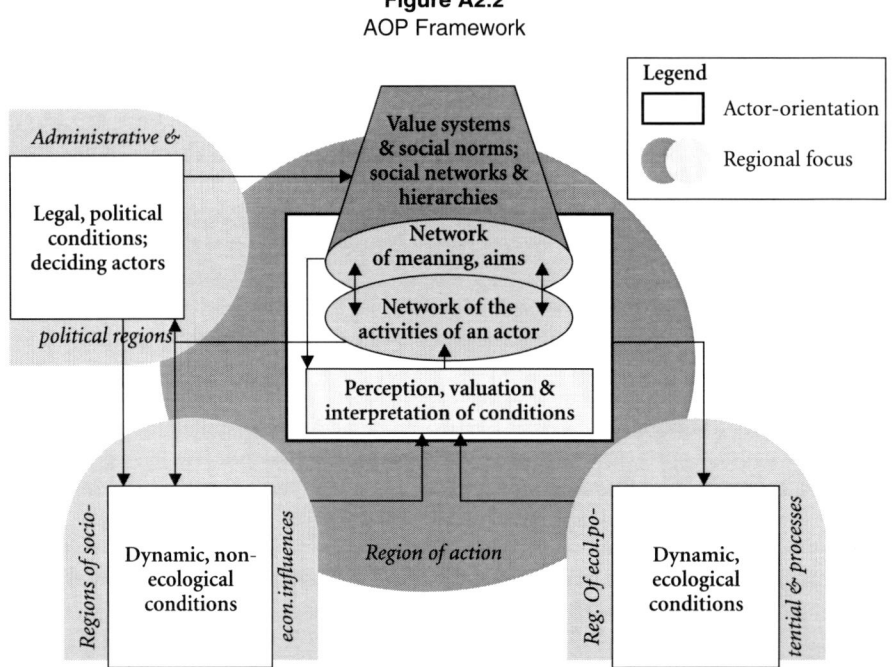

Source: Wiesmann (1998).

The AOP framework, which lies alongside the SLF, prioritises the actors themselves and also provides conceptual links with social, ecological and political contexts. It goes beyond SLF in conceptualising actor groups as units that devise strategies together. However, the action theory frameworks can also neglect:

> The orientations and preferences that inform whole sequences of action, the structures built from combinations of such sequences, the ways in which the actors themselves are configured. The action theory framework offers little purchase for establishing the patterns on which various actions converge and which they initiate and dynamically extend. It shines the analytical torch upon the strategies and interests and interactive accomplishments of individuals, and sometimes groups. While this yields important insights into how agents generate and negotiate certain outcomes, it offers no dividends on the machineries of knowing in which these agents play a part. Knorr Cetina (1999: 9)

Although this framework recognises the social and ethical dimension of action, it can leave the emotional or affective (psychological) dimensions relatively unexplored.

The Mandala is based on a home, which is used as a metaphor to study the broader, more abstract notion of a livelihoods system. It may employ different symbolisms in different cultures but is like a lens with nine focal points through which the actualities become more distinctly visible. The Mandala conceptualises livelihoods in nine squares, each denoting one aspect, as depicted in Figure A2.3.

Figure A2.3
Rural Livelihood Systems Nine-square Mandala Framework

9. Individual Orientation	8. Family Orientation	7. Collective Orientation
• Visions • Hopes • Aspirations • Fears • Self-image/respect • 'Gurus', models	• Ancestors • Caste, social status • Aspirations to leadership, education, jobs • Aspiration to power, wealth, social mobility	• Subsistence agriculture • Food security • Religion, traditions • Common property resources, state laws • World views, school • Capitalistic values, city new prosperity
6. Inner Human Space	**5. Family Space**	**4. Socio-economic Space**
• Integrity, identity • Awareness • Selfishness, compassion • Responsibility • Affection • Curiosity, courage	• Gender relations • Nutrition distribution • Health • Family planning • Distribution of work • Solidarity	• Production relations • Systems of cooperation, Community organisations • Government institutions • Markets of goods, land labour and capital
3. Emotional Basis	**2. Knowledge and Activity**	**1. Physical Base**
• Memories • Attachments • Feelings • Anxieties • Boredom	• Technology • Agriculture patterns • Experiences, skills • Traditional knowledge • Labour, crafts, services • Modern professions	• Natural environment (topography, climate) • Natural resources • Animals, habitat • Accumulated wealth

Inner ←――――――――――――――――――――→ Outer

Source: Högger (2004).

The bottom row represents its foundation. This includes the physical, emotional, knowledge and activity bases. The physical basis refers to all the resources, economic and natural, available, the accumulated wealth and remittances from migrant members, and so on. The physical basis includes the natural environment and resources, and knowledge and activity basis refers to the crafts, trades, skills and traditional knowledge of the actors themselves. The emotional basis encompasses the feelings, emotional attachments and the sense of belonging actors feel towards their home. The knowledge and activity basis refers to the crafts, trades, skills and traditional knowledge.

The middle row delineates the different spaces in society; Indian socio-economic space comprises the several caste hierarchies, the *panchayat* and relations with government, neighbourhoods. The family space deals with gender relations, seniority within generations, distribution of workload and finally the inner human or intimate space encompassing personal awareness, integrity and responsibility. The uppermost row deals with all the mental/collective perspectives that shape and guide actor strategies, including the collective, family and the individual orientations. While societal rules and family values govern general behaviour patterns, revolutionary change could originate from one strong leader only. The Mandala depicts the 'outer' and the 'inner', creating an awareness of both the physical and psychic constituents of all livelihoods systems. From the bottom to the top of the Mandala is the transition from the physical and emotional basis to the mental apex, making it a heuristic tool that recognises the multidimensional reality of a livelihoods system and alerts researchers/practitioners to certain conflicts which arise in development (Högger 2003).

The use of three frameworks allows for person-centred, multi-levelled and flexible approaches to help understand the complexity and diversity of rural livelihoods and also enable movement beyond rational economic thinking to in-depth analysis of inner realities of women and their experiences. All three approaches explicitly acknowledge that to minimise or avoid risk, actors tend to develop multiple strategies for their livelihoods. They take cognisance of the dynamic and holistic nature of the processes and structures that influenced and shaped livelihoods. Thus, the frameworks are potentially flexible, adaptive and relational.

NOTE

1. For different applications of AOPs across country contexts, see Kuenzi et al., (1998: 54), Ludi (2004), Messerli (2004) and Wiesmann (1998).

Glossary

Amavase	New moon night
Amrith Amavase	New moon night in February
Appa	Father
Ashraya mane	Shelter—a house given by the government
Avaralli Hechu Rokka ithi	He has lot of money
Baananthana	Recovery period after delivery, normally observed for 40 days
Baddi	Interest on loan
Badigar	Carpenter
Baksa	Box money
Basava Jayanthi	A festival in May
Basavi	The local term for *devadasi*, meaning a woman with no restriction for having sexual relations
Beedi	Local cigarette
Bhagya Jyothi	A government scheme, for free electricity to the poor families
Billi muthu	A chain of white pearls
Bindi	A red round spot on woman's forehead
Block/Taluk	A group of 40–80 villages, which form an administration unit of 6–8 *panchayat*s
Bund	Soil and water conservation structures, usually 2–3 feet-high walls built of stone and soil
Coolie	Casual human labour
Dai	Local nurse and midwife
Dalit	People belonging to lower caste
Dalit Seva Sangha	A membership-based organisation of Dalits
Dasar	Hindu sub-caste
Deepawali	Festival of lights
Deerga Avadhi Sala	Long-term loan
Devadasi	Women who have been dedicated to the local deity and are not allowed to marry, but can have sexual alliances with men
Dhalali	Broker/a private lender
Duddu, Rokka, Hana	Money
Finance Sala	Short-term loan
Galeamma	Hindu goddess

Ganga Kalyana Yojane	A government scheme
Gouda, Gowda	Landlord/head of a village
Gram Panchayat	A group of 6–10 villages forming an administrative unit and having elected local representatives at village level
Hammali	Porter
Hammali Sangha	Porter's union
Hani Hani Koodidare Halla, Thene Thene Koodidare Rashi	Small drops of water make a mighty ocean
Hechu Rokka Beku	Need lot of money
Hingari	Late monsoon
Holige	Sweet made with flour and jaggery
Huligemma	Goddess
Jamkhane	A thick bedsheet or bedcover
Janatha Mane	House constructed as a part of government-subsidised scheme for people living below the poverty line
Jangamaru	Hindu sub-caste (grazing cattle and trading milk is the main occupation of these people)
Jathre	Mela, fair
Janatha house	A house built under government scheme
Jhakammana kadaga	A bangle worn for religious regions
Jogamma	Lady priest
Jowar	Millet
Kaigada	A loan with no interest on it; can be repaid whenever there is money in hand
Kankana	Thread tied during marriage around the bride/groom's forehead
Kari kallu	Black stone
Karthik Amavase	New moon night in December
Kasuti	Hand embroidery
Keri	Street
Kowdis	Local thick bedsheet
Kuruba	Hindu sub-caste (general caste of shepherds, rearing sheep and goats)
Lagna maadidhane	Arranged the marriages
Lingayat	General caste
Luncha	Commission
Madar	Hindu sub-caste (scheduled caste [SC])
Madhyama Avadhi Sala	Medium-term loan
Mahanavami	Festival
Mandala	Universe
Mannethina Amavase	New moon night in July

Manthras	Charms
Marata	Hindu sub-caste (OBC)
Mungada	Cash advance without interest
Mungari	Early monsoon
Muthu	A chain made of white and red beads
Naalige	A pendant of a female goddess's tongue
Nagar Panchami	A festival to worship snake God
Nammaduddu	Our money
Nanage Ondu Savira Rupai Sala Kodi	Give me a loan of Rs 1,000 ($22.22)
Nanna Maga Nanage Hola Iddahange	My son is my biggest property, like land
Novodaya school	Subsidised school provided by the government for meritorious children
Oddaru	Stone cutter
Oni	Street
Paddathis	Practices
Panchami	A festival in August
Panchayat	A group of 6–10 villages forming an administrative unit and having elected local representatives
Pinjar	Sub-caste of Muslim
Puja	Worship
Pujari	Priest
Rashi	Wealth
Rathikuli	Family granary
Reddy	Hindu sub-caste (general caste)
Rokka	Money
Rotti	A bread, made with *jowar* flour
Rupai	Rupee
Sajje	Millets
Sala	Loan
Sammandha	Relationship
Sampathu	Wealth, asset
Samsara	Sexual relationship
Santhe	A local market
Sarai	Local alcohol
SC keri	Street of the SCs
Shavkar	Landlord/money lender in a village
Stree Shakti	Women's empowerment project funded by central government
Sulagi	A local derogatory term, meaning prostitute
Taluk Panchayat	A group of 6–10 *panchayat*s forming an administrative unit and having elected the representatives at taluk level

Talwar	Hindu sub-caste (scheduled tribes)
Thali	Pendant
Ugadi	New year celebrated by Hindu people
Undi	A sweet, prepared with jaggery, groundnut, oil and rice
Vathi	Mortgage
Vathi Sala	Loans given against security of land, jewels, and so on.
Vijayadashmi	A Hindu festival, in which people worship goddess Durga
Vyapara	Trading/business
Yellu Amavase	New moon night in January

References

Acharya, Binoy and Smita Premchander. 1999. *Evaluation of Training Programme on Strategic Business Planning: A Review Report*. Ahmedabad: Friends of Women's World Banking.

AFC (Agricultural Finance Corporation Ltd). 2005. *Report on Impact Evaluation of Swashakti, MWCD*. New Delhi: Agricultural Finance Corporation Ltd.

Agarwal, Bina. 1994. *A Field of One's Own. Gender and Land Rights in South Asia*. New Delhi: Cambridge University Press.

Aguilar, Veronica Gonsàlez. 1999. *Is Microfinance Reaching the Poor? An Overview of Poverty Targeting Methods*. Luxembourg: ADA.

AIMS (Assessing the Impact of Microenterprise Services). 1998. 'Learning from Clients: Assessment Tools for Micro Finance for Practitioners'. Available online at http://www.mip.org (downloaded on 6 February 2003).

————. 2001. 'Study Shows Strong Impact on SHARE Clients Credit for the Poor'. CASHPOR Newsletter. Available online at http://www.gfusa.org/gbrp/share.html (downloaded on 10 June 2002).

Akhter, Salma. 2003. 'Impact Assessment of NGOs Micro-credit Based Women Entrepreneurship: Methodological concerns. Enterprise Impact'. Available online at http://www.enterprise-impact.org.uk/conference/Abstracts/Akhter.shtml (downloaded on 15 January 2003).

Albu, Mike, Abdur Rob and Anisur Chowdhury. 2003. 'Learning to Improve Business Services for Rural Micro Enterprise. Enterprise Impact'. Available online at http://www.enterprise-impact.org.uk/conference (downloaded on 22 March 2003).

Alvesson, M. and S. Deetz. 2000. *Doing Critical Management Research*. London: Sage Publications.

Andharia, Jahnvi, Sejal Dand and Linda Mayoux. 2003. 'Area Networking Event by ANANDI, India. Ways forward in Impact Assessment and Livelihood Enhancement', paper presented in conference on *New Directions in Impact Assessment for Development: Methods and Practice*, University of Manchester, Manchester, November 24–25.

APMAS (Andhra Pradesh Mahila Abhivruddhi Society). 2001. *SHG Movement in Adilabad, Cuddapah & Vizag Districts*. Hyderabad: APMAS.

————. 2003. *Minutes of the Meeting of the Advisory Group of APMAS, June 24, 2003*. Hyderabad: APMAS.

————. 2005. *A Study on Self Help Groups — Bank Linkage in Andhra Pradesh*. Hyderabad: APMAS.

————. 2007. *SHG Federation in India, A Perspective*. Delhi: Access Development Services.

Appu, P.S. 1996. *Land Reforms in India: A Survey of Policy, Legislation and Implementation*. New Delhi: Vikas Publishing House.

Arunachalam, Ramesh S. 2008. *Scoping Paper on Financial Inclusion — Consideration and Recommendations for UNDP*. New Delhi: UNDP.

ASA (Activists for Social Action). 1999. *Annual Report, 1999–2000 ASA—Grama Vidiyal Spring of Hope*. Tiruchirapalli: ASA.

————. 2000. *Annual Report, 2000–2001: ASA—Grama Vidiyal Spring of Hope*. Tiruchirapalli: ASA.

Atkinson, Robert. 2004. 'Life Story Interview', in Michael Beck S. Lewis, Bryman Alan and Liao Timfuting (eds), *The Sage Encyclopedia of Social Science Research Methods*, pp. 566–69. London: Sage Publications.

Baker, Wayne, E. and Jason B. Jimerson. 1992. 'The Sociology of Money', *The American Behavioral Scientist*, 35(6): 678–93.

Banerjee, G.D. 2002. 'Self Help Groups—A Novel Approach for Reaching and Empowering the Unreached and Underserved Poor in India. Alternative Finance'. Available online at http://www.alternative-finance.org.uk/cgi-bin/summary.pl?id=88&language=E (downloaded on 6 February 2004).

Barrientos, Stephanie. 2003. 'Labour Impact Assessment: Challenges and Opportunities of a Learning Approach', paper presented at Conference on *New Directions in Impact Assessment for Development: Methods and Practice*, University of Manchester, UK, November 24–25. Available online at http://www.enteriseimpact.org.uk/conference/Abstracts/Barrientos.shtml (downloaded on 10 January 2004).

Barry, Nancy. 1995. *The Missing Links: Financial Systems that Work for the Majority*. New York: Women's World Banking.

Batliwala, Srilata. 2001. 'Challenging Ritual Caste Oppression'. Available online at http://www.wedo.org/news/Mar01/ritual.htm (downloaded on 18 January 2004).

———. 2003. *Bridging Divides for Social Change: Practice–Research Interactions in South Asia*. London: Sage Publication.

Baumgartner, Ruedi, G.S. Aurora, G.K. Karanth and V. Ramaswamy. 2000. *Participatory Research on Rural Livelihood: Sharing Research Findings for Local Empowerment*. Bangalore: Institute of Social and Economic Change, Monograph published by 'Indo Swiss Project on Rural Livelihood Systems'.

Baumgartner, Ruedi and Ruedi Högger. 2004. *In Search of Sustainable Livelihood Systems: Managing Resource and Change*. New Delhi: Sage Publications.

Baviskar, B. and D. Attwood. 1995. *Finding the Middle Path: The Political Economy of Cooperation in Rural India*. Boulder, CO: West View Press.

Bayes, Abdul. 1999. 'Beneath the Surface: Microcredit and Women's Empowerment. Alternative Finance'. Available online at http://www.alternative-finance.org.uk/cgi-bin/summary.pl?id=88&language=E (downloaded on 6 February 2004).

Bebbington, Denise Humphreys and Arelis Gomez. 2006. 'Rebuilding Social Capital in Post-conflict Regions: Women's Village Banking in Ayacucho, Peru and in Highland Guatamela', in Jude L. Fernando (ed.), *Microfinance Perils and Prospects*, pp. 112–32. Oxon: Routledge.

Berbenbach, Shari and Craig Churchill. 1997. 'Regulation and Supervision of Microfinance Institutions: Experience from Latin America, Asia and Africa', The Microfinance Network Occasional Paper No. 1, The Microfinance Network, Washington DC.

Berger, Marguerite. 1989. 'Giving Women Credit: The Strengths and Limitations of Credit as a Tool for Alleviating Poverty', *World Development*, 1(3): 1017–32.

Beverly, S.G. Sherraden. 1999. 'Institutional Determinants of Saving: Implications for Low-income Households and Public Policy', *Journal of Socio-Economics*, 28(4): 457–73.

Bhagwati, Jagdish. 1997. 'The Global Economy and American Wages', *The New Republic*, 19 May.

Bhatt, Ela R. 2005. 'Keynote Address at the Inauguration of Indian School of Microfinance', Ahmedabad, 12 September.

———. 2006. *We Are Poor but So Many: The Story of Self-employed Women in India*. Delhi: Oxford University Press.

Bhatt, Ela R., R. Armaity Desai, Mrinal Pande Thamarajakshi, Jaya Arynachalam, and Veena Kohli. 1988. *Shramashakti: A Summary of the Report of the National Commission of Self Employed: Women and Women in the Informal Sector*. Ahmedabad: SEWA.

Bhuiyan, Abul Hossain Ahmed, Aminul Haque Faraizi and Jim McAllister. 2005. 'Developmentalism as a Disciplinary Strategy in Bangladesh', *Modern Asian Studies*, 39(2): 349–68.

Blank, Lorraine. 1998. *Client Monitoring Systems for Microfinance Institutions: AIMS Assistance to the Workers Bank of Jamaica*. Washington: AIMS.

Blankenberg, Floris. 1998. 'Impact Assessment Cutting through the Complexity', in Peter Oakley, Brian Pratt and Andrew Clayton (eds), *Outcomes and Impact: Evaluating Change in Social Development*, pp. 82–97. UK: INTRAC.

Bond, Philip and Ashok S. Rai. 2009. 'Borrower runs', *Journal of Development Economics*, 2(88): 185–91.

Bose, B.K. and K.C. Ranjani. 1998. 'Banking with the Poor—SIDBI's Initiatives', paper presented at Conference on Kick-starting Microfinance: A Challenge for the Indian Banks, Bankers Institute of Rural Development, Lucknow, October 26–28.

BRAC (Bangladesh Rural Advancement Committee). 1997. *Savings and Credit Guidebook*. Dhaka: RDP, BRAC.

———. 1999. *Impact Assessment Study—I and II* (CD-Rom). Dhaka: BRAC Research and Evaluation Division.

———. 2002. *The Pro-poor Microfinance Sector in South Africa*. Johanesberg: Finmark Trust.

Brett, John A. 2006. 'We Sacrifice and Eat Less: The Structural Complexities of Microfinance Participation', *Human Organization*, 65(1): 8–19.

Brewerton, Paul and Lynne Millward. 2001. *Organisational Research Methods: A Guide for Students and Researchers*. London: Sage Publications.

Brigg, Morgan. 2006. 'Disciplining the Developmental Subject: Neoliberal Power and Governance through Microcredit', in Jude L. Fernando (ed.), *Microfinance Perils and Prospects*, pp.64–88. Oxon: Routledge.

Buch, Nirmala. 2002. *Poverty, Gender and Micro-credit: A Study of the Experience of Rashtriya Mahila Kosh*. Delhi: Rashtriya Mahila Kosh.

Burra, Neera, Joy Deshmukh Ranadive and Ranjani K. Murthy. 2005. *Micro-credit, Poverty and Empowerment. Linking the Triad*. UNDP. New Delhi: Sage Publications.

CARE and Access. 2007. *Microfinance Marketplace: A Resource Directory of Emerging MFIs in India*. Delhi: CARE India.

CARE and FAO. 2007. *Moving from Micro-credit to Livelihood Finance: A Report Prepared by CARE India in Collaboration with FAO Livelihood Support Programme*. Delhi: CARE India.

CARE India. 1997. *A Project Document on Credit Rotation for Empowerment and Development through Institution Building and Training (CREDIT)*. Delhi: CARE India.

———. 1999. *A Project Document on Credit and Savings for Household Enterprises (CASHE)*. Delhi: CARE India.

———. 2000. *Report on Participatory Mid Term Evaluation of CREDIT Project of CARE—Bihar, Ranchi*. Delhi: CARE India.

Carney, Diana. 1998. 'Sustainable Rural Livelihoods: What Contributions Can We Make?' paper presented at Natural Resources Advisers Conference, DFID, London, July.

CASHPOR. 2001. 'Study Shows Strong Impact on SHARE Clients Credit for the Poor. CASHPOR Newsletter'. Available online at http://www.gfusa.org/gbrp/share.html (downloaded on 15 April 2004).

CCA (Canadian Cooperative Association). 2000. 'Measuring Transformation: Assessing and Improving the Impact of Microcredit. Abstracts of Impact Evaluation Tools and Selected References'. Available online at www.microcreditsummit. org/pdfs/impactpaper_abstract.pdf (downloaded on 25 June 2003).

Census of India. 2001. 'Country Profile: Republic India'. Available online at http://www.apcdproject.org/countryprofile/india/india_intro.html (downloaded on 10 August 2005).

Centre for Management Development. 2003. *Concurrent Evaluation of Swarnajayanti Gram Swarozgar Yojana*. Thiruvanthapuram: Centre for Management Development.

CETZAM (The Christian Enterprise Trust Zambia). 1999. 'Measuring Transformation: Assessing and Improving the Impact of Microcredit. Part II. Implementing Impact Assessments and Monitoring Systems: A Practitioner Perspective from Zambia', paper prepared for the Microcredit Summit Meeting of Councils, Abidjan.

———. 2000. *Understanding Impact: Experiences and lessons from the Small Enterprise Foundation's Poverty-alleviation Programme, Tshomisano. Tzaneen, South Africa: Small Enterprise Foundation*. Bath, UK: Center for Development Studies, University of Bath.

CGAP (Consultative Group for Assisting the Poor). 2002. *Helping to Improve Donor Effectiveness in Microfinance: Microfinance Transparency and Reporting to Donors*. Donor Brief No. 7, Washington DC.

———. 2007. 'Beyond Good Interventions: Measuring the Social Performance of Microfinance Institutions', in Prabhu Ghate (ed.), *Microfinance in India: A State of the Sector Report*, Delhi: Access Development Services.

Chambers, R. 1991. 'Shortcut and Participatory Methods for Gaining Social Information for Projects', in M. Cernea (ed.), *Putting People First: Sociological Variables in Rural Development*. pp. 513–37. New York: Oxford University Press.

Chambers, R. and R. Gordon Conway. 1992. 'Sustainable Rural Livelihoods: Practical Concepts for the 21st Century', IDS Discussion Paper No. 296, The Institute of Development Studies (IDS), Brighton.

Chavan, Pallavi and R. Ramkumar. 2002. 'Microcredit and Rural Poverty: The Evidence', *Economic and Political Weekly*, XXV(3): 110–18.

Chen, Martha Alter. 1997. 'A Guide for Assessing the Impact of Microenterprise Services at the Individual Level'. Available online at http://www.mip.org/pdfs/aims/fin-52mc.pdf (downloaded on 2 January 2004).

Chen, Martha Alter and Donald Snodgrass. 1999. 'An Assessment of the Impact of SEWA Bank in India: Baseline Findings. USAID Microenterprise Development'. Available online at http://www.mip.org/pdfs/aims/brf26acs.pdf (downloaded on 20 September 2003).

Cheston, Susy and Lisa Kuhn. 2001. 'Managing Resources, Activities and Risk in Urban India: The Impact of SEWA Bank Executive Summary. USAID Microenterprise Development'. Available online at http://www.usaidmicro.org/pdfs/aims/India%20Core%201A%202%20Executive%20Brief.pdf (downloaded on 20 September 2003).

———. 2002. 'Empowering Women through Microcredit (Part 1/2)'. A Draft Paper Commissioned by the Microcredit Summit Campaign.

Chetson, Susy and L. Reed. 1999. 'Measuring Transformation: Assessing and Improving the Impact of Microcredit', Microcredit Summit Meeting of Councils, Abidjan, 24–26 June. Available online at http://www.microcreditsummit.org/impactpaperH.htm (downloaded on 25 September 2002).

Cheston, Susy, Vanessa Harper, Lauren Hill, Nancy Horn, Suzy Salib, and Margaret Walen. 2001. 'Measuring Transformation: Assessing and Improving the Impact of Microcredit. Part II. Implementing Impact Assessments and Monitoring Systems: A Practitioner Perspective from Zambia', paper prepared for the Microcredit Summit Meeting of Councils, Abidjan.

Chidambaranathan, M. 2002. *Livelihoods of Devadasi Women and Sexual Health in the Villages of Koppal District*. Bangalore: Sampark.

Christen, Robert Peck. 2000. 'Commercialization and Mission Drift: The Transformation of Microfinance in Latin America'. Available online at http://collab2.cgap.org/gm/document-1.9.2700/OccasionalPaper_05.pdf (downloaded on 8 February 2003).

Christen, Robert Peck, Elisabeth Rhyne, Robert Vogel, and Cressida McKean. 1994. *Maximizing the Outreach of Microenterprise Finance: An Analysis of Successful Microfinance Programs*. USAID Program and Operations Assessment Report No. 10. Washington, DC: USAID.

CMF (Centre for Microfinance). 2001. *Preliminary Synthesis Report from the Asian Region Workshop on Micro Finance and Impact Assessment Methodology*. Nepal: CMF.

Cohen, Monique and Gary Gaile. 1997. *Highlights and Recommendations of the Virtual Meeting of the CGAP Working Group on Impact Assessment Methodologies*. Washington: AIMS.

Conroy, J.D., K.W. Taylor, and G.B. Thapa. 1998. 'Best Practice of Banking with the Poor: A Review of Asia-Pacific Experience in Implementing Banking with the Poor'. Conclusions and Recommendations Adopted at the Third Asia-Pacific Regional Workshop on Banking with the Poor, Brisbane, November 21–25.

Copestake, James. 1996. 'Poverty-oriented Financial Service Programmes: Room for Improvement?' *Savings and Development*, 19(4): 417–36.

———. 2000. 'Impact Assessment of Microfinance and Organizational Learning: Who Will Survive?', *Journal of Microfinance*, 2(2): 36–45.

Copestake, James. 2002. 'Inequality and the Polarizing Impact of Microcredit: Evidence from Zambia's Copperbelt', *Journal of International Development*, 14(6): 743–55.

———. 2003. 'Simple Standards or Burgeoning Benchmarks? Institutionalizing Social Performance Monitoring, Assessment and Auditing of Microfinance', *IDS Bulletin*, 34(4): 54–65.

Centre for Youth and Social Development (CYSD). 1996. 'Improving Impact of Micro-finance on Poverty: An Action Research Programme (CYSD)'. Available online at http://www.cysd.org/ImpactAss_link.htm (downloaded on 5 May 2003).

Dale, Reidar. 1998. *Evaluation Frameworks for Development Programmes and Projects*. London: Sage Publications.

Dand, Sejal, Jahnvi Andharia, and Linda Mayoux. 2003. 'Tree of Dreams to Empowerment Strategy: Participatory Action Learning, Networking and Impact Assessment in Anandi, India, Enterprise Impact'. Available online at http://www.enterprise-impact.org.uk/conference/Abstracts/Dand.shtml (downloaded on 5 January 2003).

DANIDA (Danish International Development Assistance). 2004. *Evaluation: Farm Women in Development: Impact Study of Four Training Projects in India*. Denmark: Danish State Information Centre.

Dasgupta, Nilanjana. 2007. 'Consolidated Reply in Response to Query on Collecting Evidence of Impact of Microfinance-experience', raised by Smita Premchander, Sampark in Solution Exchange.

Datt, Gaurav and Martin Ravallion. 1998. 'Why Have Some Indian States Done Better than Others at Reducing Rural Poverty?' *Economica*, 65(2): 17–38.

De Goede, Marieke. 2005. *Virtue, Fortune and Faith: A Genealogy of Finance*. London: University of Minnesota Press.

De Haan, A. 1999. *Social Exclusion: Towards an Holistic Understanding of Deprivation, Social Development Department*. Development Studies Dissemination Note No. 2. London: DFID.

Desai, V.R.M. 1967. *Social Aspects of Savings*. Mumbai: Popular Prakasham Publishers.

Deshpande, R.S., M.J. Bhende, and S. Erappa. 2003. *Output and Impact Monitoring Study of KAWAD Project Agricultural Development and Rural Transformation*. Bangalore: Institute for Social and Economic Change.

Dexter, L. A. 1971. 'Role Relations and Conceptions of Neutrality in Interviewing', in Billy J. Franklin and Harold W. Osborne (eds), *Research Methods: Issues and Insights*. pp. 400–07. California: Wadsworth Publishing Company, Inc.

DFID (Department for International Development). 2004. 'India Country Plan. Partnership for Development'. Available online at http://www.dfid.gov.uk/pubs/files/capindia.pdf (downloaded on 19 July 2006).

Dichter, Tom. 1999. 'Case Studies in Microfinance: Non-governmental Organizations (NGOs) in Microfinance: Past, Present and Future—An Essay. Geocities'. Available online at http://www.geocities.com/salahuddin223/microfinance.html (downloaded on 5 March 2004).

Dos Anjos, M. 1999. 'Money, Trust and Culture: Elements for an Institutional Approach to Money', *Journal of Economic Issues*, 33: 677–88.

Douglas, Mary and Steven Ney. 1998. *Missing Persons: A Critique of the Social Sciences*. New York: Russell Sage Foundation.

Dreze, J. and A. Sen. 1995. *India: Economic Development and Social Opportunity*. New Delhi: Oxford University Press.

———. 2002. *India: Development and Participation*. New York: Oxford University Press.

Dunford, Christopher. 1998. 'Microfinance: A Means to What End?' *Monday Developments*, 16(17): 20–25.

———. 2001. 'The Holy Grail of Microfinance: Helping the Poor and Sustainable?' *Small Enterprise Development*, 11(1): 45–58.

EDA Rural Systems. 2003. *Impact Assessment of Microfinance—Interim Findings from a National Study of MFIs in India*. Lucknow: EDA Rural Systems Pvt. Ltd.

———. 2006. *Self Help Groups: A Study of the Light and Dark Sides*. EDA Rural Systems.

Edwards, M. 1998. 'NGO Performance—What Breeds Success?' in Peter Oakley, Brian Pratt, and Andrew Clayton (eds), *Outcomes and Impact: Evaluating Change in Social Development*, pp. 104–14. UK: INTRAC.

FAO (Food and Agriculture Organisation of the United Nations). 2002. *A Guide to Gender Sensitive Microfinance*. Rome: Socio-economic and Gender Analysis Programme, FAO.

Farrington, John, Diana Carney, Caroline Ashley and Cathryn Turton. 1999. 'Sustainable Livelihoods in Practice: Early Applications of Concepts in Rural Areas', *Natural Resource Perspective*, 42(30): 100–14.

Fernandez, Aloysius Prakash. 1994. *The Myrada Experience—The Interventions of a Voluntary Agency in the Emergence and Growth of People's Institutions For the Sustained and Equitable Management of Micro-watersheds*. Bangalore: MYRADA.

———. 2003. 'Round Table: Microfinance: An Introduction by Srinivasan R and Sriram M.S.', *IIMB Review*, 15(2): 52–86.

———. 2005. *Why Sanghamithra is Different*. Bangalore: MYRADA.

Fernando, Jude L. 2006a. 'Introduction: Microcredit and Empowerment of Women: Blurring the Boundary between Development and Capitalism', in Jude L. Fernando (ed.), *Microfinance Perils and Prospects*, pp. 1–244. Oxon: Routledge.

———. 2006b. 'Microcredit and Empowerment of Women: Visibility without Power', in Jude L. Fernando (ed.), *Microfinance Perils and Prospects*, pp. 187–238. Oxon: Routledge.

Ferraro, Emile. 2004. 'Owing and Being in Debt. A Contribution from the Northern Andes of Ecuador', *Social Anthropology*, 12(1): 77–94.

Fisher, Thomas and M. S. Sriram. 2002. *Beyond Micro-credit: Putting Development Back into Micro-finance*. New Delhi: Vistar Publications.

Freire, Paulo. 1970. *Pedagogy of the Oppressed*. Harmondsworth: Penguin.

FWWB (Friends of Women's World Banking). 1997. *Translating Dreams into Reality*. Ahmedabad: FWWB.

———. 2001. *Annual Report, 2000–2001*. Ahmedabad: FWWB.

———. 2006. *Consultation on Gender and Microfinance*. Ahmedabad: FWWB.

IFP (Institut Français de Pondicherry). 2004. *Indebtedness Vulnerability to Bondage and Microfinance*. Pondicherry: IFP.

Gadenne, Lucie and Veena Vasudevan. 2007. *How do Women in Mature SHGs Save and Invest their Money*. Delhi: Access Development Services.

Gaiha, Raghav. 2000. 'Do Anti Poverty Programmes Reach the Rural Poor in India?', *Oxford Development Studies*, 28(1): 71–95.

Gaiha, Raghav and Katsushi Imai. 2003. 'Vulnerability, Shocks and Persistence of Poverty—Estimates for Semi-arid Rural South India'. Available online at http://idpm.man.ac.uk/cprc/Conference/conferencepapers/Gaiha%20Raghav_Imai_REVISED2.pdf (downloaded on 19 May 2004).

Garcia, Maria Christina. 1998. 'The Evaluation of an Ongoing Educational Programme', in Peter Oakley, Brian Pratt and Andrew Clayton (eds), *Outcomes and Impact: Evaluating Change in Social Development*, pp. 115–22. UK: INTRAC.

Garikipati, Supriya. 2003. 'Microcredit in Rural India: An Evaluation'. Available online at http://www.enterprise-impact.org.uk/conference/abstracts/garikipati.shtml (downloaded on 7 October 2003).

Geertz, C. 1962. 'The Rotating Credit Association: A Middle Rung in Development', *Economic and Development and Cultural Change*, 1(2): 241–63.

———. 1973. *The Interpretation of Cultures*. New York: Basic Books.

George, Asha, Aditi Iyer and Gita Sen. 2005. 'Systematic Hierarchies and Systemic Failures: Gender and Health Inequities in Koppal District', Conference Paper. Bangalore: ISEC. Downloadable from http://www.esocialsciences.com/Articles/displayArticles.asp?Article_ID (downloaded on 6 February 2007).

Gerristen, Peter R.W. 2003. 'Back to the Basics: Potentials and Limitations of Socio-economic Field Methods in "Fuzzy Empirical Situations"', paper presented at the Integrated Training Course of the NCCR North-South Program on Syndromes of Global Change, Centre for Development and Environment, Berne, July 15–25.

Ghate, Prabhu. 2007. *Microfinance in India: A State of the Sector Report*. Delhi: Access Development Services.

Gibbons, David. 2002. *The CASHPOR Financial and Technical Services (CFTS) Story*. Mirzapur: CFTS.

———. 2003. 'Round Table: Microfinance: An Introduction by Srinivasan R. and Sriram M.S.', *IIMB Review*, 15(1): 52–86.

Gilbert, Emily. 2005. *Common Cents: Situating Money in Time and Place*. Routledge: Taylor and Francis Group Ltd.

Gilligan, Carol. 1993. *In a Different Voice: Psychological Theory and Women's Development*. London: Harvard University Press.

Goetz, Anne Marie and R. Sen Gupta. 1996. 'Who Takes the Credit? Gender, Power, and Control over Loan Use in Rural Credit Programmes in Bangladesh', *World Development*, 24(1): 45–63.

Goetz, Anne Marie and Rob Jenkins. 2005. *Reinventing Accountability: Making Democracy Work for Human Development*. New York: Palgrave Macmillan.

GOI. 2001. *National Policy for the Empowerment of Women*. Delhi: Department of Women and Child Development and Ministry of Human Resource Development.

———. 2002. *Five Year Plan 2002–2007. Dimensions and Strategies. Vol. I, II and III*. New Delhi: Planning Commission and Government of India.

———. 2003. All India Debt and Investment Survey 2002. Delhi. National Sample Survey Organisation, GOI. Available online at http://mospi.nic.in/nsso_4aug2008/web/nsso/reports.htm (downloaded on 7 August 2004).

———. 2005. *Agricultural Cooperation*. Delhi: Ministry of Agriculture.

———. 2007. 'The Microfinancial Sector (Development and Regulation) Bill'. Available online at http://www.prsindia. org/bills.php (accessed on January 24 2008).

———. 2008. 'Eleventh Five Year Plan (2007–12) Document'. Available online at http://planningcommission.nic.in/plans/ planrel/fiveyr/welcome.html (downloaded on 7 August 2008).

GOK (Government of Karnataka). 1999. *Human Development in Karnataka 1999*. Bangalore: Planning Department.

———. 2001. *Task Force on Health and Family Welfare. Karnataka: Towards Equity, Quality and Integrity in Health. Focus on Primary Health Care and Public Health*. Bangalore: Government of Karnataka.

———. 2002. *District at a Glance, Koppal*. Karnataka: District Statistical Office.

———. 2004. *Human Development in Karnataka 2004*. Bangalore: Planning Department.

———. 2006. *Human Development in Karnataka 2006*. Bangalore: Planning Department.

Goyder, H. 1998. *New Approaches to Participatory Impact Assessment*. London: ActionAid.

Grameen Bank. 1998. 'Measuring Transformation: Assessing and Improving of Microcredit. Abstracts of Impact Evaluation Tools and Selected References'. Available online at www.microcreditsummit.org/pdfs/impactpaper_abstract.pdf (downloaded on 25 June 2003).

Granovetter, M. 1994. 'Business Groups', in N.J. Smelser and R. Swedberg (eds), *The Handbook of Economics Sociology*, pp. 454–57. New Jersey: Prince Town University Press.

Graziosi, Ascanio. 2002. 'A New Approach in Evaluating Microfinance Institutions Performance. Alternative Finance'. Available online at http://www.alternative-finance.org.uk (downloaded on 06.02.004).

Guérin, Isabelle. 2006. 'Women and Money: Lessons from Senegal', *Development and Change*, 37(3): 549–70.

Guérin, Isabelle, Caroline O'Reilly, Marc Roesch, Maria Sathya and G. Venkatasubramanian. 2007. *Staying Free from Bondage: Do Microfinance-led Strategies Work? Findings from Tamil Nadu, India*. Geneva: ILO.

Guijit and Cornwall. 1995. 'Critical Reflections on the Practices of PRA'. *PLA Notes*.

Guruswamy, Mohan and Ronald Joseph Abraham. 2006. 'Redefininng Poverty. A New Poverty Line for India', *Economic and Political Weekly*, XLI(25): 2534–41.

Harper, Malcolm. 1998. *Profit for the Poor: Cases in Microfinance*. New Delhi: Oxford & IBH Publishing Co. Pvt. Ltd.

———. 2002. *Promotion of SHGs under the SHG-bank Linkage Programme in India*. Mumbai: NABARD.

Harper, Malcolm and Gerry Finnegan. 1998. *Value for Money: Impact of Small Enterprise Development*. New Delhi: Oxford & IBH Publishing Co. Pvt. Ltd.

Hashemi, Syed, R. Sidney, S. Schuler and Ann P. Riley. 1996. 'Rural Credit Programs and Women's Empowerment in Bangladesh', *World Development*, 24(4): 635–53.

Hatch, John K. and Laura Fredrick. 1998. *Poverty Assessment by Microfinance Institutions: A Review of Current Practices*. Foundation for International Community Assistance Development Alternatives.

Hendricks, Larry. 2002. 'Designing Microfinance from an Exit Strategy Perspective. Alternative Finance'. Available online at http://www.alternative-finance.org.uk/rtf/hendricks-designing.rtf (downloaded on 12 February 2004).

Herweg, Karl and Kurt Steiner. 2002. *Impact Monitoring and Assessment: Instruments for Use in Rural Development Projects with a Focus on Sustainable Land Management*, Volume 1: Procedure. Berne: Centre for Development and Environment and GTZ.

Hirsch, Hadorn Gertrude. 2006. 'Gender and Transdisiplinarity in Research for Sustainable Development', in Smita Premchander and Christine Mueller (eds), *Gender and Sustainable Development Berne: Case Studies from NCCR North-South. Perspectives of the Swiss National Centre of Competence in Research (NCCR) North-South, University of Bern*, Vol. 2, p. 364. Bern: Geographica Bernensia.

Högger, Ruedi. (2003). *Understanding Rural Livelihood Systems as Complex Wholes*. Delhi: Swiss Agency for Development and Co-operation.

———. 2004. 'Understanding Livelihood System as Complex Wholes', in Ruedi Baumgartner and Ruedi Högger (eds), *In Search of Sustainable Livelihood Systems*, pp. 351–64. New Delhi: Sage Publications.

Holstein, J. A. and J. F. Gubrium. 1995. *The Active Interview*. Thousand Oaks, CA: Sage.

Holvoet, N. 2005. 'The Impact of Microfinance on Decision-making Agency: Evidence from South India', *Development and Chang*, 36(1): 75–102.

Hulme, David. 1997. *Impact Assessment Methodologies for Microfinance: A Review*. Washington: AIMS.

Hulme, David and Paul Mosley. 1996. *Finance against Poverty*. London: Routledge.

Hurni, Hans, Urs Wiesmann and Roland Schertenleib. 2004. *Research for Mitigating Syndromes of Global Change: A Transdisciplinary Appraisal of Selected Regions of the World to Prepare Development-oriented Research Partnerships. Perspectives of the Swiss National Centre of Competence in Research (NCCR) North-South, University of Bern*, Vol. 2, p. 468. Bern: Geographica Bernensia.

ICMC and PRIZMA. 2000. 'Executive Summary of Impact Survey of International Catholic Migration Commission (ICMC) and PRIZMA Microfinance Programme in Bosnia and Herzengovina. Alternative Finance'. Available online at http://www.alternative-finance.org.uk (downloaded on 6 February 2004).

IFAD. 2007. 'Gender: Food Security, Poverty and Women: Lessons from Rural Asia'. Available online at http://www.ifad.org/gender/thematic/rural/rual_6.htm (downloaded on 10 October 2007).

IIB Vision. 2007. 'New Plans for Inclusive Banking. IIB Vision', *Indian Institute of Banking and Finance*, 3(3): 7.

IIHRD (Indian Institute for Human Research and Development). 2003. *Impact Assessment Study of Rural Development Programme in Ramnathapuram Distcrit, Tamilnadu*. Delhi: Ministry of Rural Development, GOI.

IIMS Dataworks. 2007. 'Invest India Incomes and Savings Survey 2007: Savings Priorities of India's High Income Groups'. Available online at http://www.iimsdataworks.com (downloaded on 11 January 2008).

IIPO (Indian Institute of Public Opinion). 2005. *Evaluation Report of Swayamsidha (IWEP)*. Delhi: Department of Women and Child Development.

IIPS (International Institute for Population Sciences). 2002. 'Reproductive and Child Health District Level Household Survey 2002. Round 2 Phase 1. Koppal'. Available online at http://www.rchindia.org/rep/kar/koppal/koppal.htm (downloaded on 11 July 2006).

ILO (International Labour Organization). 2007. 'Global Employment Trends for Women 2007: ILO Study Warns on the Feminisation of Working Poverty'. Available online at http://www.ilo.org/wow/Newsbriefs/lang-en/WCMS_082692/index.htm (downloaded on 12 December 2007).

Ingham, G. 2006. 'Further Reflections on the Ontology of Money: Responses to Lapavitsas and Dodd', *Economy and Society*, 35(2): 259–78.

Jackson, Cecile. 1996. 'Rescuing Gender from the Poverty Trap', *World Development*, 24(3): 489–504.

Jackson, Cecile. 1998. 'Women and Poverty or Gender and Wellbeing?' *Journal of International Affairs*, 52(1): 67–81.

Jain, Pankaj. 1996. 'Managing Credit for the Rural Poor: Lessons from the Grameen Bank', *World Development*, 24(1): 79–89.

Jayaraman, V. and Sanjay K. Srivastava. 2003. *Poverty Mapping and Monitoring Using Information Technology: Learning and Perspectives from India*. Consultancy Report for Ad Hoc Expert Group Meeting (EGM) on Poverty Mapping and Monitoring Using Information Technology to Economic and Social Commission for Asia and the Pacific (ESCAP), United Nations, Bangkok. Bangalore: Indian Space Research Organisation. Available online at http://www.unescap.org/pdd/projects/pov_map/4b-India%20Poverty%20Mapping%20-%20Main%20Report.doc (downloaded on 19 July 2006).

Jenkins, Rob and Anne Marie Goetz. 1999. 'Accounts and Accountability: Theoretical Implications of the Right-to-information Movement in India', *Third World Quarterly*, 20(3): 603–22.

Jeyaseelan, N. 2005. 'Transforming the Lives of the Poor From Bitter to Better, Indian Bank's Special Unit for Microfinance, Usilampatti'. Available online at http://www.solutionexchange-un.net.in/mf/cr/res06090710.doc (downloaded on 15 September 2007).

Jha, Raghabendra. 1999. 'Rural Poverty in India: Structure, Determinants and Suggestions for Policy Reform'. Available online at http://unpan1.un.org/intradoc/groups/public/documents/APCITY/UNPAN013137.pdf (downloaded on 6 February 2004).

Jha, Raghabendra and Raghav Gaiha. 2004. 'Under-nutrition, Poverty and Growth in Rural India—A Regional Analysis', ASARC Working Paper 2004–2. Canberra: Australian National University.

Johnson, Susan and Ben Rogaly. 1997. *Microfinance and Poverty Reduction*. Oxford: Oxfam.

Johnson, Susan. 1999. 'Gender and Microfinance: Guidelines for Good Practice'. Available online at http://www.gdrc.org/icm/wind/gendersjonson.html (downloaded on 25.05.2003).

———. 2003. *Gender Relations, Empowerment and Microcredit: Moving on from a Lost Decade*. Extract of Impact Assessment of FINCA, completed for DFID. UK: University of Bath.

———. 2005. 'Making MFIs and Financial Markets Work for Poor Women', paper for the Consultation on *Reclaiming Leadership of Women in Microfinance*. Ahmedabad: FWWB.

Joshi, Deep. 2003. 'Round Table: Microfinance: An Introduction by Srinivasan R. and Sriram M.S.', *IIMB Review*, 15(2): 52–86.

Kabeer, Naila. 2003. 'Assessing the Wider Social Impacts of Microfinance Services: Concepts, Methods and Findings', *IDS Bulletin*, 34(4): 106–14.

———. 2005. *Inclusive Citizenship: Meanings and Expressions*. London: Zed Books.

Kamal, Md. Mustafa. 1999. 'Measuring Transformation: Assessing and Improving the Impact of Microcredit. Part III. Impact Evaluation Mechanism of the Association for Social Advancement (ASA) in Bangladesh', paper commissioned by the Microcredit Summit Campaign for the 1999 Meeting of Councils.

Karl, Marilee. 1997. *Women and Rural Development. A Resource Guide for Organisation and Action*. ISIS Women's International Information and Communication Service. Ahmedabad: Intermediate Technology Publications.

Karmakar, K.G. 1999. *Rural Credit and Self-help Groups: Micro-finance Needs and Concepts in India*. New Delhi: Sage Publications.

Keister, L.A. 2000. 'Race and Wealth Inequality: The Impact of Racial Differences in Asset Ownership on the Distribution of Household Wealth', *Social Science Research*, 29(12): 477–502.

———. 2002. 'Financial Markets, Money and Banking', *Annual Review of Sociology*, 28: 39–62.

Keynes, John Maynard. 1936 and 1970. *The General Theory of Employment Interest and Money*. London and Basingstoke: Macmillan and Co. Ltd.

Knorr Cetina, Karin. 1999. *Epistemic Cultures: How the Sciences Make Knowledge*. Cambridge, MA: Harvard University Press.

Kottak, Conrad Phillip. 1985. 'When People Don't Come First: Some Sociological Lessons from Completed Projects', in M. Cernea (ed.), *Putting People First: Sociological Variables in Rural Development,* pp. 325–56. New York: Oxford University Press.

Kraus-Harper, U. 1998. *From Despondency to Ambitions: Women's Changing Perceptions of Self Employment: Cases from India and Other Developing Countries.* England: Hants.

Krueger, R.A. and M.A. Casey. 2000. *Focus Groups: A Practical Guide for Applied Research* (3rd edition). Thousand Oaks, CA: Sage.

Kuenzi, Erwin, Yvan Droz, Fansica Maina and Urs. Wiesmann. 1998. 'Patterns of Peasant Livelihood Strategies: Local Actors and Sustainable Resource Use', *Eastern and Southern African Geographical Journal,* 8(2): 55–66.

Leeladhar, V. 2006. 'Taking Banking Services to the Common Man-financial Inclusion: Commemorative Lecture on 2 December 2005'. Available online at http://www.rbi.org.in/scripts/BS (downloaded on 5 January 2008).

Lewis, David and Shirin Madon. 2004. *Information Systems and Nongovernmental Development Organisations: Advocacy, Organisational Learning, and Accountability.* London: The Information Society.

Lingam, Lakshmi. 2006. 'Gender, Households and Poverty. Tracking Mediations of Macro Adjustment Programmes', *Economic and Political Weekly,* XLI(20): 1989–98.

LiPuma, Edward and Benjamin Lee. 2005. 'Financial Derivations and the Rise of Circulation', *Economy and Society,* 34(3): 404–27.

Ludi, Eva. 2004. *Economic Analysis of Soil Conservation: Case Studies from the Highlands of Amhara Region, Ethiopia.* Berne: Centre for Development and Environment (CDE), Institute of Geography, University of Berne.

Lyon, F. 1999. 'Cooperation and Group Formation in Processing, Marketing and Transport', PhD thesis. Durham: University of Dhurham.

Mahajan, V. 2005. 'From Microcredit to Livelihood Finance', *Economic and Political Weekly,* XL(41): 4416–419.

Mahajan, V., B. Ramola and M. Titus. 1998. 'Dhakka Starting Microfinance in India'. Workshop on Kick Starting Microfinance: A Challenge for the Indian Banks, Bankers Institute for Rural Development, Lucknow, 26–28 October.

Mahajan, Vijay and Prasanth V. Regy. 2007. 'Microfinance and Technology', in Prabhu Ghate (ed.), *Microfinance in India: A State of the Sector Report,* pp. 131–48. Delhi: Access Development Services.

Malhotra, Rakesh. 2006. *Rate and Reasons of Dropouts in Self Help Groups.* New Delhi: Agricultural Finance Corporation.

Marr, Ana. 1999. Studying Group Dynamics: An Analysis of Microfinance Impacts on Poverty Reduction and Its Application in Peru. PhD Thesis. London: University of London.

Mask, R. 2000. 'Christian Microenterprise Development, Counting the Cost and Building the Kingdom, Lookout Mountain, GA: Chalmer's Centre for Economic Development, Covenant College'. Available online at http://www.aerdo.org/pdf/christian_microenterprise.pdf (downloaded on 19 September 2005).

Matin, Imran. 1998. Rapid Credit Deepening and the Joint Liability Credit Contract: A Study of Grameen Bank Borrowers in Madhupur. Ph.D. Thesis. Brighton: University of Sussex.

Mayoux, Linda. 1997. 'Impact Assessment and Women's Empowerment in Microfinance Programmes: Issues for a Participatory Action and Learning Approach', background paper submitted to CGAP Virtual Meeting on Impact Assessment Methodologies in Microfinance Programmes.

———. 1999. 'Microfinance and the Empowerment of Women. A Review of the Key Issues. ILO Social Finance Unit', Working Paper No. 22, International Labour Organisation (ILO), Geneva.

———. 2001. 'Impact Assessment of Microfinance: Towards a Sustainable Learning Process. EDIAIS Information Resources'. Available online at http://www.microfinancegateway.org/impact/method/iss11_1.htm (downloaded on 6 June 2002).

———. 2003a. 'Empowering Enquiry', *Enterprise Impact News,* issue 16, January/February: 1–4.

———. 2003b. 'Using Diagrams', *Enterprise Impact News,* issue 22, August: 1–4.

———. 2003c. 'Grassroots Action Learning', *Enterprise Impact News,* issue 16, September: 1–4.

McGuire, Paul, John D. Conroy, and Ganesh B. Thapa. 1998. 'Getting the Framework Right: Policy and Regulation for Microfinance in Asia'. Available online at http://www.bwtp.org/publications (downloaded on 20 March 2003).

Mehta, Kapur Aasha and Amita Shah. 2002. 'Chronic Poverty in India: Overview Study. Manchester, UK: Chronic Poverty Centre'. Available online at http://www.eldis.org/go/display/?id=11189&type=Document (downloaded on 15 January 2008).

Menon, Roshni. 2003. *Impact Assessment Studies of Selected Microfinance Programmes around the World: An Overview and Analysis*. Bangalore: Sampark.

Messerli, Peter. 2004. *Alternatives à la Culture sur brulis sur la Falaise Est de Madagascar: Stratégies en vue d'une gestion plus durable des terres*. Berne: Centre pour le Dévelopment et l'Environnent (CDE), Institute de Géographie, Universitè de Berne, PhD Thesis.

MHHDC (Mahbub ul Haq Human Development Centre). 2002. *Human Development in South Asia 2002: Agriculture and Rural Development*. Karachi: MHHDC.

MicroSave Africa. 1998. 'Beyond Basic Credit and Savings: Developing New Financial Service Products for the Poor'. Available online at http://www.undp.org/sum/MicroSave/ftp_downloads/MicroSavePaper2.pdf (downloaded on 2 June 2004).

Montgomery, R.M. 1996. 'Discipline or Protecting the Poor? Avoiding the Social Costs of Peer Pressure in Micro-credit Schemes', *Journal of International Development*, Special Issue, 8(2): 225–80.

Montgomery, R.M., D. Bhattacharya and D. Hulme. 1996. *Credit for the Poor in Bangladesh*. Universities of Manchester and Reading Paper on Finance for Low-income Groups, Manchester: Institute fro Development Policy and Management.

Morduch, J. 1998. 'Does Microfinance Really Help the Poor? New Evidence from Flagship Programs in Bangladesh, Harvard Institute of International Development and Hoover Institution, Stanford University'. Available online at http://www.wws.princeton.edu/~rpds/downloads/orduch_microfinance_poor.pdf (downloaded on 24 October 2003).

———. 1999. 'The Microfinance Promise', *Journal of Economics Literature*, XXXVII(4): 1567–615.

Mosley, Paul. 1996. 'The Regional Rural Banks: India, the Policy and Institutional Background', in Paul Mosely and David Hulmi (eds.), *Finance against Poverty*, pp. 157–79. London: Routledge.

———. 2000. 'Microfinance and Poverty: Bolivia Case Study. USAID Microenterprise Development'. Available online at http://www.mip.org/pdfs/aims/microfinance_and_poverty.pdf (downloaded on 16 June 2003).

Mosse, David. 2004. 'Is Good Policy Un-implementable? Reflections on the Ethnography of Aid Policy and Practice', *Development and Change*, 35(4): 639–71.

———. 2005. *Cultivating Development*. New Delhi: Vistar Publications.

Mosse, David, Sanjeev Gupta, Mona Mehta, Vidya Shah, Juila Rees and KRIBP Project Team. 2004. 'Brokered Livelihoods: Debt, Labour Migration and Development in Tribal Western India', *Journal of Development Studies*, 38(5): 59–88.

Mukhopadhyaya, Swapna and R. Savitri. 1998. *Poverty, Gender and Reproductive Choice*. New Delhi: Ajaya Kumar Jain.

Murthy, Ranjani K., K. Raju and Amitha Kamath with SAPAP Research Team. 2002. 'Towards Women's Empowerment and Poverty Reduction: Lessons from the Participatory Impact Assessment of South Asian Poverty Alleviation Pro-gramme in Andhra Pradesh, India, UNDP'. Available online at http://www.undp.org.in/report/wkspsclmblizn/ppt.htm (downloaded on 12 April 2003).

Murthy, Ranjani K., Neera Burra and Joy Deshmukh Ranadive. 2005. *Micro-credit, Poverty and Empowerment. Linking the Triad*. New Delhi: Sage Publications.

Mutesasira, Leonard. 1999. 'Use and Impact of Savings among the Poor in Tanzania'. Available online at http://www.undp.org/sum/MicroSave/ftp_downloads/UseTanzania.doc (downloaded on 24 December 2003).

MYRADA. 2001. *The Myrada Experience: A Manual for Capacity Building of Self Help Groups*. Bangalore: MYRADA.

NABARD. 1998. *Guidelines on Self Help Groups*. Bangalore: NABARD.

NABARD. 1999. Circular on Priority Sector Lending Special Programmes, April 1. Mumbai: NABARD. Available online at http://www.nabard.org/whats/mcirc2.htm (downloaded on 25 June 2003).

———. 2002. 'Summary and Recommendations of the Task Force on Supportive Policy and Regulatory Framework for MicroFinance, 2002, National Bank of Agriculture and Rural Development'. Available online at http://www.gdrc.org/icm/country/india-mftaskforce.html (downloaded on 16 April 2004).

———. 2007. 'SHG Bank Linkage Programme in India'. Available online at http://www.nabard.org/pdf/highlights%200607.pdf (downloaded on 25 January 2008).

Nair, Tara S. 2001. 'Institutionalising Microfinance in India: An Overview of Strategic Issues', *Economic and Political Weekly*, XXXVI(39): 399–404.

Narayan, Deepa, Robert Chambers, Meera Kaul Shah and Patti Petesch. 2000. *Voices of the Poor: Crying Out for Change*. New York: Oxford University Press.

Narula, Smita and Martin Macwan. 2001. '"Untouchability": The Economic Exclusion of the Dalits in India', paper presented at the International Council on Human Rights Policy, Geneva, January 24–25. Available online at http://www.ichrp.org/paper_files/113_w_07.pdf (downloaded on 19 July 2006).

National Labour Academy-Nepal. 2006. 'Impact Assessment and the Final Evaluation of Prevention and Elimination of Bonded Labour in South Asia (PEBLISA): Nepal Chapter'. Available online at http://www.solutionexchange-un.net.in/mf/cr/res06090707.doc (downloaded on 19 July 2006).

Nigam, Ashok and Sultana Monawar. 1998. *Impact Assessment Study of the Family Development Fund*. Egypt: UNICEF.

Nissanke, Machiko. 2002. 'Donors' Support for Microcredit as Social Enterprise: A Critical Reappraisal'. United Nations University and World Institute for Development Economics Research (WIDER), Discussion Paper No. 2002/127'. Available online at http://www.wider.unu.edu/publications/dps/dps2002/dp2002-127.pdf (downloaded on 25 April 2003).

Noponen, Helzi. 2003. 'The Internal Learning Susytems for Participatory Assessment of Micro Finance', *Small Enterprise Development*, 12(4): 45–53.

Osmani, S.R. 2001. 'Growth Strategies and Poverty Reduction. Asia and Pacific Forum on Poverty'. Available online at http://www.adb.org/Poverty/Forum/pdf/osmani.pdf (downloaded on 19 May 2004).

Otero, M. and E. Rhyne. 1994. *The New World of Micro Enterprise Finance—Building Healthy Financial Institutions for the Poor*. Bloomfield, CT: Kumarian Press.

Padhi, Bibhudutt. 2003. 'Mainstreaming Microfinance: Bridging the NGO–Banker Divide. Alternative Finance'. Available online at http://www.alternative-finance.org.uk/cgi-bin/summary.pl?id=348 (downloaded on 10 February 2004).

Padia, Veena. 2005. 'Social Mobilization and Micro-credit for Women's Empowerment: A Study of the DHAN foundation', in Neera Burra, Joy Deshmukh Ranadive and K. Murthy (eds), *Micro-credit Poverty and Empowerment Linking the Triad*, pp. 161–99. Delhi: Sage Publications.

Parr, Julian. 2005. 'PEBLISA project', presentation made at a Workshop on 8–9 September, at Delhi, International Labour Office.

Parthasarathy, Soma Kishore. 2005. 'Awareness, Access, Agency: Experience of Swayam Shikshan Prayog in Microfinance and Women's Empowerment', in Neera Burra, Joy Deshmukh Ranadive and K. Murthy (eds), *Micro-credit Poverty and Empowerment Linking the Triad*, pp. 200–44. Delhi: Sage Publications.

Patnaik, Prabhat. 2006. 'Diffusion of Development', *Economic Political Weekly*, XLI(19): 1766–72.

Peredo, Ana Maria and James J. Chrisman. 2006. 'Toward a Theory of Community-based Enterprise', *Academy of Management Review*, 31(2): 309–28.

Pini, Barbara. 2003. 'Feminist Methodology and Rural Research: Reflections on a Study of an Australian Agricultural Organisation', *Sociologia Ruralis*, 43(4): 418–33.

Pitt, M.M. and S.R. Khandker. 2004. 'Credit Programmes for the Poor and Seasonality in Rural Bangladesh', *Journal of Development Studies*, 39(2): 1–24.

Pixley, J.F. 1999. 'Beyond Twin Defects: Emotions of the Future in the Organisation of Money', *American Journal of Economics and Sociology*, 58(4): 1091–1109.

Planning Commission, Government of India. 2001. *Report of the Working Group on Rural Poverty Alleviation Programmes for the Tenth Five-year Plan 2002–2007*. TFYP WG Report No. 81/2001. New Delhi: The Planning Commission.

Pogge, Thomas and Sanjay G. Reddy. 2006. 'Unknown: Extent, Distribution and Trend of Global Income Poverty', *Economic and Political Weekly*, XLI(22): 2241–247.

PRADAN. 1997. *From Self Help Groups to Community Banking: The PRADAN Project for Empowerment of Women*. Bangalore: Comunicación for Development and Learning (CDL).

———. 1998. 'Income, Expenditure and Social Sector Indicators of Households in Rural and Urban India', paper prepared as part of the MIMAP-India Project sponsored by the International Development Research Center, Ottawa. Available online at http://web.idrc.ca/uploads/user-S/10288316670india_pov.pdf (downloaded on 19 May 2004).

———. 1999. *Minutes of the Meeting of NABARD Workshop on SHGs Organized by PRADAN-Lohardaga*. Bihar: PRADAN.

———. 2006. *History and Programme Highlights*. Delhi: PRADAN.

Premchander, Smita. 1999. *Reality and Reflections on Gender and Leadership for Natural Resources Management*. Voicing Issues for Empowerment Women Series (VIEWS) No. 4. Bangalore: Sampark.

———. 2000. *Report of the Workshop for the Design of CREDIT—III Project, Bastar*. Report prepared for CARE India Delhi. Bangalore: Sampark.

———. 2002. 'Forum: Whose Parameters, Whose Standards? Evaluating the Performance of Savings and Credit Groups Through External Parameters Only Could Be a Self-defeating Process', *News Reach*, 2(7): 8–13.

———. 2003a. 'Learning from Impact Assessments: Does Understanding Women's Perspectives Change Microfinance Programmes?', paper presented at workshop in Manchester, November 24–25. Available online at http://www.enterprise-impact.org.uk/pdf/Premchander.pdf (downloaded on 19 May 2004).

———. 2003b. 'NGOs and Local MFIs—How to Increase Poverty Reduction through Women's Small and Micro-enterprises', *Futures*, 35(4): 361–78.

———. 2004. 'Pugnacious Poverty in Bangladesh', *News Reach*, 3(5): 22–24.

———. 2005. 'Competing Perspectives of Women and Micro-finance Institutions: Rethinking Organisational Forms and Capacity Building', *Mainstream*, XLIII(16): 11–12.

———. 2006. 'Exploring the Meaning of Money: A Study of the Impact of Microfinance in Koppal District of India', a poster about the PhD may be found online at http://www.nccr-north-south.unibe.ch/publications/Infosystem/on-line%20Dokumente/Upload/11_premchander.qxp_s.pdf

Premchander, Smita and Christine Mueller. 2006. *Gender and Sustainable Development. Berne: Case Studies from NCCR North-South. Perspectives of the Swiss National Centre of Competence in Research (NCCR) North-South, University of Bern*, Vol. 2, p. 364. Bern: Geographica Bernensia.

Premchander, Smita, M. Chidambaranathan and L. Jeyaseelan. 2003. 'In Search of Water: Natural Resource Degradation Leading to a Livelihoods Crisis in Koppal District, Karnataka, India', *Mountain Research and Development*, 23(1): 19–23. Available online at http://www.mrd-journal.org/issue.asp?Issue_ID=34 (downloaded on 25 May 2004).

Premchander, Smita and V. Prameela. 2007. 'Empowering Women through Microfinance: A Policy and Programme Review. Delhi: Care India'. Available online at http://www.careindia.org/ManagePublications/VisitPublicationDetail.aspx?SectionID=114 (downloaded on 20 October 2007).

Proshika. 1998. *Participatory Impact Assessment of Proshika's Development Interventions: Proshika Group Members' Perceptions and Their Analysis of the Impact of Development Interventions on Their Lives in General and on the Lives of the Rural Women in Particular*. Dhaka: Proshika.

———. 2002. *Study of Impact of Proshika Micro-credit Programmes on Employment and Income Generation. Study carried out by Shamsul Hoque Mondal*. Dhaka: Proshika.

Putnam, Robert D. 1993. 'The Prosperous Community—Social Capital and Public Life', *The American Prospect*, 13: 35–42.

Quiñones, Benjamin R. Jr. 2000. 'Microfinance as an Instrument of Poverty Alleviation: An Overview', paper presented at a conference on The Potential and Limitations of Economic Initiatives in Grassroots Development: Current Issues and Asian Experiences, INASIA and CDF, Dhaka, November 27–30.

Rahaman, Rushidhan Islam. 1999. 'Poor Women's Access to Economic Gain from Grameen Bank Loans', Working Paper No. 9/12. Dhaka: National Centre for Development Studies.

Rajagopalan, Shashi. 2003. 'Designing Secondary Institutions of Self-help Groups (SHGs) (engaged in savings and credit services)', paper for discussion at APMAS workshop of 20–21 June.

———. 2004a. *Self Help Groups—a Critique*. Hyderabad.

———. 2004b. 'User Owned and Controlled Organizations in the Field of Financial Services', Paper written for Microfinance India 2008, 24–26 February.

———. 2005a. 'Do Federations Have a Role in Financial Intermediation?' paper written for Microfinance India 2008, 24–26 February.

———. 2005b. 'Reclaiming Women's Leadership in Microfinance', paper presented at the FWWB Conference on Reclaiming Women's Leadership in Microfinance, Ahmedabad, September 8–9.

———. 2005c. 'Micro-credit and Women's Empowerment: The Lokadrusti Case', in Neera Burra, Joy Deshmukh-Ranadive and Rajani K. Murthy (eds), *Micro Credit, Poverty ands Empowerment*, pp. 245–85. New Delhi: Sage Publications.

Rajivan, Anurdha. 2005. 'Microcredit and Women's Empowerment: A Case Study of SHARE Micro-finance Limited', in Neera Burra, Joy Deshmukh Ranadive and K. Murthy (eds), *Microcredit Poverty and Empowerment Linking the Triad*, pp. 116–60. Delhi: Sage Publications.

Rajshekar. 2007. 'Aberration or Synecdoche: Reflections on the Microfinance Suicides of Andhra Pradesh'. Available online at http://www.fracturedearth.org/?p=234 (downloaded on 20 October 2007).

Raju, K.V., Uma Rani and Anil Patel. 2000. *Role of Non-economic Motivation*. Anand: Institute of Rural Management.

Ramanathan, R. 2003. 'Round Table: Microfinance: An Introduction by Srinivasan R., and Sriram M.S.', *IIMB Review*, 15(2): 52–86.

Ramaswamy, V., G.K. Karanth, R. Baumgartner and R. Hogger. 2004. 'Emerging Rural Leadership and Sustainable Management of Natural Resources. Evidence from Two South Indian Villages', in R. Baumgartner and R. Hogger (eds), *In Search of Sustainable Livelihood Systems: Managing Resources and Change*, pp. 298–315. New Delhi: Sage Publications.

Ranadive, Joy Deshmukh and Rajini K. Murthy. 2005. 'Introduction: Linking the Triad', in Neera Burra, Joy Deshmukh Ranadive and Rajani K. Murthy (eds), *Micro Credit, Poverty and Empowerment*, pp. 322–56. New Delhi: Sage Publications.

Rankin, K.N. 2002. 'Social Capital, Microfinance and the Politics of Development', *Journal of Feminist Economics*, 8(1): 1–24.

———. 2006. 'Social Capital, Microfinance, and the Politics of Development', in Jule L. Fernando (ed.), *Microfinance Perils and Prospects*, pp. 89–111. Oxon: Routledge.

Rao, Aruna and Syed M. Hashmi. 1999. 'Institutional Take-off or Snakes and Ladders: Dynamics and Sustainability of Local-level Organisations in Rural Bangladesh', INTRAC Occasional Papers Series (30). Oxford, UK: INTRAC.

RBI (Reserve Bank of India). 1954. *All India Credit Survey*. Bombay: RBI.

———. 2003. 'All India List of NBFCs Including RNBCs, to Whom Certificate of Registration under Section 45 IA of RBI Act, 1934 Have been Issued by the Reserve Bank of India to Hold/Accept Deposits from Public (Position as on 30 July 2003)'. Available online at http://www.rbi.org.in/index.dll/39179?OpenStoryTextArea?fromdate=09/20/03&todate= 09/20/03&s1secid=0&s2secid=0&secid=7/0/0&archivemode=0 (downloaded on 20 September 2003).

RBI (Reserve Bank of India). 2007a. Circular on Master Circular on Micro Credit, RBI/2007-08/38, RPCD.MFFI.BC.No. 08/12.01.001/2007-08, 2 July. Mumbai: RBI.

———. 2007b. Circular on Microfinance—Joint Fact-finding Study with the Banks, RBI 2006-07/185, RPCD.CO.Plan. BC.No. 34/04.09.22/2006-07, 22 November. Mumbai: RBI.

———. 2007c. 'All India List of NBFCs Including RNBCs to Whom Certificate of Registration under Section 45 IA of RBI Act, 1934 Have been Issued by the RBI to Hold/Accept Deposits from Public (Position as on March, 2007)'. Available online at http://www.rbi.org.in/commonman/English/Scripts/NBFCs.aspx (downloaded on 20 January 2008).

Reddy, C.S. and Prakash, L.B. 2003. 'Status of SHG Federations in Andhra Pradesh', paper presented at Workshop on *SHG Federation* Organised by NIPCCD, Andhra Pradesh Mahila Abhuvrudhi Society, Hyderabad, March 24–25.

Reddy, Venugopal. 2006. 'Annual Policy Statements for the Year 2005–06. Mumbai: Reserve Bank of India'. Available online at http://www.sadhan.org/circular/Crdt%202005-06.doc (downloaded on 15 January 2006).

Remeneyi, J. 1997. *Microfinance: A Panacea for Poverty? Development Research Briefings*. Dublin: University College Dublin.

Richardson, Pat and Rhona Howarth. 2002. *Jobs, Gender and Small Enterprises Actors Affecting Women Entrepreneurs in Micro and Small Enterprises*. Geneva: International Labour Organisation.

Riddell, Roger C. and Mark Robinson. 1995. 'Non-governmental Organisations and Rural Poverty Alleviation. Overseas Development Institute'. Available online at http://www.ratingfund.org/ (downloaded on 10 January 2004).

Rist, Stephan, M. Chidambaranathan, Cesar Escobar, Urs Wiesmann, and Anne Zimmermann. 2007. 'Moving from Sustainable Management to Sustainable Governance of Natural Resources: The Role of Social Learning Processes in Rural India, Bolivia and Mali', *Journal of Rural Studies*, 23(1): 23–37. Available online at http://www.sciencedirect. com/science?_ob=MImg&_imagekey=B6VD9-4JKYTK4-3-3&_cdi=5977&_user=10&_orig=browse&_coverDate=01 %2F31%2F2007&_sk=999769998&view=c&wchp=dGLbVtz-zSkzk&md5=e63b563e526bf85ed2468fbe247ae601&ie=/ sdarticle.pdf (downloaded on 10 March 2007).

Robinson, S. Marguerite. 1995. 'The Paradigm Shift in Microfinance: A Perspective from HIID', Development Discussion Paper No. 510, Harvard Institute for International Development, Massachusetts, Cambridge.

———. 2001. *The Microfinance Revolution: Sustainable Finance for the Poor: Lessons from Indonesia*. Washington: The World Bank.

Roche, Chris. 1999. *Impact Assessment for Development Agencies: Learning to Value Change*. Oxford: Oxfam, GB and Novib.

Rosegrant, Mark W. and Peter B.R. Hazell. 2000. *Transforming the Rural Asian Economy: The Unfinished Revolution*. New York: Oxford University Press.

Rosenberg, Jerry M. 1996. 'Microcredit Interest Rates', Consultative Group to Assist the Poorest, Occasional Paper No. 1. Washington, DC: World Bank.

Rubin, Frances. 1995. *A Basic Guide to Evaluation for Development Workers*. Oxford: Oxfam.

Rutherford, Stuart. 2000. *The Poor and Their Money*. Delhi: Oxford University Press.

Rutherford, Stuart and Staehle, M. 2002. 'Innovative Approaches to Delivering Microfinance Services: The Case of VSSU, West Bengal. Alternative Finance'. Available online at http://www.alternative-finance.org.uk/cgibin/summary. pl?id=88&language=E (downloaded on 4 February 2004).

Sahu, Gangan Bihari and Biswaroop Das. 2007. *Self-help Co-operative and Microfinance*. Ahmedabad: FWWB.

Sampark. 2000. *Participatory Mid Term Evaluation of CREDIT Project of CARE Bihar, Ranchi*. Bangalore: Sampark.

———. 2003. *Mid-term Impact Assessment Study of CASHE Project in Orissa (A Study conducted for CARE India)*. Bangalore: Sampark.

———. 2006a. *Development of the Capacity of the Future Generation: Children's Education through Sustainable Improvement of Livelihoods of Underprivileged Families in Villages of Koppal, North Karnataka, India*. project progress report. Bangalore: Sampark.

Sampark. 2006b. *Development of the Capacity of the Future Generation: Children's Education through Sustainable Improvement of Livelihoods of Underprivileged Families in Villages of Koppal, North Karnataka, India*. Project Progress Report. Bangalore: Sampark.

SBH (State Bank of Hyderabad). 2004. *Koppal District Annual Credit Plan (2004–2005)*. Koppal: Lead Bank Office.

Schmid, Juan Pedro. 2003. 'Economic Growth and Poverty Reduction in India: Effectiveness and Efficiency of Economic and Social Policies of the Centre and the States'. PhD Proposal Berne: Centre for Development and Environment, Institute of Geography, University of Berne. Available online at http://www.nccr-north-south.unibe.ch/othermedia. asp?Context=JACS&ContextID=7&refTitle=South+Asia&SearchText=Schmid%2C+Juan+Pedro+&SearchCategory =%25&submit=Search%21 (downloaded on 20 October 2003).

Schürmann, Anke. 2002. *Participatory Impact Monitoring of Self-help Groups and Watersheds, A Users' Handbook*. Bangalore: MYRADA.

SDC (Swiss Agency for Development and Cooperation). 2007. *An Era of Innovation: Thirty Years of SDC's Involvement with Rural Finance in India*. Gurgaon: EDA Rural Systems.

Sebstad, Jennifer and Gregory Chen. 1996. *Overview of Studies on the Impact of Microenterprise Credit*. Washington: Assessing the Impact of Micro enterprise Services (AIMS).

Seibel, Hans Dieter. 2000. 'Informal Finance: Origins, Evolutionary Trends and Donor Options'. IFAD Rural Finance Working Paper Series, No. A3, 1999 (Revised February 2000). Available online at http://www.alternative-finance.org. uk/cgi-bin/summary.pl?id=88&language=E (downloaded on 4 February 2004).

Sen, Amartya. 1981. 'Public Action and the Quality of Life in Developing Countries', *Oxford Bulletin of Economics and Statistics*, 43(20): 287–319.

———. 1999. *Development as Freedom*. New York: Oxford University Press.

Sengupta, Arjun, Archana Negi and Moushumi Basu. 2005. *Reflections on the Right to Development*. London: Sage Publications.

Sharan. 2000. *Power to Urban Poor through Thrift and Credit Groups: A Sharan Model*. Delhi: Sharan.

SHARE. 2000. 'Growing Stronger With Our Members, Alternative Finance'. Available online at http://www.alternative-finance.org.uk/cgi-bin/summary.pl?id=88&language=E (downloaded on 6 February 2004).

———. 2001. 'Study Shows Strong Impact on SHARE Clients. Credit for the Poor. CASHPOR Newsletter'. Available online at http://www.gfusa.org/gbrp/share.html (downloaded on 22 July 2002).

Sharma, Kalpana. 2005. 'Indian Women Pioneer Informal Justice Courts, Women's e-News'. Available online at http://www. womensenews.org/article.cfm/dyn/aid/357/context/archive (downloaded on 10 January 2006).

Shylendra, H.S. 1998. 'Promoting Women's Self Help Groups: Lessons from an Action Research Project of India' Working Paper. Anand: Institute of Rural Management, Anand.

———. 2006. 'Microfinance Institutions in Andhra Pradesh: Crisis and Diagnosis', *Economic and Political Week*, XLI(20): 1959–963.

Simanowitz, Anton. 2003a. 'Appraising the Poverty Outreach of Microfinance: A Review of the CGAP Poverty Assessment Tool', Imp-Act Occasional Paper No. 1, CGAP and the World Bank, Washington DC.

———. 2003b. 'Designing Impact Assessment Systems to Improve Understanding and Impact'. Available online at http:// www.ids.ac.uk/impact/publicationsguidelines.html (downloaded on 15 December 2003).

Singh, Jai Pal. 2006. *PEDO's SHG Programme Impact Assessment*. A Draft Report. Jaipur: Centre for Microfinance. Available online at http://www.solutionexchange-un.net.in/mf/cr/res06090701.pdf (downloaded on 11 September 2007).

Singh, Kanta. 2003. *Poverty Reduced through Microfiannce at SHARE Microfin Ltd.: Impact Assessment Study*. Hyderabad: SHARE.

Singhdeo, Kumar Subrat. 2006. *Summary Responses of Query on Impact Assessment of Microfinance Initiative*. Bangalore: Sampark.

Sinha, Frances and Meena Patole. 2003. 'Poverty Assessment—Combining Multiple Dimensions of Poverty with a 'standard' Poverty Line. Enterprise Impact'. Available online at http://www.enterprise-impact.org.uk/pdf/sinha.pdf (downloaded on 16 November 2003).

Sinha, Sanjay. 2001. 'The Role of Central Banks in Microfinance in Asia and the Pacific: Country Study for India'. Available online at http://www.adb.org/Documents/Books/Central_Banks_Microfinance/Country_Studies/default.asp (downloaded on 25 March 2004).

Solution Exchange. 2006. *Summary Responses of Query on Impact Assessment of Microfinance Initiative*. Bangalore: Sampark.

———. 2007a. *Summary Responses of Query on Collecting Evidence of Impact of Microfinance—Experiences*. Bangalore: Sampark.

———. 2007b. *Consolidated Reply in Response to Query on SHG Federations as Vehicles for Social Change*. Delhi: Solution Exchange.

Srinivasan, Girija and Robert J. Castro. 2003. *India—Sustainable Microfinance for the Informal Sector*. Washington: Office of Microenterprise Development.

Srinivasan, N. 2004. 'Organisational Development Interventions for Change Management in RRBs', presentation made at Conference on Dare to Share Fair, SDC, Berne, February.

Stiglitz, Joseph. 1990. 'Peer Monitoring and Credit Markets', *World Bank Economic Review*, 4(3): 351–66.

Stookey, Sarah Brand. 2003. *What is Money? Four Perspectives from Management and Beyond*. University of Massachusetts, Amherst.

Sundaram, K. and Suresh D. Tendulkar. 2003. 'Poverty among Social and Economic Groups in India in the Nineteen Nineties', Working Paper 118. Available online at http://www.cdedse.org/pdf/work118.pdf (downloaded on 19 May 2004).

Tankha, Ajay. 1999. 'Some NGO Dilemmas in Reaching the Poorest with Microfinance', *Search Bulletin*, XIV(1): 73–78.

TBF (The Bridge Foundation). 2002. *Annual Report 2002*. Bangalore: TBF.

Thomas, Toms K. 2007. *Social Performance in Development Interventions—Giving Life to Organisation's Mission*. Delhi: United Nations Solution Exchange. Available online at www.solutionexchange-un.net.in/mf/Events/res111007-07.pdf (downloaded on 15 October 2008).

Thorat, Usha. 2007. Speech on Financial Inclusion—the Indian Experience by Smt. Usha Thorat, Deputy Governor, RBI at the Whitehall Place, RBI, Mumbai, 19 June.

Thorat, Y.S.P. 2005. 'Microfinance in India: Sectoral Issues and Challenges'. Theme paper at the High Level Policy Conference on Microfinance, New Delhi, India, May 3–5.

Townsend, Janet, Emma Zapata, Joanna Rowlands, Pilar Alberti, and Marta Mercado. 1999. *Women and Power: Fighting Patriarchies and Poverty*. New York: Zed Books Ltd.

Townsend, J. G., Mawdsley, E., and Porter, G. 2003. 'Development Hegemonies and Local Outcomes: Women and NGOs in Low Income Countries', in E. Kofman and G. Young (eds), *Globalization: Theory and Practice*, pp. 1–19. London: Continuum.

UNDP. 1997. *Human Development Report, 1997*. New York: Oxford University Press.

———. 1999. *Financial Services for the Rural Poor: Users' Perspectives*. Study Conducted by Prompt.

———. 2002. *Human Development Report 2002*. New York: Oxford University Press.

———. 2004. *Human Development Report 2004*. New Delhi: Oxford University Press.

United Nations Office for Project Services (UNOPS). 2002. *National Micro Finance Support Development Project (IFAD Loan 538-in UNOPS Project IND/00/FOI) 2002 Supervision Mission Report*. Malaysia: UNOPS.

———. 2003. *North East Development Project (ind00fo1-IFAD Loan No. 538-in) 2003 Review Mission Report*. Malaysia: UNOPS.

Von Pischke, J.D. 1997. 'Poverty, Human Development and Financial Services'. Occasional Paper No. 25. New York: UNDP.

Vyas, Jaishree. 2003. 'Round Table: In Microfinance: An Introduction by Srinivasan and Sriram', *IIMB Review*, 15(2): 52–86.

Waghmore, S. 2004. 'Decentralised Governance in a Case Society: Implications for Dalit Empowerment', *Indian Journal of Social Development*, 5(1): 356–453.

Weber, Heloise. 2004. 'The New Economy and Social Risk: Banking the Poor?' *Review of International Political Economy*, 11(2): 356–86.

Wiesmann, Urs. 1998. *Sustainable Regional Development in Rural Africa: Conceptual Framework and Case Studies from Kenya*. Berne: Centre for Development and Environment, Institute of Geography, University of Berne.

Wilson, Kimberley. 2003. *The New Microfinance. An Essay on the Self-help Movement in India*. Delhi: Catholic Relief Services India.

———. 2004. *Optimising Self Help Groups*. Note sent out to prepare bids for a study of SHGs in three States of India. Calcutta: Catholic Relief Services.

Woolcock, Michael. 1999. 'Learning from Failures in Microfinance: What Unsuccessful Cases Tell Us About How Group-based Programmes Work', *The American Journal of Economics and Sociology*, 58(1): 17–42.

Wright, Graham A.N. and A. Dondo. 2001. *Are You Poor Enough?—Client Selection by Microfinance Institutions*. Nairobi: MicroSave-Africa.

Wright, Katie. 2006. 'The Darker Side to Microfinance: Evidence from Cajamarca, Peru', in Jude L. Fernando (ed.), *Microfinance Perils and Prospects*, pp. 154–71. Oxon: Routledge.

Yaron, J. 1992. 'Successful Rural Finance Institutions', World Bank Discussion Paper No. 150, The World Bank, Washington, DC.

Zahrai, P.M. 2001. 'A Spiritual Approach to Microcredit Projects'. Available online at http://www.ebbf.org/aspiritu.htm (downloaded on 15 February 2004).

Zapata, Emma and Janet Gabriel Townsend. 1999. 'Outsiders and Self-empowerment', in Townsend, Janet, Emma Zapata, Joanna Rowlands, Pilar Alberti, and Marta Mercado (eds), *Women and Power: Fighting Patriarchies and Poverty*, pp. 41–61. New York: Zed Books Ltd.

Zelizer, Viviana A. 1989. 'The Social Meaning of Money: Special Monies', *American Journal of Sociology*, 95(2): 342–77.

———. 1993. 'Making Multiple Monies', in R. Swedberg (ed.), *Explorations in Economic Sociology*, pp. 193–212. New York: Sage Foundation.

———. 1994. *The Social Meaning of Money*. New York: Basic Books.

———. 1998. 'Payments and Social Ties', *Sociological Forum*, 11(3): 481–95.

———. 2000. 'Fine Tuning the Zelizer View', *Economy and Society*, 29(3): 756–88.

———. 2005. *The Purchase of Intimacy*. Princeton: Princeton University Press.

Zeller, Manfred. 2003a. 'Models of Rural Finance Institutions', Invited lead paper for the International Conference on Best Practices in Rural Finance.

———. 2003b. 'Rural Finance & Agricultural Credit: Past Experiences, Lessons Learnt And Practical Examples', presentation at Inter Cooperation, Berne, August 11.

Zohir, Sajjad and Imran Matin. 2004. 'Wider Impacts of Microfinance Institutions: Issues and Concepts', *Journal of International Development*, 16(3): 301–30.

Index

About the Authors

Smita Premchander is the founder and secretary of Sampark and has 25 years of experience in development work. She has been a trainer and consultant for gender, microfinance and micro-enterprise—both in India and internationally. Her expertise relates to evaluation and design of effective and pro-poor development projects, spanning grassroots development, organisational and programme issues and policy change. She completed a short term assignment with the International Labor Office (ILO), Geneva, as a specialist in Impact Evaluation for Job Creation and Enterprise Development. She has completed about 19 impact and evaluation studies combining both quantitative and qualitative methodologies, for different agencies such as United Nations Development Programme (UNDP), Delhi; Enterplan, UK; ILO, Delhi and Geneva; Centre for Development and Environment (CDE), University of Berne, Switzerland; FAO of the United Nations, Bangkok; United Nations Development Fund for Women (UNIFEM), Bangkok; United Nations Office for Project Services (UNOPS), Malaysia, Traidcraft, UK; Department for International Development (DFID), Bangladesh and Delhi; Swiss Development Corporation, Delhi; CARE India, New Delhi; Novib, Netherlands; National Dairy Development Board (NDDB), Bangalore and Anand; World Bank, Washington and Universities of Sterling, Durham and Swansea, UK. She has worked in most states in India, including Karnataka, Madhya Pradesh, Andhra Pradesh, Jharkhand, Orissa, Chhattisgarh, Rajasthan, Assam, Meghalaya and Mizoram.

V. Prameela is a micro enterprise and livelihood specialist with 15 years of experience and has conducted various impact and evaluation studies. She has worked as a livelihood and micro-enterprise consultant for national and international clients of International Labor Organization such as (ILO), CARE–India (Gujarat, Andhra Pradesh); FAO of the United Nations, Bangkok; Christian Aid, New Delhi; World Bank and NDDB, Bangalore and UNOPS, Malaysia. She also works as a trainer and counsellor in enterprise development and conducted several enterprise development-training programmes for both front line staff and directly for women at the grassroots level. She is working with Sampark, an NGO based in Bangalore and coordinates projects on rural livelihood; running day care non-formal education centres for children of migrant families and community-based mental health programmes. She is also involved in developing proposals and fund-raising.

M. Chidambaranathan is a development professional engaged in consultancy and grassroots- based projects through an NGO based in Bangalore. His areas of expertise include sustainable rural livelihood systems, microfinance, people's organisations, gender and leadership, natural resource management and social learning process. The nature of assignments he has conducted over 15 years for both national and international agencies span research, participatory impact and evaluation studies, designing impact monitoring systems, training NGO staff, strategy planning for development projects, fund-raising and coordination of field-based poverty reduction and women's empowerment projects. He is author/co-author for more than 15 articles published in national and international journals.

L. Jeyaseelan has Masters' degree in Social Work and has been engaged with development projects for over 15 years. His areas of expertise include children's education, microfinance, enterprise development and capacity building of people's organisations. Currently he is working with Sampark, an NGO based in Bangalore as a programme manager for its rural development project in Koppal. Here he has been involved in managing programmes such as microfinance, micro-enterprise, health, children's education, vocational training and development of people's institutions. He was involved in several participatory research and impact evaluation studies conducted for both national and international agencies. He also writes which have been articles, published in journals and reports.

48